THE CFO HANDBOOK

Revised Edition

THE CFO HANDBOOK

Revised Edition

MARK E. HASKINS

BENJAMIN R. MAKELA

Boston, Massachusetts   Burr Ridge, Illinois
Dubuque, Iowa   Madison, Wisconsin   New York, New York
San Francisco, California   St. Louis, Missouri

McGraw-Hill

A Division of The McGraw·Hill Companies

Library of Congress Cataloging-in-Publication Data

The CFO handbook / [edited by] Mark E. Haskins, Benjamin R. Makela.—Rev.
ed.
    p. cm.
    Includes bibliographical references and index.
    ISBN 1-55623-851-7
    1. Chief financial officers—Handbooks, manuals, etc.
  2. Corporations—United States—Finance—Handbooks, manuals, etc.
I. Haskins, Mark E. II. Makela, Benjamin R., 1922-
HG4027.35.C43   1997
658. 15—dc20   96–22774

Printed in the United States of America

4 5 6 7 8 9 BKM BKM 9 0 9 8 7 6 5 4 3 2 1

BRIEF CONTENTS

PART 3

FINANCIAL MANAGEMENT: THE IMPLEMENTATION OF MISSION, VALUES, AND STRATEGY

PART 4

FINANCIAL MANAGEMENT RELATIONSHIPS

PART 5

INTERNATIONAL FINANCIAL MANAGEMENT CHALLENGES

CONTENTS

Chapter 3

Understanding the Business and Economic Environment   35

*Douglas J. Beck, Senior Vice President, ICF Kaiser International,
and Roger E. Brinner, Executive Director and Chief Economist,
DRI/McGraw-Hill*

Chapter 4

Contemporary Best Practices in Making Information Technology Work for Your Customer and Organization   69

Sidney Diamond, President, Diamond & Associates

Chapter 5

Challenges for CFOs in Privately Held Companies   117

*Timothy W. Stonich, Executive Vice President and
CFO, U.S. Can Company*

PART 2

DETERMINING FINANCIAL POLICIES: THE GOVERNANCE OF MISSION, VALUES, AND STRATEGY

Chapter 6

Budgeting Systems: Operationalizing Goals and Values   131

Marshall N. Morton, Senior Vice President and CFO, Media General, Inc.

Chapter 7

Defining the Enterprise's Financial Goals   143

Glenn J. Dozier, Senior Vice President and CFO, Owens & Minor, Inc.

Chapter 8

The Role of Finance in Increasing Shareholder Value   155

Robert M. Agate, CFO, Colgate-Palmolive Company

Chapter 9

Measuring and Rewarding Performance   169

William Rotch, Professor of Business Administration, Darden Graduate School of Business Administration, University of Virginia

PART 3

FINANCIAL MANAGEMENT: THE IMPLEMENTATION OF MISSION, VALUES, AND STRATEGY

Chapter 12

Income Tax Planning for the CFO   213

*Samuel P. Starr, Tax Partner, Coopers & Lybrand L.L.P., and
Steven M. Woolf, Tax Director, Coopers & Lybrand L.L.P.*

Chapter 13

Pension Management   225

William E. Dodge, Managing Director, Marvin & Palmer Associates

Chapter 14

PART 4

FINANCIAL MANAGEMENT RELATIONSHIPS

Chapter 15

Chapter 16

Partnering for Performance © ᔆᴹ   295

Martin G. Mand, Chairman and President, Mand Associates, Limited, and Executive Vice President and Chief Financial Officer, Northern Telecom, Limited (Retired)

Chapter 17

Relations with Equity Investors 309

A. Nicholas Filippello, Vice President, Financial Communications, and Chief Economist, Monsanto Company

Chapter 18

Relations with Professional Resources   325

Robert J. Chrenc, Executive Vice President and CFO, AC Nielsen

PART 5

INTERNATIONAL FINANCIAL MANAGEMENT CHALLENGES

Chapter 19

International Risk Assessment   343

Judy C. Lewent, Senior Vice President and CFO, Merck & Co., Inc., and Caroline Dorsa, Treasurer, Merck & Co., Inc.

Chapter 20

Overseas Alliances: Assessing the Potential Benefit from, Searching for, and Structuring Them   367

John L. Becker, Director of Business Development, Cummins Engine Company, and Robert J. Sack, Professor of Business Administration, Darden Graduate School of Business Administration, University of Virginia

Chapter 21

Controlling Global Operations 397

James M. Cornelius, Chairman, Guidant Corp., and Michael
Grobstein, Vice Chairman, Ernst & Young International

P R E F A C E

The premise of this book is that the CFO is a crucial member of the top-most corporate team responsible for determining and implementing a company's strategy, mission, and values. This book is a collection of writings on the nature of the various tasks, challenges, and thinking applicable to CFOs fulfilling this larger role. Since the last edition of this book was published in 1986, it is not an overstatement to assert that CFOs have become more visible, more powerful, and more vulnerable in fulfilling their responsibilities for maintaining the integrity of all the company's financial dealings and in enhancing a company's vitality. Indeed, such a backdrop has stimulated an increasing interest in understanding what high-performing CFOs do.

Many chapters in this book have been contributed by world-class CFOs while others have been authored by non-CFO thought leaders and highly successful specialists. All the chapters are applicable to a CFO audience interested in learning about the best thinking of some of their colleagues. Moreover, the chapters are also intended to be of interest to those aspiring to be CFOs as well as those who interact with CFOs and want to gain further insights into the CFO's world.

Readers should be careful not to view these chapters as recipes for success. These chapters are the sharing of ideas, processes, and purposes. They provide insights into one person's or one company's best thinking on a subject and as such they should spark your own broader and deeper thinking. We have worked closely with the authors and have learned much from them and their chapters. We believe you will learn much too.

Mark E. Haskins
Benjamin R. Makela

CONTRIBUTING AUTHORS

Robert M. Agate (Chapter 8) retired on July 1, 1996 after nine years as senior executive vice president and chief financial officer of the Colgate-Palmolive Company, whose primary products include soap and cleaning preparations, personal care products, and pet food. Agate joined Colgate-Palmolive in 1961 as a chartered accountant in the United Kingdom. Subsequent to that he served in various other positions for Colgate-Palmolive such as controller in a number of Colgate subsidiaries (including India, Malaysia, the U.K. and Australia), controller of the European Division and vice president and corporate controller.

John L. Bakane (Chapter 1) is executive vice president, chief financial officer and director for Cone Mills Corporation, headquartered in Greensboro, North Carolina. Cone Mills is one of the world's largest producers of denim fabrics, is the largest printer of home furnishings fabrics in the United States, and is the largest domestic exporter of apparel fabrics. Bakane joined Cone Mills in 1975 after having served in numerous financial staff and management positions for the company.

Alfred J. Battaglia (Chapter 15) is group president in charge of supply chain management for Becton Dickinson and Company, a global medical technology company focused on medication delivery devices and diagnostic systems. Previously Battaglia was president of VACUTAINER Systems Division. He joined Becton Dickinson in 1970 and has served in both operating and staff assignments in the United States and Europe.

Douglas J. Beck (Chapter 3) is senior vice president, business development, consulting, at ICF Kaiser International, Inc. Mr. Beck was formerly senior vice president at DRI/McGraw-Hill, Inc.

John L. Becker (Chapter 20) is director, business development, for Cummins Engine Company, Inc., headquartered in Columbus, Indiana. Becker has worked at Cummins for 23 years in a variety of positions. Prior to coming to Cummins, Becker worked as a chemist for Swift & Co. and Motorola and as a Russian linguist and analyst for the U.S. government. At Cummins, Becker has worked in the Finance, Product Management, and International groups. He has been involved in the pursuit and establishment of international alliances throughout his career. His Business Development group is responsible for Cummins's internal processes for alliance development.

Roger E. Brinner (Chapter 3) is executive director and chief economist at DRI/McGraw-Hill. Prior to joining DRI, he was a professor of economics at Harvard University, where he specialized in tax policy, inflation, and capital formation.

Robert J. Chrenc (Chapter 18) is executive vice president and CFO of AC Nielsen. Prior to this position, he was a partner at Arthur Andersen LLP, a professional services firm.

James M. Cornelius (Chapter 21) is chairman of Guidant Corporation, a global medical device company traded on the New York and Pacific stock exchanges and headquartered in Indianapolis, Indiana. He was elected to this position in September 1994 and joined Guidant full-time following his retirement from Eli Lilly and Company in October 1995. He served as vice president of finance and chief financial officer at Lilly from January 1983 until his retirement. Eli Lilly develops, manufactures, and markets pharmaceuticals and animal health products.

Sidney Diamond's (Chapter 4) most recent corporate positions were as chief information officer of Black & Decker, a global marketer and manufacturer of quality products used in and around the home, and vice president of international information technology (IT) for Bristol-Myers, a diversified worldwide health and personal care company. Mr. Diamond has over 30 years of diverse IT experience. He is now president of Diamond & Associates, an IT consulting practice specializing in IT strategic planning based in Stevenson, Maryland.

William E. Dodge (Chapter 13) is senior managing director and portfolio manager at Marvin & Palmer Associates in Wilmington, Delaware. Previously he was chairman of investment policy and chief investment strategist for Dean Witter Reynolds, New York, a full-service brokerage firm. Prior to that he was director of quantitative equity strategies for E.I. du Pont Pension in Wilmington, Delaware.

Caroline Dorsa (Chapter 19) is treasurer for Merck & Co., Inc., a worldwide research-intensive pharmaceuticals company that discovers, develops, produces, and markets human and animal health products. Dorsa is responsible for worldwide treasury matters under a centralized structure. Previously she was the executive director of customer marketing for the U.S. Human Health subsidiary of Merck & Co., Inc. She began her career with Merck in 1987 in the financial area as an analyst in the financial evaluation and analysis group.

Glenn J. Dozier (Chapter 7) is senior vice president, finance and chief financial officer for Owens & Minor, Inc., a wholesale distributor of medical and surgical supplies, pharmaceuticals and other related products to hospitals, nursing homes and physicians. Dozier joined Owens & Minor in 1990 as vice president, treasurer, and chief financial officer. He serves on the Pension & Benefits Committee for the Company. Prior to joining Owens & Minor, he was CFO of AMF Companies, Inc.

A. Nicholas Filippello (Chapter 17) is corporate vice president of financial communications and chief economist for Monsanto Company, a science-based company involved in businesses that improve the quality of life. Prior to joining Monsanto in 1974, he was corporate economist at the McDonnell Douglas Corporation in St. Louis, and prior to that was an economist with the U.S. Department of Agriculture in Washington, D.C.

Michael Grobstein (Chapter 21) is vice chairman of Ernst & Young International, a professional services, accounting, and management consulting firm. Grobstein has responsibility for worldwide planning and various global initiatives.

George B. James (Chapter 2) is senior vice president and chief financial officer of Levi Strauss & Company, a clothing manufacturer. Prior to joining Levi Strauss, James was an executive vice president, group president, and chief financial officer at Crown Zellerbach. He also served as chief financial officer for Arcata Corporation and Pepsico Leasing Corporation.

Judy C. Lewent (Chapter 19) is senior vice president and chief financial officer for Merck & Co., Inc., the world's largest pharmaceutical company. Based in New Jersey, Merck is a researcher, developer, manufacturer, and marketer of pharmaceutical and health products for humans and animals. Lewent is responsible for worldwide financial and public affairs matters as well as some of Merck's joint venture relationships. Lewent joined Merck in 1980 as director, acquisitions, and capital analysis.

Martin G. Mand (Chapter 16) is chairman and president of Mand Associates, Ltd. a Wilmington, Delaware-based consulting, writing, and lecturing firm. Prior to starting his own business, Mand was executive vice president and chief financial officer for Northern Telecom Limited, a telecommunications equipment manufacturer. Before joining Northern Telecom, Mand served as vice president and treasurer for E. I. du Pont de Nemours & Company, a diversified chemicals, specialty products, and energy company.

Thomas G. Manoff (Chapter 14) is chief financial officer of Saturn Corporation, an innovative designer and manufacturer of automobiles.

Marshall N. Morton (Chapter 6) is senior vice president and chief financial officer of Media General, Inc., a publicly owned communications company with interests in newspapers, broadcast and cable television, newsprint production, and diversified information services. Morton joined Media General in 1989, having served previously in a number of executive capacities (including those as corporate vice president and controller) with West Point Pepperell.

Larry E. Pearson (Chapter 10) is senior vice president of finance at GE Fanuc Automation North America, Inc., a joint venture between GE of the United States and FANUC LTD of Japan. Pearson is also Director of the GE Fanuc Automation N.A., Inc., Board of

Directors and Treasurer of the GE Fanuc Automation Corporation. He joined General Electric Company through GE's Financial Management Program. Prior to joining GE Fanuc in 1987, Pearson was finance manager of GE's semiconductor business operation at Research Triangle Park in North Carolina.

William Rotch (Chapter 9) is Johnson and Higgins Professor of Business Administration at the Darden Graduate School of Business Administration of the University of Virginia in Charlottesville. Rotch teaches in both the MBA and Executive Education programs. He is a co-author of *Cases in Management Accounting and Control Systems* ©1995 and *The Executive's Guide to Management Accounting and Control Systems* ©1997. His current research interest is special requirements of service activities and businesses for the design of cost and management control systems. Prior to coming to Darden, Rotch was a faculty member at the Amos Tuck School at Dartmouth College and IMEDE in Lausanne, Switzerland.

Robert J. Sack (Chapter 20) is professor of business administration at the Darden Graduate School of Business Administration at the University of Virginia in Charlottesville. Sack teaches in both the MBA and Executive Education programs. His most recent publication is "Chief Financial Officers and the Ethical Issues They Face in Corporate Financial Reporting," *Ethical Issues in Accounting*, American Accounting Association, June 1995. Prior to coming to Darden, Sack was chief accountant in the Enforcement Division of the Securities and Exchange Commission; national director of accounting and auditing practice at Touche Ross & Company, and director of professional standards, Touche Ross International.

Douglas A. Scovanner (Chapter 11) is senior vice president and chief financial officer for Dayton Hudson Corporation, headquartered in Minnesota.

Samuel P. Starr (Chapter 12) is tax partner in Coopers & Lybrand L.L.P.'s Tax Consulting group in Washington, D.C. Coopers & Lybrand is an international professional services firm. Starr serves as a departmental editor for Warren, Gorham & Lamont's *Journal of Taxation* and serves on the board of the *Journal of S Corporation Taxation* and the *Journal of Limited Liability Companies*. He wrote the two current BNA Tax Management Portfolios on S corporations and co-authored the BNA Tax Management Portfolio on limited liability companies.

Timothy W. Stonich (Chapter 5) is executive vice president of finance and chief financial officer for U.S. Can Company. He is also chairman of the U.S. Can Foundation. Stonich joined the company in 1987 as senior vice president of finance and CFO, with 17 years of progressive financial and accounting management experience. Prior to his appointment at U.S. Can, Stonich was senior vice president and chief financial officer of the Line Group, Chicago, a medical and telecommunication equipment lessor.

Katherine Ann Woodall, (Chapter 2) is director, corporate communications, for Levi Strauss & Company, a manufacturer of men's and women's apparel. Woodall oversees LS&CO's global employee communications and financial communications functions. She directs employee publications, global meetings, the annual stockholders' meeting, financial reports, and communications for the company's global strategic business plan. Prior to coming to Levi Strauss, Woodall worked for Hewlett-Packard Company in a variety of regional, corporate, and group marketing communications positions.

Steven M. Woolf (Chapter 12) is a tax director in Coopers & Lybrand L.L.P.'s National Tax Services office in Washington, D.C. Coopers & Lybrand is an international professional services firm. Woolf edits several annual books and periodicals including *International Tax Summaries, Strategies for Your Personal Finances* and *Tax Strategies with Year-End Planning*. Woolf joined C&L in 1986 after working for several years in the National Tax group at Laventhol and Horwath, CPAs and in the Washington office of the American Institute of CPAs.

I

CREATING MISSION, VALUES, AND STRATEGY

⑥ THE HIGH-PERFORMANCE CFO ROLE OR "ZEN AND THE ART OF BEAN COUNTING"

by John L. Bakane
Executive Vice President and CFO, Cone Mills Corp.

Defining one's own high-performance CFO role is not a technical undertaking but rather a personal philosophical question. There are no objective standards or benchmarks, only judgment. And, ultimately, defining one's own high-performance role is not a one-time issue but rather a process. As some of my Eastern culture colleagues remind me, if the CFO is focused on the tools, he is a "bean counter," but to focus on the process of organizational success is to become the Zen CFO.

Over the past six years of my role as CFO, my company has restructured its LBO debt and ownership, discontinued its second-largest business, gone public, established an investment-grade balance sheet, and made a series of investments in global expansion. As a result, I have often found myself awake at 3 A.M. asking, *Now* what is my role as CFO? I am writing this chapter not to tell anyone else how to define the high-performance CFO role, but rather to share some experiences that have shaped my perspective.

THE CFO PERSPECTIVE

It has occurred to me, in my role as CFO, that just as I thought I was getting proficient at something, such as cost cutting, the organization shifted to a new agenda, such as growth. Rather than become obsolete, I have tried to identify those elements of the CFO's

3

role that are constants that can endure change. I have concluded that the CFO provides an organization with a perspective that is not only different from other functional perspectives but unique as well. Because of traditional roots in control and treasury activities, the CFO is trained in the processes of performance assessment and resource allocation. In other words, marketing and manufacturing executives are generally focused on achieving functionally defined objectives, while the CFO is focused on a comprehensive view of how effectively the organization is progressing in the pursuit of those objectives and how efficiently it is allocating financial resources.

In regard to control activities, the Committee of Sponsoring Organizations of the Treadway Commission has defined control as the process of assuring shareholders, the Board, management, and others that the objectives of the organization are being achieved in an effective, efficient manner.[1] To execute oversight responsibility for this process, the CFO must be able to identify key objectives and determine if the assessment and measurement processes for their attainment are adequate. These assessment activities are not confined to a single function but cut across all activities of the organization.

In regard to treasury activities, the perspective is one of allocation on both a macroeconomic basis and a microeconomic basis. The macroeconomic allocation is focused on funds available to the organization from the general economy at any time. Once available funds are defined, the microeconomic allocation process of where to commit funds within the organization becomes the focus. Like control activities, treasury activities cut across all functions of the organization.

An example of this difference in perspectives was highlighted when a real estate manager asked to expand the operation because the business had a high return on equity. The CFO noted that earnings had benefited from the low historical cost of sales of land inventories acquired long ago, low historical-based land asset values, and a higher leverage that was not characteristic of the industry. As

---

1. Committee of Sponsoring Organizations of the Treadway Commission (COSO), *Internal Control—Integrated Framework: Evaluation Tools* (New York: American Institute of CPAs, 1992).

a result, the real estate activities were split into two operations: one recognizing the gains on a historical cost basis and the other recognizing development gains on a replacement cost basis. The new measurement techniques provided valuable benchmarks for assessing return on investment for development activities requiring the purchase of land and allowed better estimates for determining return on investment proposals and ranking the attractiveness of investment alternatives.

Having defined the value of the CFO as providing a vision for and guidance on assessment of activities and allocation of financial resources, I believe that to be successful, the CFO must be a team player with quality relationships among members of the management team. In essence, the CFO has no turf and the CFO's value results from an ability to move throughout the organization with a unique objective perspective. This approach does create a crucial management balance in that a CFO must be accepted as a full-fledged team member in order to have access to issues, while at the same time the CFO must preserve the role of an objective assessor of the organization's progress toward goals, often for people outside the organizational team.

HELPING SHAPE CORPORATE MISSION AND GOALS

As a member of the senior management team, the high-performance CFO accepts a leadership obligation to the organization. According to Plato, the leadership obligation is based on the individual's willingness to accept personal risks for the benefit of the organization. Based on these requirements, I do not believe it is possible for the CFO to lead without having a vision for the organization; and I do not believe it is possible for the organization to follow unless there is a clearly articulated vision.

In 1983, our company was the target of a hostile takeover attempt. To me, this was the ultimate lesson in the need for balance among the company's culture, mission, and goals, and the expectations and requirements of investors who allocate capital in the macroeconomy. As a result, I believe the high-performance CFO must be involved in defining the mission and goals of the organization, particularly from the perspective of fit with expectations of investors in the macroeconomy. This requires the

CFO to develop, maintain, and communicate a model of how the organization fits with the macroeconomy.

My definition of this model is a set of relationships between the company and the rest of the economy. It is the responsibility of the CFO to determine expected returns required by equity investors in general, the expectations for returns among equity investment alternatives, the risk variables identified by the investing community, and the magnitude of these risks. The company's expected returns, growth, and risk variables need to be constantly compared to those of the general economy to determine the attractiveness of investment in the company and the resulting valuation. I believe that if the company's posture along these dimensions is out of line with the general economy, the value of the company will be adversely affected. I categorize such differences as falling into three categories: communications, strategy, and performance.

In regard to communications, the CFO must determine if shareholders adequately understand the strategy of the company and the expected performance. Gaps between management's expectations and investors' understanding should be eliminated via the investor relations programs.

In regard to strategy, problems typically arise if strategy is wrong or if investor support is unsustainable. If the CFO believes there is a problem here, then the issue must be raised and ultimately resolved through the interaction of the CEO, the CFO, and in some cases the board of directors.

In regard to performance, gaps between investor expectations and company results typically revolve around tactics for strategy implementation, individual manager performance, and investor patience. If the CFO believes there is a problem in this area, then the issue must be raised and ultimately resolved through the interaction of the CEO, CFO, and sometimes the board of directors.

An example of the use of this model came in 1991 when our company was balancing in its strategy a need to enter the public marketplace to fund growth, satisfy liquidity needs of investors in closely held stock, and turn around a major business unit. It became apparent that from a timing standpoint all three goals could not be accommodated and that the highest value to shareholders was to pursue the first two goals and discontinue the business unit rather than turn it around. In the broadest sense, the CFO's perspective on how the investment community values the mission and performance of the organization is one of the strongest ways the CFO adds value to the process of setting corporate goals and mission.

In addition to the perspective of capital allocation, the CFO brings an assessment perspective to the formulation of mission and goals. This closes the loop in the planning, executing, and assessment process from two vantage points. First, in the role of assessing the progress of goal achievement, the CFO picks up a great deal of both internal and external information about the organization that is helpful in setting reasonably achievable goals and assessing risks and probability of success. Second, the accelerating rate of change in the U.S. economy is such that the mission and goal setting process is no longer a periodic undertaking but rather a continuous process. This makes assessment of progress an integral part of the continuous closed-loop, goal setting process.

In our company, we have found that communicating goals and objectives to external, as well as internal, constituencies is as important as setting goals. Since, for our company, return on capital employed is a key element in matching company performance with investor requirements, the CFO must work very closely with the CEO in communicating how return on capital is measured, why it is important, what is an acceptable return, and what is the value to shareholders when the return on capital targets are reached. In our organization these concepts also reach into the determination of compensation for key employees.

Once goals and objectives are set for an organization, the CFO then has the responsibility for prioritizing the specific objectives and ensuring that there are adequate controls in place to assess performance in reaching these goals. The high-performance CFO ensures that there are no surprises in the assessment of performance against goals and objectives. If the analogy is that the CEO is captain of the organizational ship and is responsible for passionately articulating vision and setting direction, then the CFO is the navigator with responsibility for being an objective soundboard for where the organization is and the prospects for achieving the vision.

THE CFO AND THE MANAGEMENT TEAM

In recent years, it has become common for economists to describe the economy in terms of two dimensions: Wall Street and Main Street. I view the CFO as the bridge between these two worlds, with one foot on Wall Street and one foot on Main Street. If one accepts this view of the CFO role, then it follows that the CFO has as much responsibility to understand the business as to understand the capital markets. To understand the business, the CFO must work very closely with the CEO to thoroughly understand where the organization is being taken and the pressures for change to which the organization will be subjected. In this interaction with the CEO, the CFO provides an important perspective on availability of financial resources that match the needs of the organization as defined by the CEO and, in turn, the requirements of the capital community. It is within this context that the CFO must also consider appropriate control systems.

Good control systems usually incorporate multiple channels of assessment to ensure information's accuracy and objectivity. For example, a CFO can usually corroborate earnings estimates during an accounting period by monitoring cash flow trends. Likewise, a CEO uses multiple channels of assessment to corroborate and further define issues arising in line management responsibilities. The high-performance CFO must integrate the traditional accounting information systems with the CEO's operating control channels. For example, line managers typically gauge productivity and cost reduction trends on a project-by-project basis. But within a complex product and business unit environment it is often difficult to calculate broad measures of cost trends. In our business units, we have developed a method for deriving cost deflators to calculate FIFO to LIFO inventory conversions for financial reporting purposes. These deflators are good gauges of cost trends and provide another channel of information to the CEO in order to corroborate operating cost measures. Practices such as this integrate the concepts and processes of functional accounting with other control activities to assess important management issues facing a business.

In recent years, our organization has utilized both divisional and functional organizational structures. I strongly believe that close interaction with line managers, whether they be divisional or functional, is an absolute necessity in validating the organization's control systems and in allocating financial resources. Good control systems are not based in the science of accounting but rather in the art of sociology and psychology.

In working with business unit executives who have profit and return on investment responsibilities, the relationship between the CFO and the division executive is much like that between the CFO and the CEO. The focus is on defining mission, developing control systems, and setting goals. I spend much of my time with divisional executives in the broad areas of systems and defining their funding needs in the context of the entire organization.

Our divisional executives are strong implementors. They have a bias toward direct action, whereas the CFO has a focus on process. Here is a recent example: A division president was tired of being late on international shipments and focused on credit clearance (letter of credit) as a bottleneck and wanted credit to compromise procedures and ship the goods. The CFO role became one of focusing on the system and recognizing that (1) delays in the process were most often in preparing the goods and arranging for shipment and (2) since documentation was the last process, it became the vehicle for compromise. Rather than destroy good policies, we have set up a credit risk pool with merchandisers having responsibility for a defined risk line of credit. Both merchandisers and credit managers review this pool to better understand how to balance credit risks with risks to customer goodwill.

An example of collaboration in resource allocation comes in the area of facility planning where capital availability determines the configuration of facilities. Division executives get insight from the CFO in regard to what is feasible, and the CFO gets a better understanding of long-term financial needs. In addition, ideas about new financing techniques such as joint ventures and supplier consignment programs have been direct outgrowths of these discussions.

Relationships with functional managers for me revolve around three issues:

1. Providing overall business perspective to functional experts.

2. Gaining opportunities to add value by using tools in the financial tool box.
3. Revival of the cultural bonds that hold the organization together.

In regard to adding general business perspective, I recall the comment of a vice president of manufacturing: "I would have never believed you can cut efficiency and increase profits—but it is sometimes true." These remarks grew out of a project we worked on together that determined that at certain high-efficiency levels of operation, the marginal cost of additional labor and other costs required to increase machinery efficiency or output per machine hour was higher than the profitability on the increased output. Prior to this exercise, plant managers believed that an increase in efficiency was synonymous with increased profitability.

In marketing, we have changed the focus of information systems to report profit contribution per (bottleneck) machine hour as opposed to profit per yard, in response to the addition of new product lines in a plant.

Also, in marketing, when we entered into a new print technology that we felt would have bright long-term prospects, we changed the markup procedure for price quotations from a percentage markup over costs to a target return-on-capital-employed markup to ensure adequate returns to reinvest and expand.

By working with functional executives to define and measure risks, we are able to use financial derivatives and other financial tools to hedge currency and other risks. While transaction risks can be assessed by financial staff members, overall business risks such as market share risk can only be gauged with line management's assessment. By maintaining close relationships with functional executives, the CFO can more effectively steer the technical financial staff into value-producing activities.

My regard for the value of cultural bonds stems from the experience of our LBO years. We framed the battle during the hostile takeover attempt as an effort by a "would-be financial owner" to compromise our long-term customer relationships as well as the strategies and cultures of the organization for the exclusive purpose of earning a short-term trading profit. Like many other manufacturing companies subject to hostile takeover attempts during the

1980s, our company developed a siege mentality. During this period the CEO defined the role of the CEO and CFO as gatekeepers charged with keeping outside forces from entering the organization and, as he put it, "ransacking the organization and destroying the vitality of the operating company." So, to balance the organization's needs to attract capital and to fulfill responsibilities to shareholders while preserving the operating vitality of the company, I believe the CFO must understand the culture to determine which values are negotiable and subject to change, and which are not. To understand the culture of the organization, the CFO must spend time with functional executives, plant managers, and salespeople as well as on the shop floor.

THE CFO AND ORGANIZATIONAL EMPOWERMENT

The value of organizational empowerment was driven home for me in the early 1990s when our company faced a large debt amortization schedule during an economic downturn and during a period of inadequate liquidity in the capital markets. We knew our mission of survival was to focus on liquidity management throughout the organization. To address this problem, we set up a financial group of control and treasury managers to train 150 key employees on the fundamentals of cash management, working capital management, and fixed asset management. The 150 key employees were then asked (1) to think about how their day-to-day decisions affected cash flow and (2) to set goals for cash generation in their respective areas. Over the next year, the team documented incremental cash generation exceeding $70 million or about 15 percent of the total assets!

Over the past two years the need to shift to an empowerment and business advocacy style has become even more apparent as our company has moved from an LBO organization to a well-capitalized company seeking growth and expansion. We have determined that in a fast-paced, continuous-change environment, we need to shorten the command chain and press decision making further down into the organization.

At Cone Mills, this has resulted in three broad initiatives:

1. Our mission is being defined much more broadly in terms of principles, values, competencies, and capabilities. This

has opened up growth opportunities as compared with a previous focus on products.

2. Our seven business units are accepting greater responsibility for proposing specific goals and objectives.

3. The company is decentralizing much of its support staff to improve coordination with business units.

Based upon discussions and observations with other members of the financial community, there appears to be a strong general business trend in this direction. As a key contributor to these three initiatives, I find myself working more closely with our business unit presidents as a bridge between corporate mission and objectives, and business unit objectives. Recently we overhauled our annual business plan review with the board of directors to focus on (1) corporate mission, goals, strategy, and evaluation and (2) individual business unit goals, strategies, and evaluation. A financial forecast accompanies this review and serves as a scorecard on consequences of corporate and business unit initiatives. As a result of this approach, we in the corporate finance group are becoming involved in reasonableness tests for key objectives and the development of key indicators for measuring success. An example of this role was demonstrated when a key strategy for one of our operating units became the rapid modernization of facilities in order to hold nominal manufacturing costs constant through the remainder of this decade. After studying historical and forecasted cost trends as well as the specific capital investment plans, we determined that this was a feasible undertaking. Then we developed measurement tools that track progress toward this goal by measuring the manufacturing cost for a typical product in the business unit, taking into consideration that over 400 products are manufactured in four different locations. The strategy has been approved and the business unit is proceeding.

As business units become more empowered with their own objectives and decentralized resources, we in the corporate finance group are becoming more focused on ensuring the adequacy of functional expertise and maintenance of functional skill levels among the financial workers. To do this, we in the corporate finance group are focused on (1) what are the best practices in finance and (2) how we communicate and develop financial workers in the business units. One way of doing this is through formal forums twice a year to exchange experiences and practices among business unit financial workers. Another method is through audits of financial practices to ensure that business units have the practices in place to ensure that their goals are being achieved effectively and efficiently.

Even more important than the recognition of specific changing roles in the financial group is the need to change the entire organization's attitudes on control and assessment. Simply put, we must break the lingering notion that the need for controls is a reflection of questioning personal integrity or capabilities; we must substitute the concept that along with the greater responsibility of empowerment comes greater accountability. Likewise, the CFO's perspective of funds allocation is evolving to one of finding resources to meet business needs as opposed to husbanding the treasury's cash.

To be effective in this environment, a CFO must forge strong working relationships with business unit managers. Instead of focusing on what the business units shouldn't or can't do, the CFO and business unit managers must develop mutually agreeable objectives to create an advocacy role for obtaining resources to support the business unit. The dimensions of this new relationship encompass teamwork, partnering, and information sharing.

THE HIGH-PERFORMANCE FINANCIAL ORGANIZATION

One of the most significant roles for a CFO is to shape attitudes of the financial staff to be compatible with the overall direction of the business organization. Thus, I do not believe that a CFO can be effective in an empowered company unless the financial organization is likewise empowered. Technical proficiency of the financial organization must be a nonnegotiable given, but the shaping of the attitudes of the financial staff can only be achieved through the example and coaching of the CFO.

The CFO has the never-ending responsibility for maintaining a general business perspective among the technical experts on the financial staff. The CFO also serves as a bridge between high-level business problems and technically based financial solutions. And, like the role within the overall organization of balancing passion with objectivity, within the staff of treasury and control, the CFO must balance the optimism of the investor relations function with the conservatism of the controller's function.

In our company we see a growing overlap between traditional financial goals and measures and business goals and measures. In the empowered organization, I believe we will see the disappearance of the term *financial goals* and the adoption of the business goals nomenclature to encompass all goals. As the empowered organization moves in this direction, there is a need for new practices. For example, our controllers and accountants are developing systems that capture market share data, cost indexes, replacement value estimates, and so on as well as traditional P&L and balance sheet data. In addition, our financial staff is developing information systems that can be accessed by operating managers to share information and provide a consistent view of an organization's performance throughout the company.

Based on research conducted by the Financial Executives Research Foundation, it is becoming apparent to the financial community that behavioral patterns among financial workers are undergoing a major change from past behaviors.[2] The traditional behavior of finance workers has been perceived as rigid, aloof, impersonal, and isolated from the mainstream of the business organization. This perception does not facilitate the integration of financial workers into the mainstream business movements toward empowerment, participative management, and teamwork. My own belief is that the high-performance CFO must take on the role of high-visibility leadership in modifying behaviors and styles of the financial professionals.

MISSION AND VALUES OF THE FINANCIAL ORGANIZATION

Based on the trends of overall business practices, it appears to me that the high-performance CFO must embody the philosophy and vision for the financial organization in a formal statement of

---

2. H. A. Davis, *The Empowered Organization: Redefining the Roles and Practices of Finance* (Morristown, N.J.: Financial Executives Research Foundation, June 1994).

financial mission and values. Based on the trends I see evolving, our mission and values statement is as follows:

1. The mission of the financial organization is the mission of the company to identify consumer needs that match the company's capabilities to provide
   a. Value to customers.
   b. Appropriate return for investors.
   c. A responsible environment for employees and communities.
2. The financial organization has no turf; it operates across business units and functions, in partnership, for the purpose of furthering the company's progress in its mission.
3. While proficient financial practices are critical tools, the value we add to the organization is our unique perspective in assessment and control systems and in matching the organization's requirements with capital sources.
4. Financial workers are not passive; they are business advocates.

For me, the high-performance CFO role is defined each morning when I match what the organization is attempting to achieve with the particular talents we have in the financial group. There is no formula or textbook solution but rather a process of discerning needs for financial support, implementing solutions, and evaluating results. As with any other product or service, when the CFO offers high-performance service that creates value for the company's stockholders, then the CFO can be labeled "the high-performance CFO."

2

MAKING ETHICAL VALUES A TANGIBLE PART OF THE ENTERPRISE'S FINANCIAL FUNCTION

George B. James
CFO, Levi Strauss & Co.

Katherine Ann Woodall
Director, Corporate Communications, Levi Strauss & Co.

Because ethical principles shape the society in which we live and work, each enterprise must make clear decisions as to whether and how such ethical principles will be incorporated into its financial function and decision making. At Levi Strauss & Co. (LS&CO.), we have learned during the past 140 years that both the decisions we make and the processes we use to make them contribute to the strength of our brands, to our corporate reputation, and to our continuing growth and vitality as a business entity.

The finance function often leads the way in providing important information and analysis for an organization's business decisions. How information is gathered and weighted not only influences decisions, it also reflects ethical choices. This in turn impacts corporate reputation, brand strength, productivity, and, ultimately, the bottom line. Measuring hard dollar costs as well as less tangible costs, such as the impact of decision making on a company's constituents, is essential for the chief financial officer of the 21st century.

ETHICAL CORPORATE VALUES IN HISTORICAL CONTEXT

As Socrates said in his "Apologia" more than 2,300 years ago, "Virtue does not come from valuables, but from virtue valuables, and all other things come to men in their private and public affairs." In modern times, many would say that this device translates as "Do the right thing, rather than do things right."

RECOGNIZING STAKEHOLDER INTERESTS IN FINANCIAL DECISION MAKING

Although seldom, if ever, taught in business schools, the potential impact on an organization's various stakeholders must be taken into account in the effective CFO's decision making and management process. As the majority of companies' public relations or corporate communications staff will be all too happy to point out, no organization operates in a vacuum; all managers must consider the ramifications of policy and procedure on each of the company's constituencies, as well as share responsibility for protecting the company's reputation.

Without the continuing support of customers or clients, there will be no demand for the organization's products or services. Without employee and supplier support, demand for products and services cannot be fulfilled effectively or competitively. Without shareholder, bondholder, and lender support, capital will become prohibitively expensive. Without the support of the communities in which a company operates, frustration will come at every legal, regulatory, and activist turn. And without the combined support of all these constituencies, the organization's most valuable asset—its brand identity, service marks, and the reputation that has taken years to develop—will be wasted.

For example, our *customers'* success is enhanced when we get to know each of their businesses almost as well as they do by listening to their needs and by working closely with them to meet those needs. At Levi Strauss & Co., our customers are the retailers who sell our products to consumers. We constantly look for ways to help them keep *consumers* coming through the doors. That usually means each of our customers has different needs, problems, and opportunities. So, instead of trying to fit the customers into one LS&CO. mold, we have broken the mold and found ways to build close relationships to ensure that the right products are delivered to the right place at the right time.

We view *financial institutions* working with us not as providers of commodities but as integral business partners in our continuing success. Thus, rather than seeking bids and striking the absolute best deal each time we want to borrow capital, we have chosen to establish continuing relationships with a narrow field of lenders and investment bankers. They are brought into management's confidence, meet regularly with the company's senior leadership, are provided with sensitive information, and are used as an intelligence pool from which we draw invaluable observations and recommendations.

Our Business Vision states that we want to be the "Employer of Choice," thereby reducing *employee* recruitment and turnover costs and maximizing productivity. We have committed to providing a workplace that is safe, challenging, rewarding, productive, and fun. Companies must come to recognize that employees are their closest and most visible intermediaries with customers and suppliers—and at every step through the manufacturing process. As a result, employees must be acknowledged as true partners in running the business, sharing a common framework for achieving and sustaining responsible commercial success. This framework includes

- A clearly defined *Mission Statement* describing why the organization exists and what businesses will be pursued to sustain responsible commercial success.
- A *Business Vision* that delineates where the organization is headed, including a broad view of what is hoped to be accomplished without prescribing how to get there.
- An *Aspirations Statement* that describes what kind of organization is sought and the behaviors that are important in conducting business with colleagues and business partners around the world.

All of this means investments must be made not only in plant facilities and equipment but also in human beings, promoting innovation and continuous improvement while anticipating and modeling change. To that end, Levi Strauss & Co.'s "Partners in Performance" compensation program links incentive pay available to employees with performance objectives aligned with the company's global strategic business plan, and integrates Aspirations into employee evaluations.

This evaluation and review process assigns a full one-third weight to the Aspirational reviews an employee receives with the remaining two-thirds assigned to one's success or failure in achieving individual and group business objectives. The point worth emphasizing is that there can be no pay raise, promotion, and perhaps even job retention without a pronounced answer of yes from subordinates, peers, clients, and bosses to the question "Does this employee incorporate the company's Aspirational values in his or her daily work?"

Levi Strauss & Co. believes this cycle of collaborative objective-setting performance review and compensation, strongly tied to not only *what* work an employee does but *how* the employee does the work, results in employee satisfaction, business success, and increased shareholder value.

INCORPORATING ETHICS IS MORE THAN JUST DRAFTING A STATEMENT OF PHILOSOPHY

Dozens of books have been written about corporate cultures and hundreds of business philosophers have offered mantras ranging from "Customers are number 1" to "If it isn't broken, break it." Manuals and seminars covering the "do's and don't's" proliferate. But an ethical business culture cannot be taught; it emanates from within as a total framework, a way of thinking, responding, and relating to all those audiences inside and outside the company who are interdependent upon one another: employees and shareholders, customers and suppliers, community neighbors and government regulators.

In 1988, Levi Strauss & Co. melded the values of its founder and his successors with a recognition of today's business realities and created its Aspirations Statement, which captures LS&CO.'s fundamental beliefs about the type of company we wish to be:

> A company that our people are proud of and committed to, where all employees have an opportunity to contribute, learn, grow, and advance based on merit, not politics or background. We want our people to feel respected, be treated fairly, be listened to, and be involved. Above all, we want satisfaction from accomplishments and friendships, balanced personal and professional lives, and to have fun in our endeavors.

The six basic leadership qualities necessary to make these Aspirations a reality are defined as

- *Teamwork and trust.* Leadership that exemplifies directness, openness to influence, commitment to the success of others, willingness to acknowledge our own contributions to problems, personal accountability, teamwork, and trust. Not only must we model these behaviors, but we must coach others to adopt them.
- *Diversity.* Leadership that values a diverse work force at all levels of the organization, diversity in experience, and diversity in perspectives. We have committed to taking full advantage of the rich backgrounds and abilities of all our people and to promoting a greater diversity in positions of influence. Differing points of view will be sought; diversity will be valued and honestly rewarded, not suppressed.
- *Recognition.* Leadership that provides greater recognition— both financial and psychic—for individuals and teams contributing to our success. Recognition must also be given to all who contribute: those who create and innovate and also those who continually support the day-to-day business requirements.
- *Ethical management practices.* Leadership that epitomizes the stated standards of ethical behavior. We must provide clarity about our expectations and must enforce these standards throughout the corporation.
- *Communications.* Internally, leadership that builds an environment where information is actively shared, sought, and used in ways that lead to empowerment that works, improved performance, and meaningful feedback. Externally, leadership that strengthens our corporate reputation with key stakeholders. All communications should be clear, timely, and honest.
- *Empowerment.* Leadership that promotes ways of working in which responsibility, authority, and accountability for decision making are held by those closest to our products and customers, and every employee has the necessary perspective, skills, and knowledge to be successful in his or her job. We all share responsibility for creating the environment that will nurture empowerment at all levels of the organization.

With the Aspirations of the company defined, a values-driven business culture approaches matters—both routine and complex—differently. Rather than trying to anticipate every possible question or issue that might arise and answer it in cumbersome policy-and-procedures manuals, a simple set of guidelines can assist people. At Levi Strauss & Co., those guidelines basically affirm that we trust people and expect them to use good judgment. We do not prescribe behaviors to be followed in their business dealings; rather, we ask that managers accept personal accountability for their actions and that they be prepared to describe for senior management the ethical principles approach and reasoning they applied to a given situation.

Our experience indicates that trusting people to operate within a set of guiding principles works. Not only does this philosophy empower managers to make their own decisions, it forces decisions to be made at the level closest to the work being performed, thereby improving the use of time and resources over those dedicated staffs that attempt to provide answers for operating units.

If the Aspirations Statement describes the kind of company we want to create, the Mission Statement reminds everyone why we are in business. The Levi Strauss & Co. mission is to

> *sustain responsible commercial success* as a global marketing company of branded apparel. We must balance goals of superior profitability and return on investment, leadership market positions, and superior products and service. We will conduct our business ethically and demonstrate leadership in satisfying our responsibilities to our communities and to society. Our work environment will be safe and productive and characterized by fair treatment, teamwork, open communications, personal accountability, and opportunities for growth and development.

Note those highlighted words in the first line, "responsible commercial success." Those words remind us all that to be successful, our employees, customers, suppliers, and the communities in which we do business must also be successful. And so we invest in these relationships and weight their interests in making decisions that affect the bottom line.

At Levi Strauss & Co. the loop providing this framework is closed with a simple, four-point Code of Ethics, ground rules that focus attention on six basic values, the Ethical Principles.

CODE OF ETHICS

Levi Strauss & Co. has a long and distinguished history of ethical conduct and community involvement. Essentially, these are a reflection of the mutually shared values of the founding families and of our employees.

Our ethical values are based on the following elements:

1. A commitment to commercial success in terms broader than merely financial measures.

2. A respect for our employees, suppliers, customers, consumers, and stockholders.

3. A commitment to conduct which is not only legal but fair and morally correct in a fundamental sense.

4. Avoidance of not only real, but the appearance of conflict of interest.

From time to time the company will publish specific guidelines, policies, and procedures. However, the best test of whether something is ethically correct is whether you would be prepared to present it to our senior management and board of directors as being consistent with our ethical traditions. If you have any uneasiness about an action that you are about to take or that you see, you should discuss the action with your supervisor or management.

ETHICAL PRINCIPLES

Our ethical principles are the values that set the ground rules for all that we do as employees of Levi Strauss & Co. As we seek to achieve responsible commercial success, we will be challenged to balance these principles against each other, always mindful of our promise to shareholders that we will achieve responsible commercial success.

The ethical principles are

1. *Honesty.* We will not say things that are false. We will never deliberately mislead. We will be as candid as possible, openly and freely sharing information, as appropriate to the relationship.

2. *Promise keeping.* We will go to great lengths to keep our commitments. We will not make promises that can't be kept and we will not make promises on behalf of the company unless we have the authority to do so.

C O D E   O F   E T H I C S — C O N T .

3. *Fairness.* We will create and follow a process and achieve outcomes that a reasonable person would call just, even-handed, and nonarbitrary.

4. *Respect for others.* We will be open and direct in our communication, and receptive to influence. We will honor and value the abilities and contributions of others, embracing the responsibility and accountability for our actions in this regard.

5. *Comparison.* We will maintain an awareness of the needs of others and act to meet those needs whenever possible. We will also minimize harm whenever possible. We will act in ways that are consistent with our commitment to social responsibility.

6. *Integrity.* We will live up to LS&CO.'s ethical principles—even when confronted by personal, professional, and social risks as well as economic pressures.

So, how do these philosophies get translated into action in the finance function, in the corporate offices, or throughout the reach of a global manufacturing, marketing, and distribution company?

The "glue" is a Principled Reasoning Approach that is dissected and digested in the ethical training that more than a thousand people go through each year. Exhibit 2.1 shows the Principled Reasoning Approach in simple diagram form. In oversimplified form, the approach embraces 11 principles for decision making:

- Honesty
- Promise keeping
- Fairness
- Respect for others
- Compassion
- Integrity
- Corporate social responsibility
- Longer-term, global leadership
- Loyalty
- Sustained profitable commercial success
- Respect for cultural diversity

E X H I B I T   2.1

Principled Reasoning Approach

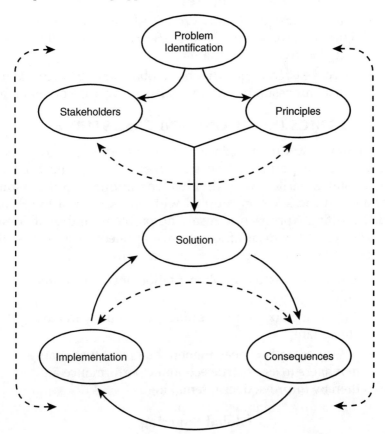

From a chief financial officer's perspective, these principles raise such decision making questions as

- Does the decision emphasize cost to the exclusion of all other factors and thereby possibly not best serve our long-term business interests?
- Have we appropriately balanced how this solution supports business strategies, brand enhancement, competitive strategy, corporate values, cost, customer requirements, quality, and service?

- How will each of our stakeholders view the problem, the alternative solutions, and their consequences in light of the company's stated principles?
- Have we adequately analyzed this business decision in the light of our external Corporate Social Responsibility goals and objectives in this matter?
- Have we encouraged diverse, global viewpoints in order to test our assumptions and balance our decision making?

ETHICS IN ACTION: MINI-CASE STUDIES

At Levi Strauss & Co., the process for incorporating ethics in decision making has permeated virtually the entire organization. The keys, as stated earlier, are individual commitment to the Aspirations and Business Vision coupled with application of the Principled Reasoning Approach to resolving problems and deliberating policy. As chief financial officer, I have applied these beliefs and concepts in a variety of specific areas including

- Establishment and implementation of global sourcing guidelines.
- An income tax model to guide the company in paying its "fair share."
- A "scorecard" or measurement blueprint that enables managers to assess true economic performance and thereby improve decision making.

Global Sourcing

As part of the globalization of Levi Strauss & Co., we have deliberately located production closer to our customers, a strategy that has required us to expand our sourcing base to more diverse cultures. As a result, Levi Strauss & Co. manufactures or sources products in more than 60 countries on all the inhabited continents. In the process of that globalization we have concluded that sourcing decisions that emphasize only cost to the exclusion of other factors will not meet customer requirements, protect our brands, or honor our corporate values, nor in the long run promote responsible commercial success.

In the early 1990s, we adopted Business Partner Terms of Engagement and Guidelines for Country Selection. This is a series of standards that provide a framework for assessing the controllable practices of individual business partners (i.e., contractors and suppliers who provide labor and/or material) as well as the political and social issues in those countries where we might consider sourcing. The Terms of Engagement act as a set of guiding principles that help us identify potential problems so that we can work with our business partners to address areas of concern as they arise. They include environmental requirements, ethical standards, community involvement, legal requirements, and employment standards.

Using employment practices as an example, Levi Strauss & Co. limits its contractual relationships to those business partners whose workers are in all cases present voluntarily, fairly compensated, allowed the right of free association, not put at risk of physical harm, and not exploited in any way. Specific guidelines include

- Wages and benefits should comply with any applicable law or match the prevailing local work hours.
- While permitting flexibility in scheduling, prevailing local work hours are not exceeded except for appropriately compensated overtime. (While LS&CO. favors partners who require less than 60-hour workweeks, we will not engage contractors who routinely require more than 60-hour weeks. Employees also must be allowed one day off in seven days).
- Use of child labor is not permissible, with *child* defined as someone less than 14 years of age or younger than the compulsory age to be in school.
- Use of prison or forced labor is prohibited.
- Employment of workers is based on their ability to do the job, rather than on the basis of personal characteristics or beliefs.
- Corporal punishment and other forms of mental or physical coercion are prohibited.

An interesting example arose in Bangladesh when these Terms of Engagement were first being implemented. After an audit of more than 600 contractors worldwide, the company became aware of one contractor that employed youngsters under the age of 14 in its plant, a practice not uncommon in many under-developed countries where children may supply most of a family's income.

This was a clear violation of the company's guidelines. After study we developed a solution that minimized ethical consequences and negative impact on the families and children involved. The contractors agreed to pay the 35 underage children their salaries and benefits while they went to school full-time. We agreed to pay for books, tuition, and uniforms. When the children reach legal working age, they will be offered jobs in the plant. In the end we were able to honor our values, protect our brand, and retain contractors that play an important role in our worldwide sourcing strategy.

As for country selection, Levi Strauss & Co. specifically assesses whether

- Sourcing would have an adverse effect on the company's global brand image.
- There is evidence that Levi Strauss & Co. employees or representatives would be exposed to unreasonable health or safety risk.
- There are pervasive violations of basic human rights.
- The legal environment creates unreasonable risk to trademarks or to other important commercial interests or seriously impedes implementation of these guidelines.
- Political or social turmoil unreasonably threatens commercial interests.

The company continually monitors and evaluates its country selections and revises these when appropriate. After a period of political unrest and the introduction of martial law in Peru several years ago, Levi Strauss & Co. became concerned for the health and safety of employees and representatives and shut down operations in that country. We continued to monitor the political situation. When the environment later improved, we resumed operations in that country.

Taxes

As the CFO of any global enterprise knows, the complexity of tax laws and corporate decision making grows geometrically with the number of government entities, cultural traditions, and business practices involved. Tax planning can become a patchwork of internal and adviser opinions, past practices, and inconsistent interpretation. This can be particularly problematical when shareholders and management have differing views over the conflict between paying the minimum tax legally possible and the long-term benefits of paying a fair and equitable share of the tax burden.

To define and incorporate a workable vision and strategy, Levi Strauss & Co. developed a framework for establishing standards for tax positions being recommended to management. The foundation for this model begins with the basics used by all companies: tax reporting statutes, case law, and standards set by tax professionals such as the American Bar Association (ABA) and the American Institute of Certified Public Accountants (AICPA). To this Levi Strauss & Co. added its own "terms of engagement" of the tax system.

The ABA standard calls for a position that must have some realistic possibility of success if litigated, before a tax lawyer should advise a client to adopt such a position. Statute, as amended in 1989, has established ethical guidelines for lawyers and accountants, in which understatement of tax liability is subject to penalty unless it is shown that there is reasonable cause of the understatement and such person acted in good faith.

The above analysis led to Exhibit 2.2's summary of US legal standards. To these generally accepted standards, Levi Strauss & Co.'s Tax Department has added a number of additional filters to address perceived company and shareholder values and the possible conflicts between them, as we see in Exhibit 2.3.

This model, applied with the Principled Reasoning Model described earlier in this chapter, has enabled the LS&CO. Tax Department to provide a worldwide tax standard that clearly exceeds the minimum standards required by the tax system and reflects balance between the company's values and shareholders' interest as well as a strong commitment to responsible commercial success.

EXHIBIT 2.2

Summary of US Legal Standards

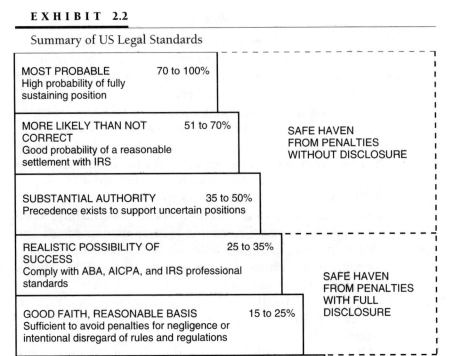

Note: All percentages of success are approximate and are determined by the Corporate Tax Department based on analysis of IRS announcements, case law, and informed professional judgment.

Supply Chain Costing and Cost Management

When making product sourcing decisions, most companies use a pure financial analysis to develop costs. But what about those intangibles that appear impossible to measure and, yet, significantly affect an organization's ability to maintain responsible commercial success?

In an organization that recognizes the importance of meeting customer service requirements, what is the value of

- A truly captive contractor who will make anything within capabilities and has reserved capacity not available to competitors?

E X H I B I T   2.3

Perceived Company and Shareholders Values

Relationship Created	Perceived Values	Adversarial	Goodwill
Environment	Wants to comply fully with all established standards, exceeding some standards when appropriate. Conscionable compliance where there are no standards.	No	Yes
Community	Wants to be recognized as a responsible leader of corporate social responsibility.	No	Yes
Employees	Wants to be a progressive role model as an employer with higher-than-average standards.	No	Yes
Suppliers of goods and services	Aggressive, reasonable, and honest	Sometimes	Sometimes
Retailers	Equitable, open, and honest	No	Yes
Competitors	Aggressive and honest	Yes	No
Tax	Aggressive and honest	Yes	No

- Proprietary positions regarding new products, production processes, product finishing or completion, and so on?
- Flexibility in lead times, changeovers, volume fluctuations, and last-minute schedule changes?
- US sourcing, which provides a hedge against import backlash, currency fluctuations, and political instability?
- Competence or expertise in which resources that can respond quickly support product development from concept through distribution?
- Risk avoidance of disruptions such as labor conflicts, natural disasters, political upheaval, and economic uncertainty?
- Protecting brand image?
- A trained, committed work force that is open to continuous improvement?

To measure the true costs of these and other supply chain characteristics, Levi Strauss & Co. has designed a scorecard that balances a simple, clear-cut view of financial and ethical performance from both internal and customer/supplier perspectives. Through its use, internal audiences such as marketing make decisions based not only on "hard" dollar costs, but also on quality, on-time delivery, environmental, and other "soft" factors. In addition, by focusing attention on return on investment—as opposed to sales and margins—truly accurate costing formulas can be developed for each product, stock keeping unit (SKU), or seasonal cycle. Finally, by broadening the definition of costs to analyze fully both the financial and ethical implications of product sourcing, company-owned plants (and their employees) can compete on a level playing field with outside contractors who often appear to present a competitive advantage on a pure dollars-and-cents basis.

The scorecard analyzes measurable areas usually neglected in purely "dollarized" costing methodology. These include

- *Partner satisfaction.* Rating and quantifying both customer and supplier satisfaction compared with that of competitors.

- *Economic performance.* Comparisons of company and competitor ratios ranging from cost of goods, inventory, profits, receivables, and assets against sales, to return on total assets.

- *Lead time.* Average number of days required to design, manufacture and deliver product.

- *On-time delivery.* Percentage of customers indicating satisfactory receipt of each product, as measured by promptness, accuracy, and completeness of delivery.

An example within our re-engineering work is our assessment and review of supplier partners. Finding those that can best meet our needs and developing strong relationships with them is an ongoing process at Levi Strauss & Co. The decision to retain or discontinue working with a supplier is based on a process that allows our employees to objectively evaluate suppliers on 16 criteria in five categories: capability, capacity, service, corporate culture, and pricing strategy. Recent results show a streamlining in the total number of suppliers through this process and we anticipate improved customer service and an increased ability to get products to market quickly.

By recognizing and managing all of the cost drivers, the organization's financial and operational performance indicators become more accurate, require fewer reconciliations, and (perhaps most importantly) provide better tools for supporting the truly important strategic financial target—return on investment.

CONCLUSION

All of our business decisions are focused on increasing shareholder value. Intertwined with this concept, we embrace a sense of shared values and ethics in everything we do. We attempt to create a "shareholder mind-set" among our employees so that they will be empowered to independently make decisions that are consistent with our company values.

Training is an important element we use to help create that mind-set. All financial managers take part in a comprehensive training program we call the core curriculum. The centerpiece is a course known as "leadership week" that helps managers practice the behavior outlined in the Aspirations Statement.

Two concrete examples of how ethics permeate our culture are the Global Sourcing Guidelines and Terms of Engagement and the tax model. We attempt to balance the "soft costs" of decisions along with other factors that affect the bottom line.

Fundamentally, we believe that "doing good" is good for business. Not only is it possible for us to act in a socially responsible manner in all aspects of conducting business, we believe it is essential to shaping the culture we've created, attracting and retaining talented employees, establishing positive relationships with retail partners and suppliers, and maintaining effective relationships with banks and financial institutions. Ultimately, our Aspirational style of business contributes to our financial success, to the image of our brands and trademarks, and to our corporate reputation.

As a CFO in a values-driven culture, the process of doing business carries a balanced weight to the financial outcomes. We benefit from a culture that allows rewarding people for both the quality of their work and work products as well as treating one another with dignity and respect. We have experienced tangible benefits from our ethical and values-driven approach to business and increases to our return on investment for all constituents. Our values contribute to the bottom line in a tangible manner and the finance function acts as a true business partner in all the enterprise's endeavors.

⑥ **UNDERSTANDING THE BUSINESS AND ECONOMIC ENVIRONMENT**

Douglas J. Beck
Senior Vice President, ICF Kaiser International

Roger E. Brinner
Executive Director and Chief Economist, DRI/McGraw-Hill

The chief financial officer (CFO) must focus on the financial decisions and operations over which he or she has control, decisions that clearly cannot be made without anticipating developments and minimizing the risks inherent in the economic and political arenas. Increasingly this environment must be understood in a global context, as corporate markets, suppliers, and competitors commonly operate within a multinational framework. Moreover, firms operating only in the domestic arena increasingly face foreign competition on their own turf as the global search for new markets accelerates. With worldwide trends toward deregulation and more open markets continuing, and as growth in emerging markets often outstrips growth in established industrial country markets, "going global" has been one of the most common strategic battle cries of the 1990s. As a consequence, today's CFO must anticipate and address economic and business environmental impact on the firm on a far larger and more complex stage than the CFOs of only a decade ago.

Within this more complex environment, it is important for the CFO to appreciate that nearly every dimension of the corporate financial position can be affected by changes in the business environment. If we look at a typical firm's income statement, for example, both the revenue and cost dimensions can be affected by numerous factors that should be anticipated in a planning exercise.

• *Revenues* are critically dependent on selecting the appropriate growth markets. Today's perspective demands an analysis of whether the appropriate industrial or consumer segments are still most fruitful in the traditional markets, or whether they lie in newly emerging markets, often in very different overseas economic and political environments.

• *Costs* are affected not only by outside effects on the traditional factors of labor and capital, but also by the wider opportunities for firms and their competitors to tap into labor and capital in new areas. They are also impacted by such factors as the multinational competitive framework of suppliers, and the complex policy environments of everything from environmental to health legislation.

• *Cost planning* in areas such as capacity expansion, inventory purchasing, and employment must reflect the stage of the business cycle in which the firm is operating in each of its important markets. Failure to incorporate such knowledge will lead to excessive fixed-cost burdens as well as gross earnings instability. While forecasts cannot be perfect in a world of random international crises and subjective domestic policy manipulation, sufficient information is available to make a material difference in corporate performance.

As a result, corporate *profits* are critically affected by the interplay of economics-driven factors affecting both the revenue and expense sides of the income statement on a global basis for larger firms or for those firms traditionally limited to domestic markets. This interplay has often expanded to an "Americas" continental basis.

To address this complexity, we believe that a CFO must approach business management as one would approach an investment portfolio. For any business there is a portfolio of revenue opportunities and a portfolio of alternative cost strategies encompassing countries and market segments globally, or regional and market segments domestically, that require a systematic assessment of risk and a careful balancing of potential opportunities against those risks. The opportunities offered by many of the high-growth emerging markets, for instance, must be weighed against the risks of operating in more volatile policy, currency, and labor environments. Many types of environmental opportunities and risks must be considered, including economic, geopolitical, and financial.

The successful firms and the successful CFOs will be those who understand the variety of opportunities that exist in the global context, and who have a healthy and well-considered respect for the risks that must be balanced to sustain growth and competitive advantage across both the upturns and downturns that inevitably occur.

To assist the CFO in evaluating today's business environment and its potential effects on the firm's revenue, costs, and profit opportunities, this chapter will address four topics:

1. *Fundamental themes.* What are some fundamental factors influencing global and domestic business environments over the next decade?
2. *Specific global market forecasts.* How do some of these key factors translate into expected outlooks for key geographic markets and sectors?
3. *Incorporating effects.* How does one link the changes in the business environment to potential impacts on a firm's financial performance?
4. *Risks.* What are the types of and approaches to risk that must be weighed against the opportunities posed by changes in the global business environment?

FUNDAMENTALS: KEY FACTORS AFFECTING THE BUSINESS ENVIRONMENT

A number of important themes concern the competitive environment of today's firms. They include the globalization of markets, constrained growth in traditional markets, remarkable growth opportunities in select developing nations, the continuation of business cycles in industrial nations, and financial and trade volatility.

Globalization of Markets

Globalization has become one of the most overused business terms in today's lexicon, but it nevertheless represents a fundamental component of business life. As most national governments continue to liberalize and encourage market behavior, and with technological changes aiding more efficient global strategy implementation, the revenue, cost, and financial challenges facing almost any firm are increasingly global in nature. Revenue patterns are shifting more quickly across regions and national markets; global competition requires that companies produce wherever it makes market and financial sense to do so; and access to capital is an around-the-clock and around-the-world business.

At the core of this trend is the increasing interaction across borders, both economically and financially. World trade, for example, has been one of the key engines of world economic growth. During most of the past decade, world trade growth has been two-thirds faster than overall economic growth, attesting to the continuing enlargement of trade as a proportion of economic activity. However, trade growth is typically more volatile than overall market growth. When domestic market segments are growing rapidly, import gains normally outperform the market as domestic capacity becomes constrained and global competitors seek to exploit the opportunities. Conversely, in shrinking market segments, foreign competitors not as close to the market often find themselves shut out more quickly. Exhibit 3.1 shows the relationship of overall real import growth with the real economic growth of the major industrial (OECD) countries. It illustrates how growth through cross-border business initiatives can present greater opportunities as well as risks to the global player.

Foreign investment has also grown rapidly as firms have moved to optimize their operations across borders. Foreign direct investment, for example, continues to grow faster than overall economic growth and international trade as well. According to United Nations' estimates of global direct investment, the world stock of foreign investment grew at double-digit rates during the first five years of the 1990s, and shows little sign of abating, especially within developing countries.

EXHIBIT 3.1

Growth Influences Imports
OECD GDP and Import Growth

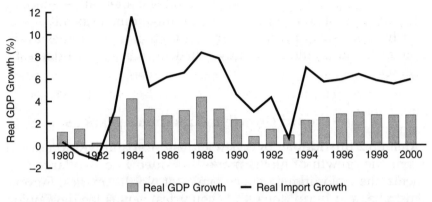

Source: DRI/McGraw-Hill

All of these factors are manifestations of a globalization process whose characteristics point to at least three key conclusions from the firm's perspective:

• Markets are changing faster and are ignoring national borders more than ever before. While sensitivity to local customs and patterns will always be critical, it is increasingly the case that market segments are viewed by product, industry, or demographic trends first and by geography second.

• Globalization of production requires new approaches to operations and cost planning. With modern ability to move across borders easily, wages and productivity will continue to play a dominant role in many production site decisions, as many developing countries offer large pools of semiskilled workers at comparably low wages. Nevertheless, political, social, and economic climates plus infrastructure and labor market stability will remain significant. Therefore, it has become increasingly important to have a "portfolio" of production sites whose potential risks and returns must be evaluated, given global market conditions.

• Global financial options will continue to proliferate. Financial market deregulation, global portfolio diversification, and increased business information flows have fostered increased international capital mobility—a trend that has hardly diminished since the explosion in the 1980s. Finance continues to involve more countries, more markets, and more instruments as regulatory barriers are still falling in both emerging and industrial markets.

"Going global" is no longer a strategic alternative affecting only the largest companies. Across all three dimensions it affects nearly every size of firm in terms of (1) the opportunities available to it and (2) the competitive challenges in its own domestic markets.

Constrained Growth in Traditional Markets

Exhibit 3.2 provides an overview of historical and DRI-forecasted economic growth of global markets divided into two large segments: the major industrial economies of North America, Europe, Australia, and Japan (the OECD countries) versus the developing economies of Asia, Latin America, the Middle East, and Africa. When viewed on a broad geographic basis, the world economy of the latter 1990s is expected to exhibit faster growth than the recession-plagued markets earlier in the decade. However, the cyclical recovery in the large industrial markets (which account for three quarters of global economic activity) is expected to be restrained compared to postwar norms.

Over the past five years (1990–1994), the industrial countries have passed through waves of slow or recessionary periods with limited market growth prospects. Unfortunately, the recovery periods over the next five years are not expected to exhibit normal postwar recovery growth rates.

Ingredients for the subdued recovery are

- Slow population growth and flat, if not declining, labor force participation rates. Even bolstered by immigration, labor force growth in North America and Europe will be approximately 1 percent per year compared to 2 to 3 percent in the 1960s and 1970s. This puts a supply-side restraint on basic market and output growth.
- The residual effects of the asset deflation of the past recession, especially in the English-speaking countries and Japan, that will continue to act as an anchor on the recovery of private investment.

EXHIBIT 3.2

Economic Growth
Industrial (OECD) versus Developing Economies

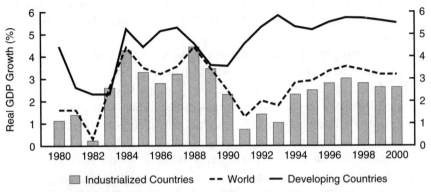

Source: DRI/McGraw-Hill

- The extremely high level of public debt constraining tax cuts or new public spending as a catalyst for growth in most of the industrial countries. The high US debt level was considered a significant hindrance to world recovery in the 1980s, but many industrial countries, especially in Europe, have now caught up or surpassed the United States in fiscal profligacy,
- Persistently high unemployment, especially in Europe, that fuels job insecurity and saps consumer optimism despite overall economic growth,

In the "G-7" nations of the United States, Japan, Canada, and Europe the implications for the medium term (1995–2000) are real growth rates averaging only 2.5 to 3 percent per year. Inflation will be held close to current rates centered on 3 percent. Thus sales and profit growth coming out of mature markets will be limited to 6 percent, well below the double-digit growth aspirations of most major corporations.

Remarkable Growth Opportunities in Select Developing Nations

In contrast to this constrained outlook in traditional markets, many of the developing-country markets have increased their ability to grow rapidly and to break their traditional linkage to industrial-country cycles and trends. In parts of Asia, Latin America, and Eastern Europe, the success of continued economic reform, coupled with high savings and investment levels, has created conditions for sustained growth 2 to 3 percent higher than in many of the traditional markets.

Increasingly open borders for goods, technology, and capital are the keys to accelerated growth in the receptive developing nations. Reductions in trade barriers for goods began with the Kennedy Round of tariff reductions in the 1960s, but these did not provide a sufficient catalyst. Indeed, the goods trade expansion produced by these early initiative locked these nations into a synchronous cycle tied to supplying raw materials and simple assembled goods to the mature nations.

The true watershed events are the political and economic reforms of the late 1980s and early 1990s that stimulated equity investment by multinationals and entrepreneurs. These factors are summarized in the accompanying box. Instead of jealously "protecting" national firms with restrictions on majority ownership by foreign firms, progressive nations began to court equity investment. With equity investment came major corporations' willingness to transfer technology, to marry it to the low-wage

---

THE NEW ECONOMIC ORDER: OPEN BORDERS FOR GOODS, TECHNOLOGY, AND FINANCE

Unprecedented technology and capital transfers plus political transformations signal high growth for selected developing nations. The earliest and most rapid advancement will occur where

- The work force is the best educated and motivated.
- Trade and investment are high to speed integration.
- The indigenous entrepreneurial climate is most positive.
- Government fiscal and monetary policies are best balanced to keep inflation and exchange risks minimal.
- The democratic heritage is strongest.

indigenous population, and to link the transplant production into sophisticated global marketing systems.

With these new ties, the value of the labor in the developing world rose dramatically. The new investment mode, equity not debt, thus promotes much more rapid convergence to the productivity and living standards of the mature industrial nations. The middle class arises and prospers, presenting huge new growth markets to international firms.

As a consequence of these varied growth patterns, many companies will and should continue to seek new opportunities for market growth outside of the traditional spheres. There will always be specific product and niche opportunities at home, but for many firms, "going global" is synonymous with the quest for the highest-growth markets of the next decade.

Along with those high-growth markets, however, there are likely to be attendant increases in the risk and volatility of those market outlooks. As we will note in later sections, addressing risk and volatility is often a defining characteristic of global economic life.

The Continuation of Business Cycles in Industrial Nations

Volatility is still an important factor in domestic and large industrial markets as well. The leading economies of the world are still subject to pronounced cycles of growth and contraction. Without exception, all postwar recessions have been caused by central bank credit tightening in response to rising prices. In the case of the 1975, 1980, and 1990 recessions, oil price "crises" occurred near the peak of US recoveries and magnified internal economic problems beyond the scope that could have been anticipated in their absence. However, the preceding recoveries had reached full maturity and rising interest rates were setting the stage for marked deceleration of growth in any event.

Because all recessions can be traced to such a fundamental cause, regular patterns can be discerned and predicted for the broad national economy and also for the sequential participation of specific market sectors. When inflation fears arise in the financial markets, the resultant surge in interest rates leads to an early decline in housing and, very shortly thereafter, to slumping auto,

---

IS YOUR BUSINESS SUBJECT TO "THE BUSINESS CYCLE"?

If you could understand and anticipate trends and cycles in sales, you could

- Avoid inventory problems.
- Budget development spending more logically.
- Manage hiring more profitably.
- Achieve greater earnings stability.
- Improve profit margins.
- Raise P-E ratios for your stock.

The good news is that you can understand and anticipate trends and cycles if you understand your links to the economy.

---

appliance, and furniture sales. Other discretionary purchases such as fast food, entertainment, and clothing then cycle lower as employment and income growth slows. Finally, business capital spending is curtailed as excess capacity materializes. Rising unemployment and falling capacity utilization gradually tame inflation, eventually leading to lower interest rates. The sequence of recovery recapitulates the sequence of entry into recession: Housing rebounds first and business spending last.

These cycles must be carefully factored into business plans to stabilize earnings as much as possible and to maximize long-run return on equity by avoiding excessive capacity investment with its high fixed costs. Many of the most respected manufacturing firms achieve these exact goals by careful anticipation and monitoring of the cycles in their key endmarkets.

Manufacturers know from experience that consumer income and business cash flow variations drive their sales, but not all know how to use this information. The results achieved by the best-practice firms are remarkable. For example, a major global manufacturer of highly cyclical goods—with $9 billion in annual sales of appliance components, process control equipment, heating and air-conditioning apparatus, and construction tools—has integrated meticulous one- and five-year forecasts into its plans so successfully that it has achieved uninterrupted earnings gains for

EXHIBIT 3.3

Is Your Business Subject to the Business Cycle?
Food Is a Necessity, but Food Sales Respond 2:1 to Cycles in Household Incomes.

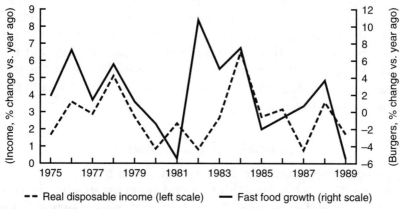

-- Real disposable income (left scale)   — Fast food growth (right scale)

Source: DRI/McGraw-Hill

37 consecutive years! Dating all the way back to 1956, this firm has been able to cut costs as rapidly as sales weaken and thus not only protect but also continuously expand earnings per share.

Service sector firms often resist such analysis because they believe they are selling "necessities" (such as food or medicine) or that their markets are driven by technology (such as computers or pharmaceuticals). These beliefs are so incomplete that they are in fact almost always dangerously fallacious. For example, the high-trend growth rates in both the fast food and software industries have masked a remarkable 2:1 or 3:1 sensitivity to growth in customer income.

A major hamburger chain, for example, based its sales plans on the premise that with women seeking careers outside the home food was becoming immune to business cycles. Sales cycles were thought to be a function of marketing campaigns. Yet further analysis revealed that hamburger sales cycles nearly perfectly match the cycle in household income, except burger cycles are twice as large as those in income. (See Exhibit 3.3). Moreover, with two-income families, fast food becomes a luxury when one wage earner is lost. This logically explains the 2:1 sales–to–household-income sensitivity through the business cycle.

A similar striking finding was determined with regard to software sales for personal computers. The industry believed that supply issues dominated. Its sales were thought to be solely driven by the revolution in computer hardware and by software product innovation. Most managers surveyed totally discounted the relevance of the business cycle. Much to their surprise, it was quite easy to show through simple statistical analysis that personal computer software growth over the past decade can be fully explained by the factors they acknowledge, plus a powerful, consistent 2:1 variation with corporate cash flow.

Financial and Trade Volatility

While economic growth in the industrial countries is expected to moderate, the global growth of capital movements and the complexity of capital markets will not. Financial market deregulation, global portfolio diversification, and the growth of the business information highway will all continue to underscore rapidly increasingly capital mobility and global portfolio diversification. Global investment will continue to be a mainstay of the global economy, but its speed, volatility, and growing range of choices all place a premium on prudent global risk management.

Volatility in global trade movements for businesses tied to them is often a less appreciated, but extremely important theme for both global and domestic firms. As shown in Exhibit 3.1, global trade has generally outpaced overall economic growth, but it is typically more volatile than the overall growth of national markets, as trade is often the swing factor between differences in domestic supply and demand. As a consequence, the CFO must accept that the trade-related opportunities presented in the international economic environment will carry a greater need to pursue diversification and other risk management strategies in light of increasing volatility of expected financial returns.

Encouraging the rapid growth of world trade are the continued evolution of freer markets and open borders plus the globalization of the world economy. General agreements to lower tariffs and trade (GATT) have gone through six successive rounds of tariff reductions since World War II, radically increasing movements of manufactured goods and activities across borders. Regional free trade agreements have also begun to take hold in the past decade after less successful attempts in the 1960s and 1970s. The European Community plus U.S. efforts with Canada and now Mexico (NAFTA) have been among the most prominent, but dozens of free trade initiatives are now underway on every continent. In Latin America alone, one can count over 20 free trade initiatives underway since 1990; among them are the Mercosur agreement in South America, numerous bilateral and multilateral agreements between Chile, Bolivia, and their Latin American partners, and Mexican free trade agreements with Chile, Colombia, Venezuela, and Central America. All of these may be building blocks toward an Americas free trade area in the 21st century.

On the minus side, it is clear that political and economic risks to the growth of world trade threaten at multilateral, regional, and bilateral levels. Most critical at the multilateral level is the renewal of the most recent (Uruguay Round) of the GATT accord. Although the World Trade Organization has now been established, continued cross-border progress in some important areas to US companies may be difficult.

The risk of stalled GATT ratification may not have its greatest impact on trade, however, where projected one-third reductions in tariffs are from relatively low levels (5 to 15 percent) negotiated in previous agreements. Rather, the more important aspects of the new agreement relate to continued progress on the cross-border movement of services (professional, tourism, financial, health, and transport), agreement on intellectual property rights, and consistency in the treatment of foreign investment. As global trade becomes increasingly dominated by sales through foreign subsidiaries, as well as the movement of information and the services to support them, the opening of these aspects becomes the new challenge for global markets. Progress is going to be much more difficult, and the multinational firm will have to pay close attention to the interplay of bilateral and multilateral policy changes that will alter this risky landscape over the coming decade.

In addition to the multilateral changes on trade, perhaps more significant will be the regional and bilateral dimensions.

Given the slow negotiating process of multilateral talks such as GATT, it is natural that many aspects of market opening and protectionist sentiments are argued within smaller groups. The proliferation of different regional and country standards about nontariff barriers has also made special bilateral and regional agreements attractive policy options. As a consequence, the multinational corporate manager still must be extremely cognizant of the variations in regional and/or national codes and behavior in implementing successful global strategies.

Our conclusion is that *mature versus emerging markets offer strategic choices*. It is clear that global competition has broadened both the opportunities and complexity of sales, production, and financing decisions faced by the international firm. Given this complexity, operating within the global environment presents two key strategic challenges:

1. *The enlarged global market offers greater opportunities to seek growth through a larger portfolio of environments in which to operate.* The domestic firm can now be less constrained by the business cycles in the home operating environment, as at any given time the global economy typically offers simultaneous high-growth and slow-growth prospects for each segment. Consequently, the quest for emerging markets outside of the traditional areas of Europe, North America, and Japan should continue to accelerate into the next decade.

2. *The ability to spread operations across more markets is often accompanied by greater volatility in many of those markets.* The risk/return trade trade-offs familiar to financial portfolio practitioners has clear analogies for the global firm increasingly operating in emerging markets. The higher average growth rates in many Asian and Latin American economies are accompanied by the increased political risk of political and policy instability, economic risks of hyperinflation and financial market fluctuations, and social risks brought on by extremely high levels of poverty and disenfranchisement amid the rapid economic growth.

The CFO facing a global marketplace must often seek higher returns in emerging or nontraditional markets, and must manage the increased risk often associated with growth expectations. Therefore, it is important to be aware of the range of opportunities and the many types of risks that should be considered and evaluated in this context. Assessing today's global environment is a systematic process of consistently weighing these two factors.

Before we address some guidelines to that process, however, it may be useful to summarize some key regional and global market trends that DRI expects firms to face over the next decade.

GLOBAL MARKET TRENDS: THE SIZE AND GROWTH OF REGIONAL MARKETS

A first step in environmental assessment is to focus on the markets in which the CFO's firm could operate from both a revenue and cost perspective. From a revenue perspective it is important to assess which markets are growing and what is the firm's ability to penetrate those markets. From a cost perspective, issues such as the cost of production (including labor and relative productivity) and the cost of capital are critical. In this section we will look at the outlook for major geomarkets for the rest of the decade and summarize some of our conclusions about the relative positioning and strengths of those markets. While this section must by necessity be a broad overview, it is meant to be suggestive of some of the factors and trends that the CFO would want to assess from the perspective of his or her firm.

Exhibit 3.4 shows the sizes of the major geographic markets over the first half of the 1990s and projects their sizes after the year

E X H I B I T   3.4

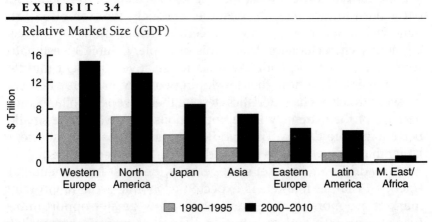

Relative Market Size (GDP)

Source: DRI/McGraw-Hill

Total and Middle-Class Population for
Three Latin American Nations, 1993

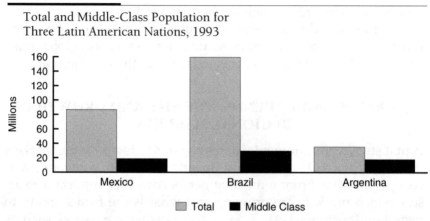

Source: DRI/McGraw-Hill

2000. Over the course of the decade, Europe and North America will remain the largest markets in absolute size, with Asia in total closing in very quickly and surpassing the other two by the end of the next decade. The less industrialized markets of Asia, Latin America, and the Middle East are more modest in size, but of course often represent the faster-growth markets for many products. While growth is certainly a key factor, market size is important, because even slow growth in a large market can make for large absolute gains.

When viewed at a macro level, market size can be deceptive. It is important to address what market segments are most relevant for particular product lines. In consumer products, for example, a firm may wish to focus on buyers with certain demographic or purchasing ability characteristics. Using this example, Exhibit 3.5 estimates some key markets in Latin America for relatively affluent middle-class buyers. Note how the developing country markets often can present attractive characteristics despite their low per capita income, because of the extremely large populations from which the smaller percentages are drawn. The middle class in Mexico, for instance, is larger than similar groups in Canada or the Benelux countries.

In addition to market size, perhaps the most fundamental attraction of target markets is expected economic growth. Growing markets are more dynamic and often allow greater opportunities for sales growth and penetration than slower-growing markets

EXHIBIT 3.6

Projected Average Annual Growth of Key Global Markets, 1994–2003

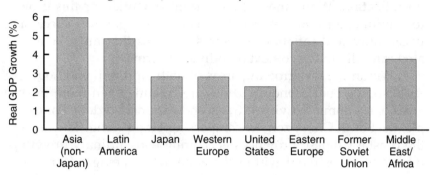

Source: DRI/McGraw-Hill

where established competitors are putting up strong defenses to maintain market share. On a comparative regional basis, DRI expects Asia to continue to top the global growth league. (See Exhibit 3.6.) The following section outlines some key market characteristics of Asia and other geomarkets.

Asia

On average, Asian economies are expected to increase their share of world output and world trade over the decade. Buoyed by high savings rates, booming middle classes, generally favorable policy environments, and relative political stability, Asia will continue to be a magnet for both sales and production activities to supply its own markets and world markets. It is just as important to note, however, that Asian countries also exhibit tremendous diversity in terms of economic performance and other dimensions that should temper any attempt to generalize on a broad basis.

Market maturity ranges from Japan to some of the poorest countries in the world. The Japanese economy, once considered an important standard for growth and export strength, is reaching a more difficult stage in its evolution. Saddled by rising capital costs and relatively weak financial and service sectors, Japanese market growth is expected to ratchet down toward the more moderate paces of its European and North American trade partners.

The highest-growth track currently belongs to China, especially in the coastal provinces which have benefited the most from liberalization. While there is significant potential for this growth to continue, an undeveloped financial sector, political succession uncertainty, and inflation pressures are risks that must be evaluated carefully in the context of individual firms.

Within the fast-growing areas of both Northern and Southern Asia, subregional economic zones are creating even more intense areas of economic activity to transcend national borders. For example, the South China zone encompassing Hong Kong, Taiwan, and the coastal Chinese provinces is creating extraordinary growth of trade and investment within the zone, while being a formidable competitor in the world economy. The Southeast Asian growth triangle also is creating strong interregional activity, although much of the investment funding is drawn from outside the region.

Latin America

Prospects for many of the Latin American economies remain extremely promising, although volatile changes around generally positive trends are to be expected. The pace of reform, including privatization and liberalization, has been critical to the evolution of the business and growth climate. Mexico, Chile, Argentina, and others have created exciting prospects for market growth, and the entire region is increasingly influenced by the opening of free trade zones and more liberal investment relationships. Yet, as the 1994–95 Mexican peso crisis suggests, the region is very vulnerable to the flow of external investment and world interest rates, while a number of structural issues (including low savings rates and lopsided income distribution) pose significant risks to the growth picture.

Western Europe

The largest industrial and trade market in the world is building momentum for economic recovery in the latter part of the 1990s. Growth in European markets is expected to be difficult relative to past trends for a number of reasons, however. High unit labor costs and relatively rigid labor markets, for example, create structural impediments to the type of competitive restructuring of industry that has occurred in the rest of the world. Moreover, with high unemployment and relatively large government deficits, the policy flexibility for instituting proactive policies is limited. Finally, European integration, a boon to investment and confidence five years ago, is now proceeding at a more cautious and multispeed pace depending upon the policy area. As a consequence, the world's largest market is also facing a range of structural issues that will constrain market and company dynamics significantly.

North America

With prospects of freer trade throughout the continent, North America faces important minuses and pluses in its market development over the next decade. Slower labor force growth, overall market maturity, and continued fiscal pressure will moderate the average growth outlook for North American markets. The ability to blend the productivity, services, and skills of the United States and Canada with the lower-wage potential and rapidly developing buying power of the Mexican economy, however, has created new dynamism in many sectors. Furthermore, North America has already undergone much of the industrial and corporate restructuring yet to be faced in Japan and Europe, and has relatively advanced private and deregulated, dynamic markets in many industries—with significant differences between regions. Thus, despite growth that is slower than the world average overall, North America will feature both the regional and sectional differences that can present important opportunities.

Eastern Europe

Eastern Europe is marked by extreme diversity, not only culturally but also by the pace of reform in the post-Soviet areas. Some reform programs now show early signs of success (as in Poland, Hungary, and the Czech Republic), whereas other regions, such as southern Eastern Europe and many of the former Soviet republics, have yet to get very far in their market development. Yet even as prospects for reform continue to improve, however, the Eastern European economies still face fundamental restructuring issues that will alter the economic, social, an political fabrics for years to come. Thus, while positive growth rates may be expected in many of these economies as they begin to turn upward, the risks and levels of market maturity will present challenges of a scale without parallel among the major economic regions.

Middle East and Africa

Here is an enormously diverse area in terms of income level, culture, and history. Outlooks here often depend on commodity prices, including oil in the Middle East and minerals in Central Africa, while progress in market reform is generally limited. Except in the oil-producing countries, income levels are among the lowest. As a consequence, this region often exhibits the smallest share of global economic or financial activity (except in mineral production), although industry-specific profiles may provide niche opportunities.

UNDERSTANDING THE BUSINESS ENVIRONMENT: GLOBAL INFORMATION REQUIREMENTS FOR ASSESSING FINANCIAL PERFORMANCE

If every aspect of the corporate financial position is affected by changes in the environment, how can one organize and address the vast amounts of economic and business inputs that could affect the firm. Certainly there are many different approaches that have been taken, but we find that a very useful organizing structure begins with an analysis of the firm's basic income statement, segmented by market. This allows a focus on the factors that affect corporate revenue by market and the factors that affect the costs. Moreover, this basic typology also provides a framework for examining how these factors may influence competitors as well.

Exhibit 3.7's three columns illustrate a template for organizing and assessing factors in the business environment and their potential impact on the firm; it is organized around the structure of the income statement. Column 1 lists the financial categories of relevant revenues and costs. Column 2 outlines the basic market or cost segments that should be defined to organize the

EXHIBIT 3.7

A Template for Organizing and Assessing Factors
in the Business Environment

Category	Segments	Variables
Revenue	Sales by market	Market size, growth, demographics, etc; market share
Expenses		
Purchased materials	Type	Price indexes, exchange rates
Direct labor costs	Location	Wage indexes, productivity, exchange rates
Indirect costs	Location	Health costs, energy indexes, service prices
Interest expenses	Produce/sell location	Transport cost indexes
Distribution expenses	Financial instrument	Interest rates, exchange rates
Taxes	Location; transfer policy	Tax rates (national, local)

environmental characteristics in sufficient detail. (For example, revenue characteristics would presumably be segmented by product line, geographic market, consumer segment, and so on.) Column 3 outlines the some of the economic, political, or policy information that should be monitored to assess the impact on financial performance.

Clearly this approach can be used for any of the firm's key financial statements. When combined with pro forma projections, it provides a picture of how future environmental changes can relate to the financial performance of the firm. In the following sections we discuss the information requirements that comprise this approach in more detail.

Revenue Information Requirements

Monitoring and projecting revenues are critically dependent on two key dimensions. Whether defined geographically or by product, industry, or consumer segment, the firm must focus on whether existing or newly emerging markets might create the best opportunities to enhance revenues. Second, for each of those selected markets, a careful analysis must be made of what market share might be gained by the firm. This involves not only a clear assessment of the firm's ability to meet each market's growth prospects, but also an assessment of what competitors will be doing in those markets as well.

Both of those analyses—the identification of markets and of market share—utilize four broad types of information: the economic characteristics of the markets; business information about competitors; policy information about the political environment; and social/demographic information about the potential consumers. All four of these information types will affect the assessment of the revenue side of the corporate income statement.

Economic Information
Key economic parameters drive the market growth for the firm's product lines. Pertinent information requirements should include the careful identification of the market measure with which expected revenue is associated (such as economic growth of a country or regional market, or sale growth of a product area) and those factors that may explain or influence changes in the market measure. Such driving factors may include a variety of demand or income characteristics as well as financial and policy assumptions that influence growth over a business cycle and beyond. These determining characteristics may be developed through a combination of quantitative or judgmental techniques, but their assessment is an important part of gauging the degree of confidence in final market growth estimates.

Business Information
Environmental impacts on revenue depend on the ability to estimate market share as well as the growth of the market itself. Market share determination is normally based on economic characteristics such as relative prices, but is also affected by business-specific information indicating the competitive position of the firm. Gaining or losing market share depends on a variety of competitive characteristics that match prices, quality, and product fit relative to the competitive environment. To provide a complete analysis, business-level competitive information is as important as the broader economic assessments.

Political/Policy Information

Political parameters affect the revenue environment of the firm primarily through changes in government policy. Consequently, monitoring and assessing those policies that relate to lines of the income statement is critical, especially in the global context. On the revenue side, the growth of various markets is indirectly affected by a variety of fiscal, monetary, and foreign investment policies. Depending upon how a firm accesses a given market, either trade policies or investment policy changes in targeting market access can be significant. Policy analysis will be discussed in more detail under risk assessment below.

Social/Demographic Information

The fourth category, social/demographic information, provides an ability to understand market characteristics that may affect both market growth and market share. Age and income levels by region, country, or metropolitan area are critical to global consumer product analysis, for example. The degree to which social/demographic data are an essential part of the CFO's tool kit depends on the product and target market characteristics of the firm.

Cost Information Requirements

Environmental information requirements that can affect the cost performance of the firm are often more complex and varied than the revenue-side requirements. Costs are affected by the traditional factors of labor, capital, and materials costs; by the patterns of suppliers; and by all the varied policies that affect overhead and benefits costs around the globe.

For cost-side environmental monitoring we again recommend that four broad information categories be considered: economic/financial, business, policy/political, and demographic/social.

Economic/Financial Information

The most common cost information relates to inflation and price indexes, but it is not sufficient for the CFO to have only a general knowledge of economywide changes in inflation. Cost information is not uniform across time intervals nor is there uniformity across the elements of cost. By focusing on the specific elements of the income statement, the CFO can determine (1) the evolution of the costs within the firm and (2) whether the components of inflation are shifting cost advantages toward or away from competitors. At a minimum, the cost components must be divided between wage indexes (by location) and materials costs by market segment. In addition, key financial information comes into play on the cost side. First, the range of long-term and short-term interest rates that affect capital costs and financial strategies must be assessed regularly on a global basis. Second, exchange rates and their evolution have become one of the most critical components for optimizing global financial performance.

Business Information
Business-level information about competitors and industry developments can often highlight cost trends that are more specific to one's firm than sectoral economic or financial indicators.

Policy/Political Information
Nearly every cost element of the firm is affected by some type of policy change within the political environment. The cost of materials may be affected by domestic content rules; the cost of labor by wage and union policies; overhead costs by reporting and health and safety requirements; selling expenses by transport and telecommunications policies; and, of course, the relative profits by tax and transfer price policies. Monitoring and analyzing the potential impact of these policy changes is key for maintaining a close watch on the firm's global cost characteristics.

Demographic/Social Information
On the cost side, the CFO is more likely to encounter the need for demographic information in conjunction with strategic rather than tactical planning. Plant location, plant expansion, acquisitions, and divestitures may require an assessment of labor force and population outlooks as part of the strategic decision process.

RISKS—INCORPORATING RISKS AND RETURNS FROM THE GLOBAL BUSINESS ENVIRONMENT INTO THE EXPECTED FINANCIAL PERFORMANCE OF THE FIRM

Monitoring and projecting the impact of changes in the economic and business environment on the financial performance of the firm must include the ability to assess risks and alternative financial scenarios. The increased complexity of the global environment for today's CFO often carries with it increased variance in the factors that may affect financial performance. Thus it is important to consider systematically the sensitivity of the firm's performance to those factors outlined in the framework above and the degree of variability that may occur. This is the key function of risk assessment.

Types of Risk

Before addressing how the assessment of risk may be incorporated into an environmental analysis, it is useful to categorize the types of environmental risk that can affect the firm's financial performance. Broadly speaking, we generally address and characterize two major types of risk: *economic risk* and *political risk.* Typically, financial risks are incorporated into the assessment of economic risk, while social risks are included within the broad context of political risk.

Economic Risk

Economic risks are changes in the economic environment that may impact either the projected revenues or costs in a given market, thereby affecting projected profitability. Depending on the characteristics of the firm, those specific factors may vary widely. The variability of energy costs, for example, may be critical to an airline or shipping company, but not a significant factor to an electronics producer.

On the revenue side, the economic risk factors that are most commonly evaluated include the factors that relate to the growth of markets (GNP or income by market, for example) or components that may influence those factors, such as interest rates and energy prices. A systematic analysis of the major markets associated with each product line sets the stage for revenue risk factor identification. For example, if single-family–home construction is the major market most closely associated with the CFO's firm's products, then mortgage rates, consumer confidence, and demographic changes are pivotal indicators to monitor.

On the cost side, economic risk factors most commonly addressed include the risks of changes in costs and prices, and financial risks associated with changes in interest and foreign exchange rates. For the global manager, this aspect of risk has grown dramatically in complexity, because these factors can vary in their level and volatility by country and region.

An additional cost risk is that of excessive or inflexible capacity that will be idled during repeated business cycles. An electric utility, for example, must evaluate not only the trend growth in peak demands over coming decades, but also the depth of the cyclical downturns that will sharply curtail industrial and household generation demands for one to two years in succession during each slump. Manufacturers have a similar need. Furthermore, "capacity" planning should not be limited to machines. All firms should adopt parallel strategies for employment—for example, explicitly planning to use temporary employees and overtime during peaks rather than hiring permanent workers and then creating unemployment compensation, severance, and morale costs when they are no longer needed.

The importance of financial risks need not be reiterated here since the literature on incorporating these risks into corporate financial planning is extensive. The risks from changes in inflation are often less appreciated, however. It is not sufficient for the CFO to have only a general knowledge of economywide changes in inflation even if it is country-by-country. Cost inflation is not uniform across time intervals nor is there uniformity across elements of cost. In the United States, for example, energy prices and costs of equipment were highly volatile during the 1970s, while labor and financial costs played a much larger role in the variance of corporate financial performance during the 1980s. Thus, detailed knowledge of a firm's cost structure and of its competitor's cost structure by the key elements of cost (labor, equipment, energy, capital, structures, etc.) is a critical tool for targeting changing factors of competitive advantage or disadvantage.

Political Risk

Political risk has two dimensions—political risk and policy risk—that relate to each other, but should be addressed separately in evaluating financial performance:

Political risk relates to the broad political environment in which political change takes place. Such factors include the stability of a particular government, the level of popular support, social factors that relate to that support, and the possibility of internal or external threats from, for example, terrorism.

Policy risk relates to changes in various government policies, such as taxation or foreign investment incentives. It includes a broad range of economic, financial, investment, and social policies that could affect the financial returns of the firm.

The broad political risk factors such as the stability of a government or the possibility of internal threats are often the most visible and broadly discussed. Indeed, in the post–Cold War environment these types of risks due to ethnic strife or regional conflict have possibly become more common, especially for global firms moving into emerging markets.

While perhaps more dramatic, risk analysis should not stop at the broad political level, however, for two reasons. First, most multinational firms do not do business in many of the more volatile areas where instability or terrorism are of reasonable probability. Some firms, such as oil companies and utilities, may have no choice but to operate in very risky environments, but for most firms this is not an overwhelming issue. Second, when considering how political change affects the firm, the key impacts occur through changes in policies directed toward the firm. A perfectly stable government may in fact have even greater opportunity to impose policies unfavorable to a given business, while a tumultuous political environment may imply few changes in current policies. As a consequence, most CFOs should monitor and address the risks of changes in policy with greater diligence than is generally acknowledged.

Exhibit 3.8 shows how the policy environment can be tied to the financial performance of the firm, much in the same way that the environmental factors discussed in the previous section relate to a firm's financial performance.

E X H I B I T   3.8

Sample Income Statement
Policy Effects on Corporate Income

Category	1994	Potential Policy Effects
Revenue	$225.0	Tariff or foreign investment allowances
Purchased materials	85.5	Domestic content regulations
Direct labor costs	61.3	Wage and union policies
Overhead costs	15.8	National health plans
Distribution expense	9.5	Transport (e.g., domestic preference) policies
Interest expenses	16.3	Credit and national bank policies
Depreciation	8.9	Tax regulations
Operating income	28.5	Capital repatriation restrictions

Whether a firm is operating domestically or globally, every line item of the income statement or balance sheet can be influenced dramatically by changes in government policy. In addition, a wide range of financial regulations can affect the capital position of the balance sheet and the financing options available to the treasurer, which are further confounded by transfer pricing and exchange rate policy effects on cross-national accounting. Thus, correctly cataloging and anticipating the policy changes that can affect the firm is the key to assessing the effects of the political environment. Broad issues about how stable a government is or who will win the next election may provide important clues about policy change, but it is the specific changes or risks of those changes within that environmental context that should bear the most scrutiny.

A Policy Checklist   As with economic risk, critical policy factors are indeed firm and location-specific in many instances. The following basic checklist should be reviewed for potential impacts on the firm's income or balance sheet performance:

- Financial policy
  Market institution regulation
  Interest rate and credit controls

- Investment policy
  Investment incentives
  Local versus allowed foreign ownership
  Government participation policies in various industries
- Economic policy
  Fiscal/monetary trends and cycles
  Foreign exchange controls
  Capital repatriation policies
  Transfer pricing policies
  Tax incentives and policies
- Trade policy
  Tariff/quota changes
  Import licensing
  Export credits and other incentives
- Operating policy
  Domestic content regulations
  Environmental regulations
- Labor policy
  Wage policies
  Unionization
  Employment regulations
  Benefit guidelines

Within each company the list of relevant policies will vary across markets. For example, an American technology components firm in Mexico may be particularly affected by wage, local ownership, and transfer pricing policies, while the same firm in Europe may be most concerned with local employee benefits requirements and tax policies.

Incorporating Risk Factors into Financial and Operating Decisions

A final step in developing a complete environmental analysis is to incorporate the assessment of risks into the financial and operating decisions of the firm. In general, we believe that the large firm should view its markets and operations as an investor would view a portfolio. That is, a portfolio of markets or operations around the globe offers a profile of potential returns. With each of those returns is an estimate of variance or volatility that represents the risk. Incorporating this risk assessment means the firm's decision makers are systematically weighing the risk/return trade-offs so they are either minimizing the risks to achieve certain returns or are maximizing the returns given certain levels of risk. As a final step, the most sophisticated decision makers also analyze the interrelationships of risk (the covariance) to offset them through a portfolio diversification strategy.

To incorporate this type of risk assessment into financial planning, we recommend a number of key steps:

1. *Array the firm's global portfolio of expected returns in a systematic manner.* To follow portfolio diversification strategy, it is of course necessary to specify the financial objectives the firm is seeking to maximize. For a particular exercise this may be investment returns, or expected net operating income (NOI) from a global array of operations, or perhaps expected repatriation of profits. This profile will then form the framework to assess the variance of those returns. For example, if the objective is to maximize the NOI from an array of global operations, then the risks should be considered in terms of their systematic effect on the various revenue and cost components that make up an expected NOI.

2. *Incorporate risk assessment by estimating the variability of economic and political factors on those projected returns.* The systematic assessment of risk on the financial performance of the firm requires an assessment of the *variability* of those returns under a variety of conditions.

For *economic risk,* the variability is best estimated by using methods of scenario analysis. Although these can be developed by different methods that range from qualitative judgment factors to formal model simulations, scenario analysis tries to interrelate how probable environmental scenarios may affect a range of relevant economic factors. For example, analyses may look at the impact of a global protectionist trend on returns to the operations of a multinational trading company, or how an oil shock caused by a Middle East war would affect the costs of operations (and hence NOI) at various corporate investment locations. Recessionary scenarios are among the most popular to assess the downside risk of lower economic growth on potential corporate financial performance.

The objective of these analyses is to get a good sense of the volatility of various financial objectives for different types of economic risk. Some corporations may formally try to calculate expected variances for each pro forma return by employing dozens of quantitative scenario analyses and simulations, while others will use broader judgmental factors. It is important, however, that under any approach, the potential variance of outcomes be considered systematically in terms of what are regarded as reasonable alternative scenarios in the context of the firm's environment. Knowing to what factors profits are most sensitive or insensitive is critical to the CFO's planning process.

For *political risk*, the variability should be viewed as how changing political or policy factors may vary the pro forma income or balance sheet statements that comprise the financial objectives in question. Employing the checklist given in the previous section can be a useful framework for evaluating which policies may need to be analyzed for their potential in affecting the financial performance of the firm.

Merely keeping track of potential policy changes is not such a simple process, however. Too often, there is a tendency to focus on the pronouncements of the government in power of the most senior individuals in that government to predict policy movements. Yet the nature of politics is to produce decisions that are the result of competing pressures among many different groups, not just one or two players. Thus once the relevant policies are identified, it is important to evaluate how the players in the political arena may force changes in those policies, if they can at all. Either systematically or implicitly this involves understanding the players who may influence a given policy, what resources they have available to influence the policies in their desired direction, and how willing they are to expend those resources. Besides understanding the players and their position on critical issues (not just the pronouncements of the government in power), assessing their relative degree of political clout and their willingness to apply it provides an additional key to determining who most affects the policy outcome. Both of these elements are important because they determine the effective pressure that a group may apply toward a policy decision. Seemingly weak groups, such as narrow interest groups, can become extremely influential on particular decisions because they target all of their available resources toward a particular outcome.

3. *Balance risks and rewards by addressing the trade-offs presented.* In utilizing the above framework, the global environment can be seen as presenting the CFO with a range of projected returns, subject to estimates of variability (or risk) of those returns. When faced with a large number of potential investments and risks, it is often more practical to deal with those investments in stages. The first stage may be conducted at the country or large-regional level to determine what areas may be eliminated or included for further analysis. This first stage can focus on broader factors of economic and political risk as they affect potential returns in order to eliminate those areas that may not merit further analysis. Then at the second stage, individual investments (characterized by an array of potential NOIs or other criteria) can be reviewed in detail as a menu of choices that possesses a profile of risks associated with given returns. In this way the management committee can consider risk minimization or return maximization strategies for given levels of risk in a more systematic process.

4. *Consider the "covariances" of the global portfolio.* The risks and returns of various investments available to the firm are rarely independent of one another. Specific risk scenarios can have positive connotations for some and negative connotations for other operations or markets within a firm's portfolio. For example, an oil crisis would more negatively impact operations in oil-dependent countries, while processing plants linked in a global production process may be more vulnerable to global movement toward protectionism. By seeking assets of investments that do not respond to risk scenarios in a like manner, a firm can actually reduce the overall risk of a given portfolio. In other words, one objective of the analysis of the portfolio of returns and their associated variances is to select investments that "covary" negatively with each other or respond differently to different risks.

This final step of diversification analysis may be addressed in the context of a few alternative global scenarios or through a series of detailed exercises across markets. This is an important final stage in the environmental assessment process as it allows the firm to balance the risks presented by the portfolio against the range of possible outcomes that can create those risks.

CONCLUSION

Understanding today's environmental forces and risks faced by the chief financial officer requires more systematic evaluation of a wider variety of influences on the corporate financial position than ever before. In this chapter we have outlined a number of components that should be incorporated into an ongoing environmental assessment strategy:

- Don't lose sight of the global context. Even if the CFO's firm's share of sales outside the home market is not large, the enlarged global market still affects every aspect of its financial performance. Competitors can now optimize their strategies and costs in a global framework of diverse markets, labor pools, and financing options even if the home firm does not.

- *Segment markets to understand revenue and cost implications of environmental changes.* On the revenue side this allows a CFO to differentiate between the growth prospects of various markets and determine what market share can be achieved. On the cost side it allows a more systematic assessment of price, financial, and policy impacts on the firm's operations under alternative scenarios. Markets are indeed more global, but the CFO's challenge is to understand the firm's sensitivity to changes in various segments of that environment.

- *Approach opportunities and risks as a portfolio.* Emerging markets have greater attraction than ever before for many firms, but greater volatility of financial results often accompanies that attractiveness. When considering both the base case outlook for the firm and the risks of alternative outcomes, consider how to balance potential outcomes so that volatility doesn't snowball in the wrong direction.

The global business environment has indeed grown more connected and more complex for most firms. With that greater complexity, however, comes an opportunity to diversify for more consistent financial results less tied to the business cycles of the home market. Systematic assessment of the economic, political, financial, and social factors that have the greatest impact on the firm's financial performance is a key component of realizing that opportunity.

CHAPTER

4

⑥ **CONTEMPORARY BEST PRACTICES IN MAKING INFORMATION TECHNOLOGY WORK FOR YOUR CUSTOMER AND ORGANIZATION**

Sidney Diamond
President, Diamond & Associates

Information technology (IT) has progressed from an accounting and record-keeping activity to a significant lever for determining the nature and manner of how you do business. This chapter briefly examines the current business environment and the role of IT, describes some contemporary best practices in applying IT to impact your business, and identifies some major IT trends.

TODAY'S BUSINESS ENVIRONMENT

"We want to be global and local, big and small, radically decentralized with central reporting and control," says Percy Barenwich, CEO of the multibillion-dollar ASEA Brown Boveri organization. I might also add "and have the highest customer satisfaction rating and the lowest operating costs" of our competition.

Using Mr. Barenwich's definition of his business and my addendum, the basis is formed for many of the trends in today's business environment: globalization, mass customization, customer centricity, downsizing and flattening, total quality management (TQM) and the empowered worker, outsourcing, and business process re-engineering. These business trends not only impact IT but are also often enabled by IT as well.

A Belgian executive recently remarked that his domestic company was going "global." When asked what countries he will now be doing business in, he replied, "France." Whatever your definition of going global may be, the reasons behind it are usually the desire for increased growth and profitability; free trade movement in Europe as well as North America; increased foreign competition in your local marketplace; and political events such as the fall of Communism in Eastern Europe. The global corporation views the world as a single marketplace for its products and services, and lends itself to a matrix management and shared responsibilities with its local business operations. Its ability to operate on a worldwide basis requires highly integrated strategies, plans, and IT systems and networks.

Our businesses have progressed over the years from just producing products and services to satisfying the customer's total experience in buying, using, maintaining, and even disposing of the product. This *customer-centric* approach pervades all aspects of our business activities and frequently manifests itself in the omnipotent "customer satisfaction" rating.

Many firms are taking this customer centric approach even further by their customizing products in large volumes for needs of local markets and even segments of their customer base. The milk industry has segmented its products into lactose-free, low-fat, skim, whole, butter, chocolate, and other varieties of milk to appeal to mass segments of their customers.

In addition to these market- and customer-oriented trends, many businesses are overhauling the way they operate internally to better serve their customers and markets.

Business process re-engineering (BPR), for example, looks at the basic steps or processes of a business and radically changes the way things are done. BPR usually aims for "10-fold" or dramatic improvement in the processes. *Total Quality Management (TQM)* also examines these business processes but with a smaller and incremental change or continuous improvement. In both the BPR and TQM endeavors, information technology facilitates both incremental and radical improvements.

Where businesses need to be more responsive to their customers and market conditions as well as be a lower-cost provider, extensive *downsizing* and *organizational flattening* are occurring.

Historically, IT has played a role in reducing the labor content of business operations in their downsizing endeavors. Today, IT facilitates this "delayering" or flattening of business organizations by increasing its managers' span of control through networks, video conferencing, database of operational information, electronic linkages with customers and suppliers, and so on. Many firms are *outsourcing* significant aspects of their activities from manufacturing to advertising to information technology. The many reasons for this outsourcing trend range from the desire to focus on the "core business" activities, to reducing costs and improving services, to minimizing capital expenditures.

With this framework of some of the significant business trends, let's look briefly at the evolution of IT and its forces on contemporary best practices in using IT to impact your business and customer.

BRIEF OVERVIEW OF THE HISTORY OF INFORMATION TECHNOLOGY

IT is a baby compared to the more mature functions such as accounting and sales, which date back to Biblical times with the shepherds counting their sheep and merchants selling their wares in the marketplace. This "infant" IT has rapidly evolved from its embryonic uses as a high-speed calculator for scientific investigations and recordkeeping for accounting in the 1950s to a lever that impacts all facets of every business.

In some businesses, such as banking, financial services, and insurance, IT has become the production or main operational component, while in other businesses, such as manufacturing, IT is the electronic linkage that ties the customer to the company. For example, mass merchants (such as Wal-Mart) are electronically linked to their suppliers (like Procter and Gamble) for a multitude of business transactions including order processing, billing, inventory management in both the retailer's and producer's operation, and distribution.

EXHIBIT 4.1

Application Software Shift

1960–1973	1973–1980s	1990s
Accounting/finance Payroll Sales statistics Cost distribution Inventory accounting	Materials management (MRP) Shop floor control CAD, CAE Analytic computation Word processing	Direct customer access Product Configurations Product customization Fast response CSI JIT EDI
Faster ledgers	**Operating efficiencies**	**Virtual corporation**

EXHIBIT 4.2

Downsizing—Platform Shift

	1960s–70s	1980s	1990s
Where	Mainframe	Desktop	Hand-held
Focus	Centralized	Distributed	Collaborative
Interaction	Keyboard	Mouse	Voice
Languages	Assembler/COBOL	COBOL/C	Objects
Applications	Functional	Integrated	Process
Data	Files	Database	Repository
Format	Character-based	Char and image	Multimedia
Performance	Response time	MHz	Accessibility
Communications	Low-band cir.	LANs and WANs	Virtual/High-band/ wireless
Service	On-site	Dealer	Seldom

Exhibits 4.1 and 4.2 show how the use and nature of IT software and hardware applications have evolved since the 1960s for Rockwell International. The software applications have evolved from back-office accounting and record keeping to customer service and product enabling activities. The hardware has evolved from a large, centralized mainframe to a small device that can be used on your desktop and/or a portable laptop or hand-held computer.

Like young children, this IT infant is changing and growing every day and will continue its exponential growth and will impact upon business for many years to come.

BEST PRACTICES IN APPLYING INFORMATION TECHNOLOGY TO IMPACT YOUR CUSTOMERS AND YOUR BUSINESS

As chief financial officer for your corporations, many of you have IT as part of your responsibilities and/or you can influence its utilization throughout your business operations through business revenues, strategic planning, capital budgeting, and so on. How can you make this IT lever or fulcrum work best for your company? What are the contemporary best practices in applying and managing IT? This section examines each of the seven IT best practices: aligning your IT efforts with the business, using IT on a global basis, controlling your IT costs, managing new development projects, business process re-engineering, insourcing or outsourcing your IT function, and establishing software contracts.

Aligning Information Technology Efforts with the Business Operations

According to a recent CSC/Index poll, the top issue facing senior IT executives is the aligning of the IT function with their business.

What actually is this alignment issue? What key levers or forces can a CIO use in bringing it about? How do you align on a global basis? Is there a framework or model that can be applied by any IT manager to his unique environment? These are some of the questions frequently asked by CFOs and IT executives concerning alignment.

Diamond and Associates (an information technology consulting firm based in Stevenson, Maryland) conducted a survey of over 700 CIOs and senior IT management positions in diverse companies such as Pepsico, Bristol-Myers Squibb, Cadbury Beverages, Massachusetts Mutual Insurance, John Hancock Insurance, Prudential Securities, Chubb, YMCA, Olympia & York, Philip Morris, Corning Inc., McCormick, NYC Transit Authority, Mutual Benefit Life, Avis, Barclays Bank, and CONRAIL.[1] The results of this survey are covered in this section (Pages 73–81) and they will help to answer the above questions that challenge so many organizations.

---

1 S. Diamond, "Aligning I.T. with Business Operations," *Financial Executive,* July-August, 1994; *Software Magazine,* February 1994; *InformationWeek,* February 1993.

E X H I B I T   4.3

Forces to Align IT with Business Operations

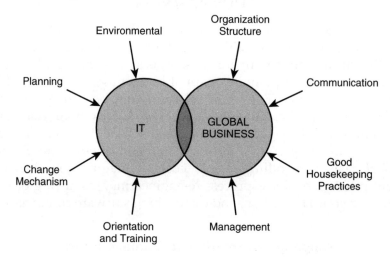

What is this IT alignment with the business operations? Alignment means fit—the fit of the IT function with the business operation's goals, needs, programs, and operating style. The IT function must totally support all these aspects of the business operations.

The entire IT function is involved in this alignment with the business, and includes such items as IT goals, organization, major programs, and personnel types and number. *Alignment means that the goals and activities of both the IT and business operations are united in one common business purpose.*

Alignment is an ongoing process. As the business needs and environment change or as new technology advances occur, the IT alignment must be also adjusted to maintain this common business orientation.

What are the key levers or forces in bringing about this alignment between IT and the business? The senior IT executives felt the critical forces were the CIO, the relationship between IT and business planning, IT organizational structure, communication, the training and orientation of both the users and IT staff, external environment, company change and control mechanisms, and best IT practices. Each lever or force is discussed below and outlined in Exhibit 4.3.

The CIO must be a business-oriented executive as well as be knowledgeable in the technology. He or she must *understand the business issues first and then present technological solutions.* For example, Jack Thompson, recently retired CIO of McCormick, introduced the "supply chain management" concept to his company based on (1) his understanding of McCormick's needs and (2) exposure to external companies and business conferences.

The CIO's role and relationship with other senior business executives is crucial. The CIO must have access to senior management and business plans, participate in key business meetings and be part of the "inner circle."

The CIO must talk the language of businesspeople and not the technocrat.

The personal characteristics and philosophies of the CIO are also important. Bill Friel, executive vice president of Prudential Securities, believes (as do others) that the CIO must have "credibility, leadership, and integrity; otherwise you're wasting time." Friel believes creditability is obtained by running the IT function as a business and by providing key impacts to the business operations.

The second critical alignment force is the *relationship between IT planning and business planning.* All the people surveyed felt that IT plans should relate to the business plans. How this integration is achieved varies from company to company.

The CIO and his IT organization must be constantly *involved with the business operation and business planning,* and with various stakeholders such as senior management, external customers, suppliers, and the IT community throughout the company. The CIO is the catalyst for bringing about this involvement of the IT organization and its environment.

A rather unique approach was successfully implemented at Chubb and Son. Senior management was asked to identify what they expected from IT. The CEO, president, and chairman then jointly wrote a one-page document on their vision, mission, and five major goals for the technology function.

What do you do if your company or individual business units do not have a formal business plan or planning process? Some CIOs have had success in preparing a "strawman" business and technology plan that supports their perceived needs of the business. The strawman document is then used for discussion purposes with the business organization.

Some companies have a business plan but have not formally integrated IT as part of the planning process. In this situation, one might use the top-down approach of reviewing the business plans and highlighting business issues where IT could help. One can also consider a bottom-up approach of recommending selected and/or new technologies to help the business.

Allan Deering (vice president of MIS for Pepsico) sums up the importance of the business planning process by saying the "CIO must understand that he and his organization have to be involved—whatever works (informal or formal approach) in your culture is OK!" Bill Friel agrees by saying, "You can't play in the game if you're not involved in the business planning process. The company needs a change in IT leadership if you're not involved, whether it is a CIO or business management problem."

The *IT organizational structure* is the third critical alignment lever at the CIO's disposal. The clear trend is to move the application development function "closer" to the business operations. By closer I mean physically putting some or all of the application development personnel in the user or business operations, often under the direct control of the users.

The extent to which the resources of application development are moved into the business operations varies from company to company. Corning Inc., has a corporate IT liaison or account executive physically residing in each business unit. The liaison's role is to work with his business unit in defining needs, setting priorities, and obtaining resources for implementing major development projects. These resources can be sourced from the Central IT and/or from external parties. Philip Morris USA, has deployed an account executive concept for key functional areas such as marketing, sales, and customer services. Another approach is to move all the development resources—management, designers, programmers, and so on—into the users' organizations and under the users' direct control. This occurs frequently in companies structured on a divisional, line-of-business, or geographic basis.

When IT resources are moved into these business units, to where do they report? One recent trend is to move the IT organization into nonfinancial functions as part of the move into the business units. In both Bristol-Myers Squibb and Black & Decker, the application development resources were moved into the customer service functions of their consumer products organization. A number of the other firms have the IT function reporting to the presidents of the business units.

Communication is another vital force the CIO can use in bringing about the alignment. The messages, audiences, and delivery vehicles for communicating are important facets.

The CIO needs to create and communicate a vision of where IT is going for his company, the major programs that move the IT function from today to the future, and periodic updates on "how are we doing" in achieving our goals and supporting the business. These "messages" need to be delivered to key audiences or stakeholders such as senior management, business units or operations, functional staffs, and the IT community.

The vehicles for delivering these messages to each audience group will vary; they need to be carefully thought out for your environment and culture. For example, the CIO can make formal presentations to the senior management community, and have one-on-one informal dialogues. Diane Smiegel, vice president of John Hancock, invites her CEO to spend a half hour or so reviewing a successful IT project at a business unit's location or a new opportunity for IT to impact the business.

For communicating with users, Bob Lobsman, system manager of Mutual Benefit Life, utilizes his company's Team Reconstruction or empowerment approach to convey messages. Here, Accounting, IT, and users from the business unit discuss mutual problems, barriers, and solutions in a joint endeavor.

A steering committee of senior level Chubb executives deals with IT strategies, direction, priorities, and so on for the 41 groups of business operations that the IT organization supports.

The CIO needs to develop a communications strategy and plan for delivering the IT message to each of his key audiences: senior management, business units, functional staffs, and the IT community. This plan should be customized to each audience group and even to important individuals within each group such as a CEO, business unit head, or large decentralized IT staff.

Another key lever the CIO can employ in bringing about alignment is the *training and orientation of both the users and IT staff.*

In the alignment process, the IT staff needs to be more business-oriented and customer-focused. Some organizations start with the hiring process. Cadbury Beverages hires managers and developers who have "business knowledge and strong interpersonal skills", while Bill Heuser, vice president of NYC Transit Authority, spends a half hour with *every* new employee on his department's mission and its orientation toward the business.

Many firms have implemented training programs to help their IT personnel and others become more business-oriented and customer-focused. At Black & Decker, IT was the first corporate functional area to adopt the Total Quality Process with its emphasis on customers, both internal and external.

At Pepsico, IT personnel go to a "chicken school" to learn about a Kentucky Fried Chicken restaurant, ride a Pepsi-Cola route truck, or work in a Pizza Hut—all to learn more about their businesses. In other industries, there are built-in mechanisms to develop business knowledge from industry training and certification programs like the LOMA program in the insurance industry.

At Mass Mutual the IT staff receives training in three areas: personal development (problem analysis, decision making, and communication), business knowledge, and technical expertise. There is a strong emphasis on technical competence in IT as a way to "add value to the company."

Orientation and training of the users in IT elicited some interesting thoughts in the survey. Many felt that their users were very literate in computing technology because of the user friendly software and desktop devices, younger work force, and greater influx of MBAs into their organizations in the past few years. To foster their users' familiarization with IT, Prudential Securities feels that a better system solution and technology encourages both the use of new systems and understanding of IT by the users. The users are to present their requests for new systems for approval, including the technical concepts.

Corning has an education program for senior management to familiarize them with PC tools, handing of files, spreadsheets, E-mail, and so on. This is done on a personalized basis. At the International Group of Bristol-Myers, all senior staff, division heads, and managers attended a two-day orientation session on computer technology. Very few firms in the survey had a formal orientation program on IT for senior executives, managers, and/or users. Are we in the IT community missing an opportunity in not adequately training and orienting the businesspeople and users in IT technology?

As for the CIO's personal development and orientation, the CIO should get out of his company's environment and "find out what's going on in the business community." He will then be able to bring new ideas and approaches back to his company.

The *external environment* is a force that can be leveraged in bringing IT closer to the business's goals, objectives, and so on. The external environment consists of the market, competitors, and regulatory, social, and demographic forces. For example, in the consumer goods and retailing market, if you do not use EDI, the customer (mass merchants) will go to somebody else.

In the pharmaceutical, utilities, insurance, banking, and other industries, there are many regulatory agency forces at the federal and state levels that CIOs can utilize. The FDA now permits pharmaceutical firms to electronically submit new drug applications to reduce the paperwork and speed the approval process!

Every company has a variety of existing change and control mechanisms that the CIO can leverage to help his alignment cause. Some of these mechanisms are the strategic planning process, TQM, operational reviews, steering committees, task forces, special interest groups, annual budgeting process, capital planning process, auditing, succession and manpower planning, and business re-engineering. At Black & Decker, there are over 20 special interest groups on a companywide basis including year-end closing, LAN administrators, security officers, IT technical standard committee, and A/R. Each special interest group (SIG) was headed by a senior manager from the business operations and consisted of representatives from the business groups and IT. Each SIG provided input in the form of strategies, new opportunities and needs, priorities, and so on to both the central IT organization and planning processes of the business and IT.

The final lever the CIO can use in his portfolio in bringing about this desired alignment is a set of "IT Best Practices" for all business operations and IT organizations in his company. Examples of these practices are an IT plan and planning process related to the business needs, IT steering committee, involvement in the business planning process, periodic reviews with business operations on their needs and IT programs, project management guidelines and standards, and a business continuance program.

The CIO role and relationship, IT and business planning, organizational structure of IT, communications, training/orientation of both the user and IT staff, external environment, change and control mechanisms, and IT best practices are all levers or forces in aligning IT with the business operations.

Some firms have business operations in many countries throughout the world. How do you align IT on such a global basis? The same key levers mentioned above are still critical; however, it is also important to understand how your company approaches globalization for your alignment process to be successful. For example, does your company extend its current domestic products and business practices to the world market, or does it provide its international subsidiaries with a great deal of autonomy on what and how they market their products? Perhaps your company uses a matrix approach to the global market with worldwide product, marketing, and manufacturing managers at the corporate level.

From an IT perspective, what business processes and applications are companywide, regional, line-of-business, or local in nature? What company data elements, standards, and IT infrastructure are required to implement your company's global approach? The "Chubb difference" to its worldwide subsidiaries is autonomy in dealing with the front end (local market) and commonality at the back end (office).

Understanding how your company approaches the globalization issue is important in deciding how to align IT on a worldwide basis. In summary, aligning IT with the business operations is crucial for the success of the CIO, the IT function, and the business.

Aligning means fitting the IT function with its goals, programs, staff, activities, and so on with the business and its goals and programs. Eight levers or forces were identified to bring about this alignment, along with numerous tactical suggestions and examples for deploying each alignment force.

Every company's culture, business operation, operating philosophies, and so on are different. These eight levers or forces comprise a model or framework for aligning IT to the business that can be adapted to each different company environment.[2]

IT executives must analyze their environment, assess which levers or forces could be most helpful in their cause, and then decide tactically how to deploy these forces. The CIO must develop alignment strategies for utilizing the levers and a tactical plan to be successful!

As the business direction and needs change, realignment of the IT function must occur. Alignment is a continuous process, not a one-time endeavor! This alignment should occur throughout the corporation on a worldwide basis. The next section covers some best practices in using IT to impact the global operations of your business.

Using IT on a Global Basis

The "Today's Business Environment" section identified globalization as a significant trend in today's commercial world. The drivers or forces for this move to global operations are economic survival, foreign competition in domestic markets, free trade movement, mergers and acquisitions, technology advances (particularly in IT), political events such as the fall of Communism in Eastern Europe, and the needs of global customers.

This section briefly describes how four organizations—the alliance of British Air, USAIR, and Qantas; Bristol-Myers Squibb; Phillip Morris; and Black & Decker—are utilizing information technology to improve their global business operations. Also discussed are some common IT strategies for impacting the global business and critical success factors (CSF) for implementing a global IT endeavor.

The Global Alliance British Air has a minority ownership of 20 percent in USAIR, 25 percent in Qantas (QF), and less than 50 percent in some European regional airlines. Regulatory and legal aspects limit the full control of these airlines by British Air (BA).

---

2 S. Diamond, "It's Time to Check Your Alignment," *CIO Journal*, September-October 1993.

EXHIBIT 4.4

Conceptual Approach to Airline Product Delivery System Integration

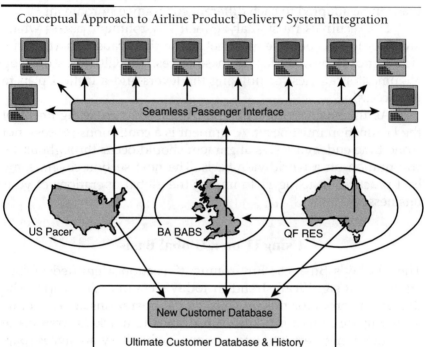

The airline business is characterized as being highly centralized from an operational point of view with one network for booking passengers and one scheduling system of their aircraft. Because of the nature and speed of their business, most systems are of a real-time and integrated nature. This environment fosters a very tight operational control of all aspects with very little ability to truly decentralize any parts of the business. Given this partial ownership, legal restrictions, and centralized operations, how can British Air maximize the economic benefits of such an alliance on a global basis?

By using IT, the alliance of these three airlines can create a "virtual" organization with one common customer database that is linked to their three existing customer databases via telecommunications, and a common way of booking passengers into their system. (See Exhibit 4.4)

This future system will enable common customer services on a worldwide basis, common frequent flyer programs, common selling of all alliance products, optimization of yield across airlines, joint scheduling and fare actions, joint target marketing to a shared customer, and elimination of some duplications.

Here, IT is an enabling lever to bring together three unique organizations in a common goal using networks, databases, and common passenger data.

Bristol-Myers Squibb—Internal Effectiveness This $12 billion pharmaceutical and health care firm operates in 150 markets throughout the world. Bristol-Myers Squibb has several internal operating needs in managing its world businesses:

• Obtaining operating information on its 350 reporting entities in a fast, accurate manner with uniform data and in a consistent format.

• Facilitating local and intercompany transactions.

• Enabling communication between, among, and within business units.

Using a worldwide network, personal computers, and common software in each field location, the firm collects 100,000 line items from its field organizations. This IT-enabled capability allows it to financially close sales on the first workday and its P&L on the seventh workday of the following month on a worldwide basis.

Some other operational applications are the internal sourcing of orders from its central plants, balancing of inventories on a regional basis, and reporting operational information on product sales, staffing levels, and adverse drug reactions. Exhibit 4.5 outlines these worldwide operational support systems that are enabled and facilitated by a global IT program.

Philip Morris As you plan to implement an IT program to help your global business operations, there are barriers you will probably encounter. Philip Morris International's IT organization has identified seven significant barriers in implementing its global IT support program. For example, most "common" application systems for worldwide use have English as the language on the computer screen. While many foreign workers are familiar with English as a second language, they may interpret some English words

E X H I B I T   4.5

Worldwide Internal Operational Support—Bristol-Myers Squibb

Financial Reporting	*Order Sourcing*
Close sales on first workday	Raw materials and domestic goods
Close P&L on seventh workday	Internal ordering from central plants
Balance sheet	Order acknowledgment,
Intercompany charges and	confirmation, ship dates
adjustments	Standard product codes
	Ordering system for external third parties
Communications	*Inventory Balancing*
Worldwide network	Stock on hand
E-mail	Export potential
Operational Reporting	*Human Resources*
Monthly product sales	"Team share" stock grant
Quarterly product P&L	Employee directory
Adverse reaction reporting	
Head count reporting	

differently than native speakers. Many firms resolve this language and understanding barrier by having the computer screen in the languages of the local countries. Exhibit 4.6 outlines other barriers you might encounter with your global IT endeavors.

IT Strategies for Impacting the Global Business

What are the key strategies and activities in using IT to impact your worldwide business operations?

The first step is to *determine the critical success factors* for your company on a global basis. Is it the common customer interface need of the Airline Alliance or the internal support needs of your dispersed organization as in the Bristol-Myers Squibb case?

Second, most global operations *require a telecommunications network* to move information between and among the operating entities, enable voice and E-mail communications among people, have access to databases, and link you with your external stakeholders.

You need to *explore "linkage" potential* both internally with your plants, research centers, market operations, distribution centers, and so on and externally with your alliance partners,

E X H I B I T   4.6

Recognize and Address International Barriers—Philip Morris

```
Language (English versus end user screens in local language)
Regulations
    Employee treatment
    Manufacturing facilities
Lack of global IT suppliers
Cultural differences
Inadequate local facilities
Modification of accounting systems
    Accommodations of local tax laws
    Currencies
Skill shortage
Local priorities versus international IT strategy
```

customers, suppliers, financial institutions, and regulatory agencies, and so on.

Also you need to *rationalize your worldwide IT* resources to make your IT organizations not only less costly but also more effective in serving your business operations and customers. This may mean consolidating data centers with their duplicate equipment, software, and facilities, eliminating redundant networks, using third-party network providers for more extensive and reliable geographic coverage, creating centers of excellence for your applications development teams, and examining the "value added" ability, service levels, and global support capabilities of your IT vendors.

Many global firms find substantial payoffs in *identifying and developing "commonality"* on a worldwide basis. Some areas for initial exploration are common data definitions, databases, applications, processes, procedures, best practices, IT facilities (hardware, networks, development resources), and outsourcing opportunities. In the Airline Alliance case, some common elements were passenger data, networks, and databases, while Bristol-Myers Squibb had common data definitions, applications, processes, and networks to facilitate their global operations.

Finally, many firms have had success in *implementing an IT standards program* to impact their worldwide business. For example,

Black & Decker: Potential Areas for IT Standardization

Companywide

Technical foundations such as computer tools, utilities, hardware platforms, and
  operating systems

Data definition and conventions to facilitate the flow of information around the
  company

Specific business applications for processes that are commonly used
  throughout the company

Line of Business

Specific business applications for processes that are commonly used throughout
  that specific line of business

Regional

For business applications covering common administrative, logistical, and
  customer service systems.

Local

Any unique items for the local operating environment and/or for compliance with
  local government regulations

Chubb Insurance Company standardized all its office technology
(word processing, E-mail, spreadsheets, etc.) for its worldwide
operations.

Black & Decker looked at the IT standards issue from an organizational perspective. Which IT standard would help the business on a worldwide basis, which in each line of business, which
in each regional area, and which on a local basis? Exhibit 4.7
shows potential areas of IT standardization within various organizational components of Black & Decker.

Implementing a global IT program to impact your business is a
complex, challenging endeavor. Some keys to success are understanding your company's global critical success factors; leveraging IT
to fit your global business needs and CSFs; enlisting all stakeholders'
participation in your planning, development, and implementation activities; and respecting the cultural and people differences.

In today's business environment, many firms are substantially reducing their operational costs, including in the IT area.
The next section covers best practices in controlling and reducing
your IT costs.

Using IT's Cost-Cutting Strategies

In this era of downsizing and restructuring, CIOs and IT managers walk a delicate tightrope as they balance improved levels of support and service for their customers while controlling IT costs.

Even the most productive IT organizations are striving to cut costs further. In a *Computerworld* survey of the premier 100 IT organizations, for example, one in six respondents faced budget cuts in 1995. Some 6 percent of respondents saw modest decreases in the range of 1 percent to 5 percent from 1993 to 1994, while another 6 percent of respondents cut budgets by 6 percent to 10 percent during that period. Four percent of respondents slashed their IT budgets by more than 10 percent in an effort to become "leaner and meaner." Meanwhile, 14 percent of respondents faced the challenge of improving service levels without any corresponding boost to their budget allocation.

Because IT services are essential to the operation of most organizations, the challenge is to cut IT costs without risk to mission-critical operations. CIOs have an urgent requirement to review the experiences of other firms to minimize the risks while improving their chances for success.

From 1992 to 1995, Diamond and Associates conducted an informal survey of 75 IT executives from Fortune 500 firms and leading industry analysts. The results provide a fresh perspective on IT cost reduction strategies in large, multiple–business-unit organizations.[3]

More than 85 strategies to cut IT costs were identified. They can be grouped by objective into five categories:
- Use low-cost technology architectures.
- Re-engineer the IT organization.
- Apply TQM principles to IT.
- Shorten IT cycle times.
- Integrate IT into business operations.

Low-Cost Technology Architectures

More flexible, responsive, and pervasive technology architectures with a low total cost of ownership are essential to meet the business

---

3 S. Diamond, "IT Cost Reduction Strategies," *Computer Economics*, June 1995; *Chief Financial Officer Journal*, Winter 1992.

demands of being global, local, big, small, and radically decentralized with central reporting and control.

Consequently, many CIOs are shifting their computing balance from mainframe transaction processing to more responsive distributed or client/server models. The long-term objective in these firms is a technology architecture without mainframes. Motorola, for example, is already "mainframeless."

The first step in this processing shift is typically a reduction in the number of mainframes through consolidation to a few large-scale systems. Examples included TRW's consolidation from 34 CPUs to 2 and Black & Decker's move from 22 CPUs to 8. Mainframe applications are then gradually offloaded to other technologies or re-engineered to adapt the mainframe to a "superserver" role in a distributed or client/server environment.

However, in successful transitions to a "mainframeless" technology architecture, IT generally retains centralized control. The reason: the high cost of unmanaged complexity. If a mainframe is like a Boeing 747 airplane, then a client/server network is like 10,000 airplane parts flying in close formation. It's no wonder firms that take a laissez-faire approach to client/server administration report IT cost increases of 15 percent to 20 percent as they migrate to client/server technology.

To squeeze out the higher costs of client/server computing, top CIOs adopt a strategy of being "lean on the desktop" and "fat on the server" in terms of function and services. Many firms also centralize their client/server support infrastructure—particularly help desk support, LAN administration, and network management.

Decentralized technology architectures are by no means universal. Firms such as AMOCO, Pfizer, Allied Signal, and Shell Oil are pursuing a "shared services model" that puts all the company's IT services under one roof.

Re-engineering the IT Organization

IT staffing is relentlessly trending downward in large organizations.[4] This trend applies to IT management as well as supervised

---

4 S. Diamond, "IT Cost Reductions," *CIO Journal*, Winter 1992; *SIM Network*, March-April 1992; *InformationWeek*, December 1992.

staff. The ratio of IT managers to IT workers is about 10:1 in large firms and is coming under scrutiny.

Outsourcing also continues its exponential growth in IT organizations. Key activity centers such as application development, application maintenance, and network management are now being outsourced, in addition to more conventional functions such as data center operations and disaster recovery.

The key to successful staff cost cutting is planning. Determine what the IT organization's key strengths are and where the IT organization brings strategic value to the business. Beef up those functions and slash everything else.

Formal business process re-engineering (BPR) methods can help with this analysis and are being applied to the internal processes and organizational structure of IT. Based on learning from the mistakes of the pioneers, BPR efforts in IT organizations start small and seek short-term payoff.

Applying TQM Principles to IT
Re-engineering the IT organization need not imply a focus on total quality management (TQM). However, TQM always requires the re-engineering of affected work groups and processes.

TQM continues to make inroads into the IT organization in the areas of quality training (with emphasis on the customer–supplier model) and the empowerment of IT employees. However, the most striking trend is the widespread use of benchmarking—the first real step to TQM. *Everybody* is benchmarking *everything* in the IT organization: traditional data center expenses, system workloads, staff ratios, programmer productivity, application quality, help desk support calls, even professional membership costs. Benchmark information is exchanged with best-of-breed organizations in the same industry for mutual benefit.

Shortening IT Cycle Time
It is no longer accepted practice for IT to take as long to develop a new application as Detroit takes to develop a new automobile. Top CIOs are pushing to shorten IT cycle times. They achieve this objective in three ways:

- Rapid application development (RAD).
- End user computing support.
- Outsourcing new development.

The most popular approaches to *rapid application development* include prototyping, reusable code, RAD tools, packaged applications, high-productivity desktop development environments, and more efficient programming languages (C++, Visual Basic, and 4GLs).

End-user computing relieves the IT department of coding special-purpose programs to produce queries and simple reports. Consequently, "green screens" are being replaced by user-friendly, intelligent desktop systems equipped with query tools, executive information systems (EIS), online analytical processing (OLAP) products, and easier, quicker access to data on disparate systems. Data warehousing is viewed as key to data delivery.

Outsourced application development entails some risk. But industry-specialized outsourcing firms can take on projects for which the existing IT staff simply doesn't have time. This type of parallel development effort requires coordination, but can be successful.

Integrating IT Into Business Operations
For IT, getting "close to the customer" means getting close to the business. CIOs can't afford to be technology isolationists in outlook. Top CIOs seek to participate in corporate strategic planning and then embed enabling, business-centered technology throughout the organizational infrastructure and beyond.

Any-to-any connectivity is key. Keith Trumbell, CIO of Alcoa, says he is busy "connecting everything" for his company—not only remote plants to corporate headquarters, but also to other plants, to customers, and to suppliers. Distributed application servers, LANs, and "glass house" systems are internetworked worldwide. ISDN (integrated services digital network) is a popular technology for interconnection thanks to significant price cuts and improved service in recent months.

Fully automated transaction processing—another major trend—leverages technology to eliminate people, paper, time, and costs from the processing of business transactions. Included among these automated transaction technologies are image scanning, bar coding, pen-based processing, and point-of-sale data capture; electronic commerce methods such as electronic data interchange (EDI) and electronic funds transfer (EFT); online imaging, viewing, and document management; work group computing; data center automation; and electronic communication via E-mail, computer-integrated fax, and video conferencing. A major New York bank, for example, eliminated all internal memos and printers with E-mail and online viewing.

It is important to note that researchers have now established a link between the profitability of a company and the degree to which IT supports the strategic objectives of the business. Within any one industry, the firms in which IT is most tightly aligned with corporate objectives are the most profitable. The business case for IT integration with business objectives could not be greater.

The accompanying box summarizes the current best practices discussed in this section on controlling IT costs. The next section covers the best practices in developing and implementing new IT applications.

TOP IT COST-CUTTING STRATEGIES

Use low-cost technology architectures.

- Consolidate mainframes.
- Distribute processing power via "lean" desktop systems and "fat" servers.
- Centralize management and support.

Re-engineer the IT organization.

- Use self-led teams.
- Outsource.
- Focus IT on adding value.

Apply TQM principles to IT

- Benchmark everything.

Shorten IT cycle time.

- Rapid application development.
- Support end-user computing.
- Outsource application development.

Integrate IT into the business.

- Have any-to-any connectivity.
- Support corporate objectives.

Beware of the Phantom User in Project Management

Industry studies indicate that over 70 percent of long-term IT development projects fail—they are not finished, are significantly late, do not deliver the promised functionality, and/or are way over budget!

After a major IT development project was halted in its second year in a major operating group of a past employer, I called a meeting of my internal IT directors from the various decentralized business units.

We brainstormed and came up with a list of do's and don'ts as guidelines for implementing large-scale IT development projects for our environment. Unfortunately, many of these guidelines were known to us, but we historically reacted too slowly or lacked the internal fortitude to "raise the flag" when things appeared to be going awry! These guidelines covering business re-engineering, planning, people, change control, and vendors are discussed in the following sections.[5]

Often IT is used to automate ineffective and inefficient business processes. These processes should first be redesigned or re-engineered before automating. While IT can be a facilitator in a business re-engineering endeavor, automation should not be the primary objective.

Do you have a comprehensive project plan? It sounds simple! But how many of us have started a major project without a thoroughly thought-out plan? Many times the demands of some 500-pound organization gorilla to get something going, response to a crisis, the "yesterday" requirements of the corner office, or even the lack of our planning expertise has caused us to pay lip service to developing a comprehensive plan.

You must take time to "plan" the plan; follow a system development methodology; establish business requirements up front; organize teams of users, management, and technicians to make decisions on critical issues; and establish measurable objectives and milestones.

Sounds rational? Why don't we do it? People!! Every project needs a cast of *people* to orchestrate its successful completion. Each

---

5 S. Diamond, "Beware of the Phantom User in Project Management," *CIO Journal*, 1993.

of these cast members must have a clearly defined role and responsibility.

Key people in the cast include a management champion; a project leader from the user community who has knowledge of the business area and project management expertise; technicians qualified in the critical technologies needed; and a supporting cast of suppliers or vendors.

Each major IT project needs a management champion or senior-level business executive to oversee the project's life cycle. This management champion should be the senior executive in the business or functional area for which the project is being developed.

Many user organizations desire minimal involvement in their application's development so they "contract out" both the project management and development activities to the IT area. Every IT project must have a strong user involvement to succeed. Preferably the project should be managed by a key user, not by an IT person.

Staffing the project team with Joe "Castoff," Susie "Woebegone," and the phantom user who frequently disappears for other priority items is another cause of an unsuccessful project. Before raising the curtain to start your project make sure you have a staff of the right size, types, and quality. The cast should have clearly defined roles and responsibilities. Any major IT project that does not have an active management champion, strong user involvement, and the right resources will not succeed.

How many say, "Change"? How many say, "Over my dead body"? The project leader, users, and sponsors must establish an environment and process to *control change* in large-scale developments. Whether one uses rapid application development, prototyping, and/or traditional design methods, changes to the user specifications, system design, and so on must be controlled. This means having a process in place to control the nature, scope, frequency, and magnitude of change. Unless a change control process is in place, not only will the project die, but so may the career of the project leader!

One unsuccessful project manager permitted users' requests to change 90 percent of the code in a purchased package. Did he buy the wrong package, was he an "easy Eddie" with the users, or both?

Here's a special note on vendors and their products and services. Are "proven" vendors who are strong in the critical geographic regions (North America, Europe, etc.) being used for this project? Do not rely on the domestic vendor's promise "We will be creating a European office to service and support your international needs."

You should buy "proven" products and services that are currently available and not "on the come" (i.e., part of vendor's development plan for next year). Involve your vendors in the planning and implementation process. Their experiences and ideas are important.

Lastly, do not assume! Check everything from the business requirements; plan milestone review points and reviewers; check people's qualifications and attitude toward this specific project; and test the commitment of the sponsors, management, and users.

Most of all, beware of the phantom user and the lack of management champion.

Another area where management champions are critical to success is in business process re-engineering. The next section covers this concept and some guidelines for successful implementations.

Business Process Re-engineering Guidelines

Corporations today are experiencing increasingly intense pressures from their competitors, customers, and work force.

Competitors operating on a global and regional basis are forcing many multinational and national firms to be more responsive, increase productivity, and lower costs.

Their customers demand both quality and low-cost products and services. They want delivery of new products in a faster time frame then ever before, and often require their products and services in a customized manner.

The corporation's labor forces are dramatically changing their mix of women, minorities, ages, and so on, and are requiring a better quality of worklife and worker empowerment.

These competitive, customer, and labor pressures are being handled by corporations in many ways. Two approaches are Total Quality Management (TQM) and business process re-engineering (BPR). Both are relatively new.

TQM involves continuous changes or incremental improvement over multiple years. These changes are usually of small scale and within an evolving culture of the firm. The TQM efforts are focused on enhancing the products and services to both customers and suppliers of the corporation.

Some firms in the past few years have recognized the need for more rapid and significant changes in the way they do things. They have instituted a re-engineering or design of their processes within their organizations as well as those processes linking them with their customers, suppliers, and other third parties.

BPR focuses on significantly changing a process by improving its effectiveness, speed, and/or efficiency rather than just automating it. It produces a dramatic or radical change in the way things are performed as well as the company's culture.

BPR may be a project or a series of projects usually being completed in a year. It focuses on the business process and the encompassing infrastructure such as policies, organization, information, technology, HR programs, culture, and staffing. The process and its infrastructure are completely redesigned rather than just automated.

TQM and BPR both focus on customers and suppliers, and process improvement. They differ in the scope, extent, and pace of change, the magnitude of benefits realized, and the role of IT. Their benefits are greater customer satisfaction, better and more innovative products, and increased revenues. The following example in the retailing industry indicates the pervasive and critical role of IT in BPR.[6]

The retailing industry in the United States has initiated BPR in the past few years with its "quick response" (QR) concept. This is a partnership between retailer (mass merchants) and supplier in providing customers with desired products and services in a more responsive manner.

Under QR, information on the customer's purchases is electronically stored at the checkout counter in a point-of-sale devise. (See Exhibit 4.8.) This information is then electronically transmitted from the mass merchant's computers to its suppliers' computers.

When the inventory of a specific product on the shelf in the retail store falls below a predetermined level, the supplier's computer

---

6 S. Diamond, "Business Process Re-engineering Guidelines," *CIO Journal*, 1993; *DEC Journal*, Winter 1992.

E X H I B I T   4.8

Quick Response Flow

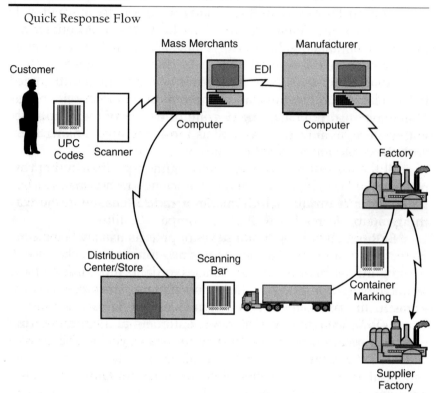

automatically issues a shipment notice. A quantity of new products is then shipped to the retailer's store or warehouse.

This incoming shipment has bar codes on the manufacturer's packing cartons which indicate the product and quantity. These bar codes are scanned at the retailer's receiving area and the information is entered into the retailer's computers to update its store inventory, accounts payable, and purchasing systems.

This dynamic replenishment of in-store stock is a key part of QR "Quick Response" in the changing levels of inventory at the retail store.

QR is a dramatic change in the way products *are* ordered, manufactured, warehoused, and distributed in a partnership between the retailer and supplier. IT plays a critical role in enabling this new partnership to work.

As with this example of business re-engineering within the retailing industry as well as other industries, there are a number of barriers to success. What walls or hurdles will you encounter in business re-engineering? How do you handle them?

A perspective is needed that covers the entire enterprise, the marketplace, and the supply chain. This vision is often difficult to find in a large organization except at the most senior levels.

A substantial resistance to change will come from all the functional areas affected, particularly from the middle management ranks and long-term personnel.

All the ingredients for successful business re-engineering are often difficult to obtain. These are executive sponsorship and involvement, organizational restructuring, and extensive resources deployment.

Most organizations do not have the internal change agents to visualize and implement a "wipe the slate clean" approach.

Finally, the technology options and enablers are not known to most business managers and executives. How many of today's managers are familiar with the potentials of electronic data interchange (EDI), imaging, workstations, optical scanning, bar coding, pen-based computing, and so on? IT plays a critical enabling role in most BPR endeavors.

What are some suggestions for success in pursuing a business re-engineering endeavor?

An overwhelming and compelling case is needed to sell the scope of change to both senior management and the organization. Often these stimuli come from external sources such as the customers, government, legislation, suppliers, unions, and competitors. Intense competition from global and regional geographic areas (Europe, North America, etc.) is forcing many firms to redesign their business policies, practices, and processes.

You need to assess your organization's readiness for change. How difficult is it now to bring about change? Is the organization aware of the need for the extensive change proposed? You may need to orient, educate, bring in new talent, reorganize, and so on to mobilize your organization for change.

The nature and scope of this change is dramatic and extensive. The support and ongoing involvement of senior management is critical. Do not attempt any re-engineering without it!

Make sure you understand the needs of your customers, suppliers, and other relevant external parties. Involve them in the planning and change process.

Design and lay out your overall plan for change, but limit your initial implementation efforts to a few areas. Focus on what is critical! You might have a re-engineering project performed in phases or a series of projects. Pilot before implementing on a wide scale in the operating environment. Try to avoid the "big bang" approach to implementing business re-engineering.

Establish a methodical process for implementation and follow it!

Eighty percent of your re-engineering success depends on a good plan and a change campaign. In assessing your organization's readiness for change, you will uncover a number of factors that must be attended to in your change campaign. These needs may be for orientations and awareness; training for new skills; bringing in new personnel with change agent abilities; reassigning personnel; organizational restructuring, downsizing, and consolidating; and so on.[7]

A whole new industry of consulting experts is evolving around this business re-engineering approach. These consultants can be helpful external forces in analyzing the needs, determining approaches, developing a plan, and guiding your organization through the change and implementation process. Senior management must still have ownership of these changes and must manage the process!

In summary, business re-engineering is emerging as a new management tool to bring about change. This change is significant, comprehensive, and dramatic as opposed to the incremental changes of TQM. Senior management must sponsor it and be involved in its implementation for business re-engineering to be successful.

In business re-engineering there are a number of barriers to overcome, particularly in the people and organizational structure areas. A good plan, change campaign, and strong management leadership are key ingredients for success.

---

7 S. Diamond, "Business Process Re-engineering Guidelines," *InformationWeek*, October 1992.

As firms are making their business processes more effective and efficient, they also are examining what activities or functions they should be doing themselves or having conducted by third-party suppliers. The next section covers this sourcing decision from an IT perspective.

Outsourcing, Insourcing, and the Entrepreneur

A study by Frost and Sullivan, Inc., projects the United States outsourcing market to increase from $4.6 billion in 1989 to over $80 billion by 1998. The magnitude of the projected outsourcing growth in this relatively short timeframe triggered a series of questions in my mind. What is causing this growth explosion? What is outsourcing, anyway? Are there any guidelines for handling an outsourcing project? How can a CIO avoid being forced to outsource? Who are the outsourcing players—now and in the future? Is anything being "insourced"?[8]

The "O" word (*Outsourcing*) is not a new concept to IT managers. Most CIOs have traditionally outsourced some aspects of their IT functions to third parties for operation and management. Historically, those functions and activities outsourced were data entry, off-site storage, microfilming, maintenance of hardware, contract programming for peak needs and conversions, documentation, facilities management of the data center, and disaster recovery "hot" sites. Today, the current items being outsourced are data center operations, application programming, network management, help desk operations, PC repairs and maintenance, and systems programming.

The cause of this outsourcing explosion lies in several areas. First, many IT aspects have become stable and commoditylike so that they can be turned over to third-party organizations for more efficient processing and management. Second, some IT technologies and activities have become nonstrategic due to the maturing of data processing technologies, distributive processing, and client/server architectures. Some firms are declaring their Mainframes and maintenance of Cobol applications as nonstrategic as they migrate to the new technologies mentioned above.

---

8 S. Diamond, "Outsourcing, Insourcing and the Entrepreneur," *CIO Journal,* June 1993.

A third reason is the tremendous downsizing and cost reduction pressures in most U.S. firms. These pressures have also hit the IT function. Finally, senior business executives are becoming more aware of the outsourcing alternative to their internal IT activities and its potential benefits and cost reductions.

As a CFO, you can handle this outsourcing of IT activities and functions in several ways: initiate an outsourcing review, have your IT area prepare an internal competitive bid, insource or become an outsourcing vendor, promote to your senior management the strategic value and importance of IT to the business, ignore the outsourcing phenomenon, or do some combination of the above.

If you initiate outsourcing on your own or are encouraged to by your senior management, what are some guidelines and critical aspects you should consider? Preparing an RFP (request for proposal), conducting a competitive bid, and specifying the nature and format of desired vendor responses are essential first steps.

Another critical area is specifying the treatment of your people in the outsourcing agreement for such items as sequence formula, timing of retention, protected employees, treatment of their pensions and benefits, and where they will be located.

Also important are (1) the pricing formula, the calculations of changes to it, and the conditions for changing it, (2) change control for the technical environment and staffing (levels, specific people, and responsibilities), and (3) service levels. (What is measured? For what time period? How do you calculate? What is the period to redress deficiencies?)

Also, disengagement or "divorce" options need to be specified and should cover under what conditions? Who is responsible for what? Who owns the resource? Who pays for set-up costs? Who prepares the transition plan?

The key in an outsourcing arrangement is to know what you want out of it and know your outsourcing "marriage partner"!

If you are requested by your senior management to conduct an outsourcing endeavor, you should also request the ability to have your IT organization present an internal bid. This step not only gives your senior management another option but also gives your IT organization the charter and motivation to come up with some creative options to dramatically improve service, reduce cost, and so on.

Most IT managers in the past have thought about or tried selling excess capacity in the second and third shifts of their data center operations. Recently, a number of IT organizations have pooled their purchasing power with others to obtain greater telecommunications discounts in filing for a Tariff 12.

Responding to this explosion in the growth of the outsourcing market, some CIOs have gone a step further. They have established an outsourcing business and are selling their IT services in the external market. These "CIO entrepreneurs" are actually "insourcing" IT work from other companies. They are trying to (1) leverage a unique skill or specialty they have developed; (2) utilize excess capacity, particularly for their large capital investments in mainframes and networks; and/or (3) creatively respond to their internal pressures to reduce their own IT costs.

A few examples of commercial firms that are in the outsourcing market as a formal business and their specialties are Mellon Bank (data center and accounting processing services for financial institutions), Sears (IT network), American Airlines (IT consulting), PKS (formerly Continental Can's IT organization–data center services), SIAC (security and exchange data processing for New York brokerage houses), and Day & Zimmerman (IT services for the engineering community).

In summary, whether or not you agree with outsourcing market projections and timing, you should address this issue within your own business organization and with your senior management. Which strategy you pursue—outsourcing to a third party, internal competitive bidding, internally promoting the strategic value of your IT activities, ignoring it, and/or becoming an entrepreneur—is up to you!

Many firms are going outside their corporations for preprogrammed software packages instead of developing the new business applications themselves. The next section offers some best practices in this area of software acquisitions and contracts.

Suggestions for Software Contracts

The IT magazines and papers are full of headlines and stories about lawsuits over software licensing between software vendors, outsourcing vendors, and companies such as Kodak and General

Motors. These lawsuits will ultimately be decided through the justice system and/or negotiated settlements among the concerned parties.

How can IT managers potentially prevent this litigation from occurring with any *new* software contract? What standard provisions might you include in any software contract? What specific conditions and/or events should you protect your company against? Here are some thoughts you might consider in your next software contract.[9]

The scope of the contracts should always cover your entire company and all its subsidiaries, divisions, and so on—not just one business unit or functional department.

As your business climate and environment change, your contract should have built-in flexibility to handle these changes. Potential mergers and acquisitions as well as outsourcing and divestitures should be considered when writing a contract. These business environment changes can be accomplished through the right to assign the product license to an outsourcer or the acquiring firm in a divestiture situation.

There should be a pricing cap and/or percentage limit on any increases for the product, maintenance, or services such as training or consulting. These price changes should always require sufficient notice to the user before the new price changes become effective.

Allowances should be specified in the contract for any successor product or cap in terms of what additional charges can be incurred in acquiring the next generation of software.

Deep pricing discounts can be obtained through competitive bidding and considering the needs of the whole corporation for this product.

Licenses for networks should be based on the active number of concurrent users at your site but not the processor size or the number of network connections. The software should record the number of users so the customer can size the growth pattern and be alerted when the usage is approaching the limits of the license.

A vendor had a contract with a company where pricing was based on the number of transactions processed. After billing the

---

9 S. Diamond, "Software Contracts," *CIO Journal*, Summer 1992; *InformationWeek*, May 1992.

customer for several periods at a constant dollar amount, he submitted a lower bill for the next invoice period since the transaction volume had dropped significantly. The auditors were unaware of the price/transaction clause in the agreement, so they initiated an audit of this honest vendor!

The up-front and long-term financial commitment to the software vendor should be minimized. Negotiate your best long-term deal on the potential number of copies, installations, and so on, but only pay and commit as the actual product/service is needed and delivered.

Build into your contract a flexibility-of-use provision. You should have the right to use the product across various platforms (open systems) and across business units as well. A product's costs should be based on how it's used versus what machine/computer it is used on.

Let's say the salesman says it will "do this and that." You should have the right to test and accept any product. Your contract should enable you to recover during the warranty period any costs incurred to date if the product does not work as represented.

A few years ago, a member of the board of directors of a company was also on the board of a computer vendor. We were encouraged to use this computer vendor's new product line. Unfortunately, the products did not work well, and we did not have any test and acceptance provisions in our "gentlemen's agreement." What a mess!

You should have the right to use the product while any dispute is being settled. A binding arbitration clause is sometimes helpful in resolving disputes. Also, termination clauses based on predetermined performance criteria are desirable.

You may be promised, "Our customer support and our development organizations will always be there to help you with a 'hot line' and product upgrades." Unfortunately, many software companies do not survive, and some are acquired by a new company with a different business agenda. You should always require source code and documentation in escrow, and have the free, unencumbered use of the product in the event the product vendor goes out of business.

These best practices covering contract scope, business changes, pricing, financial commitment, flexibility of use, product testing and warranty, disputes and termination, and vendor survival will enable you to protect your company and avoid this litigation maze.

The previous sections offered some insights, guidelines, and contemporary best practices in seven salient areas for successfully applying IT to impact your business.

The next two sections look at some future areas where IT will have a significant impact on your business. They also examine in detail the megatrend of client/server technology.

THE FUTURE OF INFORMATION TECHNOLOGY

When you look into your crystal ball and try to foretell what items will have an important impact in applying IT to businesses over the next five years, the following will probably be on the top of many a seer's list: mobile and remote computing, "super data store," linkages everywhere, electronic commerce and the Internet, the millennium issue, workflow software, event-oriented applications, and client/server technology.

Mobile and Remote Computing

As the salesman calls on his client, he will use his portable computer to find out the status of his customer's orders, enter a new order, and even conduct a product briefing using the display screen on his portable computer. During the day or from his hotel room at night, he will be able to check his office for messages, send various E-Mail messages, receive or send a fax, and compile and submit his expense and administrative reports—all on his portable computer for electronic transmission to his office, plant, or customer via a simple telephone connection. This ability to transact business and communicate via a computing device from diverse remote locations will grow exponentially, particularly with the advent of "wireless" communications.

Super Data Store

New software tools and capabilities are emerging that will permit firms to create, organize, manage, and access huge volumes of data from a data warehouse or super data store. Some retailers and consumer firms today are mining their data stores of customer information to look for patterns on purchasing and better ways to serve their customers.

Pharmaceutical firms in conjunction with health care organizations are just beginning to explore new businesses, called disease management, based on large repositories or warehouses of data about various population groups (elderly, infants, etc.) and the diseases that impact them.

Linkages Everywhere

In the BPR example we saw mass merchants electronically linked to suppliers. In the global cases British Air, USAIR, and Qantas are linked to their customers via a common database. In the Bristol-Myers Squibb scenario company plants, foreign sales and marketing operations, and headquarters are all linked together for information reporting, order sourcing, and communications. Electronic linkages are pervasive and essential for future business. These electronic linkages will be established between customer and merchant to provide services such as electronic shopping for groceries and other goods and services; between financial services providers, customers, and utilities for paying bills and money management activities, and within other consortiums of industries, companies, and third parties with a common interest.

Electronic Commerce and the Internet

The vehicles for these electronic linkages may be electronic commerce such as EDI, Internet, or private and public networks. Internet use is growing exponentially and will offer vast opportunities for companies to link up with individuals as well as other organizations on a worldwide basis for both communication and commercial endeavors.

The Millennium Issue

As we approach the year 2000, many firms are faced with a dilemma. A number of their legacy systems have programming codes and logic that is date-dependent (i.e., based upon the year code of 19xx). Some extensive reprogramming efforts are required to remedy this situation. For example, the Social Security Administration has spent 100 man years on this issue and has another 200 man years to go. Other organizations are considering replacing their entire legacy systems with newer software that better meets their business needs and also is in the technology of the future—client/service.

Workflow Software

Many firms have concluded that their business activities are critically linked together in a production-line–type environment. Insurance companies processing a new customer's application are an example. New workflow software facilitates this production process and allows the viewing and sharing of work in progress between departments within the company.

Event-Oriented Applications

Historically, most business applications are based on processing inquiries and transactions such as entering an order, and updating the inventory. The transactions were usually entered, processed, and maintained by a staff in Accounting, A/R, Order Processing, HR, and so on.

New business applications are being designed to handle "events" and place the processing responsibility in the hands of nontraditional sources. For example, human resource systems now enable the employees to maintain their own personal record in the company's computer. If a person gets married, moves, has a new dependent child, or wishes to calculate his projected pension or change his investment option for his 401K funds, he can handle these events without going through the HR department. He can enter his transactions for processing via his PC at work or at home, or use the key pad on his telephone.

Accounting, order processing, and purchase order transactions are now being handled by electronic data interchange (EDI) between customers and suppliers. The need for a dedicated transaction processing staff is dramatically redirected and/or eliminated.

For over 40 years, the computing paradigm has been a large mainframe in a "glass house" data center serving the various parts of the corporation. This centralized computing paradigm is being dramatically replaced by a distributed or client/server approach with the computing devices on the user's desktop. The following section is dedicated to this profound trend.

THE FUTURE: CLIENT/SERVER

Car bumper stickers often reflect profound social and political values with messages such as END NUCLEAR WAR, END WORLD HUNGER, and STOP ABORTION. Recently driving on the Baltimore Beltway, I saw this IT bumper sticker: END Ø USER COMPUTING.

The phenomenon of client/server computing is causing changes, anxieties, and opportunities throughout both the IT and business communities. What is client/server (C/S) computing? What are its promises? What are the myths and realities? What are its critical success factors? How do you manage and implement C/S on an enterprisewide basis?

To find out what are the leading edge and "best practices" in managing C/S, I conducted a benchmarking survey of over 50 IT consultants and CIOs of companies such as Bristol-Myers Squibb, NYNEX, Massachusetts Mutual Insurance, International Flavors and Fragrances, Carolina Power & Light, Olin, Wachovia Bank, Mead, CONRAIL, and UNUM Insurance.[10]

This survey is an informal and nonempirical one and was conducted over the previous year. It focuses on the managerial and business aspects of implementing a C/S approach on an enterprisewide basis. This survey deals with what works and what doesn't—the myths and realities, the risks, and the critical success factors!

- **How does C/S fit into the historical or "hysterical" information technology perspective and evolution?**

---

10 S. Diamond, "Hidden Costs of Client/Server Migration," *DEC Quarterly*, Spring 1994; *Client/Server Economics*, March 1994; "Client/Server," Myths and Realities," *Conference Board*, September 1995; *SIM Network*, April 1995; *Financial Executive*, April 1995; *Beyond Computing*, May 1995.

During its relatively young life, information technology has gone through some far-reaching changes. A few of the transitions include accounting machines to multipurpose computers, batch to on-line processing, file-oriented systems to relational databases, and centralized processing to PCs.

But no prior computing movement has been as pervasive as the current migration from the mainframe architecture to the multibox, client/server approach is proving to be. IT managers will need to rethink computing platforms, application development, programming languages, skill sets, security, management, and a host of other issues.

- **C/S is a profound change involving cultural, behavioral, and technical aspects in both the user and IT areas!**

The migration path, however, is uncharted and fraught with barriers and false starts. Few organizations know how to move from a large installed base of legacy systems on mainframe processors to a client/server.

- **So what is this C/S technology?**

C/S technology is where processing is distributed between a client or "front-end" device such as a PC or terminal, and a server or "back-end" processor.

The client is responsible for the user interface and data validation functions while the server handles the data repository activities. There may be a multitude of specialized servers dedicated to functions such as database, communication, printing, and naming. (See Exhibit 4.9). One CIO defines C/S and distributed computing as "a computer that has failed that I do not know about."

A common misperception in senior management ranks is that C/S is a simple linking of PCs together. In fact, a C/S architecture may be a very complex structure integrating many different technologies. (See Exhibit 4.10.)

- **What are the myths of C/S?**

As early users of C/S technologies, the survey participants unveiled a number of myths—such as the C/S approach is 8 to 10 times less expensive than mainframe approaches. Bob Woodrow, director of NYNEX's Telecommunications Group, says, "If you

EXHIBIT 4.9

Sample Client/Server Architecture

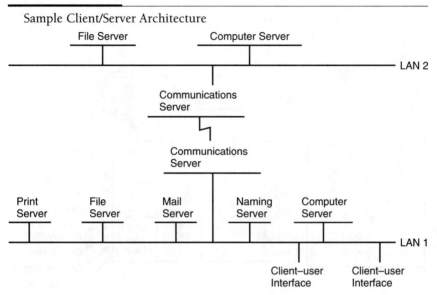

focus purely on the cost element, you can be led astray. If companies spend roughly $3,000 per user for C/S hardware and software, they will shell out three or four times that for intangibles such as help desks."

- **How do these C/S costs compare to the Cost of the mainframe approach?**

Bob Wagner, Former CIO at CONRAIL, says "In looking at CONRAIL's budget for last year and next year, they are spending more money on C/S than on the mainframe technology!" Many survey participants agreed with Wagner and also Woodrow who states, "You can make the case that it's 20 percent to 30 percent more expensive if you factor in troubleshooting, GUI experts, and support costs."[11]

The number one myth is senior management's understanding of the CIO's issues in implementing client/server technology. This lack of understanding encompasses users' need and ability to

---

11 S. Diamond, "Hidden Costs of Client/Server Migration," *CIO Journal*, November 1993.

EXHIBIT 4.10

Client/Server Environments
Complex and Expensive

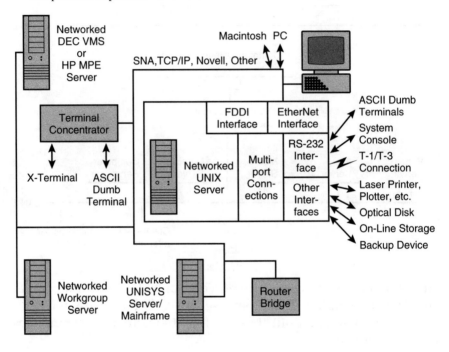

process critical applications; enhanced security and backup; extensive training of IT and the users, and IT staffing issues. The executive-suite perspective of C/S can be best summarized "as the linking together of some inexpensive and user-friendly PCs." The early users also identified eight other myths. Exhibit 4.11 presents Diamond's Top 10 Myths (à la David Letterman).

- **Given the increased cost of C/S and other myths, why are many firms pursuing it? What are the drivers? What is the promise of client/server?**

Frank Kemp (director of IT for Mudge, Rose, Guthrie, et al.) believes IS is getting pulled in the C/S direction because of the integration of the legacy system with the desktop environment—

E X H I B I T   4.11

Diamond's Top 10 Client/Server Myths

> 10. Client/server saves IT money.
> 9. Mainframes don't matter.
> 8. Mainframe approaches will work.
> 7. Client/server = UNIX.
> 6. End users can secure their own environment.
> 5. End users can run critical production systems.
> 4. Client/server is easy to implement.
> 3. Mainframe application developers can readily adapt to client/server.
> 2. Adequate client/server staff exists in the marketplace.
> 1. My senior management understands my issues about client/server, user control and staff.

graphical user interfaces (GUIs), Windows, spreadsheets, E-mail." Jim Weber (president of Omicron Center for Information Technology) feels, "The user is demanding more flexibility to make changes on the fly. IS allows the business units more freedom to do their thing." Weber also believes, "There is a desire in IS to push maintenance responsibility out to the user."

John Alexander (former CIO of UNUM states) "You can extend C/S beyond maintenance; users want to participate in the application development and maintenance processes."

Another significant reason for the move to C/S in the eyes of the survey participants is the enhanced personal productivity of the *users*. This users' productivity driver is fostered by user-friendly software and desktop devices; improved user interfaces such as graphical user interfaces; ability to use new data types, especially image; and the C/S being the first platform of choice for new applications from system development vendors. Bob Wagner feels, "Those folks who think the mainframe is the only way to go are dinosaurs. C/S is a driving force in the corporation! But don't be misled into thinking that the benefits come from cost savings. The real benefits are increased productivity and revenues!"

- **In pursuit of the promise of enhanced productivity via C/S, what is missing?**

The most cited deficiency of C/S is the ability to develop, deploy, and manage business-critical production applications in a C/S computing environment with the traditional control, security, and expertise of mainframe approaches.

Jeff Landau (CIO of Quorum) states, "We have been implementing a number of large LAN-based, mission-critical systems, and it's like skating on thin ice all of the time." Alexander believes, "You have to put together a training course for LAN administrators, set up guidelines cribbed from the data center, and have internal auditors look over users' shoulders every six months to make sure they follow procedures."

- **If we get appropriate C/S tools, will control be easier?**

One anonymous CIO says his users think "Backup is a reason for calling Roto Rooter." Jim Weber comments, "The cultural problems have to be connected not with tools but with each firm's policies from the top and user awareness. PCs are so vulnerable, it's scary!"

- **What do these early users of C/S technology suggest? What are the realities and critical success factors?**

- First, *think enterprisewide* in implementing a C/S environment in your company. Addressing an island, fiefdom or LAN at a time doesn't work. Peter Daboul (senior vice president of IS for Massachusetts Mutual) says, "You must think enterprisewide or else you're dealing with a one-off solution!"

- *Have a Plan!* The plan should cover not only the traditional components of IT plans such as platforms and operating system software and packages, but also the tools, controls, security, backup, data integrity, training of both users and IT staffs, and infrastructure support! Tom Dwyer (VP of Carolina P&L) sees C/S as a "major change over three to five years that needs to be planned and implemented well." Bob Curran (Director of IT for EG&G) goes one step further in saying "An overall C/S design or plan is paramount!"

- There are many aspects of C/S environment that must be controlled; however, it is essential to *control on an enterprisewide basis* both the configuration of LANs and the software releases. Daboul says, "You must control your release levels for your systems to be in synch." Otherwise, your C/S approach will be "alphabet soup and chaos!"

* Your senior management and users need to understand and buy into the enterprise C/S plan. The most successful approach to obtaining this buy-in is to involve your senior management and users in developing the enterprisewide C/S plan. Some firms, such as Carolina P&L, have employed companywide councils or task forces of users, management, and IT. Dwyer calls his senior management and users "knowledgeable about C/S and involved." Otherwise, you are left with the approaches Ross Anholz (CIO of Olin) calls "romancing each user" or senior management edict. Another CIO says his senior management thinks "Raid level 5 is a bug killer."

* "God created the earth in six days and on the seventh day dealt with the legacy application systems." You need a strategy for dealing with your legacy systems. One can define legacy systems as "those that work." Here are seven alternative ways of dealing with legacy systems and their migration to C/S:

* Retain—do nothing.
* Renovate—via GUI "face lifting."
* Relocate—port "as is" to lower-cost platform.
* Surround—create envelope or middleware.
* Re-engineer (code)—create new code for existing functionality.
* Re-engineer (business)—and then redesign the application.
* Replace—with a package software.

* Most firms select an individual approach for *each* application in their portfolio rather then one approach for all systems. Two commonly used approaches are to (1) re-engineer the business process first and then redesign the application and (2) replace the legacy application with packaged and/or externally developed software.

* Your C/S approach will need new software for applications and development tools, performance and network management, and security and control. The reality is that individual "point products" are available, but fully integrated product suites are two to three years away from development. Jeff Landau points out, "C/S technology available today is not industrial strength."

- **What are firms doing now?**

Three strategies are emerging for handling the software issues: (1) Go with a software vendor pursuing an integrated product suite. (2) Develop custom interfaces between best-of-breed point products. (3) Live with the current best-of-breed point products in the short term and change in years when full product suites become available. Most firms are going with alternatives (1) or (3), although a few firms cite significant gains from alternative (2).

- Client/server is not a strategy to reduce costs and should not be promoted as one in your environment. The advantages of lower hardware costs are more than offset by higher support, training, and control costs. Support is very labor-intensive due to the lack of management tools and immaturity of the C/S environment. However, some firms report significant reductions in applications development costs and time. One CIO cites those statistics for C/S application development: "The function points per user months tend to run in the 50 to 80 range versus 15 to 30 for mainframe applications—a three- to fivefold improvement in application development productivity."

- Training is extensive under C/S and could easily be classified as re-education. Users need training in productivity packages and tools, application development packages and tools, and responsibilities for operations and controls, while IT application developers need training in tools, methodologies and processes, and languages. Similar training is also needed for LAN administrators as well as data center and network personnel. Dr. Kalish Khanna (head of IT for the Society for Worldwide Interbank) puts it in perspective: "The costs of hardware and software for C/S computing are *trivial* compared to the training and control costs." You should plan on a major investment in training for your C/S program to be successful!

- Several strategies are being used for handling the C/S development staff. Some firms are growing their own C/S internal expertise via training and project experiences. Questions arise about training the entire IT development staff or just high-potential people. Other firms are supplementing their internal staff with experienced C/S hires from outside the company and/or using external contractors for major new C/S application developments. Cecil Smith (Senior VP of Wachovia Bank) is "buying

EXHIBIT 4.12

IT Development Staff—Major Changes

Individual performer	>	>	Team player
Specialized	>	>	Multiple-skill
Technology-focused	>	>	Technology- and people-focused
Incremental learning or upgrading of existing skill	>	>	Massive retraining in many different areas

outside expertise to help package the C/S approach." A few firms are taking the "Vince Lombardi approach" of having two teams: one planning for today (legacy systems) and a separate team planning for tomorrow.

Most firms are using a "blending and sorting out" process of limited training to selected staff, usually high potentials; use of contractors for major projects; hiring experienced external C/S personnel; and focusing some existing staff on legacy systems. Smith of Wachovia Bank also has a small core group of highly technical C/S staff who also have experience in mainframe technology to help his organization "bridge the two worlds."

Some early C/S users find a heavy failure rate (40 percent to 70 percent) in converting traditional COBOL programmers to object-oriented methodologies and C/S programming, particularly among older COBOL programmers. One firm with a long-termed COBOL staff even offered a bonus to their development personnel if they completed a C/S training program! Exhibit 4.12 indicates some major transitions that traditional mainframe developers must undergo with C/S technology, and the causes of their high failure rate. The re-education and behavioral issues associated with the migration to C/S are profound!

In summary, C/S is here and alive in your company and on your user's desktops. Growth will continue to be exponential in the C/S area for the foreseeable future. Data integrity, control, training, and management issues will remain with C/S for some time as it evolves and matures.

The promise of enhanced user productivity is great via C/S; however, the migration path is unchartered, has significant turbulence, and is a white-water rapid with a white-knuckle ride.

CONCLUSION

Information technology is a significant force in conducting business today and will be a critical component in shaping and operating the business of tomorrow. Whether through worldwide networks linking companies in alliances, "electronic" shopping for goods and services, conducting your personal and business financial matters in an electronic mode, or viewing the research and engineering drawings, files, and databases of your fellow scientists around the globe, information technology will be the lever or fulcrum that makes it happen.

The contemporary best IT practices and guidelines for impacting your business that are described in this chapter will enable you to significantly enhance the way you service your customers, operate your business, and potentially create new services and businesses!

5

⑥ CHALLENGES FOR CFOs IN PRIVATELY HELD COMPANIES

Timothy W. Stonich
Executive Vice President and CFO, U.S. Can Company

It might be appealing to represent the challenges of the financial function in a private company as being no different than those in a public company. And, to a large extent, that is true. CFOs, in both cases, must provide accurate financial reporting, raise capital, and perform other fiduciary responsibilities on behalf of the board and shareholders.

However, the manifestations of these responsibilities can be quite different in a private company, which, by definition, has no government-mandated standards for information disclosures that will be scrutinized by public investors. As an example, private companies have the luxury of managing their business for longer-term goals and objectives. With the absence of outside investors (often institutions whose investment time horizons can be quite short), it becomes possible to sometimes forgo short-term profit growth in return for improved long-term results. As a result, cash flow generation and creation of real economic value, instead of pressure to constantly improve reported earnings, is often the mark of a private company. Here is one reason cited for the success of Japanese business. The Japanese have taken a very long-term view of world competition, often forgoing immediate profit opportunities to build market share, enhance future growth, and ultimately improve earnings and shareholder values years down the road. While reported earnings will ultimately follow if cash flow is strong, there remains an issue between long- and short-term goals in the way public versus private companies are perceived as well as managed. It is a rare and very strong public company CEO who can sell long-term results to a short-term–oriented marketplace. Many times we have seen investors' and, ultimately, board of directors' impatience in large corporations' efforts to restructure lead to involuntary changes in management to gain more immediate results.

The more unique differences between public and private companies can be characterized by three main areas. First is corporate culture, the way things are done. This obviously involves interpersonal relationships with a host of constituents as well as the lines of communication and information requirements of the various groups. While one's main constituents should always be the shareholders, in a private company one is often dealing directly with owner/co-workers or else actively involved with very large shareholders at the board level. The depth of information to which these constituents are privy, their inputs, and their demands for information are quite different from the large impersonal institutional investors one finds in a public company. The different regulatory environment in a public company makes the issue of shareholder communication much less demanding. The second issue is the growth of the company and all that it encompasses for resource allocation, financing, strategy, and so on. The final issue is going public—that is, valuation, liquidity, capital availability, and ultimate desirability of becoming a public entity.

To explain what is challenging about these issues, some generalizations about private versus public companies need to be made. Private companies tend to be smaller in size, somewhat more entrepreneurial, and less bureaucratic. The leveraged buyout (LBO) activities of the 1980s demonstrated that going private can enhance values as private businesses can be and must be managed with an eye to cash generation to reduce a heavy debt burden. This generally has meant cutting the fat and responding quickly to the needs of the business. It also implies fewer staff and, importantly, less time and capability for analysis in the decision-making process. Therefore, while not necessarily younger than their public counterparts, private firms may tend to be less analytical or methodical in their approach to decision making. One could also argue that private firms are more reflective of their CEOs than are public companies. This can be a result of either years of family (i.e., owner) influence or elimination of the bureaucracy post-LBO. This is an important aspect of a private company. If, in fact, the CEO is also the majority owner, he or she really answers to no one, and the fiduciary responsibility of the CFO to outsiders or a board is significantly reduced.

CORPORATE CULTURE

The very nature of being private means the CEO, the board of directors, or both are not merely representatives of a diverse group of owners; they *are* the owners. Much has been written about entrenched managements attempting to protect themselves rather than enhance shareholder value. Needless to say, when these two groups are one and the same, management motivations are consistent with increased value, and this has been one of the fundamental premises of the leveraged buyout craze. The implication for the CFO is that his or her vision must be turned inside. While a public company CFO must worry about investor relations, meeting analysts' expectations, and stock prices, the private CFO must be responsive to the needs of the CEO (and/or a few investors), the organization, and, if the company utilizes enough debt, a few lending constituents. While this does not absolve one from the responsibility of properly analyzing decisions made by one's superior, it does allow the luxury of making decisions based on internal facts, not public perceptions (i.e., long-term impact versus short-term results).

This is a two-edged sword, however. While these shortened lines of communication and a rapid decision-making process can be beneficial, dangers abound. First, entrepreneurs, by their nature, like to take risks and have supreme confidence in their ability to assess risk and make the right decision quickly. While the proper decision is often made, lack of structure and accountability to higher authority creates a communication and information problem. It is not uncommon for the CEO to gather information from whatever sources available and then make a decision. This can void the normal checks and balances inherent in the business process and allow abuse of power by those with the CEO's ear.

This is a difficult problem because it will cut the CFO out of the information loop; errors can slip through the system. Most importantly, decisions based on bad information can be made and, worse yet, actions may be based on erroneous facts. There is simply a natural tendency to tell the boss what he or she wants to hear. The CFO's challenge is managing the information flow while not cutting off access of one's subordinates to the CEO and vice versa. This can only be done with everyone's cooperation, coordination, and understanding. From the CFO's staff perspective, this is a relatively simple job of explaining (and, if necessary, strongly directing) that all information passing up the ladder must be shared, if possible, prior to its dissemination and, at the very least, communicated immediately after the CEO learns of it. However, the natural tendency of the CEO to make quick decisions and bypass bottlenecks must be suppressed enough to be sure that all available inputs are evaluated. This becomes a political job that requires building strong relationships with one's peers who can impact decisions. These same relationship and trust issues must also involve the CEO; in both private and public companies, it is necessary to develop an acceptable position as the friendly opposition or voice of reason. These relationships can only be built over time with a history of favorable results. The successful CEO, while entrepreneurial and impatient to get the job done, will rely on other inputs if there is a proven track record of success and a responsiveness to the task at hand. There are no hard and fast rules here; a CFO must pick his or her spots and take a stand where there are strong supportable convictions.

The mirror image of this problem can also occur right in the CFO's office. Information must be promptly disseminated to the appropriate people up and down the organization. But without a structured environment, important facts can fall through the cracks. Because of the entrepreneurial or family orientation of many private companies, my observation is that they tend not to have a formal chain of command but rather an informal reporting structure. Take, for example, a change in tax policy that in turn affects the financial statements, which then impacts loan covenants or debt availability. All parties—tax, legal, accounting, and treasury—must be brought into the process or a technical default in the loan agreement could occur. Another example is the decision to buy a new piece of equipment. The timing of payments, capital expenditure limitations in the loan agreement, foreign exchange implications, and credit of the supplier (i.e., its ability to perform) should all be considered but will not be unless all disciplines are informed.

Furthermore, it is not uncommon for private investors/directors to communicate directly with the CFO. It is as important for the CFO to keep the CEO up-to-date on these information flows as it is for financial subordinates to keep the CFO informed. The only feeling worse than being "blind-sided" by a superior with information that one should know is having a director blind-side the CEO based on information provided by the CFO.

A further challenge in a growth environment relates to specific cultural and information integration. Acquisitions require the assimilation of people and their way of doing business as well as the form and substance of the acquired company's management information systems. Some people who may be critical to the acquired organization may not be able to cope with an unstructured environment. They may be used to the large-company mentality where decisions are often made only after interminable committee actions and levels of approval which, in turn, waste a tremendous amount of time. I have personally seen such an individual incredulously ask a CEO no less than four times, "You mean I should just go ahead and do it?" Ergo, people used to a formal approval process with written reports and decision by committee may not be comfortable actually making decisions on their own in an unstructured environment that lacks these features. This can, of course, lead to lost opportunities through inaction. Conversely, there are those who take advantage of the lack of structure to ramrod pet projects or act without appropriate approvals. As the CFO, one must be careful not to stifle creativity and entrepreneurism while, at the same time, maintaining some form of control over the commitment of resources. Loose cannons can be more dangerous than wallflowers who are incapable of making a decision on their own. In each case, positive action must be taken to nurture the employees and provide them with the time to adjust to a change in organization while, at the same time, monitoring activities to maintain a degree of control over the organization. Once again, this raises the important issue of constituents and relationships with one's peers and co-workers. It must be made clear that the CFO's interests are also the interests of the organization and ultimately of those very people whose actions he or she wishes to influence. Constant interplay and feedback to and from these constituents to build trust and convey the desire to be advised are critical.

A related issue is the integration of different management information systems' cultures. In addition to the attendant personnel-related issue described above and natural resistance to change, business combinations require adoption of common standards of financial reporting and management information systems. This can be a huge dollar-and-cents issue—conversion from multiple systems to commonality is a laborious, expensive task. Even something as simple as uniform part numbers throughout the organization can be controversial with each party feeling their original system is the best. Reaching consensus is difficult at best under these circumstances and almost requires scrapping all prior systems for an entirely new one so that each interested party suffers equally.

Each of the aforementioned issues also has a bearing on a major challenge faced by each CFO where financial leverage is an issue. Whether by acquisition or leveraged buyout, the people and culture in the resulting business entity have often come from larger, public, and, generally, well-financed companies. Many times I have heard employees of assimilated companies refer to their former employer as an almost bottomless source of funding. This is not, of course, the case in most smaller or private companies, especially those created or grown via leverage. Pennies are watched. Inventory levels increase in importance as does collection of receivables and payment terms. It is a real challenge to instill a sense of cash flow in people while not stifling their ability and enthusiasm in the new environment. Among the methods we have used is dissemination of the cash report (which includes credit availability) to those who may influence cash flow. A few reports reflecting a dearth of cash and credit will quickly sober the less discriminating spenders into rethinking their priorities. It is very important, early on, to communicate openly and frequently just how the rules have changed and what is expected of employees.

COMPANY STRATEGY

Another major challenge for CFOs (and all management in private companies) is establishing quantifiable strategic goals and then implementing and financing them. Often the CEO–entrepreneur has formulated an idea of where he or she wants to take the company. Unlike in a public company, where a concise, well-formulated strategy should be communicated to investors, an entrepreneurial CEO in a private company need not be explicit at all, leaving one's lieutenants to implement their interpretation of vague goals and objectives. While "I want to grow" may be a perfectly cogent, thorough plan in the CEO's mind, translating the amount of growth and area of growth to a usable structured plan may be a different matter. One might find entrepreneurial CEOs resisting any written strategy or official formulation of a plan because it limits their perceived flexibility in reacting to change. This is especially important where there is an active board that makes known its wishes to participate in the process. The CFO may become a referee between a board wishing to set policy and a CEO who avoids setting policy so that he or she may react quickly to changing circumstances. Therefore, the CFO is working, by necessity, with fairly general guidelines, and it is a great challenge to interpret and anticipate what the CEO really wants to do. Once again, rapport of the parties and a history of working together enhance the CFO's ability to perform in this capacity.

In a purely financial sense, this challenge manifests itself in how to fund growth with only general objectives and rapidly moving targets. It is a difficult challenge to provide flexible enough financing to accommodate a fluid, changing environment. One of the truly two-edged swords of being private is being able to provide financial institutions with projected financial results. The benefits are clear-cut. The company is able to quantify its plans and, therefore, its needs and expected financial performance. However, the downside is that lenders hold the company to those projections. The entrepreneurial CEO will also tend to exaggerate the projected performance of one's "baby." When, therefore, a scant few weeks pass between executing a new financing and a change in the company due to acquisition or divestiture, all bets are off. While the financial community may deny it, there is, in fact, a stigma attached to private companies and a lack of implicit trust in "the numbers." Why aren't they public? What's the real story here? What aren't they telling me? As a result, the private company CFO becomes the chief salesperson for the company in the financial world. A tremendous amount of time is spent getting lenders comfortable, accommodating due diligence, and explaining changes. Building credibility is one of the most important challenges for the CFO, especially in a rapidly changing environment. Because one is dealing with private constituents, one is not shackled by legal restrictions on information flow and projections. It is especially important to suppress the ego of the "organization" and provide lenders with a realistic yet conservative outlook for the future. Untold good comes of regularly "beating the numbers" year-in and year-out. Second, because one's ability to communicate is not limited by law, it is important to communicate often and in detail. No one likes surprises, and even a minor problem can take on undue importance if these constituents, including one's board, believe negative news has been withheld or hidden. A feeling of openness and candor is beneficial in most relationships but is especially important in building trust among constituents. It is a great advantage of private (versus public) companies to be able to communicate in this way.

GOING PUBLIC

Perhaps the greatest challenge, both inside the company and out, the CFO of a private firm faces is making an initial public offering (IPO) of stock. There comes a time in the life cycle of most companies when an IPO is appropriate. The owner(s) want liquidity for estate planning; growth can no longer be financed with debt; strategic plans call for acquisitions, or unusually large capital expenditures are needed in response to changing technology.

From an internal standpoint, one must recognize that the private company is akin to one's child. It is a living organism conceived by the CEO, to be nurtured and protected. Going public is akin to sending a child out into the world, and it is an emotional decision for the ownership. Taking this analogy a step further, it is often difficult for parents to loosen their control as a child gets older—to let him or her learn by making mistakes. A CEO is used to reacting quickly, and in making intuitive decisions may shy away from the scrutiny going public entails. The CFO bears a great burden on this issue. First, it is generally the CFO's responsibility and challenge to identify the need for capital well in advance of the time it is required because the ultimate process of going public can take up to a year or more, depending on market conditions. Also, the natural tendency is for ownership to say, "Let's do it the way we always have," and the CFO must internally sell the concept that new capital should be raised. The issue of company control and dilution are especially sensitive, and it is important to convey the message that, while ownership by the current shareholders will be reduced, the returns that can be made on the new capital will increase the value of that reduced ownership by more than the dilution. While the Kohlberg Kravis & Roberts's of the world clearly understand the concept of total value and know that smaller ownership of greater value can be worth more than 100 percent of current value, this is not necessarily the case with more traditional private investors. Once again, the CFO's marketing skills and credibility are necessary to overcome these hurdles.

Another internal hurdle is the reluctance to make information public. There is a natural tendency, especially by people involved day-to-day in a competitive marketplace, to worry that any information made public will be used by the competition with negative implications. Once again, the CFO must convince internal constituents that the competition probably already knows much of what will be disclosed. One way to do this is to collect the opposition's public documents, if any, which may already include estimates of one's own company's sales, market share, and so on. It also helps to point out what is already known about a competitor and ask why the competitor would not have similar knowledge of one's own operation. More often than not, however, notwithstanding all reasonable arguments, a great deal of "hand holding" (i.e., assuaging these concerns) is required. In any event, disclosing market share, customer base, and supplier information is traumatic at best and leads to a certain amount of resentment and wariness of the process by those less familiar with the process, particularly the marketing and operations departments.

Once these issues are resolved and the decision to consider going public has been made internally, it is necessary to engage one or more investment bankers to actually evaluate and underwrite the offering. (As an aside, *underwrite* is really a bit of a misnomer as the securities are pretty well presold prior to the price being set. That is, the underwriters really bear very little risk.) The process involves a tremendous devotion of time and effort by the financial staff, senior management, and board.

After internal agreement on an IPO is reached, a group of investment bankers is contacted to present their recommendations on the size, pricing, and timing of the IPO. Generally, underwriters are selected based on their familiarity with the industry, analytical capability (i.e., whether they follow your kind of stock and make recommendations to institutions), reputation, and, often, prior experience with management and/or the board. Fees for the various types of offerings are generally pretty much the same at each firm, and there is little room for negotiation. The financial staff must prepare projections on which the bankers base their recommendations. The CFO will be occupied for several weeks with "due diligence" work by the investment banking community followed by several presentations to management and a committee of the board of directors. The decision, in the end, is based largely on chemistry. As previously noted, going public is a very personal experience for the ownership of a private company. It is essential to the success of the offering that the underwriter be genuinely enthusiastic about the company (as opposed to merely underwriting it for the fee) and have credibility in the marketplace for the particular type of offering and industry. It is equally critical for management to be comfortable with the underwriter and enthusiastically open its lines of communication.

The process of underwriter selection can occur well in advance of the actual offering, which is highly dependent on both company performance and the state of the market as a whole. While the selection process will involve estimated valuations, this issue is not fully addressed until the offering is imminent.

When the decision is finally made to go to market, valuation (i.e., offering price) is the next hurdle to overcome. Initially, this is not the actual selling price but an estimate to be used in the prospectus. If I may once again characterize the company as someone's child, it is relatively easy to see that current ownership always thinks the company is worth more than do the underwriters. Many offerings have been canceled as a result of valuation differences. In some cases, however, because management and owners are much more familiar with the facts and circumstances, a higher valuation is appropriate. It is the CFO's challenge to act as an arbiter in this case and generate compromise on each side in this emotional issue. It is typical of underwriters, although they would dispute it, to undervalue an offering to both lower their risk and reduce the effort necessary to successfully market the issue. They will cite statistical comparisons supporting their valuation at lower levels than comparable companies. The CFO must sort out which comparisons are valid, which are not, and which require further analysis. With this ammunition, there is then a basis for negotiation and compromise by both sides.

In the course of preparing the prospectus and attendant requirements for going public, it is the CFO who acts as the mediator between company interests, legal (both company and underwriter counsel) interests, and the accountants. While strict rules and regulations surround an S-1 registration statement, there are a number of judgmental and interpretative issues in conflict (i.e., what must be disclosed and in what fashion). The rules are much too extensive and complicated to get into here. However, generally, they require that any statement made be supported factually, and the manner of presentation must, if anything, be slanted to the negative. For instance, we had a long negotiation with the lawyers on environmental disclosures even down to where in the prospectus they would be presented. This was particularly annoying because the five-page disclosure statement, after much ado about nothing, essentially showed the company to have no environmental problems, but the very length of the section might lead an investor to believe otherwise.

Another important function of the CFO is formulating with the underwriters the selling strategy and the presentation material to be used when the company goes on the "road show" (the one- or two-week period when personal visits are made by management to as many large institutional investors as possible). This material technically may not include any information not contained in the prospectus and is generally not distributed, but, rather, shown as slides. The road show is critical to the offering's success and lets investors actually meet management and ask questions to test their mettle. It puts people and their attitudes together with the dry and impersonal SEC filings required by law and, most importantly, allows management to actively sell its vision of the company.

A related internal issue surrounding the IPO is the necessary change in focus of the operations. In our company, for instance, the focus was an operating profit and cash flow (i.e., before interest expense). And it remains our focus because it makes solid economic sense. Cash flow does, in fact, ultimately translate into earnings and growth. However, because the public markets focus on earnings per share, a refocus at the top must occur with more attention to the impact on borrowing costs, taxes, and so on. These items, in addition to cash flow, have a bearing on the economic well-being of the corporation and, therefore, must be incorporated into one's communication with the investment community. Management must also be prepared on how to deal with the media and investors who call. Gone are the days when information could be freely communicated; an IPO enters the company into the world of press releases and conference calls with private communication most safely avoided.

CONCLUSION

To summarize, the private company CFO must perform a larger role as the conscience of the company. There is a lack of impartial public scrutiny in these situations, and, while the CFO must be loyal to his or her superiors, there is also a professional obligation to, in a sense, fill this void in the private business sector. Of course, there will be the standard oversight committees of the board of directors such as audit, finance, and compensation. However, due to the nature of private company boards, these can be less effective than in a public company. It is important, therefore, that the CFO establish a leadership position in defining the underlying values and integrity of the management team.

II

6 DETERMINING FINANCIAL POLICIES: THE GOVERNANCE OF MISSION, VALUES, AND STRATEGY

6

⑥ BUDGETING SYSTEMS: OPERATIONALIZING GOALS AND VALUES

Developing Data for Business Decision Making

Using Planning Systems for Achievement and Growth

Marshall N. Morton
Senior Vice President and CFO, Media General, Inc.

Properly organized and managed, a budgeting system, linked with the long-range planning structure and the incentive compensation system, becomes a functional tool—a tool for decision making, for engineering growth, and for achievement of objectives.

Information systems should never be more sophisticated than the situation requires. Industries that are highly and inherently profitable often consider it unnecessary to understand the elements of their profitability. So long as growth is steady and without surprise, management can generally be satisfied knowing what the results *are*, not how they were achieved. There is, however, much room within highly profitable lines of business for much to go astray without its becoming noticeable.

For many years budgets were viewed as presenting little more than targets, given annually to product line or cost center managers. They were thought to stimulate achievement but often were a source of irritation or concern. Achieving the budgeted number became the manager's all-consuming goal; explicit or not, the manager often felt that superiors equated failure to achieve the goal with poor effort. It was hard to escape the conclusion that failure to achieve the goal would result in some form of corporate punishment.

The negatives associated with budgets, and budgeting in general, led many businesses to avoid their use, particularly in industries where change had historically come slowly. However, as senior management became enlightened by a growing body of business research focusing on the impact of the communications, transportation, and data processing advances of the past two or three decades, it began searching for positive approaches that would induce desired behaviors and achieve required results. The budget process, used appropriately, should be viewed as delivering a set of accountability tools to senior managers—tools that can stimulate performance.

Integrating the disciplines of the budget process into a company's culture requires assurances that the budget will not be used as a corporate weapon. Further, it entails bringing people to understand that the budget should form a common basis for understanding management's vision of profitability, expansion/contraction, and the strategies/tactics to be used in addressing those goals. Just as important, from the financial officer's perspective, is enlightening senior management to view the budget process in such a fashion. It is easier to make a transition such as this if there are obvious trouble spots in the company's financial or operating performance or if its future holds obvious new challenges. The transition is easier for companies without a budgeting background than for those whose previous budgeting experience has left a negative legacy in its managers' minds.

DEFINING THE BUDGET

The budget is not a weapon, it is not a hurdle to be surmounted, and it is not magic.

The budget should be viewed as a *short-term* planning tool. It should, through words and numbers, describe the enterprise's expectations, performance commitments, and capital requirements over the next year or less. In a multidivisional firm the operating budget would ideally be the consolidation of the divisional budgets.

At each level the budget should represent the unit manager's performance commitment for the coming year.

Once developed and approved, the budget must maintain an active presence in operating management's decisions. It should become an ongoing framework for analysis of interim (weekly, monthly, quarterly) results and should provide early signals, not only of shortfalls or surpluses, but also of manufacturing problems (volume, cost), inventory issues, shipping, and other distribution matters. In almost all cases, a budget can provide the standard necessary to allow managers effectively to manage by exception and to take advantage of opportunities as they surface. Giving the budget a central place in the manager's decision-making process should help prevent situational, unfocused decisions.

BUDGET GOALS AND OBJECTIVES

A company has many audiences. It is important to choose budget and long-range targets that recognize and "speak to" the various audiences.

Many companies today labor under heavy debt burdens imposed by earlier leveraged buyouts, refinancings, or the heavy capital requirements of their specific lines of business, so free cash flow may be a more important focal point than the more classic measurements: operating profit or net income. Recognizing that the goals established in a budget will induce managers to attempt to meet the committed goal, it is important that the goal itself be calibrated to reflect the requirements of the enterprise.

Sometimes it is possible to join two requirements into one goal. In my company, for example, where the heavy capital cost of production equipment makes all expansion decisions costly, while, at the same time, high fixed costs deliver strong gross margin for each incremental revenue dollar, we use return on assets (ROA) as the ultimate budget goal, but that ultimate goal is the result of an established profit growth requirement and a desired level of asset investment. The profit growth target itself is the result of the company's cash flow requirements, which bear a clear relationship to its shareholders' expectations, its debt service requirements, and its capital spending needs.

While the critical inputs may be different, this process does not differ in any meaningful way whether it is applied in a manufacturing or a service environment. The important element is to ensure that the budget goals are expressed in terms that are meaningful to its users and that focus the users' attention on the most appropriate resources and constraints of the business. For example, the ROA focus at Media General sensitizes our operating managers to the resource commitment implicit in their operating and capital decisions. They quickly discover the relative power of the numerator and denominator in the ROA formula. We have encouraged them to look at ROA using the DuPont two-step formula:

$$\text{Asset turnover} \quad \times \quad \text{Oper. margin} \quad = \quad \text{Oper. ROA}$$

$$\frac{\text{Revenue}}{\text{Assets}} \quad \times \quad \frac{\text{Oper. profit}}{\text{Revenues}} \quad = \quad \frac{\text{Oper. profit}}{\text{Assets}}$$

Measuring a business by way of ROA has had an added dividend for Media General in the capital spending area. We have found that the ROA discipline forces a thorough review of the operating processes and working capital commitments involved in spending requests, in hopes of gaining further efficiencies in both. This, in turn, has often enhanced the capital project rate of return.

ESTABLISHING THE BUDGET

Setting the budget cannot be done in a vacuum. The business unit or department heads are the key people in the process. Before unit managers can responsibly establish their budgets for the year, however, they and their superiors need a *common* understanding of the company's future direction, its operational and financial requirements, and the expectations for a manager's business unit. Without such an explicit context, the unit manager is being asked to create a budget in a vacuum.

With such a view, the beginning of the budget process at Media General is to generate, at the corporate level (or similar consolidating point within the company), targeted levels of earnings, cash flow, asset returns, and so on. These targets should be developed in light of *consolidated, corporate* requirements without any particular concern, initially, about how (or whether) the individual operating units might achieve them. These targets are generally a factor of competition, corporate cash requirements, stock market expectations/requirements, and the economic/political environment. In the recent past, our practice has been to develop consolidated pro forma income statements and balance sheets that reflect the company's desired growth profile and capital structure. In that context, the responsibility of the operating unit centers on operating profit level and capital spending and working capital requirements. The ROA measurement process we use lets the working capital matter sort itself out, the capital spending is handled in a collateral process using a combination of qualitative and quantitative measures, and the consolidated operating profit is converted to a return on asset percentage.

If there is an operating unit tendency to "game" the budget (a tendency that can be magnified if bonuses are dependent on budget attainment!), this is a good place to begin dealing with it. One of the more effective ways of gaining perspective on a given budget's difficulty is to develop benchmark performance levels and, as a part of the budget preparation process, request a reconciliation between the budget and industry benchmarks. While it can be tempting to use past unit performance as an indicator of current achievement levels, unless your unit is the performance leader of its industry, it can allow you to aim too low in your profit targeting.

After the aggregate corporate requirements are determined, the next step, also handled by senior corporate management, is to make preliminary determinations as to how much of the consolidated year-to-year change should be contributed by each operating unit. Alternatively, doing nothing more than letting each operating unit know the required *consolidated* performance level for the coming year may work well; this latter approach has the merit of not asking for less than might otherwise have been delivered. In those cases where targets are handed down to the operating units, the units should be asked to analyze the causes of any difference between the target and their final budget.

To this point, the target-setting discussion has focused on quantitative measures. Qualitative benchmarks are important to the budget process also; however, they are more difficult to measure, particularly on an interim basis, and generally speaking, they are hard to establish early in the budget cycle, when the shape of unit management's plan is still being formed. Frequently—and for the same reason that it is sometimes best to let the operating unit develop its own growth targets—putting the task of establishing qualitative goals in the hands of the operating unit management may highlight otherwise unthought of factors and targets. This can be particularly important to companies operating in the service sector, where the relationship between revenues and the costs associated to produce those revenues is not so clear as it is in an industrial company. For example, my own company could choose to run low-cost syndicated programs on its television stations or it could substantially reduce the ratio of news to advertising in its newspapers, thereby generating real and immediate cost savings. The short-term benefit of such moves, however, would be ruinous to the company's future health. The corporate role here, in all companies, is to ensure that the quest for improved profitability and better investment returns does not force operating mangers to resort to such ruinous activities.

Capital spending plans are also an inevitable part of the budget planning process in that they affect free cash flow levels and asset returns. In addition, the budgeted future profit level may depend on a certain level of capital spending. Given this interaction, the capital budget for the coming year is best developed and approved in advance of the annual budget.

As a postscript, administratively we have found that it is important that all units have a coordinated set of assumptions on expense items whose costs change year-to-year, whether they are commodity items like paper, chemicals, raw materials, or a specialized item like general wage levels or merit salary increases. Company units that buy and sell their production to each other must have their transfer prices in accord.

From the corporate perspective it is important, early on, to develop a list of scheduled completion dates for the various phases of the budget. Closer to the time at which the budgets are actually being prepared it will be necessary for a centralized authority (corporate budget department, for example) to develop and distribute commonly needed information such as wage guidelines and inflation factors for supplies.

While possibly less important than the foregoing, it is worthwhile to consider developing a standard format for budget presentation. Not only is it helpful to the staff who will be developing a consolidated version of the budget, it is also very helpful for those who are less familiar with financial statements on a day-to-day basis, but will be reviewing them later.

In companies with multiple business units, inevitably one will want to know the plans of each other. Some information transfer can have positive impact, for example, in reassuring one manager that his or her unit is being treated no more demandingly than another. At Media General we use the annual meeting of senior operating unit management to discuss the coming year and the role each must play in it. We have found that information shared beyond the level of summary P&L, balance sheet, and a general summary of the business plan is generally not constructive. For one thing, each unit has a right to some privacy in its dealings with the corporate office; for another, often there is some competition between business units on the edges of their product lines or services. This kind of competition keeps managers sharp and need not be dulled by giving away parts of their business plan.

REVIEWING AND APPROVING THE BUDGET

It is important that unit managers understand that the budget is a functioning, living, planning tool that has an ongoing role in daily corporate life. The quality of effort devoted to the development of the budget and the degree of operating unit management's commitment to the budget are closely related to the budget's perceived importance to senior management.

The opportunity to present the budget to a senior audience gives unit managers the chance to bring some life to their plans and, conversely, gives senior management the chance to interact with the managers and to react to their programs. To this end, the budget is generally best presented by a group including the general manager and the chief marketing, production, and financial officials of the operating unit.

It is at this point that the importance of senior-level management's involvement in the budget process, and the positive side effects an operating budget can have, become most apparent. If senior management is merely a passive recipient of the unit management group's presentation, it will give unit management the impression that it is doing little more than going through the motions of a budget setting exercise. Ideally a budget presentation will provide a situation in which to challenge and explore the budget assumptions used and will give corporate management a chance, by a face-to-face explanation of the corporation's needs, to exhort the unit team to stronger performance.

INTEGRATION WITH THE LONG-RANGE PLANNING SYSTEM

Associating the annual budget with the company's long-range planning system reinforces the concept that the short term and the long term require trade-offs. It also underlines the fact that the annual budget is a building block of the larger, longer-term picture.

Generally speaking, the purpose of a company's long-range planning system is to keep sufficient focus on the future so that today's actions and decisions will be determined in a way that enhances the company's ability to reach its desired goals. Rethinking the long-range plan every year is necessary to ensure that changing business, market, and political climates haven't invalidated the company's objectives.

The development of a long-range plan bears many similarities to the annual budget setting process. It is important that senior management use the process as a tool for growth, strength, and stability, not as a means of creating yet one more hurdle to be climbed or as a method of imposing punishment.

Typically the long-range plan should predate the annual budget preparation, often using the most recent forecast of the current year's results as the base year of the plan. Whether the plan covers 3, 5 or 10 years is wholly a factor of the business in question. Industries dealing in high technology areas (whose whole world may change tomorrow) and commodity businesses (which are subject to the vagaries of wild cost and pricing swings) may find a detailed five-year plan to be a fruitless exercise. The long-range plan has to be tailored to the business it is covering and should provide a basis for valid decision making in the short term. At Media General, the Long Range Plan is developed during July and August and covers three years. The first year of the plan, as suggested above, is really the estimate for the current year and is made up of seven months' actual results and five months' estimate; the second year of the plan is the next full fiscal year. Thus, in the Three Year Plan we have an early look at the next year's budget—operating units and corporate management alike use the opportunity it provides. Operating management can get reactions to its early thinking (as to both degree of effort and direction); corporate management can begin to understand where the unit managers will need support (or more latitude), coming capital requirements, and likely cash generation.

DEALING WITH PERFORMANCE SHORTFALLS AND SURPLUSES

If senior management is committed to the concept that the purpose of a budget process is to provide a tool for decision making, for engineering growth, and for achieving objectives, and if the program is developed in that context, it is important that management deal constructively with variances from the budget. Frankly, dealing with performance that is better than budget requires just as much care as dealing with lower-than-budgeted performance.

Variances from budget, after all, represent nothing more than deviations from operating management's earlier view of the possibilities available to it. It is essential that management study the sources of the shortfall to determine whether the causes of the budget variances should have been obvious or could have, with additional analysis, become obvious before the budget was finalized. Budget variances are typically sending messages about dealing with the future: areas of concentration for capital spending, product redesign, staffing levels, and so on. If the lower-than-budgeted performance generates a particularly paltry bonus (or no bonus at all), consider quite carefully before making an exception to the formula payout. Making an exception can, and almost certainly will, change completely the nature of the commitment the operating managers thought they were making when they developed their budgets.

Dealing with better-than-budgeted performance requires care. However, after the ritual rejoicing over such performance this situation requires the same analysis that is indicated by lower-than-budgeted performance. Finally, it is senior management's obligation, if the better-than-budgeted performance generates a particularly handsome bonus, to pay it without question. If the bonus system is not working properly, fix it later but pay for performance now.

INTEGRATION WITH THE COMPENSATION SYSTEM

It is important to align operating-unit management's fortunes with those of the company so that unit managers are motivated to do the things and deliver the performance that senior management, the shareholders, and the securities markets deem best for the company.

If compensation is to be effectively coordinated with the budget system, it is important that it affect incentive compensation only. Our compensation system uses base pay to compensate for good work and it uses the incentive component to reward excellent performance. In this regard, it is important to guard against an atmosphere where incentive payouts come to be regarded as "givens"; if that happens, the failure to pay a bonus will be viewed as punishment and will tarnish the budget process itself.

Ideally, an integrated compensation system will have a long-term incentive program to accompany a short-term incentive program, thus helping to keep the business-unit management's attention focused on the long term as well as the immediate impact of its decisions.

The performance targets in a bonus system (long- or short-term) must be calibrated to reinforce the behavior patterns desired by corporate management. The annual budget forms a solid basis for determining what will constitute "excellent performance" in the ensuing year. Because the budget had its genesis at the business-unit level, it will largely be viewed as a reasonable point of departure by unit management. Inevitably—particularly where consolidation of all the business-unit budgets yields inadequate consolidated profitability, cash flow, and so on—the budgeted performance levels may need to be ignored for purposes of developing a bonus target. Even then, however, the business unit will inevitably view the bonus target, however arrived at, in terms of its relationship to the budget itself.

PERIODIC REVIEWS

During the course of the business year it is worthwhile to have interim reviews so that senior management can understand the current environment of the operating unit and see how it is being affected by that environment.

A quarterly or semi-annual budget review gives operating-unit management a chance to update senior management on its progress through the year and any fine-tuning steps it is taking or considering taking. It also provides an opportunity to give early warning of expected deviations from budgets. At this point some companies simply rebudget the remainder of the year; others allow the original budget and a frequently updated forecast to coexist. The right approach depends on the business involved. At Media General, in order to emphasize the commitment each manager is expected to make to his budget, we do not rebudget in the course of the year. To maintain a clear focus on the current state of the business, however, we do update income statement and cash flow forecasts quarterly. It is important that the budget process accommodate (and be able to take advantage of) changed circumstances. Handling it as a review process such as this should allow effective interaction between operating-unit and senior management. It should allow the operating-unit manager to leave the review session with knowledge that he and his superiors are moving in a commonly approved track and that he has the latitude to proceed with his program.

CONCLUSION

Budget systems are not straitjackets. They provide a plan that becomes a reference point. To the extent that actual performance exceeds or falls short of budget, the budget provides a point from which description/analysis can begin. Budgets must be coordinated with the enterprise's long-range planning system to ensure that each year is effectively contributing to the progress of the business and they must be coordinated with the compensation system to give business-unit managers an understood and understandable target of performance.

⑥ DEFINING THE ENTERPRISE'S FINANCIAL GOALS

Glenn J. Dozier
Senior Vice President and CFO, Owens & Minor, Inc.

The success of any business enterprise can be measured in financial terms. Having proper and useful financial goals that are fully communicated and well understood greatly enhances the probability of success for the enterprise. The elements of a financial goals program should consider the distinction between publicly owned and privately owned companies. Also, goals must be defined and evaluated in a manner best suited for different audiences, including investors, lenders, management, and workers. Additionally, the importance of consistency of the goals, the alignment of the goals with incentive plans, and the proper training related to the achievement of the goals must be considered.

Corporate financial goals must be consistent with the overall strategy of the company. For example, a high–sales-growth strategy probably should not emphasize cash flow generation or debt reduction. Moreover, specific financial goals for the enterprise should be tailored to suit the nature of its business as well. For example, a business with large inventories, such as a distributor, should most likely include inventory management goals among its key financial measures. A primary criteria in selecting the company's goals is to identify a limited number so that a properly focused effort and resource allocation can be brought to bear to see that these goals are achieved.

PUBLIC VERSUS PRIVATELY OWNED ENTERPRISES

The ultimate financial measure in its most simple form is cash or cash flow. The more cash an enterprise can generate, the more successful it is from a financial standpoint. It is sometimes stated that "you can't spend earnings, you can't buy food with return on equity (ROE), you can't pay for a house with return on total assets (ROTA), you can't pay wages to workers with inventory turns, you can't build the company's next factory with earnings per share (EPS), and you can't pay dividends with return on investment (ROI), but you can do all of these things with cash." However, cash is not the only relevant measurement and it can be evaluated in a number of ways. For privately owned companies in particular, cash and cash-flow–related parameters are extremely important overall financial performance measures. Publicly traded companies need to focus also on earnings-related goals (particularly EPS). The dual emphasis on cash and earnings measurements for publicly traded companies is due to the heavy focus investors place on EPS and related measures, and the resulting impact on stock price.

GOAL SETTING

Three major considerations must be brought to bear in setting financial goals:

1. The company's peer group or competition.
2. The company's cost of capital.
3. The sustainable earnings growth formula.

Owens & Minor, Inc., primarily focuses on the first two.

Peer Group

The ultimate measure of a successful publicly traded company is its stock price and its relative performance compared to a standard or to the competition. A recent disclosure indicative of this type of performance is the Securities and Exchange Commission's requirement for a graph that shows stock price performance versus a peer group and the S&P 500. Exhibit 7.1 shows the chart

E X H I B I T   7.1

Owens & Minor Stock Performance Graph, 1988–93

The performance graph compares the performance of O&M common stock to the S&P 500 Index and a peer group of companies for five fiscal years. The graph assumes that the value of the investment in the O&M common stock and each index was $100 on December 31, 1988, and that all dividends were reinvested.

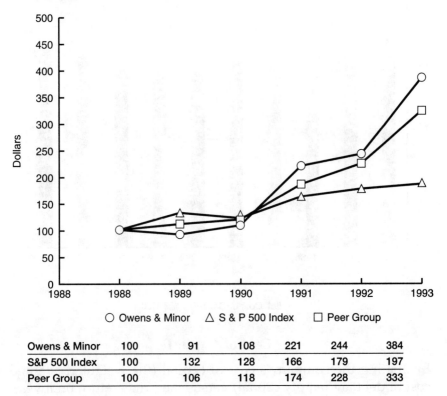

	1988	1988	1989	1990	1991	1992	1993
Owens & Minor		100	91	108	221	244	384
S&P 500 Index		100	132	128	166	179	197
Peer Group		100	106	118	174	228	333

○ Owens & Minor   △ S & P 500 Index   □ Peer Group

from our company's recent proxy. The exhibit demonstrates the importance not only of stock price performance but also of the use of comparison to peer companies or competition. Our goal is to be at or above the top quarter of performers within our peer group. We have chosen that goal because (1) we are capable of performing at the level based on our market position and operating capabilities and (2) our shareholders have invested in our company with that kind of expectation.

EXHIBIT 7.2

Owens and Minor Cost of Capital versus ROI, 1984–93

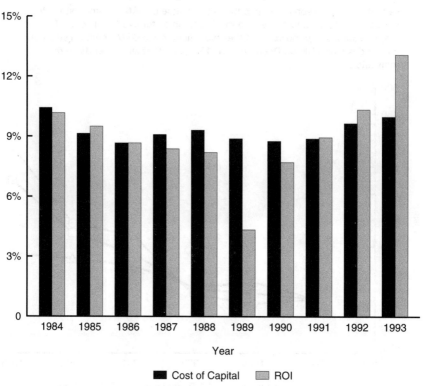

Cost of Capital

Evaluating the company's cost of capital (the weighted average cost of debt and equity capital) versus the firm's return on investment is another important overall measurement of financial performance that we use.

Exhibit 7.2 plots the cost of capital versus the ROI over a 10-year time period for Owens & Minor. Exhibit 7.3 plots the stock price performance for Owens & Minor over an 11-year period. As you can see, from 1983 to 1990 (when the ROI is approximately at or below the cost of capital), the stock price performance is approximately at or below the Standard & Poor's 500 (S&P 500) level of performance. However, in 1991–93, when the firm's ROI was at or above the cost of capital, the firm's stock performance greatly

EXHIBIT 7.3

Owens & Minor Stockholder Return per year, 1983–93
Value of $1,000 Invested in 1983 in either the S&P 500 or Owens & Minor Stock

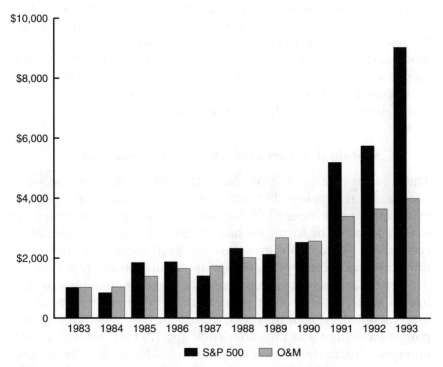

exceeded the S&P 500 performance. Of course, many factors go into stock price performance, but these exhibits certainly indicate a positive relation between ROI performance and stock price performance. This ROI versus cost of capital relationship can also be expressed as

$$\text{(Net income before interest expense but after taxes} - \text{Investment)} \times \text{Cost of capital} = \text{Excess (or deficit) contribution}$$

Note that investment in this model is defined as the total debt and/or equity funds used by the company or used for the project being evaluated. The cost of capital is defined as the after-tax weighted average cost of debt and cost of equity.

By using this model, now popularly referred to as an economic value added model, we can see the magnitude of the positive or negative contribution the company has made (expressed in dollars) for the period being evaluated. The results using this model may contradict results produced by other measures because the results from this model provide a more medium–to–long-term view since it incorporates the cost of capital which typically has longer-term characteristics. Different guidelines can be established for different business segments, but since Owens & Minor is in just one segment, we avoid this complication.

Sustainable Earnings Growth Formula (SEGF)

The concept of an SEGF has been around for quite a few years and has been developed in different ways by a number of academics and practitioners.[1] It can serve as an excellent planning tool. A number of formulas have been published to calculate a company's sustainable growth rate. Each formula is based on the same basic concept: A company having no debt, paying no dividends, and having a constant rate of return on equity would have a sustainable growth rate equal to its rate of return on equity. Customized formulas then adjust for the facts that (1) companies have debt and pay dividends and (2) their rates of return on equity fluctuate. Some of the formulas have been developed in great detail into quite complex, computer-based models. Others have taken on a fundamentally treasury-management bias by emphasizing funding needs to the exclusion of the measurement of operating profitability. Each of these formulas suits a specific purpose.

An operationalization of the SEGF concept that is relatively simple, is easy to communicate, and relates well to the needs of both operating and corporate management is

$$\text{SEGF} = \left(\frac{\text{NIi}}{\text{S}} \times \frac{\text{S}}{\text{NA}}\right)(1 - \text{D})(1 + \text{R})\left(1 - \frac{\text{i}}{\text{NIi}}\right)$$

---

1 Readers are referred to the first edition of this book (in particular, Chapter 3, "Corporate Financial Goals" by H. D. Vos and A. J. Battaglia) for an extended discussion of the SEGF. This section is based on that earlier chapter.

where

S = Sales for current year

NIi = Net income before interest expense but after taxes for current year

NA = Net assets employed at beginning of year (total assets less cash and short-term investments less all current liabilities, except any short-term debt)

D = Fraction of earnings paid out in dividends

R = Allowable debt to equity ratio

i = Interest expense after taxes

Analysis of this formula and the following example shows that a company's SEGF is improved by

- An increase in return on sales.
- An increase in asset turnover.
- A decrease in the dividend payout ratio.
- An increase in the debt to equity ratio.
- A decrease in the ratio of interest expense to net income.

The SEGF is applied to an Owens & Minor set of data in Exhibit 7.4. If the SEGF results are not adequate in terms of the company's strategic goals, analyses are performed to see what changes are required for each of the components of the formula so that a satisfactory growth rate is achieved.

E X H I B I T   7.4

The SEGF Applied to Owens & Minor Data

Income Statement Information		Balance Sheet Information		Other Information
Sales (S)	$3,000,000	Debt	$195,000	Dividend payout (D) 25%
Net income before interest expense (NIi)	34,000	Equity	200,000	Allowable debt to equity ratio (R) 1.0
		Total net assets (NA)	395,000	
Interest expense after tax (i)	7,000			
SEGF =	(.011)(7.6)(.75)(2)(.794)			
=	10%			

FINANCIAL GOALS FOR THREE CONSTITUENCIES

Owens & Minor, Inc., has three important constituencies (investors, lenders, and teammates); various financial goals are employed for each. The CFO's challenge is to focus on the right goals and institute them in the best way possible. Let's look at the process by which we establish our financial goals for each constituency.

Investors

Equity investors tend to have a wide-ranging view of an enterprise's activities. However, they tend to concentrate on a few financial measurements. The key profitability measures we incorporate in our planning process are EPS (and EPS growth) and ROE.

At Owens & Minor we compute ROE based on net income for the year divided by the beginning and ending equity divided by 2. Additionally, we focus on capital structure ratios as an indicator of risk and stability. We specifically focus on

Capitalization ratio.
Debt-to-equity ratio.

The capitalization ratio at Owens & Minor is computed as long-term debt divided by long-term debt plus equity at a particular point in time, such as the end of a quarter or a year. The debt to equity ratio is defined as total interest-bearing debt divided by total equity at a particular point in time.

Lenders

When setting financial goals, the expectations and/or requirements of lenders (including the rating agencies that lenders rely on) should be incorporated into the process. Lenders tend to evaluate an enterprise on a more conservative, risk-averse approach than equity investors do. They also tend to focus on cash flow and liquidity more than equity holders do. Consequently, the key measures we employ in this regard are

- Current ratio.
- Leverage ratios.
- Coverage ratios.

The current ratio (defined as total current assets divided by total current liabilities) is used as an overall corporate measure of liquidity and is not used by Owens & Minor as an operational divisional criterion. Owens & Minor has a high degree of liquid assets (receivables and finished goods inventory) and we have a target of a 1.5 or higher current ratio.

The leverage ratios have many definitions, but the most common are

- Total debt divided by total equity.
- Long-term debt plus total equity divided by total equity.

The coverage ratios are even more varied:

- Earnings before interest and taxes divided by interest.
- Earnings before interest, depreciation, amortization, taxes, and rentals minus capital expenditures divided by interest, rentals, dividends, and current maturity of long-term debt.

Owens & Minor uses both measures but focuses on the latter due to its more comprehensive nature. The key is to establish goals that the company can comfortably achieve, but still give adequate comfort to the lender. Typically, there is a correlation between interest rate spreads (i.e., the cost of debt) and the nature and quality of the lender's financial ratio goals as expressed in loan covenants.

Management and Workers

At Owens & Minor we call our fellow employees "teammates" because we feel we are all part of the same team, and we need to work together in a coordinated, constructive manner to be successful. It is the divisional operational teammate who really gets the work done. Consequently, it is crucial that all teammates or workers have financial goals that are consistent with the corporate goals and that they are structured to be suitable to the people doing the work.

We focus on two key operating measures: return on total assets (ROTA) and EPS at our operating decision level. Yes, we actually compute EPS for each of our 45 divisions. These two major goals are also broken down into additional goals pertaining to

- Gross margin percentage.
- Selling, general, and administrative expenses as a percentage of sales.
- Accounts receivable (A/R) days.
- Inventory turnover or inventory days.
- Accounts payable (A/P) days.

We also compute what we call a *liquidity index* in days, which is

A/R days + Inventory days – A/P days

This measure serves as a useful monitor of net cash invested in working capital.

The EPS for the division is particularly useful for a public company because it directly ties to data externally reported to shareholders. The EPS for our divisions is computed identically to our corporate EPS, which has aligned divisional management toward shareholders' expectations.

Exhibit 7.5 explodes the formula for ROTA backwards into its various components. We use this expanded formula, particularly in our annual budget process, so that Owens & Minor managers can see how changes in the various elements impact the ROTA.

For operating management performance related to our financial goals, we measure results at the local–profit-center level on a FIFO inventory basis (rather that LIFO), carry all goodwill at the corporate level, charge interest on all net assets at average interest rates (in recent times at a rather modest 5 percent annual rate), and allocate almost all corporate expenses to operating divisions on a formula basis primarily based on revenue.

COMMUNICATION, TRAINING, AND INCENTIVES

Of equal importance to the specific financial goals is the proper and effective handling of various related items.

All appropriate goals need to be communicated to all participants including managers, workers, investors, and lenders as well

EXHIBIT 7.5

Return on Total Assets Formula

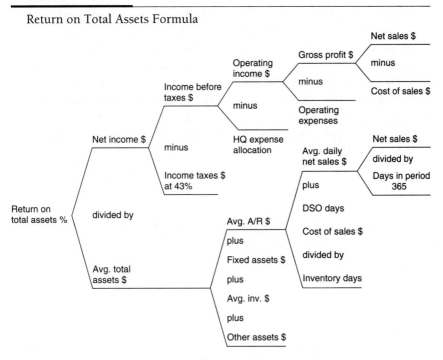

as customers. In this way, you get the "buy in" support from all parties, and you become a more unified company striving toward the established goals. Since goals are established on a participatory basis as an outgrowth of the budget process, goals achieve broader support.

Understanding the goals is basic to a successful outcome. Therefore, a necessary part of the successful enterprise is appropriate education and training related to the goals and how to achieve them. We do this through in-house training videos and seminars as well as external classes.

The work force down the line must have relevant incentives. Quantitative dollar rewards as well as recognition and less tangible rewards consistent with the goals set. For example, at Owens & Minor, officer-level personnel typically have ROE, EPS, and ROTA goals as their primary financial reward criteria. Approximately 80 percent of our incentive potential is tied to the performance of the individual or the individual's profit center. In addition, all teammates at Owens & Minor are eligible for an incentive bonus based on EPS for the entire company as well as for their respective profit center. A combination of goals that are refined and tailored based on current market and operating conditions is key to establishing a mutually beneficial goal system. In conjunction with the incentive programs, the key financial criteria discussed in this chapter should be integral to the overall management performance evaluation system, which is the case at Owens & Minor.

❻ THE ROLE OF FINANCE IN INCREASING SHAREHOLDER VALUE

Robert M. Agate
CFO, Colgate-Palmolive Company

Before discussing the role of finance in increasing shareholder value, it may be appropriate to outline the theoretical concept of increasing shareholder value. This concept initially defines for a company the theoretical minimum value improvement (dividends paid plus share price improvement) that a shareholder should expect each year. From this definition, a series of financing and operating assumptions are made so that the company's management can select suitable ranges of financing and operating strategies that will optimize the possibility of exceeding shareholder value expectations.

A hypothetical example of this concept includes the following assumptions:

1. Shareholder return expectations are, say, an annual return of 12 percent (comprising a U.S. government 30-year bond return of 7 percent plus a risk allowance of 5 percent).
2. Long-term debt cost for the company is, say, 8 percent pretax and 5.2 percent after tax of 35 percent.
3. Financing strategy determines that total capitalization (in market value terms) should be split 75:25 between equity and debt.
4. The resultant cost of capital, 10.3 percent, is arrived at as follows:

Equity	75%	×	12%	=	9.0%
Debt	25%	×	5.2%	=	1.3%
Cost of capital					10.3%

Thus, from a financial perspective, projects that return more than 10.3 percent will increase shareholder value, while those that return less than 10.3 percent will reduce shareholder value.

With this concept in mind, one of the prime responsibilities of a CFO is to ensure that the financial function at all levels is playing its appropriate role in the management team's efforts to continually increase shareholder value. This responsibility may be viewed as four interrelated activities:

- Agreement at the senior-management level on the financial and operating plans that will provide financial results exceeding the entity's cost of capital.
- The setting of financial ground rules by which progress can be measured in all divisions, locations, and levels of the business.
- The stimulation of teamwork within the financial function and the positioning of Finance as an active and valued member of the management teams that exist at various levels throughout the organization.
- The communication of appropriate information within each team to stimulate the setting of optimum financial goals and the timely measurement of business progress against those goals.

To illustrate the application of these activities I offer the recent history of the Colgate-Palmolive Company as an example of shareholder value creation. This illustration may be divided into three segments:

1. The initial turnaround from 1984 to 1989.
2. Building on success, embodying strategies for the more focused business, and incorporating more refined financial methodologies.
3. The challenge of the future.

INITIAL TURNAROUND

The initial turnaround was called for because, in the early 1980s, Colgate was trying to shed the remnants of a number of unsuccessful diversifications undertaken in the 1970s. We wanted to refocus our attention on our traditional consumer products businesses. By 1984, a start had been made, but—both internally and externally—there was great skepticism that Colgate would be successful in this refocus and even survive as an independent company.

Indeed, the capital market's patience with Colgate was running out. With a shareholder return of 80 percent from 1974 to 1984, compared with an S&P 500 return of +300 percent over the same period, shareholders were quite disenchanted. Thus, for Colgate, 1984 was not a time for complex strategies but a time to emphasize the need for continuing efforts to refocus on traditional businesses and, at the same time, restructure to improve profitability and cash generation. To simplify this focus and provide a rallying cry for internal and external consumption, a number of financial goals were established. These goals comprised a challenging eight-year plan to be achieved by 1991:

	1991 Goals	Average for Prior 25 Years
Annual earnings per share growth	15%	6.0%
Return on equity	18	13.2
Return on capital	15	
Net profit return on sales	5	3.6
Pretax margin improvement	5	
Annual sales volume increase	5	

There was little science applied to the selection of these goals. For the most part they comprised simple, round numbers that could be easily remembered and that represented an approximation of the best achievement of selected peer companies.

In early 1985, the CEO and other senior executives made a whirlwind trip around the globe to personally meet with all operating managers to ensure understanding of these goals. These meetings were supplemented by videotapes for local operating heads to use with their own management teams.

The definition of these goals did not, in itself, identify the plans for their achievement. However, the goal focus provided a simple way to evaluate business plans by quantifying their contribution, if any, to the goals. For example, local attractive projects in a nonfinancial sense such as new product plans or plant expansions were challenged against alternatives that, while apparently less attractive in a traditional sense, contributed more to achieving the financial goals.

Two other important ingredients in this approach were

1. The linking of incentive compensation to the achievement of business goals supporting these total-company plans in place of bonus payments that had had a significant discretionary element. An executive incentive program was introduced which was primarily dependent on the achievement of budgeted results, consistent with the company's financial goals.

2. Disclosure to the investment community that these were the financial goals for which the company was aiming. Discussions with financial analysts incorporated the targets, including the aim to grow EPS at 15 percent per year.

By 1989, results indicated that we would meet our goals. Consider

- Return on sales (ROS) was 3.2 percent in 1984 and was targeted for 5 percent by 1991. The actual 1989 ROS was 5.6 percent.
- Earnings before interest and taxes (EBIT) was 5.6 percent in 1984 and targeted for 10 percent by 1991. The actual 1989 EBIT was 9.2 percent.
- Return on capital (ROC) was 9.1 percent in 1984 and targeted for 15 percent by 1991. The actual 1989 ROC was 12.7 percent.
- Return on equity (ROE) was 11.7 percent in 1984 and targeted for 18 percent by 1991. The actual 1989 ROE was 24.6 percent.

From 1984 to 1989, the compound annual growth in earnings per share had been over 17 percent, compared with the goal of 15 percent. In the five years ending in December 1989, the annualized return to Colgate shareholders was 25 percent compared with a comparable return on the S&P 500 of 20.3 percent.

However, all was not perfect! By the end of 1987, there had been no significant improvement in the EBIT and ROS profitability ratios. Therefore, in late 1987, it was determined that two actions had to be taken:

1. Attention was focused on the trends of selling price increases versus inflation and, temporarily at least, the earlier 5 percent volume increase goal was de-emphasized.

2. Added emphasis was placed on the necessity for achieving the 5 percent ROS goal. This message was made clear by creating a simple percent to sales analysis for the corporation. This demonstrated that, at a 5 percent ROS level, sufficient cash would be generated to fund working capital growth, capital spending, and dividends. Using this simple financial model, every operating unit was able to factor in its alternative growth and investment parameters to identify profit requirements.

To illustrate this analysis, consider the fact that Colgate, at that time, was looking to grow sales at 10 percent per year, with net working capital at about 15 percent to sales. Annual capital spending was targeted at 4 percent to sales and depreciation charges were 1.6 percent to sales. Dividend policy was aimed at 45 percent of profit payout.

Thus, the 5 percent profit level represented the sum of funding needs as follows:

Capital spending	4.0%
Depreciation	(1.6)
Net working capital (15% of 10%)	1.4
Accruals and deferrals	(1.0)
	2.8
Dividends 45% (45% of 5%)	2.2
Net profit to sales	5.0%

Therefore, we were able to demonstrate clearly to our managers that, unless 5 percent profitability was achieved, capital spending or net working capital would have to be reduced, sales growth would have to be curtailed, and/or dividends would have to be cut.

This same analysis was utilized in an overseas operating unit to determine profitability needs under alternate assumptions.

In a country with higher inflation this approach would highlight the need for higher profits and/or lower net working capital. As examples,

	Hi Growth	Lower Growth
Capital spending	5.0%	3.0%
Depreciation	(1.2)	(1.2)
Net working capital (20% of 20%)	3.3	1.3 (10% of 15%)
Accruals and deferrals	(1.9)	(0.8)
	5.2	2.3
Dividends 45%	4.3	1.9
Net profit to sales	9.5% or	4.2%

From these examples, it can be seen that the alternative to achieving a 9.5 percent profit to sales was to reduce capital spending from 5 percent to 3 percent to sales, sales growth from 20 percent to 10 percent and net working capital from 20 percent to 15 percent. This combination made profitability of 4.2 percent to sales sustainable. It should be emphasized that this is a simple financial plan that enables the concept of profitability to be linked to the cash impacts of basic operating assumptions.

The resulting effects on profitability ROS can be seen in the trend:

	Profit ROS
1984	3.2%
1987	3.3
1988	4.1
1989	5.6

Some of the underlying operating and financial changes that contributed to this significant improvement were:

1. Major business restructurings in 1984 and 1987 which concentrated manufacturing locations and reduced corporate organization layers and expense.
2. Divestments (accounting for business representing one-third of 1984 sales) realizing $1.4 billion and its reinvestment in stock repurchases and acquisitions.
3. Greater marketing discipline in focusing investment funds on global brand equities, resulting in more advertising dollars spent on fewer brands.

4. More emphasis on appropriate profitability rather than on defending or building market share at all cost.
5. Concentration on a rigid capital spending discipline, whereby at least two-thirds of each year's program is devoted to savings projects with at least a 20 percent after-tax internal rate of return.
6. Introduction of a methodology for managing business in U.S. dollar terms in hyperinflationary environments.

BUILDING ON SUCCESS

The building on success segment had its roots in late 1988. At that time, with total business momentum building successfully and with a more cohesive understanding across all our operating units of the need for higher profits and their underlying relationship to cash funding, the senior financial group set about looking to the future to try to identify any changes in financial emphasis that may be required. Some issues considered were

1. The recent profit focus had moved management emphasis from sales growth to balance between sales and profit growth, with funding and cash generation as drivers.
2. Financial measurements were largely based on short-term accounting data. There was a strong feeling that this had to be extended to incorporate longer-term cash- or economic-related data.
3. As in most companies there was a proliferation of mostly accounting-based criteria for supporting business decisions. The financial function felt a responsibility to introduce greater clarity into business and financial reporting to lead to faster and enhanced decision making.

These issues were embodied in the consideration that, as a company, Colgate had begun improving shareholder value for several years. The next challenge was therefore to establish a *simple methodology to measure value creation* on a total-company basis. It was clear to us that the methodology must be

- Consistent internally and externally.
- Comprehensible to nonfinancial people.

- Applicable across the range of business decisions that managers at any level (corporate, operating, or project) may face.
- Applicable to a variety of activities such as acquisitions, restructurings, new product development, and capital investment.

After significant effort from the senior financial group and an outside consulting firm, a methodology was defined. Titled Colgate BASICS—*Building Added Strength Into Cashflow Streams*, it fundamentally is a conventional cash-based methodology that values the cash flow from activities at a present value, discounted at the firm's cost of capital.

The first step in the methodology itself was to identify Colgate's cost of capital. At that time, a weighted cost of capital of 11 percent was arrived at by combining after-tax long-term borrowing costs with an equity return. The equity return comprised the market risk premium and beta applicable to Colgate, factored over the 30-year Treasury bond yield. The debt and equity weighting was based on the market values of Colgate's debt and equity.

Implementing this methodology presented a number of challenges, not the least of which was the global nature of Colgate's operations that spanned over 70 countries. For an overseas location with possibly very different tax, inflation, and interest characteristics from the United States, questions arose regarding what cost of capital, tax, and interest rate assumptions should be used. We finally concluded that

1. The U.S. cost of capital was to be used everywhere.
2. Overseas projects would be assessed on a U.S. dollar basis, reflecting estimated longer-term exchange and inflation differentials and so on.
3. U.S. income tax rates would be used, reflecting the ability in the United States to utilize foreign tax credits on a consolidated basis.

The central rationale behind these conclusions was that, as a U.S. company with shareholders investing in U.S. dollars, it was important that shareholder value be viewed in U.S. dollar terms. Thus, overseas business opportunities had to be viewed with the ultimate U.S. dollar impact in the United States after all local and U.S. taxes had been accounted for. Therefore, it is necessary to take a view on the future local relationship of inflation with local currency devaluation and the global effective tax rate to which future earnings will be subject when finally remitted to the United States.

The only exception to these guidelines is that for some overseas countries, a premium would be added to the basic U.S. cost of capital to risk adjust for individual-country political/social risk (as opposed to economic or project risks, which are embodied in the project assumptions). The risk adjustment premiums are determined periodically from data published by international trade or economic organizations or international banks.

In the introduction of this methodology throughout Colgate, the challenge was not its creation but its communication. The initial step in the communications process was the design of a logo. More significantly, it was critical to garner support for the BASICS methodology across the organization's management. At Colgate's first global management meeting after BASICS's development, the senior financial group made a five-hour presentation on BASICS. This included personal-computer–assisted case studies covering an acquisition or a new product where teams of general managers bid against each other. The methodology was extremely well received. To further the project's marketing, each participant then received a hand grip strengthener with a BASICS logo engraved to emphasize "Building Added Strength." To further drive home the message, BASICS T-shirts and mugs were distributed.

Over a two-week period prior to this meeting, six two-day seminars were held in different parts of the world to introduce BASICS to the 200 top financial managers in the company. This gave them the opportunity to endorse the project to their managers and provided them with a sense of participation in the project. As part of this marketing effort, they were each presented with a clock with the inscription BUILDING VALUE OVER TIME.

Shortly after these meetings, a BASICS presentation was made to Colgate's Board of Directors, so BASICS became a part of the Colgate Board's vocabulary. Additionally, the chief operating officer and chief financial officer made a videotape outlining and endorsing the BASICS philosophy.

Another step in marketing BASICS was series of half-day presentations to business groups in corporate departments in New York and the Technology Center in New Jersey, combined with a series of presentations covering all of Colgate's worldwide operations. No formal presentation of BASICS was made to the external financial community. However, banks and financial analysts were reminded of our discounted present value criteria whenever investment announcements were made.

Thus for Colgate, BASICS came into existence as a methodology to link operating decisions to the optimization of shareholder value. This improved concentration of management effort when evaluating acquisition or restructuring opportunities. All attention can be focused on the operating assumptions because the methodology behind the justification is now understood right from the managers making the initial estimates to the final decision makers—the board of directors.

Examples of this can be

- *An acquisition opportunity in a developing country.*
  Management is provided with the risk-adjusted return required and agrees on the future inflation/local-currency/dollar relationships. It then focuses on the future business assumptions, such as category growth, market shares, margins, advertising, local infrastructure, fixed assets, and working capital. To provide sensitivity to the analysis, three projections may be prepared and weighted to arrive at the single projection. The three projections are to simulate best-case, most-likely, and downside scenarios.
- *A range of restructuring opportunities.* There may be an opportunity to close a plant in country A and service its needs from either country B or country C or a combination thereof. Future cash flows have to be evaluated in terms of costs and savings as well as sale and tax write-off of equipment, future capital needs, working capital differentials, severance costs, government incentives, and so on.
- *Divestment opportunities.* After-tax proceeds from the divestment of a business or product have to be evaluated against the present value of the future cash flows projected from retaining the business or product.

In the absence of a clearly understood methodology, decisions on the above topics would be clouded and delayed by debate not only about the business assumptions but also about the criteria on which the evaluation should be made.

Up to the end of 1994, the impact of all of Colgate's shareholder value initiatives can be seen by comparing compound annual shareholder returns (stock price appreciation plus dividends):

	5 Years to 12/31/94	10 Years to 12/31/94
Colgate	17.7%	21.3%
S&P 500	8.7	14.4

For Colgate, the impact of business methodologies such as BASICS on these real increases in shareholder value can be attributed to four simple steps:

1. The identification of longer-term business and financial goals.
2. Having each operating unit understand and embrace its part in those goals.
3. Relating compensation to goal achievement.
4. Having the goals externally understood so that they were consistent with stock market expectations.

The link between these steps and the shareholder value achievements is provided by the improvement in the percentage to sales ratios that operating management had been focused on from 1984:

	1984	1989	1994
Gross profit	39.2%	43.6%	48.4%
EBIT	5.6	9.2	12.7
Net profit	3.2	5.6	7.7

Although return on equity had increased from 11.7 percent in 1984 to over 30 percent by 1994, the use of this ratio and the return on capital ratio was de-emphasized during the period under review. It was felt that, at times, the use of these book-value–based ratios could be a distraction from cash- and value-oriented methodologies such as BASICS.

Today, several years after its initial introduction, BASICS is still being used in essentially its original form. Refinements are being introduced that can enhance its utility in special circumstances. For example, in acquisition scenarios the total value can be broken out by major time period (first five years, next five years, residual) and by source (regular business, new products, synergies) to provide more qualitative information to aid decision making. Similarly, what-if variations can be built into acquisition or new-product scenarios to show the cost or benefit of potential moves by competitors.

Periodically, comparisons are made with similar methodologies such as EVA (economic value added). In principle, EVA is identical to BASICS but has many refinements (e.g., treatment of R&D spending) that we have found add to the complexity of its use and understanding by a broad range of our management, without appearing to significantly add to its value to us.

THE CHALLENGE OF THE FUTURE

The challenge of the future comes for companies like Colgate that have a successful track record in creating shareholder value because past achievements only act as a spur to find opportunities, initiatives, strategies, and methodologies that will blend to continue to provide exceptional future growth for their shareholders.

The pressures on these companies will intensify from every conceivable direction. Exhibit 8.1 lists some aspects of future operating uncertainties that are likely to affect businesses over the next decade.

It is essential that the role of the Finance Department is focused and understood, not only by Finance professionals, but also by general managers and team partners in other functions. For Colgate, this focus has been crystallized into a simple vision for Finance: *"to be a valued partner in identifying and optimizing business opportunities."* In a formal sense, this vision is supported by the identification of personal, professional, and managerial competencies, as well as global career tracks, training menus, disciplined succession planning, and career planning processes. These efforts have been distilled into three essential and timeless qualities for financial professionals in Colgate known as the three C's: *Challenge, Communication,* and *Credibility.*

E X H I B I T   8 . 1

Operating Uncertainties in the 90's

Environmental	Ethnic groupings
Consumerism	Recession
Health	Taxation
Aging populations	Regional stock markets
Pensions	Advertising claims
Medical care	Unions
Inflation	Communications
Insurance coverage	Regional legislation
Investment trends	Third World Finance
Competition	New geographic markets
Cross-border mergers	Interest rates
Computers	Cross-border advertising
Nationalism	International accounting
Religion	

By implication, these three qualities embody knowledge of business strategies, cross-functional understanding, sharing of financial understanding and techniques, the ability to communicate financial issues to nonfinancial partners, and a change agent mentality with overall credibility.

By this means, the Finance function at Colgate is positioned to play its part in ensuring the continuity of the shareholder value creation that has been a feature of the past 10 years.

ⓖ   # MEASURING AND REWARDING PERFORMANCE

William Rotch
Professor of Business Administration
Darden Graduate School of Business Administration
University of Virginia

As defined in Chapter 1, a CFO is a key member of the top management team, manages the financial function, and oversees the general design of information systems. The CFO's interface and understanding of operations, marketing, and other important activities are also essential parts of the job. This chapter examines another part of the job: measuring and rewarding performance. In carrying out this function the CFO draws on the other functions: being a team player, handling financial management, overseeing information systems, and maintaining a deep knowledge of the business. As we shall see, performance measurement is not just a passive activity, for when insightfully carried out, it can be part of a firm's competitive advantage.

WHY MEASURE PERFORMANCE?

There are two basic reasons for measuring performance:

1. To see how things are going compared to some level of expectation. The monitoring of performance is done in different ways but always to assess how we are doing.
2. To motivate those who are responsible for or can influence the activity. What gets measured, gets attention. If we do not measure cash flow, quality, or customer satisfaction, for example, people may not pay the desired attention to those aspects of performance.

In this chapter we first look at the performance monitoring purpose, considering both financial and nonfinancial measures. Then we examine the motivation purpose and review some of the issues relating to use of incentives. And, finally, we come back to the important but less concrete process of reviewing strategic and organizational performance.

FINANCIAL MEASURES

CFOs have found a variety of measures useful for different purposes. Exhibit 9.1 lists some key measures.

Each of these measures has its special function for helping management achieve its goals. *Contribution,* for example, is a useful short-term measure of the effect of a decision on profit. Contribution may also be related to a unit of activity, such as an hour of machine time or space in a baker's oven. If the activity is at capacity, contribution per unit of capacity will help in deciding how best to use the activity. Contribution is a short-term measure because it assumes that the fixed costs stay fixed, whereas over time they are likely to vary. It also considers only those variable costs that vary with sales volume (or, more precisely, production volume). As activity-based costing has shown us, some costs vary with or are driven by other measures of activity, such as orders, setups, and product complexity. Nevertheless, contribution is widely used to measure the impact of short-term, small-change decisions.

Throughput, which assumes that only material costs are variable, takes on a kind of black box perspective. Throughput analysis assumes that (1) it costs a certain amount to run the black box that produces products and services and (2) the objective is to maximize the amount that revenue minus material cost contributes to covering that cost. Eliyahu Goldratt applies this approach to the bottleneck in an operation. When you maximize the bottleneck's throughput, you will get the most profit out of the whole factory.[1] Champion International's Hamilton Mill uses the throughput as a key performance measure for its premium paper

---

[1] Eliyahu M. Goldratt, *Theory of Constraints* (North River Press, 1990).

E X H I B I T　9.1

Financial Measures

The Measure Defined	What the Measure Highlights
Contribution Revenue minus variable costs, which are usually material, direct labor, and some variable overhead.	Shows how much the activity (or the product, service, division, branch office, etc.) contributes to covering all other costs (usually considered fixed) and then profit. Increasing contribution usually increases profit or decreases loss.
Throughput Revenue minus material costs.	Similar to contribution except that direct labor is considered fixed and, hence, a part of the total cost of capacity.
Profit Revenue for the period minus expenses of the period.	This is generally seen as the bottom line and, hence, the financial results available for debt repayment, further investment, and rewarding share owners.
Return on Capital Employed Profit divided by capital employed, which is usually assets minus current liabilities.	Shows the rate of profitability or how much profit per dollar of invested capital.
Residual Income or Economic Value Added Profit minus an amount reflecting the cost of capital used by the activity (e.g., profit minus total assets used times the estimated cost of capital or, for example, 10 percent).	Emphasizes the need for profit to cover the cost of capital used before any real economic value is created. Can be used throughout the organization but requires training.
Cash Flow Profit with noncash expenses like depreciation added back, and noncash revenue subtracted.	Shows cash income. Profit can be negative while cash flow is positive. Considers the business activities as a cash flow engine without distortions from artificial depreciation or amortization policies. But, by the same token, cash flow does not reflect the wearing out of assets.
Cash Flow from Operations Same as cash flow, but in addition reflects changes in accounts receivable, inventories, and other elements of working capital.	By including changes in working capital this measure considers the management of working capital to be part of business operations.
Free Cash Flow Usually computed as operating cash flow minus capital expenditures.	Shows the amount of cash a business generates that can be used for purposes beyond operating that business(for dividends, reducing long-term debt, buying back stock, or acquiring other businesses).

business.[2] The perspective is that the company has a collection of paper machines and related equipment that can produce a variety of sizes and grades. With that black box of production capability it aims to maximize throughput. The firm makes no distinction between direct labor and other conversion expenses, which are all incurred within the black box.

Economic Value Added (EVA) is a term coined by the consulting firm of Stern Stewart. Its success at companies such as Coca-Cola, Quaker Oats, and Scott Paper seems to come from the way it has helped connect stockholder value and cash flow with operating decisions. Managers who are cognizant of EVA make operating decisions in ways that maximize EVA, not just volume or profit. For example, EVA may influence decisions on payment terms (longer terms increase the capital used), combining production in one line or one plant, divesting profitable activities whose return is less than the cost of capital, or expanding activities that earn more than the cost of capital used. EVA can go up while the rate of return on capital goes down if the capital base is expanding and producing a return higher than the cost of capital.

This sounds very logical, but G. Bennett Stewart says,

> You can't implement EVA overnight. Companies sometimes don't disseminate EVA knowledge widely enough through the organization. Those that understand EVA know how important it is to train everyone in the organization because even those with the smallest jobs can help create value. This means linking EVA to key operating metrics like cycle time or inventory turns and making sure the people involved understand how EVA fits in.[3]

The key point is that the mindset produced by knowledge of EVA can influence decisions by people throughout a company, many of whom do not themselves have direct responsibility for EVA though their actions and decisions can influence EVA. EVA becomes more than a financial measure; it becomes a guide to operating decisions.

---

[2] See William Rotch and Kim Constantinides, "Champion International Corporation's Hamilton Mill: A New Reporting and Control System," University of Virginia, Darden Business School case (UVA-C-2105), 1994.

[3] G. Bennett Stewart, III, "EVA Works—But Not If You Make These Common Mistakes," *Fortune*, May 1, 1995, pp. 117–18.

Cash flow is an important measure for many CFOs because it is closely tied to the operating success of the enterprise. Dennis Dammerman, General Electric's CFO, has said,

> If I could have only two measurements, the two I would choose would be customer satisfaction and cash flow.[4]

Free cash flow highlights what is left over after satisfying the working capital and capital expenditure needs of a business. This measure would be most useful in a multidivisional company where some divisions generate positive free cash flow and others are absorbing cash. It is also a way to measure the amount of cash available for acquisitions, or for the reduction of long-term debt.[5]

NONFINANCIAL MEASURES

Managers are finding that careful development of an array of nonfinancial measures is a key part of improving performance. Careful development is important because, as we have said, what gets measured, gets attention. If you measure something that's not vital, managers will waste time giving it attention or, worse, take suboptimal action (detrimental to overall performance) to be sure they look good.

GE's CFO Dennis Dammerman has said,

> We as finance people have to recognize that there are more measurements than machine output per labor hour, or contribution margin on widget A. There's a whole range of things that are becoming more and more important to managing the business. The focus on time, for example. Are we managing our speed of getting something done? If we make tape recorders, how fast do we make them? What are the steps? How do we do it? Are we as good at measuring that and understanding the ramifications of that measurement as we are on cents per light bulb? Similarly, are we as good understanding

---

[4] "Fast Times at General Electric," *CFO*, June 1995, p. 33.

[5] For a more detailed discussion of the merits of the free cash flow measure, see Tom Copeland, Tim Koller, and Jack Murrin, *Valuation: Measuring and Managing the Value of Companies* (New York: John Wiley & Sons, 1990). The authors define free cash flow as "equal to the after-tax operating earnings of the company plus noncash charges less investments in working capital, property, plant, and equipment and other assets" (p. 100).

how we measure customer satisfaction as we are measuring returns in customer concessions?[6]

The level and scope of nonfinancial measures will vary with the scope of responsibility of the managers who have influence on the outcomes. At the plant level, measures such as those used by a frozen food processor in Exhibit 9.2 might be considered.

A recent Conference Board study showed that an international group of companies were using these key nonfinancial measures of performance:[7]

- Quality of output.
- Customer satisfaction/retention.
- Employee training.
- Research and development investment and productivity.
- New product development.
- Market growth/success.
- Environmental competitiveness.

Robert S. Kaplan and David P. Norton have written about the "Balanced Scorecard,"[8] which a number of companies have successfully used. This approach uses measures of performance from four perspectives:

1. *Financial (the shareholders' perspective).* Measures such as return on capital employed, cash flow, EVA, sales growth, and profit forecast reliability.

2. *The customer perspective.* For example, measures of customer satisfaction, response time, delivery reliability, and quality.

---

[6] "Fast Times at General Electric."

[7] Carolyn Kay Brancato, "New Corporate Performance Measures: A Research Report" (Conference Board, 1995).

[8] Robert S. Kaplan and David P. Norton, "Balanced Scorecard—Measures That Drive Performance," *Harvard Business Review,* January–February 1992, p. 71, and "Putting the Balanced Scorecard to Work," *Harvard Business Review,* September–October 1993, p. 134. See also Robert M. Curtice and George T. Kastner, "Balanced Performance Measures: Tracking the Pathway to High Performance," *Prism,* second quarter 1995 (Arthur D. Little), pp. 57–69.

EXHIBIT 9.2

Plant Key Trends Recap
Monthly Report, November

Quality Measures	
Hold % (excess production held in inventory)	0.9
Complaints: retail/MM lbs.	5.0
Complaints: food service	1.0
Write-offs/rework	$10,000
Clean pay scores (housekeeping)	3.5
Product cutting failures	1
(from lab samples of finished product)	
Safety/Turnover	
Lost-time accidents	0
Medical incidents	2
Turnover (hourly)	4.5%
Financial Measures	
Yield vs. history	.02
Yield vs. plan	(0.001)
Pounds produced	7,500
Overhead cost per lb.—actual	$.15
Run rate vs. plan	98%
Hours earned (lost)	(36)
Actual absorbed vs. planned absorbed	30
Over (under) absorbed vs. planned over	10
(under) absorbed	
Gainsharing/person (perfect attendance)	$180
Other	
Uptime %	92%
Planned run-rate mix in pounds per hour	4,100
Actual run-rate mix in pounds per hour	4,000

3. *The internal business perspective.* For example, measures of process reliability, rework, inventory level, and employee turnover.

4. *An innovation and learning perspective.* For example, measures of percentage of revenue from new products or services, number of employee-generated new ideas, progress on process changes, and improvement programs.

At first glance the Balanced Scorecard seems to be just a variation on management by objectives. However, a closer look at how it is used shows that it is more than identification of multiple objectives and measurements. It is really a system for managing strategy. Successful use in a number of companies shows the following:

1. The process of identifying the measures is often more important than the scorecard data. At Apple it is a planning device. If that planning process involves managers from a variety of functions, the scorecard provides a basis for examining the interdependence of the functions. Key objectives in each perspective must be identified and their interdependence with other perspectives put on the table for discussion. A target for improved customer response, for example, will have an impact on internal objectives. Innovation and learning will require management attention, time, and costs. The scorecard provides a useful template for choosing and building management initiatives.

2. The balanced scorecard helps clarify the links between strategy and action. For example, if the strategy is to enter new markets or design new products, each of the four perspectives will be affected. The scorecard encourages managers to be specific about what they want to accomplish and how to measure progress.

3. The impact of using the balanced scorecard seems to be strongest if it is part of a process of change. It provides a discipline to help managers coordinate to bring about the desired change.

PERFORMANCE MEASURES, MOTIVATION AND REWARDS

The act of measuring results provides motivation to make the results at least acceptable. Of course, the motivation may be weak if no one comments on the results. One plant manager said, "Each month I prepare a report, carefully explaining the key dimensions, but no one at headquarters ever says a word about it. I wonder if they read it." For him the performance measures received little motivational reinforcement.

Sometimes publicizing the results can by itself contain motivation. In its staff lounge Fairfield Inn by Marriott posts survey results of guests' ratings of front desk service and room cleanliness as captured at checkout by a "Scorecard" system. Each staff member learns quickly how he or she compared to the desired score and to other staff members. Friendly competition and personal pride supply motivation to keep one's score up.

It is important to show that somebody cares. Once that is done, motivation may be strengthened if a reward system is attached, but reward or bonus systems are tricky. There are a number of key challenges in the design of a bonus system.

Challenges in the Design of a Bonus System

Avoiding the Entitlement Mentality

A reward such as a bonus does not necessarily provide incentive. What has been called the "entitlement mentality" can mean that the bonus is expected and only the absence of the bonus provides incentive and that may be negative. However, clearly linking rewards to performance can help dissipate the entitlement mentality since it will be well known that inferior performance will deserve no rewards, and superior performance, even if achieved year after year, *should* be entitled to a reward.

Designing the Reward to Encourage Desired Behavior

Linking pay or rewards to performance is an attractive concept that few will dispute. When a job can be narrowly defined and output significantly influenced by the worker, the linkage can work. For example, piece-rate pay works for agricultural fruitpickers; it has also worked for years in the Lincoln Electric Company making welding equipment.

However, when the job is more complex, measuring performance is more difficult. In his classic article, "On the Folly of Rewarding A While Hoping for B,"[9] Steven Kerr cites numerous instances in which managers hope to achieve one thing but install a

---

[9] Steven Kerr, "On the Folly of Rewarding A While Hoping for B," *The Academy of Management Executive*, February 1995, pp. 7–14. This is an update of the original article published in *Academy of Management Journal*, vol. 18 (December 1975), pp. 769–83.

system that rewards different behavior. For example, he says, "We hope for teamwork but we often reward individual achievement," and "We hope to set challenging 'stretch' objectives but reward achievement of goals and making the numbers."

The objective, then, is to design the reward to encourage what you really want to happen. To achieve that result, many companies go for the macromeasures (such as enterprise profit, EVA, and shareholder value) and let the managers figure out how to achieve it.

Recognizing the Short- and Long-Term Dimensions

When the macromeasures are used with senior managers who can influence those figures, they are attractive bases for reward. But even those measures present the possibility that the basis of rewards will encourage short-term behavior while the owners hope for long-term value enhancement. And such short-term behavior can even impede long-term results. Rewarding on the basis of annual profit, for example, may not encourage managers to build for long-term growth in shareholder value.

Both the *basis* for reward and the *nature* of the reward have short- and long-term characteristics. The basis is the defined performance on which the reward is based. The nature of the reward is its content: cash, stock, options, and so on. Exhibit 9.3 gives examples. There is, of course, nothing wrong with short-term rewards for short-term results. What is to be avoided is rewarding short-term results while hoping for longer-term achievement.

In the past few years, many companies have required their senior managers to own a significant amount of stock in the company, stock often costing several times their annual salary.[10] Two advantages are cited. First, stock ownership provides an automatic link between company performance and the manager's wealth. Second, unlike stock options, this pay–performance link has downside risk for the managers, more closely aligning their interest with that of the shareholders.

---

[10] See John Mintz, "Lockheed Martin Will Order Stock Purchases: 1,400 Executives Must Own Stake in Company," *Washington Post,* August 30, 1995, p. F1, and Vernon R. Loucks, Jr. (CEO of Baxter International), "An Equity Cure for Managers," *The Wall Street Journal,* September 16, 1995, p. A19.

E X H I B I T   9.3

Basis and Nature of Rewards

Short Term	Long Term
Basis of Reward	
The year's profit, sales, economic value added, and achievement of other stated objectives with minimal effect beyond the current year.	Development of organizational capability, market penetration, R&D results, building customer and supplier relationships, and other achievements that are expected to have a payoff beyond the current year.
Nature of Reward	
Cash bonus, salary increase, shares of stock with no holding requirements, and other forms of compensation that have little long-term incentive.	Stock options, stock appreciation rights, shares of stock with holding requirements, deferred compensation conditioned on future events or achievements, and forms of compensation whose value is linked to future performance.

Using Single or Multiple Bases

Multiple bases for incentive pay could include elements such as profit, market share, customer acquisition, and employee morale. More than three or four bases are generally believed to dilute the force of each measure. The advantage of multiple measures is that they can encourage attention to both long- and short-term performance dimensions. Employee morale and customer satisfaction may not affect profit in this quarter, but are worth working on now to improve future results. In 1993, Courtyard by Marriott used the bases shown in Exhibit 9.4.

Deciding Whether to Base the Bonus on a Formula or on Judgment

Managers must choose whether to base the bonus on a predetermined formula or on judgment applied after the covered period is over. Use of a predetermined formula has the advantage of being unambiguous and the bonus is predictable when the base figures are known. However, use of a formula may grow to imply that the full essence of performance can be captured in a few numbers. Managers may begin to manage for this period's bonus numbers and pay less attention to building the enterprise. The flexibility of a judgment-based bonus can avoid this narrow focus. Furthermore, basing the bonus on judgment avoids having the bonus fail to reflect properly

E X H I B I T   9.4

Courtyard by Marriott
Summary of Bonus Plan for Unit General Managers

Maximum bonus potential: 30+ % of eligible earnings

Components for FY1993:

Property guest satisfaction	Weight 25%	Payable quarterly
Payout matrix to be developed		Award 0–75%
Property total revenue	Weight 25%	Payable quarterly
Measured by accomplishment vs. budget:	Below 85%	No bonus
	85%	0.9%
	97.5%	3.8%
	103.0%	7.5%

Each percentage point above 103% will be paid on year-end results and is worth .7% of eligible earnings. Uncapped portion is paid *only* if property's annual house profit is 100% or above.

Property House Profit	Weight 25%	Payable quarterly
Measured by accomplishment vs. budget:	Below 85%	No bonus
	85%	.9%
	97.5	3.8%
	103.0	7.5%

Each percentage point above 103% will be paid on year-end results and is worth .7% of eligible earnings.

Property Employee Satisfaction	Weight 15%	Payable annually
As measured by annual Employee Opinion Survey		
Payout matrix to be developed	Award 0–4.5%	
Individual Accomplishments	Weight 10%	Payable annually

As measured by supervisor's assessment of performance against specific measurable objectives. Objectives should be limited in number
Award 0–3.0%

the effects of positive or negative unforeseen circumstances that arise during the period. Of course, if postperformance judgment is to be used effectively, the boss is obliged to explain the judgment, which may not be easy, but it's an important part of management.

Extending Performance Measures and Rewards throughout an Organization

While a CFO will have direct responsibility for the performance measures and reward systems applied to senior managers, a CFO also has much to do with developing the process that extends the measures and rewards systems throughout the organization. This CFO function is a key part of the re-engineering and restructuring processes that many companies are working on.

The process during the turnaround of the Bank of Montreal provides an interesting example of how a new approach to performance measurement was implemented.[11] CFO Robert Wells said the idea was to take both financial and nonfinancial goals and derive relevant operating metrics that "mentally enhance understanding upwards and downwards through the chain of management about what can be managed and what can be delivered." There were several steps in the process:

1. Analyze key stakeholder groups, which for the bank included the usual shareholders, customers, and employees, but also local communities.

2. Design performance measures that would tell how well the bank was doing at meeting the goals and objectives it set for each group. These measures included not only the usual "primary" measures that focused on results, but also "secondary" performance indicators that focused on what Wells called "causes or drivers of results." For example, customer satisfaction might be a primary measure and customer wait times in the retail division might be a drive or cause. Each division or operation would have its own secondary indicators.

3. Build connections in two ways: (1) between what people do or can do and improvement in the measures and (2) between the measures at each level and reaching overall corporate goals. This takes time because it is a learning process. For the Bank of Montreal it took more than two years.

4. After the performance measures have been understood, perhaps modified, and accepted, then a reward system can be layered on top. In this way, the reward system is not expected to drive the changed approach to doing business, but rather to strengthen and reward the changes that are already well understood. Wells's next step was to work on tying performance measurements to team-based pay throughout the bank.

---

[11] See Bill Birchard, "Making It Count: How Innovative Companies Really Use the New Metrics," *CFO*, October 1995, p. 43.

There is no universal answer to the issues surrounding financial incentives. Individual and small-group incentives can be accompanied by conversation; large-group gain sharing or profit sharing plans can involve all employees. However, Robert McNutt, manager of compensation and benefit initiatives at DuPont put it this way: "There is no one-size-fits-all plan. They must be customized. A financial incentive should reinforce and support corporate culture, not drive it." In fact, McNutt believes a corporate environment in which employees are encouraged to contribute their ideas must *precede* the financial incentive. "The really successful plans," he says, "aren't the ones that make the most money for the employees. They're the ones where there's a high level of employee involvement in the design and implementation of the plan.[12]

MONITORING THE PERFORMANCE OF STRATEGY, STRUCTURE, AND PROCESSES

There are really several levels or domains in which performance needs to be monitored. On one level are the operating performance measures that test whether the currently defined strategy is being effectively implemented. These are the financial and nonfinancial measures we discussed earlier. On a different level, three other areas of activity need to be monitored: the development of strategy, organizational structure, and organizational processes.

Strategy

Having gone through a process of defining and promulgating strategy, managers need to monitor performance to test whether the strategy itself is appropriate. A number of companies have been known to focus so intently on the elegance of their strategic planning process that once the strategy was set, there was little inclination to review it. To avoid such a myopic view strategic performance measures are designed to help answer the question, *If we were to invent the strategy all over again, would it come out the same*

---

12 Quoted from Lynn Brenner, "The Myth of Incentive Pay," *CFO*, July 1995, p. 29.

way under current conditions? So the measurement process tests those current conditions to see if they have changed. Such conditions would include economic and competitive conditions, the technological landscape, and the evolution of the enterprise's core competencies. The measurement process could also test the rational linkage between a firm's overarching vision and the currently defined strategy. Does that connection still make sense? Of course, to do that, the linkage must be clearly enough articulated in the first place to be tested at a later time.

Organizational Structure

Since strategy often includes organizational structure, another domain of performance review may include the firm's structure, especially if new structures are being tried out.

Here structure refers to the assignment of authority and responsibility. Monitoring structure means reviewing whether the structure is working properly to support the strategy. For example, if management changes the strategy from a product focus to a focus on processes (perhaps customer service or new product development), the structure—the designation of responsibilities—is also likely to be changed. Performance measurement in this domain would periodically review the new structure to see if it was working. While using it, management would be testing it to see if it needed revision. Such tests would go beyond casual conversations and look at communication patterns (Do people get and give the information needed for their jobs?), clarity of tasks (Do people understand how their work can and should contribute to the total enterprise?), and speed of accomplishment (Do things get done promptly or are there delays due to uncertainty or bureaucracy?).

In 1984, when General Motors changed its structure from divisions focused on single brands to divisions grouped in larger, more autonomous units, the new structure never worked as well as management had hoped. There was confusion about tasks, relationships, and communication. Yet people in the middle management ranks seemed used to dealing with a cumbersome bureaucracy—that was part of their jobs—and the new structure was never really challenged until years later. GM's experience reinforces the notion that when change has been implemented in an organization's structure, it is particularly important to measure the effectiveness of that change.

Organizational Processes

Monitoring organizational processes is an increasingly important domain for performance measurement. For years academics, consultants, and business managers have described new organizational processes that are intended to enable companies to deal effectively with the changing environment. Competition, global markets, technology of production and communication, and an emphasis on customer satisfaction have all been changing rapidly. If a company's management moves in the direction of these new organizational processes, it follows that management should devote attention to assessing the effectiveness of the processes. Here are some examples of processes that managers might choose to give attention to.

From C. K. Prahalad:[13]

1. Democratizing strategy creates a new way of thinking about a process for pooling collective knowledge and commitment in an organization and channeling it. Many people say there is no natural constituency for change in a large company. We argue the contrary, that there is a natural desire for change in all companies, but there are *no forums for mobilizing that desire for change.* We say that [mobilizing and directing] the desire for change should be seen as an integral part of the strategy process involving both substantive and organizational issues.

2. The dilemma is in being efficient in the short term, and simultaneously having a point of view about the future and also providing consistency in resource allocation over time.

The goal is not to give up short-term orientation and operational efficiency. The goal is to add strategic and long- term perspective to it. I must say that in some parts of the world companies are even in the reverse trouble—neglecting operational efficiency in favor of a long-term perspective. Senior management must constantly maintain a balance.

---

[13] From "An Interview with C. K. Prahalad," *European Management Journal,* June 1995, pp. 132–33, 137.

3a. . . . translating these concepts into capabilities in large companies (i.e., operationalizing concepts). At the present time much of the toxic side effects of concepts being widely used in companies is poor operationalization and procedurizing of these concepts. The result is that only a small number of people can practice them and, even then, imperfectly.

3b. One of the major innovations the Japanese have made in management is to take a broad idea or concept and spend five years working out how to make it happen across the whole organization. To me, this skill is basically a deployment skill—how to make things happen, provide the tools and procedures, the training and commitment and understanding to a large number of people around the world so that strategies and concepts can be deployed.

From Samantra Ghoshal and Christopher Bartlett:[14]

1. The entrepreneurial process requires a close interplay among three key management roles. The front-line *entrepreneurs* are the spearheads of the company, and it is their responsibility to create and pursue new growth opportunities. The *coaches* in middle and senior management positions play a pivotal role in reviewing, developing, and supporting the front-line initiatives. Corporate *leaders* at the top of the organization establish the overall strategic mission of the company that defines the boundary within which the entrepreneurial initiatives must be contained, and also sets the highly demanding performance standards that these initiatives must meet.

2. . . . the entrepreneurial process alone is not sufficient for effective corporate entrepreneurship: the new management approach also requires the creating of a strong integration process to link the company's diverse assets and resources into corporate competencies, and to leverage these competencies to pursue new opportunities.

3. To remain successful over time, companies must establish mechanisms in which internalized wisdoms and established

---

14 From Christopher A. Bartlett and Sumantra Ghoshal, "Changing Role of Top
   Management: Beyond Systems to People," *Harvard Business Review*, May–June 1995,
   pp. 145, 148, 151.

ways of thinking and working are continuously challenged. If the integration process links and leverages existing capabilities to defend and advance current strategies, the renewal process continuously questions those strategies and the assumptions underlying them and inspires the creation of new competencies to prepare the ground for the very different competitive battles a company is likely to confront in the future.

Monitoring the effectiveness of processes such as these does not require precise measurements. It does require a statement of objectives and a conscious effort from time to time to take a reading on progress. Thus performance measurement is not a process confined to precise measurements in finance or on the factory floor. Whenever there is a defined desire to achieve something, the process will be strengthened by monitoring progress along the way.

THE CFO's ROLE

With regard to strategy, structure, and processes, the CFO's role can vary from an indirect one of ensuring that someone is in fact monitoring these three areas to a more direct one of managing the monitoring process. The CFO acts as the conscience of the organization, a kind of auditor to see that what was planned is actually happening as planned and, if not, find reasons for the deviation. To a large extent the CFO's role here is to see that the necessary questions are in fact being asked. More than with operations monitoring, these questions may require external information. The CFO may need to help make sure that the need to look outside the company does not hide the importance of information such as competitive trends, technological evolution, and market dynamics.

In the management of strategy, structure and processes, the CFO's auditing role is important not only for ex post review but also for the influence on ex ante preparations. If the CFO knows that he or she will direct a review of progress in these three areas, the CFO will push for clarity of objectives. This ex ante discipline will help to avoid vague plans and facilitate ex post recognition of what works and what does not work.

CONCLUSION

In this chapter we started by pointing out the link between measuring performance to monitor progress and measuring it to provide motivation. While closely related, often using the same information, the two purposes are not the same. Though it's at least as important, the motivational purpose often receives less attention.

We examined commonly used financial measures, showing that each had a distinct purpose. We also noted the development and increasing attention to nonfinancial measures. Along the way we recognized some of the issues relating to tying these measures to incentive or bonus systems.

Finally, we noted the importance of extending performance measurement to domains other than strategy implementation. We suggested that the current strategy itself should be tested, that organizational structure should be reviewed (especially if changes had been made), and that when new organizational processes are to be tried, measuring their performance (though difficult to carry out) was an essential part of managing the changes.

III

FINANCIAL MANAGEMENT: THE IMPLEMENTATION OF MISSION, VALUES, AND STRATEGY

10

⑥ MAKING WORKING CAPITAL WORK

Larry E. Pearson
Senior Vice President–Finance, GE Fanuc Automation North America, Inc.

Cash is the lifeblood of any business. Effective management of working capital affords the inflow of cash to meet the needs of the business and its shareholders. True to the traditional definition, we define working capital below as current assets minus current liabilities:

Current Assets	Current Liabilities
Cash/short-term investments	Accounts payable
Receivables	Other short-term liabilities
Inventories	
Other short-term assets	

It is important to distinguish between cash generated by a business and working capital funds generated. Figure 10.1 depicts a simple income statement illustrating the difference between these concepts.

This chapter emphasizes working capital generated from business activities, limiting the discussion to receivables, inventories, and payables. For most companies, these areas represent the most significant elements of working capital and the principal opportunity to improve working capital performance. There is a strong interdependence between the three working capital areas and cash flow. In an ideal state, the time it takes to collect on products sold to customers should be equal to or less than

F I G U R E   10.1

A Simple Income Statement

Income Statement		Net Income	Cash Generated	Working Capital Generated
Sales: Cash	$40,000		+$40,000	+$40,000
On account	10,000	+$50,000		+10,000
Cost of goods sold:				
Goods purchased for cash	18,000		−18,000	−18,000
Goods purchased on account	7,000			−7,000
Reduction in inventory	3,000	−28,000		−3,000
Gross margin	22,000			
Expenses:				
Paid in cash	10,000		−10,000	−10,000
Accrued (liability)	2,000			−2,000
Depreciation	4,000	−16,000		
Net income		$6,000		
Funds generated from operations			$12,000	$10,000

Source: Glenn Welsch, Walter Harrison, Jr., and Charles Zlatkovich, *Intermediate Accounting*, 5th ed. (Homewood, IL, Richard D. Irwin, Inc. 1979), p. 784.

the payment terms agreed to with material suppliers, plus the business manufacturing cycle to convert inventory to finished goods. Management of working capital is a total-business initiative, not just a finance initiative. First and foremost, the business team (normally the CEO and direct reports to the CEO) must acknowledge that less working capital is better. Having cash tied up unnecessarily as working capital restricts business flexibility to reinvest elsewhere. For example, directing cash from working capital toward product development or adding capacity to meet growth initiatives will yield a greater return to the shareholders.

Working capital is the repository for the results of many decisions a company makes, both good and bad. A working capital turnover of 10 turns or higher in a manufacturing business indicates that a company can quickly convert product to customer collections, which allows more capital to be invested in growth opportunities. Thus, working capital turnover (defined as annual sales divided by average working capital employed) reflects the viability of the business. As financial executives consider the controllable factors that are likely to affect such a metric, attention is usually drawn to such issues as

- Overdesign of the product which increases the manufacturing cycle and adds cost to the product.
- Proliferation of product features that increase inventory requirements and complicate the manufacturing process.
- Less disciplined manufacturing processes that add cycle time and costs to the product.
- Payment delays caused by selling to high-risk customers.
- Sole source material suppliers that force you to incur higher product and inventory costs since there are no competitive bids with alternative suppliers.
- Low inventory turnover that increases risk of obsolescence due to technology changes.

However, sometimes the CFO will take an active role for the business team in agreeing to changes in payment terms or other factors that temporarily increase working capital balances for the benefit of the business. Normally, these actions are customer- or supplier-specific and in response to some unusual situation such as temporary financial difficulties of a customer. The following sections of the chapter detail the needed steps to make working capital work for your business.

BENCHMARKING

Every business needs to benchmark its business processes against peers and competitors in its industry to identify best practices. As stated previously, the health of the various processes in your business will determine the amount of working capital required to manufacture and sell the product. Industry groups, government, and consultants all provide insight into business process information of peers and competitors. Common benchmarking information includes

- Order to remittance times. The time required to process orders, manufacture and deliver products to customers, and receive payments from customers.

- Manufacturing cycle times. The time required to convert raw material to finished goods inventory.
- Cost of the product manufacturing processes (as detailed and specific as practical). This information permits intelligent decisions on make-versus-buy analysis of production operations.
- Customer payment practices include form and method of payment and their own customer payment practices.
- Supplier payment practices.
- Product quality, cost, and performance. You can get such data from discussions or surveys with customers and suppliers.

Following this self-examination and comparison with the best-in-class practices, the CFO should support a process that is structured to improve target areas identified during benchmarking.

INVENTORY INITIATIVES—THE PROCESS

Reducing the manufacturing cycle time is critical to avoid unnecessary capacity expansions and maintain low inventory levels (and associated obsolescence). Short manufacturing cycles afford (1) increased flexibility to satisfy changing customer demand, (2) reduced cost of labor and equipment to manufacture product (more output per installed base), (3) reduced scrap and rework through quicker feedback of quality issues, and (4) reduced raw and in-process material levels (less capacity, inventory, and overhead).

Typically, a business team focusing in this area will find cycle time improvement opportunities in the following categories:

- Operator training needs, particularly in a business experiencing high employee turnover or rapid growth.
- Equipment bottlenecks where throughput of the machine is slower than for the rest of the factory production equipment.
- Factory equipment in need of maintenance or replacement.
- Material shortages due to product forecasting difficulties in specifying correct volume and mix of product to be sold.

- Factory scheduling problems creating suboptimum production runs and numerous set-up delays.
- Unplanned or unscheduled prototype assembly on the factory floor that interrupts production process flows.
- Process flow disconnects resulting from space limitations and/or rapid growth.
- Production scheduling inefficiencies (from both operator and machine points of view). Production scheduling may fall victim to special requests made on the manufacturing operation (e.g., customer delivery promises with short lead times, special branding requirements of customers, nonstandard test and inspections requested).
- Product designs that complicate the manufacturing process and increase product costs. Normally this occurs when products are overdesigned and therefore require more testing or extensive calibration of the production equipment.
- Processes that add little value and can be eliminated. These situations normally result from temporarily working around other problems in the material flow or manufacturing process without correcting the essential problem.

Teams should be assigned to review cycle time performance on a regular basis. It is important to assign personnel outside the manufacturing process to the team to ensure that the best solutions are obtained. People too close to the process don't always see the need for change. Process maps detailing the steps followed in each manufacturing process are effective tools for a team to develop and study ways to streamline and reduce cycle time.

Further internal analysis is also helpful to identify ways to improve cycle time. For example, analysis of scrap and rework might indicate that (1) production operators need retraining, (2) there are equipment calibration problems, or (3) supplier material is falling short of specified quality standards. An examination of machine downtime and associated maintenance logs might indicate that an aging piece of equipment needs replacement. Lengthy queues of in-process material at a work center might indicate set-up and/or operator training issues, or the need for additional equipment to break the bottleneck in the process. Investigation of the manufacturing process cost might point to a noncompetitive subassembly that is a candidate for farm-out. Farm-out is an effective way to make the process more competitive once other avenues have been exhausted.

Material shortages can bring production to a standstill and seriously affect your cycle time. Correcting material shortages might require (1) an adjustment of buffer stock levels held by the business (i.e., ordering more raw material to cover unforeseen demand surges), (2) a product redesign because of scarce supply of the material or component, or (3) attention to a new supplier issue that may result from the change (e.g., making sure the supplier's manufacturing process meets established engineering specifications for the material or assembly). Making changes to cover material shortages often bloats inventories and hurts working capital. Besides determining the cause of the problem and tracking its solution, the CFO must highlight the urgency of the problem and request reports on sales value and aging of missing parts as well as inventory lockup due to material shortages.

INVENTORY INITIATIVES—PROCUREMENT

Another major element in minimizing inventory levels is the qualification of suppliers. Material qualification includes meeting certain quality standards, cost targets, delivery expectations, and buffer stock levels to cover demand spikes on your business. Qualified suppliers must understand your business and manufacturing process so they may suggest alternative materials to improve your product's performance, reduce material lead times, or lower your cost. Also, the supplier must have a strong understanding of the market and customer demands on your business to provide the most cost-effective material for new product releases at the right times. Effective supplier qualification includes

- Periodic audits of the supplier's manufacturing process to be sure it complies with your quality standards.
- Assurance through thorough test and inspection by the supplier that material shipments to your plant meet expected quality standards, are counted accurately, and are packed appropriately.

- Agreement on productivity goals necessary to keep your product and your customers competitive.
- Assessment of the supplier's financial viability and technical development capability.

Having the above understanding promotes long-term partnering and allows a business to minimize costs by relying on suppliers to deliver quality material on time. An increasing number of suppliers recognize the importance of being flexible and providing varying quantities of material to accommodate their customers' manufacturing processes. This can be achieved through (1) an on-site inventory of supplier-managed material, (2) consignments of material located in your warehouse, or (3) a warehouse location nearby where suppliers stock your material. Each method makes you, the customer, better able to meet increased demand with a relatively short turnaround time. This is especially critical to businesses with short manufacturing cycles and erratic demand surges.

In the first method, supplier-managed inventory, a customer pays the supplier when material is taken from the supplier's inventory to the manufacturing process. Typically, businesses pay an administrative fee for this service (10 percent of material cost or less) and mutually agree with the supplier on the level of inventory maintained. The supplier's on-site representative works hand-in-hand with the purchasing and production employees to make sure that adequate production material is present when needed. All paperwork and communications with the supplier are channeled through the on-site representative. Conventional payment terms may be accelerated for this service, but the trade-off in reduced purchasing and handling costs plus reduced inventory levels normally make this method attractive for both the supplier and customer.

Consigned material is similar in concept to the supplier-managed inventory except that (1) an on-site representative from the supplier is not present to handle paperwork and correspondence between the supplier and its customer, (2) the risk of damage or loss of material rests with the consignee or the supplier's customer, and (3) the supplier's customer must determine specific material types and quantities to be included in the consignment. The administrative fee is also eliminated in this supplier inventory initiative. Generally accepted accounting principles (GAAP) may require that the consignment be recorded as inventory depending on the terms of the agreement. However, in any event, the business enjoys a ready supply of material and deferred payment terms for the consignment that would otherwise be counted as inventory.

To have a supplier locate material close to your manufacturing site (1) eliminates the risk of damage or loss of material as is the case with consignment and (2) requires some delivery and additional handling effort to get the material to the customer's manufacturing floor. All other aspects of this inventory method are identical to supplier material consigned at a customer's manufacturing site.

Once the qualification process is complete, the selection process begins. At GE Fanuc Automation North America, Inc., a five–step sourcing process (Five Steps to Effective Procurement™) has been developed that is now used as a standard within the company. The process has significantly cut incoming material costs by ensuring the lowest competitive cost levels for material used in manufacturing.

Five Steps to Effective Procurement™

To be successful, the five-step process requires (1) multiple qualified material sources, (2) hard work from both the business and suppliers, (3) a disciplined approach, (4) setting tough cost targets, and (5) convincing suppliers of the benefit of doing business with you over time. From the beginning, one must convey serious intent to award the entire contract to the lowest bidder. The five step process works best when purchasing standard commodity-type items that are available from multiple sources.

Step 1. Solicit initial bids from at least four global reputable suppliers. Note that breaking personal relationships and brand preferences built up over time can be a difficult and emotional process. The CEO or someone independent in the procurement may be needed to assist the sourcing qualification process.

Step 2. To be sure that at least three suppliers meet those minimum specifications, involve a cross-functional team comprised of purchasing, engineering, finance, and marketing staff to be sure that quotations received were submitted according to the technical specifications in the bid request. This may be the most important step. This is where specification changes can be implemented for cost reduction purposes and productivity and quality improvements can be factored in! Transfer creative ideas from your team into a new bid. Issue the new bid to all competing suppliers to ensure a uniform basis for the quotations. From this point forward, secure a team agreement to use any of the remaining suppliers.

Step 3. Remove the team from the bidding and turn the process over to the procurement professionals. Finalize all other remaining terms and conditions. Then analyze the latest bids and set very challenging target price reductions between 15 and 50 percent lower than the lowest bid.

Step 4. Call in the suppliers, assign their target prices, and require their best and final offer on a very short schedule—72 hours maximum. Be sure they understand there is no second chance. In other words, turn up the urgency to the highest possible level to obtain the best price possible.

Step 5. Review the results with the team and award the contract to the lowest bidder 48 to 72 hours later.

At the heart of success in the five step process is a realization that collaboration with suppliers to reduce cost is hard work. It requires a disciplined process that involves continuous and dedicated efforts from both parties. Major savings are not realized simply by asking for lower costs. It is important to follow the process exactly and put a lot of emphasis on Step 2, which is where the supplier can really reduce its cost. Also, don't underestimate the benefit of Step 4, where the cold reality of winning or losing with no second chance against a tough target prompts suppliers to submit their best bids.

Again, letters simply requesting price reductions from incumbent suppliers do not go far enough. First of all, you will not likely ask for enough, and to succeed, you must have the pressure of real competition. Since we know that not all procurement initiatives are totally perfect, let's recognize there are potential problems that need to be managed, including

- Unique parts from a sole source require that new sources be developed and incremental qualification costs be incurred. The upside is that free market conditions determine costs for competitive products and should more than offset the qualification and redesign costs over time.

- Further, the procurement may require you to shift suppliers, thereby creating new tooling costs.
- The introduction of quality and delivery problems from new suppliers can cause incremental cost and customer satisfaction issues.

There will be an impact on electronic data interchange/just-in-time programs with incumbent suppliers creating new cost pressures. In some cases, you may have to make multiyear procurement commitments to get the price that is needed. Finally, there could be price-increase pressures from the supplier downstream after the initial deals, so be prepared to pick up the pieces.

INVENTORY INITIATIVES—DEMAND FORECASTING

The next stage toward effective inventory control is to work with key customers so you can more accurately forecast demand placed on your factory. This cooperation, in turn, increases the accuracy of orders you place on suppliers. Ordering material is an inexact science that will never be perfect. A business is only as successful as its customers are successful. Having your product available when your customer needs it is critical for the continued health of both companies. Working closely together will improve the forecast accuracy and allow product deliveries to customers when needed. Areas of cooperation include agreement on (1) minimum order quantities, (2) lead times including a price premium for shorter delivery cycles, (3) annual order commitments, and (4) restocking privileges. Inventory risk sharing may also be a solution for the business and its customers. Risk sharing is common for products sold through distributors and many original equipment manufacturers. These business customers agree to maintain a certain quantity and level of inventory to serve their customer's needs, generally in exchange for pricing discounts.

Following an examination of a business's manufacturing, material sourcing, and associated inventory processes, the CFO should develop a report card of key measurements to determine working capital progress and process corrections that need to be made. Someone independent of the processes must maintain the reporting database to ensure the most accurate and unbiased interpretation of the trends or results.

INVENTORY INITIATIVES—THE MEASUREMENT

Place inventory measurement in the hands of the person who can influence the process and make the necessary trade-offs—normally a product manager or product line manager. Establish aggressive turnover goals; for example, dollar inventory balances of well-managed manufacturing companies generally turn over 10 times or more in a fiscal year. To set stretch targets, encouraging and/or empowering employees to challenge the status quo, and placing the measurement in the hands of the person capable of making changes are two critical elements in improving inventory turnover. Most marketing forecasts of shipments tend to be optimistic. To determine material input based on aggressive sales projections will bring material in earlier than needed in the manufacturing process and create unnecessary tie-up of cash in inventory. The experienced product manager (understanding business processes and customers' needs) will make decisions on the appropriate amount of input to satisfy customer demand. Focus accordingly on material input factors that you can reasonably estimate to achieve your inventory turnover objectives. Use information regarding customer demands to control the material input from suppliers to help you meet your turnover goal. Tying compensation to achievement of the inventory measurement will also improve results.

SUPPLIER PAYMENTS

Benchmarking best-supplier payment practices will facilitate discussion of overall payment terms and needed support from your supplier. Ideally, supplier payment terms should be greater than or equal to the time it takes to convert material to product and collect from your customers. Unfortunately, it may take longer to convert the material to product than suppliers will allow in payment terms, and many suppliers are unwilling to be flexible in this area. Many times, partnering with key suppliers can yield flexibility. Again, having suppliers understand your business processes and customer payment practices will improve overall results and cooperative efforts. Convey the importance of longer payment terms to your suppliers and they may take the same "push back" approach with their own suppliers. This strategy will enable them to respond to your business's needs by granting term concessions. Other considerations to improve supplier payments include

- Payment by credit card to suppliers demanding 30-day or earlier payments. This method is especially beneficial for smaller accounts. Usually, this practice extends the average payment cycle to 45 days.
- Payment in product or services. Although rarely used in large business transactions, there may be opportunities for smaller suppliers to improve their factory processes by using your product and services.

RECEIVABLES INITIATIVES—THE REPORT CARD

While overall working capital is the thermometer of business health, receivables is the report card that shows management and shareholders how well the business is performing. Breakdowns in business processes hinder receivables collection performance. In my experience, one or more of the following situations have occurred that handcuff collectors and make it nearly impossible to receive payments according to agreed-upon terms:

- Early/late shipment of product.
- Incomplete/incorrect product shipments.
- Damaged/deficient product upon receipt.
- Invoicing errors.
- Nonpayments due to customer financial condition.
- Temporary payment terms extension offered by sales/marketing personnel.

As you can see, there are many business process breakdowns that can impede customer payment performance. Collectors discover most of these process breakdowns as they encounter roadblocks in collecting outstanding payments from customers. Payment disputes by customers need the attention of the total business. Cross-functional team members should work with the collector to resolve the outstanding payments and, more importantly, fix the process to prevent the situation from occurring again in the future. Resolving the disputed receivable without fixing the process is counterproductive. The CFO can facilitate the dispute resolution, but responsibility for the process repair must be embraced by the business team.

RECEIVABLES—THE RETURN ON INVESTMENT

Businesses must continually look for the best way to invest their excess cash resources. One way to differentiate among all of the available options is to calculate the rate of return each investment will generate. To assist in the evaluation process, most companies establish minimum hurdle rates that any particular investment decision must meet or exceed. That is, the rate of return for an investment must be greater than or equal to a percentage predetermined by management.

Poor investment decisions by the company, particularly in the areas of establishing payment terms or extending special terms to a customer, can result in a large receivables balance. To explain how investment decisions can affect working capital, let's examine an extended-terms investment request.

Assume the following figures have been approved by business management and shareholders for the annual operating plan. Management has determined that the minimum hurdle rate for investment decisions is 15 percent.

		Amount
Sales		$10,000
Income before taxes		$1,500
	% to sales	15%
Net income	$900	
	% of Sales	9%
Shareholder's equity		$6,000
Return on equity		15%
Standard terms of sale		30 days

Assume a customer who buys $1,200 of product annually requests an extension in payment terms to 60 days and offers to pay a 1 percent higher price in return for the longer terms of payment. Should the business accept the customer's offer? To answer this question, we must calculate the rate of return generated by accepting the offer and determine whether it meets the minimum hurdle rate. Consider the following details:

- If the business sells an even flow of products to the customer during the year, a 30-day extension represents one-twelfth of $1,200, or $100, which we have loaned to the customer.
- Customer offer of 1 percent higher price equals $12 in additional sales for the year.
- The cost of debt financing is 5 percent.
- The tax rate is 43 percent.

Using this information, you may calculate return on equity:

Sales increase:	$12
5% debt financing	(5) (or $100 × .05)
Taxes @ 43%	(3)
Net income	$4
Return on equity	4% (or $4 ÷ $100)

To achieve 15 percent return on equity, the business would need to raise prices to the customer by 2.7 percent as shown below:

Sales increase	$32 (or 2.7% × $1,200)
5% debt financing	(5)
Taxes @ 43%	(12)
15% return on $100	$15

Too often, the business thinks of term extensions as only having an impact on borrowing costs. If a business must borrow money to grant this term extension, then indeed its cost for granting this favor is the added expense ($5 in this example). In reality, that $100 is a lost opportunity for the business to reinvest elsewhere that would achieve the targeted rate of return (15 percent) for its shareholders. To achieve the 15 percent ROE requires more than recovering or slightly improving the business's debt financing position. Companies and their employees must understand the difference between recovering lending costs and achieving returns acceptable to management and shareholders.

To illustrate the need for employee education, let's look at a common problem experienced in the sales force. Because measurements on sales performance are determined from orders received, sales personnel may be tempted to offer term extensions to increase their orders. It is important that the CFO communicate the minimum hurdle rate concept to all employees to gain their support to prevent unnecessary increases in payment terms. Customers and the sales force continually challenge terms extension in order negotiations and there must be a control in place to ensure proper working capital management. This concept is especially difficult to convey to those who naturally think in terms of net income and the impact of incremental volume. Only through a careful, continued education process for all employees and customers will this concept be understood.

RECEIVABLES—OTHER INITIATIVES

To supplement our discussion of receivables, here are further steps to improve collection performance:

- Establish electronic data interchange (EDI). This method is especially helpful for high-volume accounts and customers receiving special payment considerations. Agreement to wire transfer funds eliminates postal delays and counterproductive follow-up by collection employees.
- Restrict approvals for terms extensions to the CFO. This policy will provide consistent high-level education of the investment return expectation of shareholders to both customers and employees.
- Allow credit card payments by small, low-volume customers. Credit card payments eliminate needless paperwork and collection effort for immediate payment. Generally, the price premium for the product or service sale and the associated collection effort on late payments more than offset the discount charged by credit card companies.
- Share best practices with customers. Customers can make more timely payments to your business if they improve their own cash flow by implementing best practices in the cash processes. Volunteer your own cash flow experts to help key customers improve their cash generation.

- Find alternative forms of payment to cash. A customer's product or services may be of value to the business and may be used for payment in lieu of cash.

CONCLUSION

Hopefully, you now have a better understanding that working capital is more than several balance sheet accounts that only accountants can understand. Working capital is the product of key business processes and employee decisions. Quantum improvements can only be realized through keen insight into the business processes that drive inventories, payables, and receivables. Only then can changes occur to improve working capital turnover. Cross-fertilization of ideas with employees, suppliers, and customers for working capital improvements is critical. Without a shared understanding of the issue or the objective, progress is hindered. Keep in mind that effective working capital management is a continuous process, not a periodic project. The business team must ensure that process changes to improve working capital performance continue on track. The process of continual improvement is the key to making working capital work for you.

Ⓖ   **FINANCING WITH DEBT**

Douglas A. Scovanner
*Senior Vice President and Chief Financial Officer, Dayton Hudson
Corporation*

Debt financing decisions for most corporations involve balancing
a series of trade-offs involving cost, liquidity, choice of maturity,
and the basis and frequency of interest rate resets. In this light, the
decision process of financing with debt typically represents a
very-large–scale, multivariable risk management exercise. Effective planning to optimize these trade-offs requires a debt financing
plan well integrated into the operating and strategic fabrics of the
firm. Maintenance of adequate capital resources to meet diverse,
ongoing funding needs and to deal with unforeseen contingencies
is among the primary objectives of any CFO.

A typical corporation funds its debt needs through a combination of instruments. A committed revolving line of credit may
provide liquidity directly or indirectly by supporting the issuance
of commercial paper. Term debt may have been issued in the public capital markets or through a private placement, or it may be
provided by the bank or group of banks that provided the revolving credit. Interest rate swaps may have been arranged to hedge
the interest rate risk of certain underlying debt. The possibilities
are diverse and sometimes complex.

This chapter is structured to approach the concept of financing with debt from a conceptual and structural vantage point—to
explore issues to consider in formulating a debt financing plan.
These issues are by nature inextricably intertwined with capital
structure considerations.

LIQUIDITY

The foundation of a debt financing plan is a cash flow forecast to determine expected funding needs. Additionally, an assessment of factors that might cause funding needs to change is necessary. The importance of carefully weighing the amount of flexibility needed in the future depends on the degree of risk of having insufficient funds available offset by the cost of providing more funds than are necessary. Failure to meet a future payroll due to lack of liquidity represents an obvious and severe problem. Maintenance of excess liquidity to guard against this risk is not free.

The most common means of providing liquidity is a committed line of credit facility with a bank or syndicated among a group of banks. Such an arrangement will specify the term and maximum amount of the commitment. It will contain a negotiated set of financial and other covenants, and it will specify pricing considerations on both a drawn and undrawn basis.

The market for such facilities among lenders is highly developed and reasonably competitive. For most investment-grade corporate borrowers this means that material economic aspects of the agreement can be predicted within a fairly tight range of likely outcomes by analysis of comparable deals before attempting to syndicate a facility. While pricing ebbs and flows with liquidity and competitiveness in the banking system, generally this product has evolved to be somewhat of a loss leader. Accordingly the appetite of lenders to bid aggressively on a proposed facility is often a function of the extent of existing and potential overall relationships.

The assessment by a CFO of the appropriate amount of liquidity should include an analysis of the possible extent and likelihood of material deviations from a base cash flow forecast. If such a deviation were to occur would it most likely be a temporary timing difference or the result of a more permanent change (i.e., shortfall) to the forecast?

A key element of this overall assessment is a judgment regarding the firm's flexibility to augment traditional external sources of liquidity by internal means as needs arise. Beyond basic belt-tightening this could include the sale of non-strategic assets, temporary reduction of working capital investments or deferring planned capital investments. Obviously consideration of such possible actions naturally includes careful thought regarding the probable effect on the execution of a corporation's overall strategy.

MATURITY

For corporations with sufficient credit quality to access longer maturities in the U.S. public debt markets, the 30-year maturity has typically defined the limit to investor appetite for many years. Two notable exceptions are recent 100-year maturity debt offerings by Disney and The Coca-Cola Company.

Corporate debt issues tend to be bunched into several specific maturities that correspond to the when-issued maturity of debt issued by the U.S. Treasury (e.g., 2, 3, 5, 10, or 30 years). This is because corporate debt is typically priced at a yield spread to comparable maturity "on the run" (i.e., most recently issued) U.S. Treasury instruments.

While these are the most common choices, usually offering the best pricing and execution in the public market, many instruments are issued with odd maturities of 4, 8, 12, or 20 years. The choice of maturity for a given debt issue balances the likely duration of the need for funds with the relative cost of various maturities in the context of the maturities of existing debt. This context is a very important consideration.

The basic framework for a maturity analysis is a review of the pattern and extent of future cash flows from operations net of financing costs (interest expense and dividend requirements), but *before* accounting for the effect of debt maturities. On this basis, in a perfect world, one could simply match amounts and timing of debt maturities to the respective projected dates of positive future cash flows. In the real world needs change, creating mismatches. Additionally, moderate intentional mismatches appropriately result from balancing future refinancing risk against current funds availability and cost considerations.

When faced with this series of trade-offs, some CFOs opt for the longest available maturity when the need to borrow arises on the belief that risk is minimized by this technique. Refinancing risk (that is, the risk of providing adequate liquidity in the future to refund the excess of a maturing debt obligation over available funds from operations) *is* minimized. The cost is potentially severe. Longer maturities typically carry higher interest rates through a combination of higher-reference Treasury yields in a positive-slope yield curve environment and higher spreads to Treasuries demanded by investors in longer-maturity corporate debt. Beyond these measurable costs lies a loss of funding flexibility. For example, if faced with the decision of how to apply the cash flow generated by the sale of an asset, a CFO who "goes too long" must then choose between two bad alternatives: (1) to reinvest the proceeds in typically lower-yielding debt of others while awaiting a convenient maturity of his or her own to apply the proceeds or (2) to incur explicit or implicit prepayment penalties associated with prepayment of longer-maturity debt.

INTEREST RATE RISK

In its simplest terms a borrowing is priced at either a fixed interest rate or a floating rate that resets periodically based on prevailing market rates. In a sense, the terms *fixed* and *floating* are not precise because a floating rate is actually fixed for a short time (say, one month). Fixed rates offer the luxury of certainty. Cash flows necessary to service the interest component of fixed-rate borrowings can be forecast with precision.

Floating rates in contrast can and do change, sometimes abruptly. Three-month LIBOR, a benchmark against which many floating-rate borrowings are priced, has ranged from just over 3 percent to just over 10 percent during the past 10 years, with a mean of about 6½ percent. Cash flow necessary to service a liability priced against this benchmark is inherently imprecise to predict.

In view of this, why would anyone choose a floating rate instead of a fixed rate? The answer is that a series of floating-rate borrowings sequentially rolled over will more often than not cost less than fixed-rate borrowing. This is due to yield curve and credit spread issues previously discussed. In other words, there is an expected cost to be paid for the certainty of the fixed-rate borrowing.

The development over the past decade of a vast and efficient interest rate swap market allows the CFO the luxury of completely segregating considerations associated with the maturity profile of a corporation's debt from those associated with the mix of fixed- and floating-rate instruments. No longer is long-term debt necessarily priced in fixed rates and commercial paper or credit facility borrowings priced in floating rates. In essence, the *repricing risk* of debt can be isolated from all other aspects of financing with debt so it merits specific analysis.

It is axiomatic that the more interest rate risk a firm is willing to assume, the more *expected* interest savings will accrue to the benefit of the firm. Striking the appropriate balance requires an analysis that models the effect of reasonably possible changes in interest rates on hypothetical mixes of fixed- and floating-rate exposure.

The key to settling on an appropriate balance lies in defining risk and establishing tolerable parameters. As with most other forms of risk, no one definition fits all circumstances. To some CFOs, volatility of net debt portfolio interest rate will be the controlling factor. To others, next year's—or next quarter's—EPS volatility will control. To yet others, cash flow volatility or other considerations are most important. In all cases, the fundamental proposition suggested here is to insert as much floating-rate exposure as is prudent in light of one's definition of, and tolerance for, interest rate risk.

CONCLUSION

The trade-offs described in this chapter form the basic strategic considerations in approaching the topic of financing with debt. Formulation of a debt financing plan that considers disparate and often conflicting aspects of funding needs is necessary to judge debt financing risk in an organized, thoughtful way. Finally, in the absence of such a plan, the quality of implementation cannot be adequately assessed.

12

⑥ INCOME TAX PLANNING FOR THE CFO

Samuel P. Starr
Tax Partner, Coopers & Lybrand L. L. P.

Steven M. Woolf
Tax Director, Coopers & Lybrand L. L. P.

Taxes are among the most important components of any corporate profit-and-loss statement. Traditionally a significant cost of doing business, taxes take on increasing importance in today's corporate environment as federal, state, and local governments search for new and increased sources of revenue. Longstanding tax planning ideas may no longer be appropriate in light of frequent changes in the income tax laws. Rapid expansion overseas broadens the scope of planning considerations. State and local tax authorities have become increasingly aggressive in their pursuit of revenue from business.

This chapter will discuss ways to measure and increase the effectiveness of the corporate tax function. It will also highlight issues to consider in organizing and staffing the tax department as well as discuss ways to ensure that adequate tax information flows to corporate managers. In addition, it will outline some strategies and techniques to help maximize tax planning and corporate profitability.

In today's complex and changing business environment, the corporate tax department must do more than file tax returns and handle tax audits. The tax department must be an integral part of the corporate business team; tax planning strategies must mesh with overall corporate strategy. Because of the broad scope and complex nature of income taxes, it is often difficult to evaluate the effectiveness of the corporate tax department. Constant change at the federal and state levels exacerbates this difficulty, especially for a CFO who lacks substantial tax expertise or who has not stayed current with shifting income tax laws and regulations.

How do you know whether the corporate tax department is performing up to speed? How should the corporate tax department be staffed and organized? Who should the corporate tax department be serving? It is your responsibility as CFO to determine the answers to these and other questions.

MEASURING THE CORPORATE TAX FUNCTION

Effective Tax Rates

One key performance indicator for the corporate tax department is the effective corporate tax rate. At first blush, it would appear that such an objective standard should serve as a reliable measurement. However, the effective corporate tax rate varies widely from industry to industry as well as from company to company within a specific sector of the economy. A study published in 1991 by Tax Analysts of Arlington, Virginia, found that the average U.S. effective corporate income tax rate was 26.1 percent. This compares to the statutory rate of 34 percent. The average effective tax rate ranged from just over 15 percent for motor vehicle companies to over 26 percent for communications companies to just under 32 percent for retail department stores.

A company's effective tax rate can reflect investment and operating decisions, prior economic performance, as well as strategic tax planning. Achievement of an effective tax rate below the statutory rate could be the byproduct of poor business results as well as a capital investment or expansion program.

Because certain components of the tax equation can be controlled, reducing the effective tax rate remains a primary goal for most corporate tax departments. A relatively small reduction in the effective tax rate often translates into a significant dollar savings for large corporations. Indeed, in recognition of the bottom-line impact of significant tax savings, some companies tie incentive compensation for tax managers and other financial officers to an overall reduction in their cash outlay for taxes.

It is important to note, however, that the effective tax rate is a book or accounting concept. For many companies the so-called book-tax difference (the discrepancy between the tax provision for book purposes and the actual cash outlay for taxes) can be significant. It is therefore critical to determine the amount of actual cash savings achieved through the implementation of tax planning strategies.

Wherever possible, planning strategies should attempt to reduce rather than merely postpone taxes. This will reduce both the effective tax rate as well as any current cash outlay for taxes. Examples of permanent reduction strategies are the purchase of tax-free bonds and the utilization of net operating losses by filing consolidated corporate income tax returns.

Permanent reductions in both the effective tax rate and the cash flow for taxes can increase earnings per share, return on equity, and after-tax return on assets. These factors, in turn, raise the company's perceived value in the marketplace in relation to other investment opportunities. The astute CFO will ensure that the corporate tax department puts a reporting system in place that shows how much the company has paid and has saved in taxes for the quarter and the year.

Reducing the annual cash flow for taxes also can improve reported earnings. Tax deferral strategies that increase expenses or losses that are deductible for tax purposes before they are recognized in financial income should also be considered. Investment in depreciable assets or depletable resources and intangibles when accelerated depreciation methods are employed is an example of such a deferral strategy. The "timing difference" between book and tax reporting generated by the use of accelerated depreciation will ultimately "turn around" for individual assets. However, expanding companies that continue to purchase fixed assets can benefit from the cumulative impact of such investments.

Analysis of the effective tax rate should not be attempted in a corporate vacuum. The CFO should work with the corporate tax department to ensure that tax strategies blend with overall business strategies. Attempts to increase pretax earnings that are enhanced by intelligent tax planning will produce superior after-tax returns.

In today's increasingly global economy, a discussion of corporate tax rates must recognize the impact of foreign investment and taxes. The corporate tax department must be concerned with international tax planning strategies. The practicality and success of virtually every domestic planning strategy must be reviewed and measured with foreign statutory and effective tax rates in mind. Continual domestic statutory changes such as those that limit the utilization of foreign tax credits to reduce domestic taxes or rules that accelerate or recharacterize the repatriation of foreign earnings must be reviewed before business decisions are finalized. In turn, it is essential to be aware of changes or potential changes in foreign tax systems.

While industry competitors can act as preliminary benchmarks for measuring performance, it is important to remember that differences in corporate structure, international location, product mix, and investment goals can cause wide variations between companies.

Similarly, state and local tax issues need to be considered when analyzing pretax, after-tax, and effective tax calculations. It is essential that tax professionals assess opportunities to reduce local income taxes, sales taxes, and gross receipts taxes, as well as property taxes.

Audit Results

Tax audit results often serve as another benchmark for measuring the corporate tax department's effectiveness. Again, the CFO should be able to answer basic questions: Was the audit conducted in a timely and an uneventful manner? Were interest and penalties incurred? Will the controversy continue in the next level of appeals? Answers to these questions, however, only provide one level of analysis. A "clean report" may not always be the best or represent the work of the most efficient tax department.

While tax compliance performance remains one of the chief roles of most corporate tax departments, the planning and implementation of tax reduction strategies is also a primary responsibility. The successful corporate tax department approaches tax return positions aggressively, with a realistic appraisal of risk. Indeed, it may be difficult to view the corporate tax department as effective if the IRS accepts tax returns as filed without levying any additional assessments against the company. The tax laws are replete with areas that are open to interpretation. Most corporate executives would wish that their tax managers adopted those interpretations that are most favorable to the company and then defend those positions on audit.

The CFO should be intimately involved in setting the tax goals of the company. A primary concern is helping to define the acceptable level or risk for the company when analyzing planning strategies or contemplating transactions. The CFO should also be involved in determining the provision for taxes in the company's financial statement. Such decisions will impact effective tax rates as well as corporate earnings. However, future events (including audit disallowance or cash flow needs) could reverse the prior beneficial corporate financial statement consequences.

The CFO should be familiar with the overall audit potential for the corporation. In recent years the IRS has revised its approach to the complex task of auditing large, often highly diversified corporations with multiple business locations. A Coordinated Examination Program (CEP), commonly referred to as the "large-case program," has been established that attempts to redefine issue resolution authority, expand industry and issue specialization, encourage settlement initiatives, and improve functional coordination.

The CEP audit team reviews all types of tax returns and tax liabilities for a company and its subsidiaries. Interrelated with the CEP is an Industry Specialization Program (ISP) that promotes IRS expertise in the accounting and business practices peculiar to various industries. This enables the IRS to better identify and develop examination issues and ensure that companies receive consistent treatment on identical issues.

The continued evolution of the large-case audit program will have a dramatic impact on corporate audit tactics and strategies. Corporate tax departments, as well as the CFO, should monitor this evolution. The elements of a successful audit strategy will enable tax departments to (1) avoid issues leading to potential litigation, (2) achieve the earliest possible issue resolution consistent with a prompt and overall settlement, (3) identify potential issues, (4) manage the audit including document and information requests, and (5) maintain effective working relationships with appropriate IRS personnel.

Source of Information and Planning

Many corporate executives first learn about tax developments from their senior tax managers. Indeed, this information and communications function is another important yardstick for measuring tax department effectiveness. It almost goes without saying that the tax department must attempt to avoid last-minute surprises and unforeseen consequences. The efficient tax department will provide senior management with information on pending legislative and regulatory tax developments. This information should be supplemented with contingency plans detailing how to deal with potential changes. At certain times, such changes are easily identified and alternative plans can be developed. For example, in the fall of 1992, the astute corporate tax manager and CFO would have scrutinized candidate Bill Clinton's tax proposals and their likely impact on the company's business plan. Similarly, today, a leery eye should be given to the alternative tax regimes advocated by House Majority Leader Armey and others. Often important potential changes are buried in other legislative proposals, such as (1) a contemplated change in inventory accounting rules that surfaced as a means for financing the implementation of the worldwide General Agreement on Tariffs and Trade in 1994 and (2) the technical correction hidden in the 1995 budget reconciliation tax provisions that would permit the deduction of certain redemption costs in corporate acquisitions.

Productive interaction must extend beyond that between the CFO and the senior corporate tax manager. Tax managers should interact with other corporate committees and regularly attend policy group meetings. They should keep senior management abreast of tax issues and developments on a regular basis. Such communications should highlight tax savings opportunities and legislative and regulatory developments as well as tax savings generated and the status of audit and litigation issues.

Annual and long-range tax plans should be developed through concerted efforts. Key assumptions and projections should be reviewed periodically and the plans should be monitored to ensure that current and long-range issues are resolved. Where appropriate, other corporate managers and executives, including in-house counsel and outside advisers, should join in deliberations.

In sum, the tax department—through the tax director and others—needs to work with management to create an environment where everyone strives to minimize taxes. It is incumbent upon tax department personnel to understand the company's business as well as its plans for the future. The financial and operating groups of the company, in turn, must work to involve the tax department early in the planning process. Such collaboration can help to minimize tax and risk while maximizing bottom-line results.

ORGANIZING THE CORPORATE TAX FUNCTION

Every corporate tax department performs a variety of functions and provides services to many different customers, including government taxing authorities, senior management, and corporate shareholders. In addition, it is essential that the corporate tax department serve and integrate with the business divisions of the company. It is this interrelationship that ensures that tax planning ideas become entwined with business operations and overall corporate strategies.

One can assert that the current trend toward outsourcing the corporate tax department is a recognition by some companies of the inability to adequately integrate the tax function. Instead of "purchasing" tax compliance and planning services from in-house experts, such companies have turned to outside firms and professionals. Concepts such as re-engineering, consensus building, and customer service must be re-enforced in the relationship between the tax department and the rest of the corporate structure.

Many corporate tax departments and chief tax officers view outsourcing, not as a threat, but as an opportunity to address perceived weaknesses in their current structure. The process permits the tax executive to review existing communications with senior management. Again, increased involvement of the tax department in overall strategic corporate planning can result. Further, some companies that examine outsourcing soon determine that alternatives to full or partial outsourcing can provide practical benefits. For example, the tax function can be redesigned to increase efficiency through better implementation of technology. Parts of the compliance function or the expatriate function can be outsourced to third-party providers.

Structure and Staffing

Most corporate tax departments face a variety of different types of compliance and planning work including federal income, state, local, international, payroll, property, sales and use, and excise taxes. Many companies assign specific professionals to accomplish specific tasks and, in the process, create technicians with particular areas of expertise. Other companies attempt to balance the work load, providing experience in both planning and compliance as well as exposure to different areas of taxation. While it may not be possible to achieve the latter method without sacrificing some cost efficiencies, tax departments that follow this model foster more technical expertise.

There is no proper number of tax staff that need be employed at corporate headquarters. Staff size is subject to many variables, not the least of which is the degree of use of outside advisers. Effective use of the tax staff, however, can be enhanced if it reports directly to the CFO and is fully involved at an early stage in the investment and planning functions of the company.

The chief tax officer plays a pivotal role in the success of tax planning strategies. Knowledge of tax laws, relevant experience, general business acumen, and understanding of linking of business and corporate goals with tax strategies are essential. This foundation enables the tax manager to build a more secure understanding of company operations and also to plan for the future. This ensures that planning for new tax legislation, IRS regulatory or audit initiatives, corporate contractions (such as through spin-offs or liquidations) or expansions (such as through acquisitions or overseas investments) will benefit from insights that recognize the need for both technical and business perspectives.

TAX PLANNING STRATEGIES

In most large corporations, management devotes considerable effort to the fundamental business issues: new products and markets, pricing strategies, and investment in plant and equipment. Tax concerns often impact such fundamental decisions. The effects of careful tax planning should be considered. For example,

• *Factors in selecting the form of business.* Often a threshold question, choosing the most appropriate form of entity for new or existing business operations can be complicated due to state and local as well as federal tax issues. Increasingly, companies are turning to joint ventures as the business form to conduct new operations. Corporate joint ventures can provide immediate access to technology, financing, new markets, and many other benefits that otherwise might take years for a company to obtain. The vehicle chosen to conduct these joint venture operations is frequently either a partnership or a limited liability company (LLC).

When forming a partnership or LLC, corporations must consider the tax effects of the specific provisions of the agreement. Several key issues must be considered: What type of entity should be used? Is there appreciated or depreciated property being contributed to the joint venture? Are special allocations of income, gain, loss, or deduction going to be made among the partners? How will members that provide services be compensated?

• *Business operations concerns.* Strategies can be employed to maximize tax savings and minimize record-keeping costs through inventory elections. Once a business is established or acquired, it must be managed to provide an acceptable rate of return on investment. The management function includes analyzing a range of considerations, which—if handled effectively—can help the business yield the desired return. Tax law changes over the past several years have increased the importance of tax accounting considerations. Such rules often dictate the timing of taxation and impact alternatives for tax accounting planning. In addition, there are many record-keeping requirements that may necessitate changes in accounting systems.

• *Purchases, sales, and other transfers of business operations.* Stock and asset acquisition strategies can vary depending on the objectives of the buyer and seller as well as existing and future liabilities. Merger and consolidation strategies can also vary depending on corporate objectives.

• *International operations.* Businesses involved overseas through either manufacturing or sales can face a host of issues. In addition to dealing with U.S. tax rules concerning multinational businesses, the corporate tax department must deal with foreign taxes, tariffs, and rules and regulations covering exports and business operations in other countries. While U.S. companies are generally subject to tax on export income, opportunities may arise to exempt certain income from export sales by using a foreign sales corporation. Another potential tax benefit can be derived from exports if sales of U.S. manufactured goods are structured so that title to the goods passes abroad. If foreign subsidiaries are involved in sales, companies can expect both IRS and foreign revenue authorities to carefully scrutinize intercompany transfer prices that impact corporate profitability. Repatriation of foreign earnings and foreign tax credits are also areas where corporate tax department expertise is essential. Unwanted and unnecessary cash flow and financial statement costs can be incurred if dividends from foreign subsidiaries to U.S. parent corporations are not properly structured and timed.

FACING THE NEXT CENTURY

Corporate financial officers and corporate tax departments may be faced with an entirely different tax system in the future. Fundamental tax reform is beginning to generate considerable interest both in Washington and throughout the country. While consensus on the shape of any new tax system remains to emerge, there appears to be virtual agreement among proponents of change that the current income tax system is too complex, is biased against savings and investment, rewards consumption, and hinders U.S. businesses competing in a global economy.

Fundamental tax reform promises to be a key component of contemporary political debates. It is further apparent that such reform will more than likely feature moves to better integrate business and individual taxes in an attempt to improve the competitive position of the U.S. economy. A move toward consumption taxes (whether in the form of a flat tax, national sales tax, or value-added tax) and away from income taxes seems to be the favored path.

Introduction of a new tax system would raise a myriad of questions and concerns for tax professionals and corporate executives. Transition from one system to another could be chaotic absent detailed rules. Important financial and tax considerations that would need to be addressed include treatment of deferred tax liabilities, survival of existing tax attributes, and the disparity of effective tax rates among different business taxpayers. The answers, as well as proper formulation of the questions, to these and other issues must be considered by lawmakers and others during the coming debate over tax reform.

CONCLUSION

Today's tax environment is ever-changing. This challenges the CFO and the corporate tax department to work together to ensure that the company deals with existing challenges and plans for the future. The corporate tax department must prepare federal and local tax returns, calculate the financial statement tax provision, outline tax planning objectives, and handle IRS and state audits. All this needs to be done in an environment where the tax professional is an integral part of the corporate decision making function.

13

⑥   PENSION MANAGEMENT

William E. Dodge
Managing Director, Marvin & Palmer Associates

Pension management is about managing the interaction of two portfolios: the pension liability and pension asset portfolios. Unfortunately, the behavior and returns of both portfolios are dynamic and uncertain. Moreover, the health of the pension plan and the economic requirements and accounting implications for the corporation are determined by the correlated or uncorrelated behavior of these portfolios and the resulting shortfall or surplus of pension assets over pension liabilities. Consequently, the challenge for the high-performance CFO is to provide a framework to manage the shortfall/surplus position in the most predictable manner possible and in a way that is consistent with the nonpension operations of the corporation.

While the interaction of the asset and liability portfolios is at the heart of pension management, the CFO must also understand the income and outgo aspects of the pension management problem. Mr. Joseph Applebaum put it best when he wrote, "Over the life of a plan, both defined benefit and defined contributions plans satisfy a simple relationship between income and outgo." As he puts it,

$$\text{Contributions} + \text{Return} = \text{Benefits} + \text{Expenses}^{[1]}$$

---

1 Joseph Applebaum in *Trends in Pensions 1992,* edited by John A. Turner and Daniel J. Beller (U.S. Department of Labor Pension and Benefits Administration), 1992, pp. 509–17.

The left side of the equation is the income side; the CFO strives to minimize the contributions and maximize the return from the pension asset portfolio. The right side of the equation is the outgo side; here the CFO strives to keep benefits arising from the liability portfolio low and also to anticipate the distribution of pension benefits with as much certainty as possible.

The high-performance CFO finds it essential that senior management recognize that the requirement to manage pension assets would not exist were it not for the corporate operating decisions that give rise to liabilities. This reality demands a pension management paradigm that views (1) pension management as an operating problem and (2) pension assets and liabilities as operating assets and liabilities. The need for this pension management paradigm is reinforced by the scale and growth of pension assets and liabilities relative to operating assets and liabilities. For example, pension assets and pension liabilities may be as large as the assets and liabilities of an operating division. It is estimated that at the end of 1993, pension assets represented roughly 10 percent of total corporate assets and 14 percent of total corporate liabilities.[2]

This chapter begins by presenting a pension management paradigm and strategic planning framework. It then discusses the management of liability and asset portfolios plus some odds and ends. It closes with a summary of the key issues covered in the chapter.

A PENSION MANAGEMENT PARADIGM

Everything about the management of pension assets flows from the operating decisions that give rise to the pension liabilities. The proper pension management paradigm therefore must recognize that the pension assets simply collateralize the collective operating decisions of the corporation embodied in the pension liabilities. It is the responsibility of the CFO to move this paradigm into the mainstream of management thinking and to ensure that senior management is aware of all pension management issues and how they relate to the day-to-day operations of the company. Mr. Jack

---

2 Based on a survey of S&P 500 companies that reported pension assets and liabilities as separate items on the COMPUSTAT Database for fiscal year 1993.

Quinlan (recently retired CFO of E. I. duPont de Nemours & Company) puts it this way:

> The issue most important to keep in front of senior management is that pension expense is as much an expense of the corporation as wages and salaries. Pension expense impacts all aspects of product sourcing (costs) and product pricing.

Indeed, pension costs can find no deeper penetration of the company than at the product level so they must be evaluated as operating costs that result from the interaction of the return from the pension assets and the expenses associated with the pension liabilities.

Unfortunately, the rules of ERISA, and the language of pension management deflect the focus away from operating status for pension assets and liabilities. ERISA, for example, stresses the segregation of pension assets, while its interpretation raises questions about the corporate claim on those assets.[3] Well-known pension investment consultant Mr. John Casey of Rogers & Casey Associates believes, "ERISA makes you think differently about pension assets than you do about the operating assets of the corporation. It should not!" Additionally, the language of pension management undermines the proper paradigm by creating the impression that pension assets, liabilities, and net worth are outside the domain of normal financial statement terminology; funded position substitutes for assets, obligations substitutes for liabilities, and surplus substitutes for net worth.

Admittedly, Statement of Financial Accounting Standard (SFAS) No. 87 has helped to focus attention on the need to view the pension asset/liability problem from an operating perspective by increasing the disclosure requirements for pension cost and the funded or collateralized position of the pension liability. But SFAS No. 87 does not mandate the proper pension paradigm; it simply gives management incentive to adopt it and avoid the embarrassment of increased volatility to Generally Accepted Accounting Principles (GAAP) earnings or, worse, the embarrassment of bringing the pension liability out of the closet onto the balance sheet.

---

3 For an early discussion of this issue see J. Bulow and M. Scholes, "Who Owns the Assets in a Defined Benefit Pension Plan?" *Financial Aspects of the United States Pension System* (Chicago: University of Chicago Press, 1983), pp. 17–36.

The implication for the management of plan assets is clear; everything about the strategic asset allocation policy, evaluation framework, and feedback mechanisms for quality control of the pension management function flow from the operating decisions of senior management that give rise to the pension liabilities. Strategic planning for pension management must begin with acceptance of this reality and it must include the elevation of both pension assets and liabilities from the swamp of segregated thinking to the high ground of operating status. This will ensure, with the highest probability, that the performance of plan assets is consistent with the objectives of the corporation as it discharges its obligations to the shareholders, employees, and customers.

STRATEGIC PLANNING FOR PENSION MANAGEMENT

Success is often the simple consequence of sharp execution of a well-conceived plan.

—an anonymous stock picker

Strategic planning for pension management should be no different than the strategic planning process for any other area of the business. The challenge is how to get organized; the purpose is to develop a target plan including goals, objectives, and tasks that guide the pension management process and its key functions.

Seven Steps for Strategic Pension Management Planning

There is no uniform or standard format for strategic planning in general or for pension management in particular. The adaptation of strategic planning formats used in other areas of the enterprise is highly desirable because (1) the format is familiar to the CFO and senior management, (2) usage demonstrates cultural continuity, and (3) it will enable the pension management strategic plan to be integrated easily with the overall strategic plan and operational control systems of the corporation. Whatever specific planning format you use, most probably it will follow the general form of Exhibit 13.1, which is provided for illustrative purposes.

The creation of the mission statement is the opportunity to simplify the complex issues of pension management. It's about

EXHIBIT 13.1

Pension Management Strategic Plan

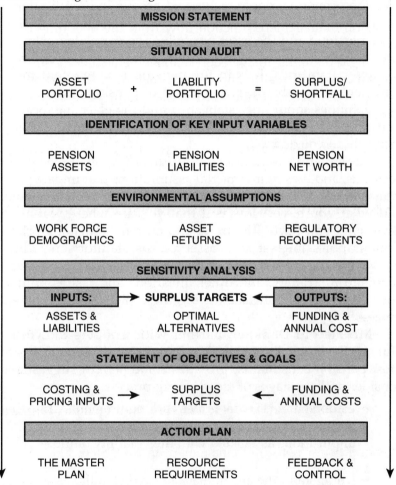

finding a focal point. The statement should include an expression of the pension management paradigm discussed above. But the paradigm is like a picture frame—active thought of the mission statement must also step into that frame and draw attention to the central focus of the picture, a focal point.

That focal point is the health of the pension plan and the economic requirements and accounting implications. For the corporation, the economic requirements and accounting implications are determined by the correlated or uncorrelated behavior of the liability portfolio and the asset portfolio. The correlated or uncorrelated behavior is reflected in the shortfall or surplus of pension assets over liabilities. It is in the pension management mission statement where the operating status of pension assets and pension liabilities should be established and the objective focal point of the pension management function, shortfall/surplus management, should be defined.

The situation audit is about the identification of the key input variables, and the environmental assumptions that impact pension management. These steps involve taking stock of where you are and what you have. How is it that you are where you are and have what you have? The trend and current status of work force demographics, interest rates, asset returns, statutory and administrative law, the growth of your business (or lack of it), merger and acquisition strategy, and other questions and issues unique to your situation will surface during these phases of the planning process.

Mr. Harold Dankner, partner with Coopers & Lybrand's Human Resource Advisory Group and one of the world's foremost pension consultants, provides some helpful suggestions to consider in these stages of the planning process.

- Understand: (1) what issues and requirements drive the numbers, and (2) the economic costs and accounting implications associated with the volatility of those numbers.

- Understand the general lack of predictability associated with pension costs and recognize that the challenge to the CFO in creating a well-managed pension plan is to create a framework where the behavior of the liability portfolio and the asset portfolio is as reasonably predictable as possible.

- Ask yourself, Are the issues that drive the numbers prioritized to what the corporation wants to be? Given the current priorities and policies, where are they leading you in terms of corporate cash flow? Is the asset allocation policy in proper alignment with the issues of work force demographics, funding policy, and the predictability of results?

Sensitivity analysis is the laboratory where the reactive characteristics of the key variables and environmental assumptions are quantified. It's about the input–output analysis and it's about examining your current situation. Given your policies, inputs, and assumptions, what is the optimal configuration of the asset and liability portfolios and how does that optimal configuration compare to your present structure? Where will you be down the road if the current trends and policies continue and is that where you want to be? There is a tremendous amount of software available to handle the evaluative and what-if elements of this phase of planning. Consult your local actuarial consultant, accountant, or investment banker for details.

Since it is the operating decisions of the corporation that give rise to the liabilities and the statutory and administrative law that guides their treatment, most work in the sensitivity analysis phase will focus on simulating liability portfolios. It may at times seem like a leap of faith, but the returns from the normal array of investment classes are reasonably predictable. This is particularly true given the long-term characteristics of the pension liability, which allows the holding period or investment time horizon to be extended and creates the tangential benefit of lower volatility of expected asset returns and lower risk.

Sensitivity analysis enables the CFO to select from analytical output the best combination of asset and liability portfolios including worst-case scenarios that best fit the corporation's economic and accounting requirements. From this information probabilities and outcomes can be established, thus ensuring that the pension plan is well managed in as predictable a manner as possible.

At the next stage of strategic planning the task is to establish the objectives and goals for the pension management process. Everything comes together here. The focal point of the pension management paradigm is defined in explicit terms. It's time to target specific surplus/shortfall objectives and goals at which you will direct corporate energies. What funding requirements and annual costs will follow from the target surplus/shortfall strategy and what are the accounting implications? Finally, what are the general implications for the operations of the company, and product costs and product pricing strategies, in particular?

The strategic plan concludes with an action plan. This stage involves how the objectives and goals will be reached. Capital and human resource requirements flow from the plan and must be outlined. How will the pension management function be staffed and what role will actuarial and asset management consultants play in the execution of the plan? Will you employ asset management as a cost-effective alternative to outside asset managers? Finally, what information feedback structure will you implement to ensure quality control of the pension management function? What range of conditions will you tolerate before corrective action is taken?

The final step of the action planning phase is to throw the switch and turn the process on. Remember, success is often the simple consequence of solidly executing a well-conceived plan.

THE LIABILITY PORTFOLIO

The high-performance CFO will recognize immediately that the nature of the pension liability and the liability portfolio depend on the type of pension benefit provided. There are two classes of pension benefits and benefit plans: the defined benefit (DB) plan and the defined contributions (DC) plan. The character of the corporate obligations, the substance of administrative costs, and the management of the asset portfolio under these plans are as different as night and day.

The Limited Liability and Expanded Use of DC Plans

Under DC plans, the liability is limited to periodic contributions triggered by the employee's voluntary contributions to the plan. The administrative requirements are limited to the forecasting and record keeping of employee participation and contribution rates. Under DC plans, the employee bears all the investment risk, actuarial requirements are nonexistent, and regulatory requirements are minimal. With DB plans, the company bears the entire contribution burden and all the investment risk under intense regulatory and

EXHIBIT 13.2

Workers Covered by Pensions by Plan Type

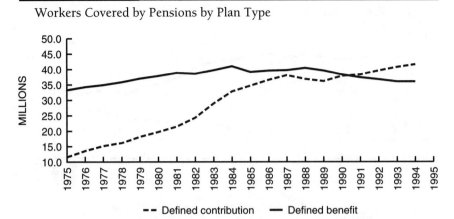

-- Defined contribution   — Defined benefit

record-keeping requirements. Actuarial services are enormous and essential. The treatment of the asset portfolio becomes complicated by the need to control both liability and asset return volatility in a shortfall/surplus management framework. Is it any wonder that the popularity of DC plans is soaring over that of DB plans.[4]

While DB plan assets still exceed those of the DC plans, the gap will continue to close and DC plans will exceed those of DB plans by the end of the 1990s if not sooner according to Michael Goldstein et al. at Sanford C. Bernstein Research.[5] (See Exhibits 13.2 and 13.3.) This trend has been influenced by the rapid growth in the number of small firms over the past decade simultaneous with the downsizing of larger corporations. The costs of the DB plan are prohibitive for firms with fewer than 1,000 employees. For example, the administrative cost of a DC plan are 50 percent less than the costs of a DB plan for firms with fewer than 50 employees. But just as startling is the fact that firms with 10,000 employees have seen the administrative costs of a DC plan fall from

---

4 For an insightful discussion of the trade-offs between DB and DC plans, see Z. Bodie, et. al., "Defined Benefit versus Defined Contribution Plans: What Are the Real Tradeoffs?" *Pensions in the U. S. Economy* (Chicago: University of Chicago Press, 1988), pp. 139–62.
5 Michael L. Goldstein, et. al., *The Future of Money Management in America,* 1994 ed. Sanford C. Bernstein Research, pp. 28–30.

EXHIBIT 13.3

Plan Assets by Plan Type

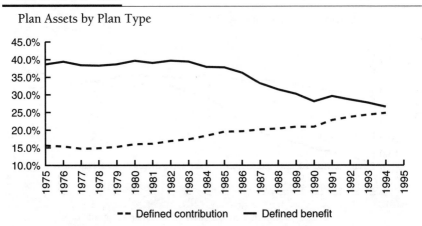

-- Defined contribution   — Defined benefit

110 percent of comparative DB costs in 1981 to less than 75 percent 10 years later.[6]

It's perhaps more than coincidence that the relative growth of DC plans has occurred during the most intense period of corporate restructuring in American history. The catalyst is the unprecedented expansion of competition from Japan, the Pacific Rim, and other emerging production centers around the globe. The incentives to understand the sources of product costs and get those costs down has never been higher and the problem will not soon go away.

Given this competitive business environment and the high costs of the DB plan, the high-performance CFO's principle task might be to lower benefit costs by changing the character of the liability portfolio. This can be accomplished in several ways. The DB plan might be terminated and assets reverted to the plan beneficiaries, with a DC plan in its place. The DB plan might be closed to new hires and a DC plan made available to the new workers. Or the high-performance CFO might choose the middle ground, one that preserves the DB plan but lowers its cost by reshaping the volatility characteristics of the liability portfolio. This might be accomplished through early retirements, new pay scales, work (job) elimination— in short, through steps involving those work force demographics that give rise to the pension liabilities and annual contribution

---

6 Ibid., p. 31.

requirements of the plan. What the CFO should do will be shaped and influenced by the mix of union and non-union workers, the mix of retired versus active lives, the financial health of the corporation, the corporation's growth prospects, competitive wage and salary considerations, and generally the corridor of legal options.

Know the Complexities of the DB Liability

Nevertheless, it is unlikely that there will be a broad-based trend toward DB plan termination due to the political ramifications if for no other reason. Consequently, DB plans will remain a challenging management problem for the CFO so a brief review of the DB liability portfolio, its volatility characteristics, and the pension costs that flow from its existence is warranted. Exhibit 13.4 shows an analytical framework for DB liability management.

There are two ways of looking at the DB pension liability: on a historical or cumulative basis and on a projected basis. The differentiating characteristic of the approaches is that the former assumes the plan is terminated, a going-out-of-business assumption, while the latter assumes a going concern. The former is called the accumulated benefit obligation (ABO); the latter is called the projected benefit obligation (PBO).

The PBO is the present value of benefits earned by employees based on the plan's benefit formula prior to the plan's valuation date. The ABO is the measure used to ascertain the minimum required funding level or funding floor for the plan; as such, it is a pension fund balance sheet concept and minimum target funding level. The PBO looks forward and projects years of service wage inflation between now and retirement. Under SFAS No. 87 it is the fundamental measure of accrued liability and it must be used in calculating annual pension expense. Its relevance is closer to the pension fund income statement as a consequence.

There are six components of pension expense: (1) service costs, (2) interest costs, (3) return on plan assets, (4) amortized prior service costs, (5) actuarial gains and losses, and (6) amortized shortfall/surplus asset position at the time of adoption of SFAS No. 87.[7] Service cost is the present value of the future pension benefit

---

7 Mark J. Warshawsky in *Trends in Pensions 1992*, pp. 497–5045.

E X H I B I T   13.4

Managing the Liability Portfolio

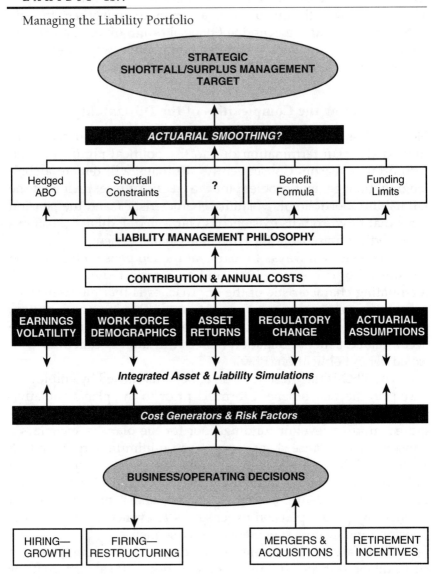

that arises from an additional year of employment (service) assuming the employee's wage increases at some assumed rate. Interest cost is the cost of carrying the PBO that was outstanding at the beginning of the year. Return on plan assets is the actual return on plan assets plus or minus a charge or credit to a deferred return account that is acceptable and allowable for smoothing the actual return on plan assets. Amortized prior service costs are costs arising from plan changes/amendments that can be amortized over the remaining estimated years of employment for currently active employees. Actuarial gains and losses arise from results that differ from original assumptions used to calculate the PBO and the expected return on plan assets. Finally, amortized shortfall/surplus that existed at the time of adoption of SFAS No. 87 is essentially the difference between the ABO and the plan assets at the time SFAS No. 87 was adopted divided by 30 or 40 years.

In addition to understanding the general components of pension expense, the high-performance CFO must probe the nuances of each and understand how the characteristics of the firm's work force demographics can and do influence each component. It's vital to develop an appreciation for what is controllable and what is not. Together, SFAS No. 87, the Omnibus Budget Reconciliation Act (OBRA) of 1987, and original ERISA legislation provide both the boundaries of pension funding and the corridors that the CFO can build and modify within. By understanding both the rules and the characteristics of your company, you are thoroughly prepared to manage the pension function in response to changing operating requirements.

Pension Liabilities and Overfunding as Corporate Assets— Use Them

It is not inconceivable that the high-performance CFO might even take steps that increase pension expenses and funding requirements as a means of optimizing the performance of the company overall. Does that sound crazy? Well, it's not. Consider the example of a company under intense competitive pressure, experiencing profit margin erosion in a weak pricing environment, and having low sales output per employee. Assume that new information technology is available that enables the company to reduce the number of people employed in the Finance Department and in the Management Information Services Department. Assume that these are not production line employees and that the company's ability to generate sales will be unaffected by their dismissal. Finally, let's assume that the technology cost is 5 to 10 percent of the jobs that can be eliminated.

Enter the human resource (HR) director. He explains the detrimental effects that such a restructuring will have on employee morale and reminds senior management that many of these employees have been with the company for 15 to 20 years, some are over 50, some are women, and some are minorities. The HR director worries that there could be age, gender, or race discrimination issues. Under these circumstances, what are you willing to pay if the cost savings is material and how will you do it so as to keep the HR problem within manageable bounds? The maximum price that you are willing to pay is the equilibrium price (the present value of future employee expenses).

With respect to the HR problem, one approach might be to view the pension benefit as an asset, one that enables management to shift costs from the wages-and-salaries account to the pension account. The HR problem might be resolved with gratuitous increases in the employees' years of service which increase the employees' pension benefit and may enable them to retire with a full pension. The pension management paradigm discussed earlier will encourage the high-performance CFO to think about the interrelationship of operating (wages and salaries) and pension expense in the context of restructuring the company.

In addition to using the pension expense in a cost-shifting exercise, the high-performance CFO will also recognize that the pension asset is valuable as a resource, particularly in overfunded situations. The reversion of overfunded assets to the corporate accounts is significantly restricted under current regulations which might lead to a view that the assets are just there, untouchable and unusable.[8] But what if your company was considering a merger with a company that had a pension that was in

---

8 The Department of Labor restricts reversions of surplus pension assets to those amounts exceeding 150 percent of the accrued benefit. See M. Alderson, "Corporate Pension Policy under OBRA 1987," *Financial Management* Winter 1990, pp. 87–97.

a shortfall or underfunded position. Perhaps your surplus could be applied to the merger candidate's shortfall funding position and a reduction of the merged company's cash requirements for pension expense.

Both these examples illustrate the creative thinking that should be applied to the pension management question. That creativity can mean more profits and cash flow, more shareholder value, and, in the long run, a more secure environment for your employees. By developing a deep understanding of the factors that influence pension costs and funded position in the operating context prescribed by the pension management paradigm, the performance of the CFO is elevated.

No Target, No Feedback Means No Control

The final point about the pension liability is that it has outputs—outputs that provide for feedback and control, outputs that can aid operating conditions like the work force restructuring and merger examples, and, finally, aid in providing a target for the management of the other pension portfolio, the asset portfolio. Remember, everything about the requirement to manage pension assets flows from the operating decisions that give rise to the pension liabilities. The high-performance CFO understands that a sharply defined target is a lot easier to hit that a fuzzy one. Let's move now to the asset portfolio and the management of the assets.

THE ASSET PORTFOLIO

The pension asset management problem is about how the pension assets will be allocated across the various classes. For the high-performance CFO, the central issue of pension asset management and the asset portfolio is the establishment of an asset portfolio structure that provides for a reasonable level of predictable portfolio behavior—the foundation for control. The shortfall/surplus strategy (target) discussed previously is the axis around which the processes that control the asset portfolio turn, and around which the allowable boundaries of asset portfolio performance are defined.[9] Remember, you cannot reflect too much on the fact that the requirement to manage pension assets arises out of the existence of the pension liabilities that result from the operating decisions of corporate management.

The problem of how to best allocate pension assets depends on the type of benefit and benefit plan: defined contribution (DC) or defined benefit (DB) plan. How to best allocate assets under a defined contribution plan is about providing investment options more than allocating assets. The task is straightforward. You must establish a menu of investment options from the spectrum of asset classes, use due diligence respecting the quality of investment management in each class, and ensure that the choices are broad enough to let a prudent employee establish a reasonable level of portfolio diversification. The toughest questions that the high-performance CFO will face are (1) the domain of investment (asset class) options that will be made available to the plan beneficiaries and (2) who will provide the professional management of those investment options (classes). The employee allocates the assets across the various investment options. While it is a good idea to provide training and guidance with respect to the risk and reward characteristics of each investment option, it is not the responsibility of the corporation to allocate the assets.

Develop the Target for DB Plan Asset Management

The complexity of the asset management process under DB plans mirrors the complexity of the DB liabilities. Indeed, as stressed throughout this chapter, the DB liabilities drive the need for asset management in the first place so the CFO's asset management policy should be targeted at the behavior of the liability portfolio and how senior management has defined its pension liability funding policy. Most probably the funding policy seeks to minimize both the long-term economic costs of the plan and the volatility of annual

---

9 From the asset management perspective, see Martin L. Leibowitz, "Pension Asset Allocation through Surplus Management," *Financial Analysts Journal*, March-April 1987, pp. 29–40. Also see "Portfolio Optimization under Shortfall Constraints" in *Asset Allocation*, edited by R. Arnott and F. Fabozzi, pp. 257–81, and "Setting the Stage," *Managing Asset Liability Portfolios*, AIMR, 1992, pp. 6–13.

contribution requirements. This is not usually expressed as a single dollar amount; rather it is usually expressed as an acceptable (predictable) range of volatility for annual pension contribution requirements. In seeking to minimize the volatility of annual contributions, management has made short-term predictability a priority.

These two criteria (minimizing long-term economic costs and annual contribution volatility) define the objective function for the pension asset portfolio. The first demands a structure that minimizes the need for annual contributions; the second demands an asset portfolio structure that minimizes the volatility or range of annual pension contributions. The high-performance CFO will note that the first is opposed to the behavior of the liability portfolio while the second is aligned. The first is opposed because the objective to minimize the level of contribution creates an objective for the asset portfolio to maximize the return from, or growth of, the asset. The second criterion, however, aligns the volatility of the liability portfolio and the volatility of the asset portfolio. If they are not aligned, the behavior of the two portfolios will not be correlated. Since the periodic and cumulative effect of the interaction of the liability and asset portfolio is expressed as the net worth or funded position of the plan, a lack of correlated behavior will produce (1) substantially more volatility of the shortfall/surplus position than if they were correlated and (2) in turn result in more volatile annual pension requirements.

Note that uncorrelated behavior and a resulting increased volatility of surplus and contributions may not be all bad. No doubt there will be instances when the uncorrelated behaviors of the assets and liabilities improve the funded position and cut the annual pension contribution requirement. But there will be other instances where the opposite is true and pension contributions will be higher than planned. In either instance, however, the predictability of the level of annual pension contribution requirement is undermined when the behaviors of the pension liability and asset portfolio are uncorrelated.

Minimizing both contributions and the volatility of contributions requires that the asset portfolio produce maximum return and minimum risk. Maximizing return and minimizing risk is of course the objective function of modern portfolio theory—particularly in the context of finding the optimal combination of reward and risk. The link between—managing the asset portfolio and managing the liability is this information—and the shortfall/surplus management strategy must provide it to properly target the asset portfolio as illustrated in Exhibit 13.5.

The ABO—to Hedge or Not to Hedge

Perhaps the most important asset management issue that flows from the specific information in the shortfall/surplus strategy is the decision to hedge the accumulated benefit obligation (ABO). The amount of these liabilities and their future behavior are highly predictable. At the risk of oversimplifying the issue, a lump sum purchase of an annuity could cover the obligation. Assuming there is no cost-of-living adjustment for the retirement benefit, the assets employed to fund the ABO do not need to grow, albeit the return of principle and credit quality considerations remain significant. Bonds and other fixed-income alternatives are suitable for the investment pool that funds the ABO. The projected benefit obligation introduces significant complications because errors in estimating wage inflation, retirement age, mortality, service years, and other elements of work force demographics as well as asset returns can have a multiplicative effect on misestimating the PBO. To the extent that inflation is at the center of the estimation errors, the need to grow the assets is increased and the need to incorporate equities and real assets in the asset portfolio structure rises.

The most conservative asset structure would include a bond hedge for the ABO and a diversified stock/bond/real asset mix for the PBO. The portion of the asset portfolio allocated to the bond hedge would depend on the ratio of the ABO to the PBO. This strategy would satisfy the requirement that the volatility of annual pension contributions be minimized. But what about seeking maximum return? Since the pension asset portfolio is a tax-sheltered pool of assets, why not pursue a strategy that generates growth? Growth of plan assets beyond the assumed rate of return and the interest rate necessary to settle the ABO would help PBO funding requirements, create increments to pension net worth, and aid the shortfall/surplus position. In short, it would improve the health of the pension plan, and reduce the economic drag of the pension plan on the corporation overall. The argument can be

Managing the Asset Portfolio

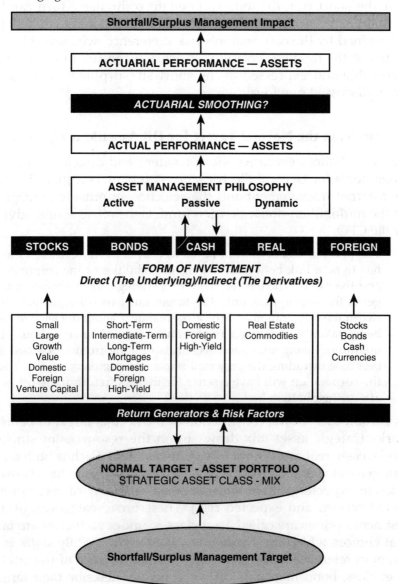

compelling. Even though the inclusion of noncorrelated or weakly correlated growth assets such as common stock carries higher risk over the short run, the long-run benefit of higher return can be substantial. What the high-performance CFO chooses to do will be determined by the corporation's risk preference, which will be reflected in the range or volatility of pension contributions deemed acceptable and expressed in the shortfall/surplus management target discussed previously.

Construct the Normal Target for DB Asset Management

Mr. Gene Bolton, executive vice president and director of equity investments for General Electric's pension plan, is responsible for the internal management and the selection of outside managers for the multibillion-dollar pension fund. Gene offers sound advice for the CFO:

> The pension assets can not be viewed in a vacuum. There clearly has to be a link between the pension liabilities of the corporation and the assets. The development of a strategic asset allocation target is the appropriate link. The target must reflect agreement between the corporation and the asset manager about the level of risk being taken with respect to asset allocation. The risk should be quantified using simulated scenarios ranging from worst case to best case including the projected impact on company results. Thus the corporation will have a sense for the risk/return trade-off as it affects their bottom line.

As Exhibit 13.5 shows, construction of the normal target or benchmark strategic asset mix draws upon the resources of stocks, bonds, cash, real assets, and foreign investment. Each is both a return generator and a risk factor, which is to say each has its own discrete expected return and expected volatility of return (expected reward and expected risk). These broad categories of investment options are called asset classes; under each class are tactical choices which are frequently called styles. While *styles* is a common reference to tactical choices in the instance of the stocks asset class, bond managers do not generally describe their target strategies as styles. It is certainly not going to undermine the CFO's performance by thinking about classes and then styles even for bonds, real assets, and foreign investments, however.

The field of investment management and performance evaluation has evolved to a point where historical performance benchmarks are available for all the asset classes and most of the tactical style choices. Data that describe the return and risk characteristics of each are available to illustrate the portfolio returns of any combination of classes and styles that your creative juices desire. Of course, the objective of the simulations is to create an asset portfolio return profile that in any given year will match the range of allowed negative impact on the shortfall/surplus-funded position of the plan discussed previously while at the same time maximizing the return on plan assets and thereby satisfying the objective to minimize the annual pension contribution.

The selection of investment styles and the style managers should be guided by and evaluated on the basis of benchmarks. The selection of an investment style and a manager should be based on a performance expectation that is quantified or expressed as a target or benchmark. For the small-stock style and manager, a representative benchmark might be the Russell 2000, (a popular equity benchmark formulated by the Frank Russell Company, Consultants, Tacoma, Washington). The purpose of the benchmark is to ascertain the value added of the portfolio-style manager. If he cannot beat the benchmark but the benchmark does well, perhaps a Russell 2000 index fund manager will make better sense. The key issue is control of the process that strives to hit the strategic DB asset target. If the target is based on the performance of the Russell 2000 small-stock index, then you had better match the Russell 2000's performance or you'll miss your target. If you miss your target, you might be out of control and that is something the high-performance CFO should not stand for.

A Counterintuitive Free Lunch—Uncorrelated Assets

The high-performance CFO should be familiar with one counterintuitive aspect of constructing the asset portfolio, using assets with known risk and reward characteristics. Two assets with equal expected return profiles and high risk or annual volatility characteristics under certain circumstances can be combined to produce the same or sometimes higher average expected return but with a lower risk characteristic than either asset held separately. The expected return for each asset is defined as statistical mean returns; the risk characteristic of each is defined as the mean variance of that mean return. Most often in the field of investments, risk is stated as the standard deviation of the expected return, which is nothing more than the square root of the mean variance. These statistics describe the discrete performance of the asset class or style; what is left out is how each behaves relative to the other—their correlated behavior. The statistical portrayal of this behavior is in the correlation statistic R^2. What is important to understand is that two assets with low correlation to each other (one or both of which might be regarded as too risky when viewed in isolation) when combined in the same portfolio will sometimes lower the volatility and therefore lower the risk of the total portfolio substantially while maintaining or even increasing expected return of the portfolio. Does this sound like a free lunch? Well, it is a free lunch—one that the high-performance CFO must be aware of so as not to reject asset classes or asset styles based on their individual behavioral characteristics.

The two areas of pension asset allocation receiving increased asset emphasis in the mid-1990s are foreign investments and real assets. Foreign investments in particular are often justified on the basis of providing lower asset portfolio risk or volatility while maintaining or increasing the expected return on portfolios. When considered independently, foreign investments often reveal higher historical mean variance risk and (because the pension liability for U.S. companies is almost entirely dollar-denominated) the foreign investment option was previously bypassed for inclusion in the portfolio. The high-performance CFO won't make this mistake and will grasp the generic significance of adding uncorrelated asset classes and tactical styles to the menu of possible investment options.

One caveat to this approach to asset allocation is warranted. History is a useful guide for the future—those who do not know the past may repeat the mistakes of history. In the world of finance, however, remember that while history is a useful guide for the future, it's sometimes unreliable. Mean returns are not usually stable. They change year-to-year. Neither are the mean variance risk characteristics and correlations between asset classes stable. Because the tools used today in simulating portfolios provide discrete solutions based on the inputs, it's often a good idea to evaluate the recent trend of the return, risk, and correlation assumptions. The high-performance CFO will question the validity of the inputs based on casual observations of the corporate business environment.

For example, the export competitiveness of U.S. manufacturing is on the rebound in the mid-1990s in part because of cost reductions and in part because the U.S. dollar has collapsed versus the currencies of the principal Cold War success nations (Japan and Germany). If American export competitiveness is on the rebound, what does it mean for the competitiveness of Japanese and German products whose costs are rising relative to the American competition? It is reasonable to assume that the rate of return on Japanese and German domestic investment will be below that of recent years with consequences for their stock markets. Japan in particular represents a major weight in global stock market indexes; if returns there are likely to be below the recent average, perhaps you should consider reducing the mean expected return for Japan in particular and foreign equities in general. Maybe you will decide not to make this adjustment, which is fine. However, the high-performance CFO will feel comfortable asking the questions and considering the implications of the answers.

Forms of Investment—Derivatives and the Underlying

You have run your simulations and you have found the ideal asset structure that is most likely to provide the magnitude and pattern of returns dictated by the shortfall/surplus management strategy. Before moving on, you should consider the form of investment that you will employ.

As far as the financial markets are concerned, we are living in the golden years of financial engineering and derivative products like futures and options. Derivatives are contracts between you and the issuer wherein the issuer agrees to provide the upside return of a specific financial instrument like a stock or index of stocks, a bond or index of bonds, or a commodity or index of commodities, and you agree to cover the downside price movement. The derivative is designed to mimic these underlying financial instruments and commodities, but you do not usually intend to own them. If you were to own them, you would be said to own the underlying assets from which the return of the future or option is derived—hence the name *derivative*.

Leverage is deeply and significantly imbedded in these instruments. As a result, the buyer can obtain a great deal more exposure to the behavior of the underlying than the required investment outlay. While the most active markets for derivatives are listed and regulated in options and futures markets in Chicago, New York, Philadelphia, and London, a very real, dynamic, unregulated, and unlisted over-the-counter market has also evolved. There you can virtually create your own derivative to mimic any underlying asset or combination of assets—domestic and foreign—that you want. At a price, you can literally engineer return and risk profiles.

These instruments, whether sold on the exchanges or over the counter, offer great advantages that can aid the fine-tuning of your investment returns. They should be included in your asset management strategy. But you must understand how to price them, you must understand that they are not always liquid, and, most importantly, you must understand that they represent first and foremost a credit instrument. Recognize that, in exchange for your extending funds to the issuer of the derivative (even if it's for only a small portion of the dollar value of the underlying), you accept the word of the issuer to make good on its side of the bargain. If an issuer goes out of business, you could be out of luck. Otherwise derivatives can—and in most situations should—be used in the implementation of your asset strategy.

Selecting Investment Managers—Including Yourself

The next question is *who will manage the pension assets?* This raises the issue of whether the CFO will choose internal management for a portion of the money with current or prospective employees of the corporation. Fortunately, there are a number of highly sophisticated consulting firms that manage databases of investment managers including key information like their performance track records, their investment styles, the number of investment professionals in their employ, and how long they have been in business.[10] The key is how to use the consultants. The first rule to live

---

10 There are a number of asset manager selection consultants including Rogers Casey, & Associates, Frank Russell, SEI, Callan Associates, and most actuarial and benefit consulting firms.

by is that it's possible to delegate too much. The right balance can be defined by asking yourself a simple question: If this were about delegating responsibility for the operating assets of the corporation, how far would I go? Yes, you will need the professional assistance provided by the pension manager selection consultants, but you will be a better client, achieve a better level of overall control, and manage the pension management problem in the most predictable manner possible by staying personally involved or keeping your subordinates closely involved. Know why you chose the managers that you did; know what role they will play in achieving the returns that are expected from the normal target or strategic asset mix that you have chosen.

The option to manage assets internally is often overlooked. While it can present certain management challenges, it can be economically rewarding in situations where the value of the asset portfolio exceeds $1.5 to $2.0 billion. At that level, (assuming an average management fee of 0.35 percent), the fee paid to outside managers is $5.25 to $7 million annually, or the equivalent of 15 employees with salaries and benefits costs of $350,000 per year. You'll need two to four very senior people and 6 to 10 analysts, a trader, and some support staff. Yes, some of the very good portfolio managers make $1 million or more a year, but some of them do not and some of them do not like the travel schedules that multiple client meetings require. As a captive investment manager, you can use incentive stock options in your company to provide incentive to prospective internal portfolio managers.

It is unlikely that all of your assets will be managed internally and probably it would not be wise either. It might be appropriate to manage passive funds such as index funds internally. It might make sense to manage internally large U.S. stocks and style-based index fund strategies that employ disciplined selection criteria. However, it most probably does not make sense to manage global assets, private placement bonds, venture capital investments, real estate, or commodities internally because of the marginal costs involved. Each requires unique analytical skills and exponential growth of the staffing relative to the assets involved. Using outside managers for the specialized and nontraditional investments makes sense because the economies of scale are on their side, not yours.

The disadvantages of internal management are largely cultural where employee turnover can be a serious problem, a salary structure above those of some middle managers can create morale problems, and new internal auditing, legal, and record-keeping requirements can emerge. Generally, however, the problems are not insurmountable for the high-performance CFO. If the scale of your plan assets is large, you should take a close look at internal asset management versus external asset management.

Rebalance to the Normal Target—Function and Frequency

There is one major policy decision left with respect to managing the pension asset portfolio. You have run your simulations, you have selected your normal target for the strategic asset mix of the portfolio, and you have lined up the money managers. Let's assume you start the process and one year later you look at the mix of assets and they are no longer aligned with the structure of the normal target. What do you do? There are four choices. First, you could exercise benign neglect and do nothing, which assumes you set the normal target with the intention of evaluating its success or failure at some longer and unspecified time interval. Second, you could rebalance the structure back to the original normal target. In this instance you have adopted a fixed–time-interval rebalance frequency of one year, a passive decision. Third, you could decide that the outlook for the stock market will continue to be very good and, even though the above-normal equity performance over the past year means the equity allocation is also above normal, you leave it be. You wait for what you believe would be a more propitious time to rebalance the equity position back to normal. In this instance you have made an active asset allocation decision based on judgment and timing skills. Fourth, you could rely on predetermined asset valuation criteria, systematically derived if–then decision rules that cause rebalance to be contingent on the presence of certain conditions: conditions related to the financial markets, the shortfall/surplus management strategy, or the operating conditions of the corporation. This is an active decision based on the dynamic interplay of diverse financial markets, the pension asset portfolio and liability portfolio, the business environment, or all of the above. This is a dynamic rebalance decision, contingent on predetermined decision making criteria.

The high-performance CFO will keep in mind the expected return assumptions as he evaluates the rebalance alternatives and reflects on the inputs used to construct the normal target for the asset portfolio. What was the assumed holding period for the asset classes and style choices used to calculate the annual returns, risks, and correlations? What was it for the asset classes and style choices? Were the simulations of various alternative strategic asset allocation mixes evaluated on an annual basis? If so, are you going to evaluate the success or failure of your plan's real-time asset portfolio performance on a fixed-interval annual basis also? If you do not, can the value added of active or dynamic management reasonably be defined by the return above or below the normal target's performance?

The answers to these questions are far less important than the fact that they are asked in the first place. Explore the issues that surface as you ask them and understand that your normal target or strategic asset allocation mix requires servicing. That servicing requirement is about when, how, and why you rebalance the pension assets. One thing is certain. At the end of the year it is almost impossible that the mix of assets will be the same as it was at the beginning of the year. What will you do then?

Delegation of the Rebalance Function— The Asset Overlay Manager

In the mid-1980s the transaction costs of individual asset managers and the transactions costs of rebalancing the strategic mix of the fund developed considerable attention. The attention was focused on controlling costs.[11] At the same time the evolution of derivative products gathered momentum as the volume of contracts traded exploded, particularly for those derivatives written against the broad asset classes of stocks and bonds. The efficiencies and liquidity of the markets improved dramatically and the costs of acquiring exposure to stocks and bonds plunged as a consequence.

---

11 For a thorough discussion of taxonomy, origins, control, and standing of transactions costs in pension management, see Wayne H. Wagner et al., *The Complete Guide to Securities Transactions,* (New York: Wiley, 1989).

Compare, for example, the cost of buying S&P 500 equity futures contracts with the cost of purchasing the underlying 500 stocks. For illustrative purposes, assume that the average price per share of a stock in the S&P 500 is $45 and that we will buy only round lots of 100 shares for each stock for a total of 50,000 shares at a total cost of $2,250,000. Let's assume that it costs us only 5 cents per share for a total of $2,500. Each S&P 500 futures contract represents 500 shares of the S&P 500 Index, which we assume is 453. This means that (1) each contract represents $226,500 of S&P 500 value and (2) we need to purchase 10 S&P 500 futures contracts to equal the equivalent $2,250,000 of underlying common stocks. The typical S&P 500 futures contract commission is $15 to $20 per round turn, which covers both the purchase and sale of the contract. To be consistent, so to be consistent with the purchase of the underlying, we should include only 50 percent of the $15 to $20 or $7.50 to $10. The cost of purchasing the equivalent of $2,250,000 of S&P 500 common stock using futures, or 10 S&P 500 futures contracts, is $75 to $100, only 3 to 4 percent the cost of buying 100 shares of all 500 stocks in the S&P 500 Index. A similar magnitude of cost savings is available when purchasing bond derivatives.

Moreover, the amount of cash needed to gain exposure to the $2,250,000 of S&P 500 stock value using derivatives is restricted to the collateral requirement of the futures contract, usually 15 to 20 percent or a maximum of $450,000. Both the transactions cost of acquiring stock and the outlay required are substantially lower using the futures contract. This creates a very useful opportunity for managing the strategic asset mix of the portfolio.

Rather than buying and selling the underlying stocks and bonds required to rebalance the strategic mix or normal target, the high-performance CFO might use futures as an overlay strategy. For example, if the rebalance required the sale of bonds and purchase of stocks, then the sale of futures (a short) in an equivalent amount of bonds, and the purchase (a long) of an equivalent amount of common stock would do the trick at a fraction of the cost and cash outlay of implementing the rebalance via the sale and purchase of the underlying bonds and stocks.

The asset overlay strategy can be implemented in-house or it can be delegated to an asset allocation overlay manager. The asset manager selection consultants discussed previously can help you if required. Once you become comfortable with the approach, it can be used to adjust exposure to some of the tactical choices or styles such as small-stock exposure, provided there are actively traded and sufficiently liquid futures (and options) markets available for the tactical style.

Incidentally, the asset managers will find the strategy easy to accommodate. Instead of having to sell and purchase their stocks or bonds to meet your strategic mix change or rebalance requirements, they just go on managing their portfolios.

ODDS AND ENDS OF PENSION MANAGEMENT

While the central focus of pension management must be the issues of the liability and asset portfolios and their outgo (expense) and income (return) characteristics, a number of subtle but potentially time-consuming issues add to the challenges of pension management. They include social responsibility, proxy voting, and shareholder activism.

Social Responsibility

It is seldom required by statute, but shareholders, employees, and the media can elevate social and cultural issues to the center of pension management. South African investments yesterday, Chinese investments tomorrow—issues of human rights can influence the management of the pension assets. Issues involving the environment, local enterprise investing, and animal rights can also create intervening pressure to influence how you invest plan assets or the investment options for your beneficiaries. Most corporations today realize that their constituent obligations include the diverse needs of shareholders, employees, customers, and the general public. How do you respond to them? How will you respond to them if they arise in the future? Must the return on plan assets be subordinated to fulfill the demand of a member of the broad constituent base? Contingency thinking and contingency planning will be part of the high-performance CFO's pension management process.

Proxy Voting—You Need a Policy

You will certainly delegate the securities processing and record-keeping requirements to a plan trustee, probably a bank. The trustee will record the sales and purchases of your investment managers, collect dividends, handle stock splits, and collect interest and dividends. It will also vote the plan's proxy; how it casts those votes should be of concern to you.

Will the trustee vote automatically with management on all issues coming before shareholders—issues ranging from the election of directors to incentive compensation to takeover proposals? If it automatically votes with management, will the interests of plan beneficiaries be properly served? What are your fiduciary requirements? Do you need a formalized proxy voting policy including a review process? Probably.

Shareholder Activism—Corporate Governance

The dramatic growth of public pension plans has spawned a revolutionary class of shareholders and bondholders.[12] Their loyalties are not corporate—their loyalties are to the state, local, and federal government's pension beneficiaries. As shareholders (often your largest shareholders), their concept of shareholder rights sometimes extends to governing the day-to-day operations of the corporation by demanding representation on your board of directors. Their power has sent more than one chief executive officer packing in the name of realizing shareholder value.

Their emergence redefines the concept of pension liability for the high-performance CFO way beyond the technical issues of ERISA, OBRA, and the IRS. How will you deal with them? Think about it—the high-performance CFO does.

CONCLUSION

The high-performance CFO finds it essential that senior management recognize that the requirement to manage pension assets

---

12 See "Can Pension Funds Lead the Ownership Revolution?" *Harvard Business Review*, May-June 1991, pp. 166–83.

would not exist were it not for the corporate operating decisions that give rise to the liabilities that the assets collateralize. This fact and their size demand that the pension liabilities and pension assets be evaluated from the swamp of segregated thinking to the high ground of operating status.

The goal of pension management is to create a framework to manage the income/outgo and shortfall/surplus position of the pension plan in the most predictable manner possible. Remember, success is often the consequence of executing a well-conceived plan.

Whether the focus is the asset portfolio or the liability portfolio, it is imperative that you know the factors that give rise to their respective costs and returns and the volatility of those returns. You must understand that the health of the pension plan and the economic requirements and accounting implications of it are determined by the correlated or uncorrelated behavior of these costs and returns.

Think creatively. Use the pension plan as an asset of the corporation in connection with other corporate decisions and activities like restructuring and merger and acquisition strategy. Understand leading-edge investment strategies and products like derivatives. Look for a free lunch—you might find one in uncorrelated assets like foreign investments.

Understand that the existence of the pension liability and the pension assets creates issues and liabilities that extend beyond the dollars involved and into the realm of social responsibility. Contingency thinking and contingency planning will prepare the high-performance CFO for these time- and cost-consuming issues if and when they arise. Finally, whether it's about rebalancing the asset portfolio back to its normal target mix, tracking changes in the law, or restructuring your work force, understand that pension management is a dynamic process. The high-performance CFO will use feedback and retargeting to maximize the predictable control over the dynamic pension management process.

CHAPTER
14

⑥ ## MANAGING
HEALTH CARE

Thomas G. Manoff
CFO, Saturn Corporation

Health care costs in the United States, both alone and as a percentage of total corporate expense, have been increasing at tremendous rates over the past decade. The industry average through the late 1980s and into the 1990s reached a trend of 15 percent per year. This trend has begun to decrease as the efforts of national health care reform have grown, but still far exceeds the inflation rate of the national economy. On the other hand, Saturn Corporation has experienced a downward trend in health care costs since introducing its own benefit plans in 1992. Here I relate the different measures tried by the Saturn Corporation to help start and sustain this trend.

Saturn Corporation is a wholly owned subsidiary of General Motors. Its mission is to make small cars competitively in the United States. Saturn was given the opportunity to seek a more competitive, better-quality, cost-effective approach to all areas of the business, including manufacturing, vehicle design, systems integration, human relations, and benefits for employees. This allowed Saturn to look at the parts of the General Motors organization that were working well and that would be effective in meeting this goal. It also permitted Saturn to begin again in areas that were not as competitive or were ripe for potential cost savings ideas. This second area is where the benefit programs fell.

Many of the ideas and techniques that helped Saturn control its health care cost can be used by other companies facing that same rising cost if they are willing to look to areas within their control to help start solving the problem. There are steps that can be taken to reduce costs and that build on each other, but that can also be used individually to augment existing plans.

One step when designing or redesigning a benefits program is to decide that there are no sacred cows. The whole operation must be open to internal as well as external review. The idea that new, novel, or simplistic approaches are what is needed must be allowed to grow—especially when looking at parts of the business that have already been identified as uncompetitive. The group given the task of reconsidering existing processes and procedures must have free reign to question all existing customs.

An example of traditional thinking is that the benefits function should be a part of the human resources group, while the payroll group should be a part of the finance area. Since many functions of a flexible benefits plan, such as deducting plan coverages from employee payroll, are part of the payroll process, there is considerable advantage to combining these two functions into one area. The rising cost of health care, as well as the fact that benefits are administered through the payroll system, spawned the idea that the natural owner would be the one best able to integrate these functions.

At Saturn, benefits administration has been combined with payroll administration and placed in the financial function area. The role of the chief financial officer at Saturn is then twofold with respect to benefits administration. First, along with the Human Resources organization, the CFO is responsible to ensure that the concerns and needs of the work force are expressed, understood, and addressed within the benefit plan. The CFO must also balance this need with the requirement to remain competitive in total benefit plan design and cost.

Another aspect of designing or redesigning a benefits program is the cost to administer the plans. A company must decide what is its core line of business and what functions it can do and still be competitive in its functional area. Certain portions of benefits administration are very clerical in nature. Depending on the company's line of business, other tasks may or may not blend with the core line of work.

Since Saturn's core business is automotive manufacturing, not benefits administration, Saturn decided to outsource day-to-day administration of its benefits plan to our on-site administrator, NationsBank. Saturn is responsible for designing and implementing its benefit plans (where we believe we can add value to the process) but we have outsourced the administrative duties. Saturn then spends its time identifying trends in the industry and querying its work force to understand the needs of its members.

HEALTH CARE NETWORK APPROACHES

There are three general network approaches that can be used when establishing or modifying an existing health care program: the *traditional plan (TRAD)*, the *preferred provider organization (PPO)*, and the *health maintenance organization (HMO)*. The exhibit on page 260 summarizes their key aspects. The traditional option, if structured properly, can provide co-pays and deductibles to ensure that the employees are aware when they are spending health care dollars, but there is little else that is involved in a traditional plan to help cost sharing or pass information to the employee about the cost of health care. However, the traditional plan is least invasive to the employee's decision of the provider network as there are few or no restrictions on which doctor or hospital the employee can use. Reasonable and customary charges are the only means for managing the cost of health care, but these also have increased tremendously in recent years.

One type of managed care is the PPO, where a defined network of providers is formed; employees are encouraged to use this network for health care treatment. The plans can be structured with co-pays and deductibles to ensure a form of cost sharing with the employees. There is the additional benefit, over the traditional plan, that there should be a reduced cost to the company negotiated when the network is established due to the increased customer base utilizing the PPO network. The PPO network is more restrictive to the employee in the choice of provider than the traditional plan, but still does not impose a great amount of restrictions on the provider network. Employees can be encouraged to use the PPO network to gain the maximum reimbursement from the plan. Note that the incentive for the health

Key Attributes of Health Care Network Types

	Traditional	**PPO**	**HMO**
Member's ability to select own provider	High, all doctors included.	Must select preferred provider for highest benefits	Must use specific physician to reimburse costs.
Provider willingness to join plan	High, does not restrict fees.	Some fee reduction for increased volume potential.	Limited. Must be area of high competition.
Cost to company	Highest.	Discounts on fees to company when members use approved providers.	Capitated plan. Transfers risk of cost from company to the HMO. Offers potential of lowest cost if managed correctly.
Co-pay coverage level	Plan can be structured so member has co-pays.	Can modify behavior by reducing cost/increasing coverage for using preferred provider.	Usually offers highest coverage with limited co-pay to encourage members to join.

care provider to become involved in a managed care network is very dependent on the amount of competition in the medical community. It is difficult to recruit providers to the network and have them accept reduced reimbursement when there is a shortage of providers within a given area.

A second form of managed care, the HMO, is very restrictive in the number and variety of providers in the network, but can offer reduced co-pays and deductibles or added coverages as incentives for employees to join. The HMO option has received much attention as a vehicle for cost savings, but the proposed money to be saved has not always been realized. HMOs are also the most intrusive plan to the participants due to restrictions as to whom the employee can see to get plan reimbursement. It is also the most disruptive plan from a health care provider perspective as the risk of the patient's health is transferred from the company to the provider of the plan. Finally, to form an HMO there must be a high level of competition in the medical arena. It is difficult to encourage medical providers to join an HMO with capitated reimbursement schedules (versus full-paying customers) unless they can benefit from an increased customer base.

MAKING A CHOICE

Saturn concentrated its efforts in a PPO network for a couple of reasons. The traditional plan had been popular with many employees in their former work locations, and a PPO plan was a step toward managed care with the fewest differences from traditional coverage. Also, the PPO network was well suited for the widely distributed geographic area where Saturn employees live. A large number of physicians were attracted to the increased patient load that Saturn could offer. Finally, there were few existing HMOs in the central Tennessee area and not much acceptance of them from the provider organization. Although Saturn is by some standards a large employer, the level of competition in the rural areas was not high enough to support an HMO form of managed competition. Since many of the physicians in rural areas already had a full patient load, the offer of additional patients at a reduced fee structure was no incentive to them. Thus a PPO provided the best compromise plan for providers and employees.

The next step for health care management is involving the community in finding the solution. A company needs to be involved in the local community, in its problems, and in its solutions to combat its problems. This is true of many different aspects of the community, from educational needs to citizen responsibility as well as in health care usage and the associated cost of health care. A company can become involved in identifying needs for the provider community, such as additional health care providers in particular fields or after-hour clinics for its members. If a company is too small to make this type of difference, much can be gained by combining with other local companies. Once the community and the companies are working together, many new and untried areas of interest can be explored, such as centers of excellence. This type of plan modification would again depend on the presence of competition in the health care fields. If there is a limited number of providers, it is much more difficult to start this process, but not impossible.

Saturn wanted a network that incorporated Nashville-area hospitals that are leading providers of certain types of specialized care, but it also realized that many of the small community hospitals would be needed in the network due to its work force's geographic dispersion in the middle Tennessee area. To meet these needs, Saturn formed the Community Health Consortium (CHC) organization.

When Saturn moved to the middle Tennessee area, there was no established health care network that would meet our needs. This involved a wide geographic area since team members were relocating into this area and settling in all directions from the plant. Some went toward Nashville, where there were extended health care networks. But team members also settled south of the plant toward Alabama, where there were no large population concentrations. In addition, some members were transplants from Kentucky or Alabama facilities, and decided to maintain their homes in those areas and make a long drive to the plant each day. Saturn had to be sure that the network offered to our members could support this geographic dispersion with a high level of quality.

Saturn members were also used to a high level of benefits in GM plans as well as quality health care treatment. They would expect this same standard with any network set up for them in Tennessee. This high standard covered not only primary care facilities but also medical centers, clinics and hospitals.

Finally, the Nashville area boasted established health care facilities in certain specialties that Saturn wanted to take advantage of and offer to our members. Using the claims administrator that Saturn had selected, Metropolitan Life, we began talks with the major middle Tennessee hospitals as well as existing provider networks to develop a network for Saturn team members. It was important that this network be focused on the specific needs of the Saturn community, and be able to influence the health care providers in the area.

These talks ended with the development of the Community Health Consortium, a company formed to provide health care to the Saturn team members and their families. It ties together eight major Nashville facilities, including specialist care facilities, as well as all local hospitals in surrounding middle Tennessee. In addition, it offers team members a wide selection of physicians to choose from as it combines two local area networks of physicians supplemented by some aggressive recruiting of doctors in areas that eventually had a concentration of Saturn members. The consortium, by being a collection of these organizations, enables Saturn to access many different resources to help manage its health care problems. It is the only organization in the area that combines this many competing organizations for the benefit of its members. CHC has been used to address lack of certified care in outlying areas, quality of care of member providers, as well as sanctioning of member doctors who do not comply with the network limitations. The CHC has also became a valued resource in identifying ways to contain the cost of health care in the middle Tennessee area.

Thus far CHC's sole responsibility has been in providing health care for Saturn team members, but in recent years there has been talk of allowing other customers access to this network. This would spread out the costs of the organization as well as increase the network's local influence. Saturn is a voting member of the CHC board and takes an active role in investigating quality control and expanded services for employees.

While the CHC relationship is unique to the Saturn organization, this type of relationship is one that many organizations are finding a need for in an attempt to reduce the growth of health care costs. Health care costs can be influenced on the local level in addition to the national level. There are advantages to the various providers to assure themselves they are meeting a local need, both now and in the future, as well as ensuring that competition is working on the local level. Part of local solutions is being able to work with the business community to identify facility and professional expansion needs in a timely manner. This aligns two major forces (the company and the community) to identify future problems and work together to solve them. These groups can identify the type of provider network that may be needed, and together plan the future of health care in the community.

HOW THE COMPANY INFLUENCES COST

Structure of the Plan

Controlling health care costs can be attributed to three areas of benefit management:

Creation of a flexible benefit plan.

Education of the work force.

Involvement of the work force in the design and implementation of the plan.

A flexible benefit program is one that offers employees a cafeteria selection of coverages to fit many different needs, as well as involving some level of cost sharing with the company. The Saturn flexible plan can cover surgical, medical, dental, vision, vacation, optional and dependent life insurance, and personal accident insurance, as well as healthy lifestyle credits, disability coverages, and health care and dependent care spending accounts. Employees have a choice between HMOs, PPOs, and basic care. They choose the amount of cost sharing, from a minimum to a maximum as defined by out-of-pocket limits, in addition to their purchased level of health care coverage. A flexible benefit plan is structured to take advantage of the existing tax laws that allow pretax spending for benefit expenditures and for pretax spending of an employee's co-payments.

Saturn chose a cafeteria-style plan so that each member could tailor the plan to fit her lifestyle. A single member just out of college needs something different from her benefit plan than a young family with three small children. While health care may be important to one member, additional vacation may appeal to another. A flex plan allows the members to spend their dollars where it best suits their needs.

The work force should be educated in identifying their lifestyle, their health care needs, and the scope and level of coverage for each of the plans as well as their level of risk aversion. Employees should be encouraged to select the appropriate level of coverage to fit their benefit needs. Employees can be given benefit credits or benefit dollars, which they can use to purchase benefits. Purchasing flexible dollars offsets the cost to members and can also reward employees for reducing their spending by returning unspent dollars to the members in cash.

Many different programs are used in flexible benefits plans across the company: credits to employees who lead healthy lifestyles, increased co-pays for dangerous activities (drunk driving, not wearing a seat belt), penalties for employees who are injured in dangerous activities specifically not covered by the plan.

There are no unique provisions offered in the Saturn flexible benefit program, but Saturn has made a conscious decision to ensure that (1) the selections are varied and diverse and (2) Saturn employees are well educated in their role in impacting health care costs. We found that there is a slow learning curve with providers and employees in understanding new and different programs. When changes are made to a plan, they must be communicated well. The need for the change must be explained. If a change in behavior is expected, that should be included in the communication plan. Monitoring is needed to determine if the expected change happens. These results should be communicated to the work force, to keep them involved in the solution.

The Saturn plan gives members flexible dollars equal to $780 plus 2 percent of base salary. On average, the amount of credit dollars given to employees is comparable to a standard GM benefit plan. This formula was developed because it reduces the variation between what members pay for top-of-the-line care. The out-of-pocket expense for any employee to receive top-of-the-line care varies from 1 to 3 percent of base pay. Employees who do not spend all their credit dollars have them returned as cash in their paycheck. Employees are given additional credit dollars if they maintain a healthy lifestyle. This encourages employees to do their part in maintaining healthy lifestyles and reduce the long-term health care cost of the company.

Educating the Work Force

The second and most important control a company has to affect the cost of health care is the time spent educating the work force on their role in impacting the plan cost. Education is not merely to assist enrollment and to ensure that employees select the plan best suited for their needs. It is critical for employees to understand how they can influence the rising cost of health care. This includes what they pay for health care, but also extends into what the company is paying for their health care. This ranges from the advantages of using network providers, to calling for predetermination of treatment when necessary, to understanding how much the company will pay, which exceeds what the member is asked to pay. It also involves providing employees with an explanation of benefits (EOB), so they understand the medical treatment they have received and the associated cost. It means that employees see their health care expenses rise based on their usage, making them the first line of discrimination as to what type of health care treatment is needed. At this level of the process, recipients of health care can question the need and propriety of the treatment they receive. This process involves short, pointed educational classes on the rising cost of health care and the means available to the employee to combat it.

There is more education needed beyond how to get the most out of your company's benefit package, but this is a good start. Employees must understand how their behavior can affect the amount of money spent on health care as well as their share in that cost. This education could range from methods as simple as encouraging employees to use medical network providers, to encouraging employees to check for an after-hours clinic versus using an emergency room. Employees are specifically not discouraged from seeking health care treatment, but rather are encouraged to seek preventative treatment to maintain a high level of wellness. Also, they are encouraged to eliminate discretionary forms of spending on health care or to control the amount of health care dollars that they spend when the opportunity arises—for example, is there a generic drug available, can this surgery be done on an outpatient basis, and if I lift properly, is there less chance of a back injury?

An example where Saturn has educated the work force to be knowledgeable and understand how to use the programs has been in the area of health care spending accounts. Since Saturn moved to a cost sharing plan with our employees, this type of program that lets employees use pretax dollars to pay for health care expenses is a much higher concern to the work force. Only about 2 percent of the work force had utilized spending accounts prior to moving to a flexible benefits plan. With education and awareness of the advantages to the employee of the spending accounts, particularly for a pretax expense, that percentage increased to 14 percent of the work force in the first year of the plan, 20 percent in the second year, and currently 27 percent of the work force. We continue to emphasize the advantages of these cost saving opportunities to our employees.

Creating a work force that is concerned and interested in the cost of the health care package is essential. This means spending time educating and training all the employees in how to best use their health care plan. Employees are very interested in tips on how *not* to spend more money. You might create a forum where employees can discuss the company benefits and how to use them efficiently. This creates an open environment, and employees share their experience and lend credibility to the idea that all benefit plans were not created equal. Examples of this type of assistance include advice on (1) what expenses are eligible for reimbursement from flexible spending accounts and (2) how to use the local community health care program to cover the cost of child immunizations.

Although these are very commonsense approaches, many employees and dependents have never had to look at the cost of health care, and lack the knowledge to challenge the costs. Helpful ideas and suggestions to the employees are very welcome as a means to help them decide how to reduce health care costs. This education is accomplished in many different forms. Leaders are educated as an additional resource to members. The main thrust to the work force is a two-to-three–hour presentation each year to tell members the changes in the coming year. In addition, topics of interest are selected such as how to best use their health care plan, how to use a spending account, and how to get the most out of the vision plan if they wear contact lenses. Education is Saturn's key to success in maintaining health care costs. Saturn is teaching employees to be knowledgeable and to maintain costs, while at the same time explaining to employees the need for plan design changes that affect their plan cost.

Involving the Work Force

The third effort of cost containment is to make the work force an integral part in the design of the health care plan. To facilitate this, employees offer suggestions or modifications to the program each year based on their own experience. This can be accomplished as a task force or in the form of benefit representatives from the work force at large. Involving work force representatives has furthered our educational objectives as well.

This employee group at Saturn is responsible to review the current plan, look at health care trends within the industry to ensure our plans remain competitive, review current and forecasted cost increases, and explore suggestions that have been submitted by other employees.

Since benefits is a very specialized area, there is a good chance that the company will spend quite a bit of time in training and educating this group of employees, but the team can then be given the freedom to help make some of the tough decisions involving health care costs. The group can be empowered to make decisions that help general understanding as well as implementation among a potentially diverse work group. The employees are given guidelines about the limits of the plan, and are then allowed to make innovative and responsive suggestions. This type of forum has provided a credible voice to members that the plan is competitive, is cost-effective, and identifies abuses, which allows peer pressure to begin to work.

The task force can also review enrollment in existing plans and gauge how well these plans suit the work force. Finally, the task force can review carriers for quality of service, customer satisfaction, and cost-effectiveness.

This is how many benefit changes at Saturn are developed. A volunteer cross-functional team of employees, representing the work force at large, forms a benefit task force concerned about the outcome on the members of the program. This allows the group the freedom to develop solutions from a multidisciplined approach. The task force is given parameters to operate the benefits plan as a small business would: the cost increases of benefit changes cannot cause the price of the car (our product) to become uncompetitive, and the benefits to the employees must be prioritized and weighted. In other words, this task force must weigh the cost of the changes versus the benefits to the employees.

Suggestions considered in the past include increasing preventative care coverages to 100 percent (reducing co-pays for this type of coverage) to encourage usage, providing long-term (elder) care to employees and their dependents, expanding well baby care, increasing pretax savings options, raising wellness credits for healthy employees, and providing employees with prescription drug EOBs to help educate them about the rising cost of prescription drugs. In addition, Saturn has implemented a hospital bill audit program that (1) rewards employees for finding and correcting errors on hospital bills and (2) allows employees to receive a discount on mail order noncovered prescription drugs to encourage them to use the mail order prescription drug program.

This task force method of modifying a plan is time consuming, as most employees have little knowledge of the tax laws that structure benefit plans. A great amount of time is spent educating the members of the task force. But there are many advantages to going through this type of employee review each year. It allows employees who are concerned about the benefit program to have a peer present to represent their concerns. It lets employees become part of the decision making process addressing a very important part of their daily lives. There is much energy and concern from most work forces in the benefits areas. There is also knowledge that, with the task force, team members can affect and influence their program as the need arises. This ability to make changes to the program keeps employees interested and involved in the benefit plan. Also, they know that if they are going to be involved in cost sharing, they must understand how to control cost.

RESULTS

When Saturn implemented its benefit plan, the intent was for the new plan to be comparable in cost to the existing General Motors plan. Our objective was to understand the effects of moving to a flex benefit program and not to immediately change the scope or definition of the plan.

However, during the first year of the program Saturn's health care costs decreased 7 percent while GM's rose 8 to 12 percent.

Based on this information the first task force recommended a reduction in health care costs to employees in the following plan
year. This reduction was followed in the next year by a slight increase of 3 percent in costs, followed again by decreasing costs in
1993, so that Saturn's current employee health care costs are less
than the 1991 cost. This change from the national trend of rising
costs was welcome information to the employees and helped
them understand that cost sharing can also reduce the cost of
health care.

Another plus for the program was that in 1991–92, employee
benefits was a major employee concern as expressed in a member
survey. Members were concerned with change and feared that
they would be held responsible for rising health care costs.
Through education and member involvement in the program, as
described here, in the survey for 1994, benefits were listed as an
item the employees were by then comfortable with.

AREAS OF CONCERN

Be aware that there can be strong opposition from dissenting
forces. Some people do not want to know the details of the plans;
they want a plan that costs them little and covers their needs to
the fullest. They believe there have been too many benefit take-
aways, and they are not receptive to further changes. This is
where trust in the company is important. Employees must believe
that the company is looking out for their best interests. In addition, the employees must have the best interest of the company in
mind when they recommend changes to the package. The goal is
for both employees and the company to remain competitive to ensure that both individual and company goals are met.

It is important to understand how this information is received
by the work force. Many employees are concerned about the rising
cost of health care and the trend toward shifting the increase in the
cost burden from the company to the individual. Educating employees assists in these areas also. Primarily, it helps employees understand that the rising cost of health care is creating a crisis within
the United States. Shifting the burden of costs to the larger industrialized companies has been a solution up until now, but is not
one that can continue and allow the automotive industry to remain

competitive. More than ever before, a company's work force is aware of the issues surrounding health care and of the repercussions of corporate and national policy decisions that affect business and industry.

There is a definite advantage in having a knowledgeable and interested work force. Employees see that problems are identified and are addressed. There is a constant stream of questions and suggestions as Saturn employees gain a better understanding of the issues. This requires a close relationship with Saturn employees so management can understand their problems and concerns and return a constant flow of information to the employees about the plans.

In summary, there are no easy answers or quick fixes that will reduce a company's future health care costs. Educating and training the work force requires time, commitment, and more than an annual brochure. Besides the financial portion of the equation, rationales behind why decisions are made must be explained and understood. This hurdle is not always easy, and there are many concerns about the people side of the benefits issue. But the ability to educate and inform a company's work force encourages them to voice new concerns, stay current in industry trends, talk to associates for new approaches to similar dilemmas, and become a part of the team. In fact, simply stated, benefits can be a win–win situation for both parties!

Finally, the community and the health care providers must take an aggressive approach to managing costs and the options available within their resources to address them. It is critical that the company be a part of the process to develop a community solution to ensure that the many diverse needs of all parties are considered.

⑥ FINANCIAL MANAGEMENT RELATIONSHIPS

15

⑥ SUPPLY CHAIN MANAGEMENT

The Role and Responsibilities of the CFO

Alfred J. Battaglia
Group President, Becton Dickinson

Beyond being expert in financial matters, it is imperative that the high-performance CFO understand the *business processes* that are critical to organizational success as well as his or her responsibilities in this regard. Business processes cut across an organization's functional and departmental boundaries. An obvious example is the product development process. Product development is not an R&D function. It is, in fact, a multifunctional process that requires effective integration of several functions in addition to R&D including, but not limited to, marketing, manufacturing, finance, logistics, and law.

Among the most important business processes in most manufacturing companies are the systems and tools used to develop, produce, sell, process orders, and deliver products. They also include processes to allocate an organization's shared resources—most notably, financial, information technology, and human resources. This chapter addresses the concepts and value of supply chain management (SCM) and the role and responsibilities of the CFO in formulating, supporting, and implementing SCM. To begin, SCM is defined as

> An integrating process, used to build competitive position, based on the delivery to customers of basic and unexpected services. Led by senior operating executives, SCM optimizes information and product flows from the purchase of raw materials to the delivery

(and disposal) of finished goods with a vision of achieving significant strategic objectives involving productivity, quality, innovative services, and alliances. Total SCM includes the implementation of sales and marketing activities to share the benefits with all of the participants in the supply chain.

Supply chain management has evolved from the excellent work by Michael Porter, who describes the *value chain* as the basic tool for disaggregating a firm (and its trading partners) into its relevant activities in order to better understand costs and sources of differentiation.

As firms have begun to implement value chain concepts and techniques, SCM has evolved as the strategic management approach to organization, integrating, and operating business activities. In its basic form, SCM is a strategic concept that involves understanding and managing the sequence of activities—from supplier to manufacturer to customer—that add value to the product supply pipeline. Since these activities are often "cross-functional" or transcend traditional departments, SCM represents a new initiative—and a new challenge—for many companies.

Some companies have adopted the term *logistics* to represent an SCM initiative. Others term it *product supply* or *value chain management*. However, SCM means much more than these terms. In fact, to implement world-class SCM, a company must define its strategy, select an implementation framework, resolve how it wants to manage change, and commit to work over a long period of time to achieve these levels of operational effectiveness. The CFO must understand these concepts to support them. This support, as will be explained in this chapter, involves building on the concepts, finding approval, and directly assisting in implementing certain SCM programs. These four actions can be characterized as follows:

- *Strategy.* What strategic trends are being faced that give rise to new management approaches? Generally, strategic responses fall into one of two categories: (1) reactive, when competitors' actions increase customer satisfaction, are recognized as points of differentiation, and thus become threats or (2) proactive, when new opportunities are identified to lead the company's industry segment. An example of the latter is identifying customers' "unmet needs" and responding with tailored, value-added services. In either case, a significant degree of dissatisfaction must be present to *implement* a new management approach. Dissatisfaction, however, is not enough. A company must also have a *vision* of where it would like to be—and a plan to get there.

- *Implementation framework.* What is the best implementation approach? In this chapter, I will describe an implementation framework (a conceptual "blueprint") used by a few leading companies. Because each company is unique, the blueprint must be tailored to meet individual needs. In any event, *all* elements of the framework must be addressed.

- *Change management.* By definition, the SCM initiative will require (and cause) significant changes. How should the management of change—organizational, functional, and behavioral—be addressed? This issue is complex but critical for success. The Total Quality Management process, now so prevalent in U.S. industry, is often adopted as the change platform, although other approaches also exist.

- *Performance measurement.* This is an area of particular significance to the CFO. How should SCM performance be measured to reflect the value of the new approaches? Traditional measures of departmental or functional activity, product cost, or service cost are not as meaningful in the SCM context. SCM performance involves expected gains in such business measures as *total* cost savings, market share, cash flow, return on assets, and service improvement—all by product, by market, and by customer. This means identifying new critical success factors and performance measures that will be evaluated across the business.

The manner in which these areas are addressed, and refined over time, will determine the effectiveness of implementation. If either the strategy, framework, change process, or performance measures are inadequate, it is my experience that the implementation of SCM will not achieve the desired results. On the other

EXHIBIT   15.1

Contribution of Service Quality to Relative Performance

	Low Third in Service Quality	High Third in Service Quality	Difference in % Points
Price index relative to competition	−2%	7%	+9%
Change in market share per annum	−2%	6%	+8%
Sales growth per annum	8%	17%	+9%
Return on sales	−1%	12%	+11%

Source: Strategic Planning Institute, Cambridge, Mass.

hand, proper management attention to these areas, coupled with relentless executive commitment and leadership, can yield powerful results. For example, as reported by Philip Kotler in his classic textbook, *Marketing Management*, companies that provide high-quality *service* will outperform their less service-oriented competitors. Exhibit 15.1 provides data to support this conclusion. The Strategic Planning Institute selected several industries and, within each, sorted out the top third and the bottom third of the business units according to customer ratings of "relative perceived service quality." The exhibit shows that the high-service businesses managed to charge more, grow faster, and make more profits on the strength of their superior service quality.

In addition, by achieving the highest levels of quality in all areas that determine interorganizational operational effectiveness, a few leading companies are reaching new heights of performance. For example,

- Procter & Gamble has estimated that up to $500 million in operating costs savings are possible.
- Bergen Brunswig—a major distributor of pharmaceuticals and health care products—has achieved a remarkable 12-hour order-cycle time (the amount of time from when an order is placed until it is delivered to the customer).
- Xerox Corporation achieved cost reductions of 12 percent and improvements in inventory turns of 30 percent.

- Many companies, including Becton Dickinson (BD), are building stronger productive long-term relations with trading partners.

SCM AND THE MANUFACTURING COMPANY

One element of a manufacturing company's competitive strength is a strong base of proprietary, technology-based products. Nonetheless, because of the role that *service* can plan in a *manufacturing* company's strategy, Becton Dickinson identified the opportunity to implement an SCM strategy. BD realized that with services it could enhance its products' value to customers. However, it was determined that SCM had to be viewed as an operating function at every organizational level in the company. In other words, executives at the corporate headquarters, divisions, and plants needed to develop jointly and implement the SCM program.

Understanding the rationale for a manufacturer's SCM initiative begins with the belief that having the best *products* is not enough. These quality products need to be delivered where and when the customer wants them—with near perfect administrative and physical quality. Such delivery is one of many customer expectations. These expectations may be called "basic services." BD's goal is to achieve *basic service excellence*—not only regarding logistical services, but also for all the other services provided along with its medical device and diagnostic products. As BD moves toward achieving basic service excellence, it can also satisfy needs that customers may not expect the company to serve. Providing an unexpected service that customers value is the definition of a *value-added service*.

SUPPLY CHAIN MANAGEMENT FRAMEWORK— THE SCM PYRAMID

Given the importance of communicating new concepts to several layers of management, it was very important that a conceptual framework be developed to guide the process. Several Becton Dickinson executives were familiar with the well-known McKinsey "7 S" model which includes these seven factors: shared values, strategy, structure, systems, staff, style, and skills.

Starting with this conceptual framework and adding additional factors, we created a useful framework called the Supply Chain Management Pyramid. (See Exhibit 15.2). This model is being used by BD in its efforts to implement leading edge SCM in the health care industry. This goal has become one of our company's most important "shared values" and is represented as the top layer of the pyramid. I will discuss each layer, giving specific examples using our (as well as other companies') experiences and will highlight concerns of particular relevance to the CFO. There are three points to emphasize as an introduction:

1. The "blocks" in the framework are excellent representations of basic building blocks for most businesses. Of course, each company will have its own unique factors that must be taken into consideration in implementing SCM.
2. The framework should be used as a checklist or a discussion outline by a multifunctional team to explore the advantages and implementation of SCM. Some discussion questions are suggested.
3. With most blocks in the pyramid, I do not describe how to implement each step. For example, it is beyond the scope of this chapter to explain how a company determines which services its customers want.

BASIC ELEMENTS OF SCM

Supply chain management really comes down to two steps:

1. Developing and producing the products and the services customers want.
2. Delivering these products and services on a timely, effective basis.

It is important to consider each of these straightforward statements very carefully. First, note that this is a customer-driven strategy. The road to successful implementation of SCM begins with a commitment to serving the customer by *everyone* in the organization.

It may also seem obvious that "service" is an automatic element of a company's product offering to its customers. I reject this notion. It is not an exaggeration to suggest that we are facing a

Supply Chain Management Pyramid

Shared Values — Implement world-class supply chain management in the health care industry

Measurements

Supplier performance	Manufacturing performance	Capacity utilization	Inventory investment	Cost-effectiveness	Service levels	Customer satisfaction

Staff/Skills/Style

Ensure adequate staff resources	Build required skills	Create multifunctional integrated teamwork approach

Subsystems

Forecasting	Capacity planning	Production and vendor scheduling	Inventory status	MRP	Warehouse management	Lead time management	Logistics maps	Order management

Master Systems

Business planning systems	MRP systems	DRP systems	Customer service systems

Structure

Suppliers	Marketing	Logistics	Manufacturing	Transportation	Internal distribution	Sales administration	Distributors	Health Care providers

← Information technology →

Policies/Objectives

Inventory	Manufacturing	Purchasing	Distribution	Transportation	Product handling	Service level

Strategies

Customer and supplier alliances	Superior relative quality	Productivity/Cost effectiveness	Innovative products and services	Best customer service in the industry

Basic Elements

Develop and produce the products and services our customers want	Deliver these products and services on a timely basis

service crisis in this country. That is the bad news. The good news is that many companies are "stepping up to the plate" and addressing the service issue. We are in the midst of an awakening as to the importance of service. Progressive companies are using service to build competitive position. One of the most obvious services performed by a manufacturing company is the logistical process of delivering its products in an outstandingly effective manner—where, when, and how each customer wants them.

As a senior member of the management team, the CFO needs to help ensure that the company is customer-focused and, if the company produces a product, the CFO must also understand the role that service plays in building competitive advantage. One way to accomplish this is to visit your customers—spend a few days every year working with a salesperson in the field.

SCM STRATEGIES

A strategy is basically a comprehensive plan to achieve a specific goal. In order to achieve SCM goals, it is necessary, through business planning systems, to identify and document the required strategies. For example, Becton Dickinson has identified five strategic areas to be addressed:

1. Customer and supplier alliances.
2. Superior relative quality.
3. Productivity/cost-effectiveness.
4. Innovative products and services.
5. Best customer service in the industry.

Customer and Supplier Alliances

In order to manage the supply chain most effectively, progressive companies are beginning to address their relationships with suppliers and customers. They realize that the chain begins and ends with these players. Traditional ways of interacting with suppliers can often be characterized as adversarial and must be changed to a partnership or alliance relationship based on trust, cooperation, and teamwork. These relationships tend to produce win–win outcomes.

With regard to customer alliances, among the most common problems facing businesses today are challenges to selling prices.

This has given rise to the notion of "value-added selling," which involves a central theme of moving customers away from only price by considering how a company's total offering can add real value to its customers and its customers' customers.

With regard to building supplier partnerships, many companies have begun a process through which the qualifications of key suppliers of raw materials, parts, supplies, capital equipment, and services are being reviewed to examine the total cost and strategic advantages of reaching new agreements with fewer suppliers. These agreements have already yielded benefits in terms of improved quality, lower cost, lower inventories and, not to be underestimated, significantly improved day-to-day working relationships. Also, these ideas apply equally well to internal customers throughout the organization.

Superior Relative Quality

The competitive necessity and advantages of offering superior relative quality are well understood in the business community because of the exposure and discussion of these important topics over the past several years. The key question is whether manufacturing companies have applied quality concepts to their *service* offering. This is being done by many companies in several industries. For example, the automobile industry heavily promotes its quality vehicles ("At Ford, quality is job one.") and has begun to promote the service that goes along with the automobile (for example, 24-hour road service). Quality standards can be applied to logistical operations just as easily as manufacturing operations. Specific quality standards should be developed covering such areas as transportation and warehousing. For example, do product handling and storage specifications exist in your warehouses? What is an acceptable shipping container? The strategic approach of *continuous improvement* in service quality must be promulgated by supply chain leadership.

Productivity and Cost-Effectiveness

This is another strategy that does not require substantial explanation. Historical approaches to the management of purchasing, materials management, transportation, warehousing, and so on have traditionally emphasized minimizing costs. These "staff" departments have been treated only as cost centers. Progressive companies and their CFOs are now beginning to realize that total cost must be addressed. More importantly, these companies are converting and integrating these functions into customer-driven operations that contribute to the achievement of competitive advantage. Yet, there are significant financial benefits to a greater commitment to managing costs throughout the supply chain. Several studies indicate that total cost reductions from 5 to 30 percent or more are possible through SCM. At Becton Dickinson, one example of benefits derived is the success of a joint effort with a key distributor which led to a 36 percent reduction in inventory, while simultaneously improving services from 94 to 98 percent order fill.

Innovative Products and Services

Innovation is not only the province of product development. Given the appropriate strategic direction, companies have come to realize that innovative service can be developed and implemented through the supply chain. For example, more suppliers are pre-inspecting and guaranteeing the quality of their component parts. Freight companies have begun to guarantee scheduled deliveries. Market research in the service area is just as feasible and desirable as it is in the product area. Yet, how many manufacturers assemble a focus group of key customers to brainstorm how to improve logistical services or to identify services that would be of value to the customer?

Best Customer Service in the Industry

The important point here is that a specific strategy must be developed and communicated through the entire company if customer service is going to receive more than lip service. Here again, this may appear to be obvious, but the question remains, Can a company achieve outstanding SCM without an *explicit* strategy to have the best customer service in its industry?

Obviously, the high-performance CFO will play a major role in developing strategy. Too many CFOs concentrate on only productivity and cost-effectiveness strategies. Many CFOs have come to realize the importance of building alliances with supply chain partners and the rewards of higher relative quality. Far fewer

CFOs can verbalize the importance of service innovation and the significance of customer service for their businesses.

POLICIES AND OBJECTIVES OF SCM

Strategy development is incomplete without specific measurable objectives. Many companies express these objectives in the form of policies. How should objectives be set? Some companies use benchmarking techniques to compare themselves with outstanding performers both within and outside their industries. However, it is at this point in the pyramid that many companies begin to fall short of the best practices that lead to superior SCM. To be sure, most companies have specific inventory objectives and policies. If there were no other reasons, the visibility on financial statements as well as the carrying costs focus attention on inventory levels. Also, many companies have articulated specific manufacturing policies regarding, for example, capacity utilization.

It is my experience that some companies have ignored areas involving transportation, logistics, and customer service. For example, are there specific inspection criteria for trailers and containers? What conditions are deemed to be unsatisfactory regarding transportation equipment? How are proper pallet loading procedures defined? What are the procedures for handling visibly damaged products? What is the policy regarding the stacking of pallets? In the area of customer service, what policies empower individuals who deal directly with customers to respond to customer concerns and problems? Do specific objectives exist for complete order fill, line item fill, and cycle time?

Even if a company has its full range of policies and objectives, an important challenge exists: how to balance the inevitable trade-offs that need to be made. If manufacturing policy is determined only by manufacturing, for example, it is possible that capacity utilization will tend to be high, even if excess inventory exists. On the other hand, if customer service goals are determined by the marketing department alone, this may place unacceptable burdens on manufacturing or yield unacceptable inventory investment levels to the finance department. Someone or some function (in this best-case scenario) must be held responsible for recommending solutions to these trade-off issues. I will address this question.

MEASUREMENTS

This pyramid layer, perhaps more than the others, is of particular relevance to the CFO. In many organizations, the CFO either directly or indirectly, significantly influences the measurements used in the organization. Having understood the importance and relevance of the concepts addressed up to this point, the CFO is in a position to ensure that the appropriate non-financial metrics are being used by his or her company.

Whether or not specific policies and objectives exist, all companies measure and control many elements of their businesses. Because of its visibility, inventory is actively managed, and inventory or service levels are consistently measured. However, it is interesting to note that many companies are not able to measure, within a reasonable time frame, inventory or service levels by specific catalog number. Yet it is principally at this level that corrective actions can be initiated.

Manufacturing cost is another area that is actively managed. Here again, it is my experience that measurements involving performance-to-schedule and capacity utilization, for example, are often ignored. Some companies actively manage supplier performance. These companies are able to determine which suppliers are most reliable, are most accurate, and provide the best overall service and value. A new measurement involves customer satisfaction studies or customer service audits. Interestingly, these studies have shifted from only measuring customer satisfaction with the product itself to measuring all aspects of the customer interaction with the company, including service. Very often, companies determine that their measurements involving customer service are inadequate. The CFO, as a senior executive, should insist that order cycle time, fill rates, or whatever measures are appropriate for his or her business exist and are being used.

Most companies that have rigorously developed specific strategic SCM objectives and then compared these long-term goals with current measurements have determined that there is a significant gap. How can we close the gap between where we are and where we would like to be? The answer to this question rests with a better understanding of the remaining layers in the pyramid, which address structure, systems, staff, skills, and style.

STRUCTURE

The road to implementing SCM begins by accepting the fact that SCM is more than logistics, materials management, purchasing, and transportation. In the health care industry, the "structure" addressing supply chain opportunities *starts* with suppliers and *concludes* with health care providers and other end users. In leading companies, internal functions (especially marketing and manufacturing) play an important role in SCM. If this notion is accepted, internal as well as external alliances can be more easily formed to create optimal results.

Most companies are missing a major opportunity to gain maximum advantage from their SCM strategy because they do not involve their sales and marketing functions actively enough in their implementation programs. Viewing the features and benefits of service offerings as "service products" can be a very powerful, thought-provoking analogy. Shouldn't sales and marketing people be involved in promoting and selling our service products? It makes no sense to achieve basic service excellence (for example, the most reliable delivery system in the industry) or to create unexpected new value-added services (for example, electronic data interchange capabilities) and then not obtain the appropriate return for these services in the form of higher sales, market share, and profitability.

It is important to realize that most other functions are involved, at least indirectly, in SCM. We have highlighted the importance of market research and quality assurance. Later, in the description of staff and skills, the importance of human resources will become evident. For one other example; it is ironic that facilities and engineering management will plan manufacturing sites with excruciating care where a product is produced in minutes, but then virtually ignore the warehousing sites where products can be held for weeks and shipments delayed by days because of poor design!

A function receiving much attention, especially for its role in building competitive advantage, is information technology (IT). Since the IT function often reports to the CFO, my observations about IT and systems should be of significant relevance to the CFO. If effective SCM is a "business within a business," then its "R&D" and a large part of the "operations" functions are provided through IT. To state this more strongly, information flows are just as important as product flows. In leading companies, costly inventory is being replaced by timely information. Therefore, IT is fast becoming the backbone technology of SCM. In addition, there is an enormous opportunity to have SCM act as a functional integrator if it is properly managed. The senior executive responsible for SCM activities must be able to work with and gain the cooperation from several functions.

SYSTEMS

There are four master systems directly involved in SCM: business planning systems, customer service systems, manufacturing resource planning (MRP) systems, and distribution resources planning (DRP) systems.

Business Planning Systems

I stated that specific strategies to implement SCM must be developed. Strategy development is part of a planning system and covers both near-term and longer-term time horizons. Most companies issue guidelines and standard procedures that the organization follows for executing its planning activities. I believe that it is very useful to include specific guidelines regarding SCM concepts. Here are some specific examples:

- In the review of competitors' performance, it should be suggested that the operating unit go beyond an analysis of the competitors' products and include an analysis of each competitors' service capabilities.
- During planning activities, we list our customers' desires for product features, assign a weighted value to each, and compare ourselves with our competitors. Planning systems should include the same type of analysis of customer service needs. The more "commoditylike" a product offering is, the more important the service aspect will be in achieving customer acceptance.
- In the annual plan guidelines, we often identify specific financial objectives. Should we not also include a requirement that specific nonfinancial objectives (such as the service metrics previously discussed) be established which support our supply chain management initiatives?

Customer Service Systems

As stated earlier, SCM is customer-driven. Hence, it is appropriate that we address those systems that most directly interface with the customer. In order management systems, order entry deserves significant attention. It may be obvious that it is common sense to make it as easy as possible for a customer to place an order! But, do we make it easy? To be sure, many companies have been very creative about implementing state-of-the-art order entry systems. One area receiving particular attention is electronic data interchange (EDI). At Becton Dickinson, for example, more than 70 percent of U.S. sales are transmitted electronically into one computer and then electronically sent to operating units. Interestingly, leading-edge companies are also exploring ways of connecting "internal" customers electronically as a means of more efficiently and effectively managing their information flow requirements.

As we consider systems, it is important to emphasize that I am not only referring to *computer* systems. There are many organizational systems. For example, it is critical that compensation incentive systems be aligned with business strategies and goals. For a manufacturing company, if product availability and service are important to competitive position, manufacturing bonus programs must take this business need into consideration. If these executives are rewarded and recognized only by reducing their plant costs, the company's customers will probably experience service failures.

Another example worth discussing in more detail involves lead time management. One of the highest payoff opportunities in SCM is to reduce the total time between the customer order and delivery. Not only will the customer be better served by rapid response time, but also the supplier will be able to remove significant inventories from the supply chain and provide more flexible service. Logistics "maps" have proven almost indispensable in documenting information and product flows for specific product lines. These maps are essentially flowcharts that depict every location, starting with raw material and concluding with the customer, where inventory is kept or is in transit. The map should also reflect information such as the average transit time between locations and the average day's supply and value of inventory at each location.

After these maps are created, it is more feasible for a multi-functional, multiorganizational team to formulate ways to reduce leadtime and, in doing so, achieve benefits as previously described. This process may not be as easy as it may appear. If the supply chain has never been documented in this manner, chances are that no one department would be capable of creating the map without assistance. This implies that several people from various locations may have to come together to go through the effort of creating the map. Furthermore, it may not be obvious to each of these departments (especially in different organizations) why they should take the time, unless the "vision" of implementing SCM is promulgated. Without a vision, each operating unit will do its best locally to optimize its own results. This translates into additional buffer stocks and an overly conservative time schedule—all of which add up to less than optimal results and, in the worst case, disastrous results. The CFO can play an important role in supporting the preparation and use of logistics maps.

Manufacturing Resources Planning (MRP) Systems

It is well beyond the scope of this chapter to describe MRP systems in any detail. However, it is important to realize that MRP must be integrated into overall SCM implementation. It is my experience that significant opportunities for improvement exist by simply doing a better job of integrating customer and manufacturing requirements. The body of systems that can accomplish this goal most effectively are often called distribution resources planning (DRP) systems.

Distribution Resources Planning (DRP) Systems

I have stressed that several functions should be actively involved in SCM. To repeat, the risks of managing each function separately are significant:

- Customer service suffers unnecessarily.
- Each location attempts to compensate for uncertainty by carrying excess inventory.

- Production, product sourcing, and distribution activities are subjected to wide variations in demand that are managed at significant additional costs.
- Under these circumstances, business is conducted in a reactive mode, scrambling to avoid lost sales and/or damage to customer relationships.

The value of DRP-based SCM is that the process itself can create an integrated, internally consistent view of market requirements. Properly executed, all functions are involved in managing the supply chain in a more cooperative, collaborative manner. This managerial style is a vital element of successful implementation, as I discuss later.

STAFF AND SKILLS

Implementation of world-class SCM will require a significant investment in staff resources. The originators of the 7 S model defined staff to mean the "demographic" description of important personnel categories. For example, some organizations are known to be led by technical personnel, whereas others may be dominated by staff who are marketing or financial types. Very few companies would identify logistics or customer service personnel among their top five categories. Worse, if these activities are viewed basically as cost centers and a necessary evil, some firms may inadvertently create ineffectiveness by underestimating the potential contribution of this operating function and, therefore, underinvest in it.

The body of knowledge and the skills required to operate in a more effective manner have become more complex. Although some fundamental questions remain the same (What will we sell? What do we have? What do we need?), the advent of global markets, foreign competition, more demanding customers, and the realization of greater strategic benefits of service—to name just a few of the significant environmental factors impacting SCM—all demand better and stronger skills. Realizing that firms must invest in stronger staff and skills to achieve world-class SCM is a major milestone that must be verbalized and believed by senior management, especially the CFO.

STYLE

An organization's style may be described as how key managers behave in achieving their organizational goals. It is sometimes referred to as the company's "culture." With SCM (and, for that matter, all business processes), excellence cannot be achieved without creating a multifunctional, integrated teamwork culture. In most companies, this will require a significant change. Change management skills must be learned and implemented by senior management. The probability of achieving the required culture is significantly enhanced as the various S's are properly implemented. For example, if management creates, as an important shared value, the vision of implementing SCM, energetically communicates its vision, backs it up by developing specific strategies supported by rigorous policy and objective initiatives, modifies measurements, and ensures that staff, systems, and skills are in place to understand and be rewarded, then there is a greater probability that the teamwork approach is headed in the right direction.

AN EIGHTH S—SYNERGY

The preceding comments regarding style suggest that there is another S to consider, namely synergy. Synergy may be defined simply as a group of independent people (or activities) coming together for a common cause to achieve a specific goal—and in coming together achieve results that are greater than the sum of their parts. If the essence of organizational analysis resides in the 7 S's, then the essence of management art is to ensure a proper fit so that the 7 S's complement, support, and reinforce one another. I have made reference to our belief that even well-managed, but discrete, activities will yield less than optimal results and could actually cause significant adverse effects. For example, a strategy involving the development of the best customer service in your industry without the appropriate systems, staff, or skills is not achievable. Or, as mentioned earlier, manufacturing, inventory, and customer service policies must be analyzed and trade-offs must be made.

Who will lead this effort? Before the effort can be led, who will undertake the challenge to develop a vision and firm understanding of supply chain management as I have described it?

Surely, we cannot expect that a miracle will happen whereby everyone in the structure suddenly comes to realize that by working together, significant competitive advantage can be gained. Nor is it reasonable to expect that the chief executive officer or the chief operating officer can take on this leadership responsibility alone—especially in large organizations.

It is my belief that a new operating function should be created that will lead the organization toward world-class SCM. Which functions are the breeding ground of these new supply chain executives? This new breed of manager could logically arise from operations and manufacturing—which are probably the sources of the limited number of visionaries who exist today. However, it is my opinion that there is significant opportunity for managers and executives who are currently in the logistics, materials management, customer service, or management information systems functions to rise to this new level of leadership. For this to happen, this group of executives must achieve a new plateau of academic and business experience. This will involve a significant effort and commitment well beyond what has been demonstrated to date.

CONCLUSION

The examples of significant benefits represent compelling reasons for more companies to commit to achieving and sustaining excellence in SCM. There is little doubt that substantial opportunities exist for tangible improvements in operating costs, inventory savings, time-based competition, customer service, service quality, management information, and ultimately competitive position.

Several management concepts and approaches have been described that may seem obvious. Achieving better quality, higher productivity, faster throughput, quicker market response, and best customer service has become a competitive mandate for every U.S. manufacturer. In my opinion, only a small percentage of U.S. (and, for that matter, non-U.S.) manufacturers are well into strategies and implementation programs that are resulting in their gaining ground from their current positions.

New leadership roles among operations executives are required to gain the synergies necessary for effective SCM implementation. Accordingly, a new operating function should be established.

In my view this step is critical if companies seek to hasten the pace of execution. In each case where SCM benefits are being realized, a driving organizational leadership focus is in place or is evolving.

This chapter concludes by emphasizing the same major points with which it started: The high-performance CFO must gain a greater understanding of the business processes that must be executed in an outstanding fashion, first, to survive the onslaught of continuous competitive and environmental pressures and, second, to build and sustain competitive position. Today's CFO must assist his or her CEO and his peer senior management in analyzing and implementing these important ideas.

16

⑥ PARTNERING FOR PERFORMANCE©SM

Martin G. Mand
Chairman and President, Mand Associates, Limited (a consulting, writing and lecturing firm), Wilmington, Delaware, and Executive Vice President and Chief Financial Officer, Northern Telecom Limited, Toronto, Ontario (Retired)

In today's very competitive, complex, government-regulated world, the chief financial officer and his or her Finance team are uniquely situated to help their companies and individual business units achieve their goals and objectives.[1] But this can only be done effectively if (1) businesses can overcome their traditional reluctance to involve the Finance team in their decision-making and (2) businesses view the Finance team as a full and equal partner, not just a supplier of services. This means that Finance must have a new mind-set as to its role in an organization.

Why have businesses been reluctant to involve Finance? Justified or not, they have traditionally viewed Finance as the custodian of the company's assets and as a historical financial reporter; in other words, just keep the books and report the numbers. (Have you ever heard of members of the Finance team referred to as bean counters or green–eye-shade clerks?) In addition, there has

---

© Mand Associates, Limited, 1995.

SM "Partnering for Performance" and "Partners for Performance" are service marks of Mand Associates, Limited.

1 Although this chapter covers many issues in the context of profit-making business situations, the concepts are equally applicable to all organizations, profit or nonprofit, private or government, small or large. All organizations have two common characteristics: (1) They were established for a purpose and have objectives to achieve that purpose. (2) They have finances. (In its simplest form, finances means revenues must exceed or equal expenditures, or the organization will cease to exist, no matter how worthwhile the purpose.)

been a fear that Finance will tell senior corporate management (including the chief executive officer) of issues or plans before the businesses are ready to do so—call it a lack of trust!

When Finance personnel have become involved, often only because company policies require their participation, they have been viewed as junior players or as simply the doer of certain tasks ("just grind the numbers") or as "rubber stampers" called on to give their blessing (as may be required by the corporate bureaucracy). This limited participation is not what I call "Partnering for Performance"SM and not a recipe for success.

Finance teams are not free of guilt for these traditional views of businesspeople! Indeed, this predicament was more than likely created by their behavior. How many times has Finance told a businessperson he or she could *not* do something the businessperson thought was right for the business? Perhaps they said no because (1) it violated company policies and procedures, (2) it would have adverse tax effects, (3) it was against the law, or (4) you name the other reasons. More importantly, when giving such "negative" advice to businesspeople, did Finance ever say, "Tell me what you are trying to achieve so that I can help you do so"?

Similarly, does anyone doubt that Finance of the past told senior corporate management of issues or plans they learned about within a business unit when such issues or plans were still embryonic and under development by the businesspeople—and that as a result, such senior corporate people got involved prematurely to the great displeasure of the businesspeople?

Beyond the relationship issues, there is another reason why Finance has traditionally been absent from the business decision-making table. Many businesspeople have not invited them because they—that is, the businesspeople—believe they fully understand finances and have no need for Finance specialists. Why is this so? Simple. Each of us, regardless of what we do in life, has personal finances—we collect our paycheck, pay the bills, reconcile the checkbook, borrow money (as in a mortgage for the home), and save or invest (as in call your broker). What more could there be to the finance field that we haven't had exposure to in our personal lives? So, why invite in a Finance specialist? No doubt he or she will contribute little that we don't know and may even create problems we don't need.

Getting from this past to the future I envision where businesses (1) eagerly seek the Finance Team's participation at the beginning stages of any activity, (2) welcome Finance as a true partner in their endeavors, and (3) achieve the results they desire due in part to Finance's involvement. But this requires both the business units and Finance to change behavior and past practices. My views as to how this can be done follow.

BELIEFS

People with different viewpoints attempting to agree on something must share an implied or expressed set of beliefs underlying their agreement (e.g., each person will do what he or she promises to do). Set forth below are my beliefs as to how the business units and the Finance team can be "Partners for Performance"[SM] and some suggestions toward accomplishing this mutually advantageous relationship.

Finance team members are first and foremost businesspeople. They simply have expertise in some area or areas of finance based on education and/or experience, not unlike other businesspeople who have expertise in areas such as sales, marketing, manufacturing, research, or technology. Without such recognition, the concept of equal partners is difficult to achieve.

All functions in any organization are of equal value to the enterprise. If this is not so, then eliminate those functions believed to be of lesser value. The concept of operating and staff functions is a red herring if it in any way suggests or implies that staff functions are subordinate to operating functions. Traditionally, operating functions develop, make, and sell products or services (R&D, manufacturing, marketing, etc.), while staff functions provide administrative services (finance, legal, human resources, advertising, etc.). Despite such categorization, all functions are like cinder blocks in a dam. If one block weakens from water pressure and fails, the valley is flooded whether the block is located in the center, left, right, bottom, or top. Similarly, no enterprise can achieve its objectives if one of its functions is weak and fails. Thus, if a function such as Finance is required, then by definition, it is of equal value; if not required, then it should be jettisoned for the sake of productivity and efficiency.

All partners—including Finance—must help the sales and market-ing efforts. The most important activity of any enterprise—for profit or not—is to obtain revenues. Without sufficient revenues, the organization ceases to exist, no matter how worthwhile its ob-jectives. This being so, every employee, regardless of his or her job, should be customer-focused, that is, always thinking of how he or she can help increase revenues. After all, without revenues, there is no employer and no jobs.

How can Finance, which hardly ever sees a real live cus-tomer, help? Just extend yourself! Here are a few examples. At Northern Telecom, a European accounting manager invited two Finance executives from one of our largest European customers to accompany him to North America for two weeks to show them Northern's management accounting systems. He then assisted them in developing their finance systems strategies when they re-turned to Europe. His initiative to do this was recognized in sev-eral ways by this large European customer. This is Finance proac-tively supporting the sales effort through customer service. For another Northern Telecom example, one of Finance's credit repre-sentatives took it upon herself to solve a major collection problem by visiting a consistently late-paying customer. She learned that the problem was poor billing accuracy. Working first with the cus-tomer to determine its needs and then with Northern's billing group, she was able to resolve the billing problem (and, thus, the collection problem) quickly as well as ensure a happy customer. At DuPont, Finance always took time to describe for customer representatives how we did things—from capital appropriation re-views to cash management.

Here's a personal story. As CFO of Northern Telecom, I initi-ated personal relationships with the CFOs of our largest cus-tomers worldwide—in North America, Europe, and Asia. These top customers represented more than 50 percent of the company's business. The purpose was to have alternate access into the cus-tomer, beyond the usual marketing–purchasing door, to generate business and resolve issues as they arose. Although this alterna-tive door was not used often, our businesses (and, I believe, the customers) appreciated knowing there was another route to do business. So, Finance can be proactive in interfacing with real cus-tomers if it takes the initiative. There is no doubt it should.

Information is a competitive weapon if it is timely and insightful. It is critical that the Finance team provide information on this basis. Data per se, however, is almost useless, while lack of timely, insightful information is undoubtedly a competitive disadvantage! Timeliness means usefulness in decision-making. For example, if January operating results are available the first week of February along with interpretative information, there is still time in the quarter to take corrective action if January did not go according to plan. Let's assume in this example that sales were lower than anticipated, suggesting that manufacturing schedules be modified to reduce inventories. Reviewing the same January information in late February or early March leaves little time to reduce inventories by quarter-end.

To be insightful, information must suggest some action or at least confirm the desired result from prior actions. For example, reporting quarterly selling expense versus budget and the prior year may show that results are on-budget and at the same level as the prior year. This could be good news, but not necessarily. If sales were down significantly from budget and from last year, then selling expense as a percentage of sales would be much higher than planned (and than the prior year), which would indicate a potential problem. Thus, reporting this percentage over time—instead of just reporting selling expense dollars—provides the business manager with the information he or she can act on (1) to reduce selling expense to reflect lower than anticipated sales or (2) to increase such expense in an effort to get back on the sales plan. When it comes to financial reporting, the Finance team must provide timely, insightful information—not merely data—as part of their contribution to the partnership. Other types of information Finance can and should provide include analyses of competitors' results, predicted impact of announced competitive actions, and comparisons between different businesses in the company.

The size or organizational structure of a company has little impact on "partnering"—but its culture does. Let's define *culture* as how people work together to achieve results. It is not necessarily good or bad—it simply exists in all organizations. It has nothing to do with the size of a company (the number of employees) or how it is organized (who reports to whom). What matters is how motivated employees are to work together toward the common goal—that is, to partner.

It should be obvious to all that size is irrelevant in the success or failure of a company. Small companies succeed and grow while large companies can and do fail and vice versa. Success or failure depends on many factors including how well people work together. Organizational structure's role is not so obvious, as some people, particularly chief executive officers, believe it can make a difference in achieving results. Why else would so many new CEOs totally reorganize companies shortly after taking the helm? However, I have my doubts as to whether it makes any difference how a company is organized in getting people to work or partner together. Successful companies can be highly centralized, be highly decentralized, or fall somewhere in between. Some successful companies are organized by product, others by geographic market; still others we say are matrixed. Sometimes staff groups, such as Finance, report "straight-line" or "dotted-line" to business groups, but no one company seems to have a permanent organization structure. Obviously, people do or do not work well together for a number of reasons other than organization structure. I believe that any organization structure will work if people want it to; moreover, I see benefit in reorganizing the structure periodically because it creates change, which can be very healthy for an organization. Perhaps that is why new CEOs reorganize.

Organization cultures, however, can and do affect partnering. Suppose a culture resists outsiders and a new CFO or manufacturing VP comes in from the outside. Initially, partnering will be difficult. But when a culture welcomes outsiders, they are likely to find instant partnering. As the CFO and his or her Finance team attempt to partner with the business units, they would be well advised to consider fully all aspects of their organization's culture if they hope to succeed.

Diversity of opinion within a partnership team adds strength. People from different backgrounds—gender, race, socio-economic, educational, business specialization, experience, or whatever—bring unique perspectives to solving problems. In other words, two heads are better than one, three better than two, and so on, even if everyone starts out with entirely different perspectives and solutions. Although everyone cannot work on the same problem, the best solution to the problem will arise if the decision-maker acts with input from others—rather than alone.

The 1995 San Francisco 49ers would not have been Super Bowl champions if every player was Steve Young, their left-handed quarterback and the league's Most Valuable Player. A championship team needs running backs, fullbacks, wide receivers, interior linemen, defensive linemen, linebackers, cornerbacks, safeties, punters, placekickers, and special teams. Fifty-three all-star quarterbacks, no matter how good they are, lack the necessary skills to win a championship. It's no different in the world of organizations. In diversity there is strength.

The CFO and his or her team are the "conscience of the company." They must have unquestioned integrity and very high credibility, and must bring these attributes to their partnerships. Many times in the business world, honest people are faced with decisions and judgments that may turn out in hindsight to (1) be embarrassing, (2) raise ethical considerations, or (3) even be illegal.

If you have some doubts when making such decisions and judgments, take my newspaper test: Would you be happy and proud to have your family and friends read about your decision in the newspaper—with full disclosure? If so, you are making the right call, even if some should disagree with your decisions. If you are not sure you would like this public exposure, then the decision is probably not the right one and you should reconsider. Keep in mind, it is not whether others might disagree with your decision, as we read every day about disagreements over political decisions, but rather how you would feel under the spotlight of full disclosure—happy and proud or not!

Ethics and integrity are certainly personal issues, and it is individuals who make organizational decisions that impact an organization's ability to achieve its objectives. For example, charges of price fixing or overcharging on government contracts (whether they result in convictions or not) adversely affect organizations in many ways. Thus, it is imperative that "conscience" be a part of each partnership's decision-making as an organization's reputation is at stake. The Finance partner on the team must bear the ultimate responsibility to see that the right decision is made. It goes with his or her job, whether he or she wants it or not. This should not imply that other partners do not bear such responsibilities or would do anything that would raise ethical or integrity issues. It is simply a belief that the Finance partner does not have the option to waiver on matters involving ethical issues.

Agreement means one thing, alignment another. When partners work together to achieve a desired result, there will be differing opinions. But how do you implement a decision when there is lack of agreement without destroying working relationships and, thus, the partnership? At Northern Telecom, I was introduced by a consulting firm, the DiBianca-Berkman Group, to the concepts of "agreement" and "alignment," which I found useful. My understanding of the concepts follows:

- *Agreement*—When people have strongly held beliefs about the way to accomplish a goal or objective, they should not be expected to surrender their beliefs and agree with everyone else. That is neither realistic nor healthy.
- *Alignment*—But once the debate has been held and a decision has been made, it is expected that every team partner will "align" with the decision. This means they will support the decision and work to make it successful, even if they continue to disagree with it. The alignment concept is essential to the effectiveness of any partnership striving for outstanding performance. In other words, when the time for debate is over, it is time for all the partners to pull together as a team and make the chosen decision a success.

You are assigned accountability for certain actions by the team, but you should assume responsibility as a full and equal partner. The DiBianca-Berkman Group also helped me form my views regarding the difference between accountability and responsibility.

- *Accountability* is directly linked to an individual's specific day-to-day role and position in the organization. Accountability is assigned to an individual by the organization. An accountable person is counted on for a particular result. As such, it is his or her phone that rings first when an accomplishment or breakdown occurs.
- *Responsibility,* on the other hand, goes beyond the limit of one's accountability on an organization chart. Responsibility is assumed, not assigned. It is a commitment you make and a risk you take to make things happen, report breakdowns, influence decisions, and partner with those who are accountable.

The Finance representative on the business team, in order to be accepted as a full and equal partner, must share responsibility for the team's outcome with all other partners. In other words, to be an equal partner on the team, it is essential that one be willing to help all the other partners.

The partners must have a sense of urgency to achieve results. The old adage "time is money" is true. The longer it takes to do something, the more costly it is. Moreover, additional time provides greater opportunity for mistakes, which also are costly. In the business environment, the lowest-cost provider of goods and services has the competitive advantage regardless of conditions in the marketplace. For example, at any competitive price level, the lowest-cost provider will have the highest margin and the most flexibility to take pricing actions. Not only does moving forward with urgency save dollars, it also provides a competitive advantage in responding to the marketplace quickly. The message is brief: Equal partners on a team must not delay decision-making or implementation of plans with endless debates and inaction. The inherent risk of endless debate when "Partnering for Performance"[SM] must be recognized.

The Finance partner must be accountable and responsible for being the agent of change. Let's acknowledge up-front that change is difficult to foresee and also difficult to implement. For example, someone told me, and I assume the statements are true, that in 1921 baseball all-star Tris Speaker said, "Babe Ruth made a big mistake when he gave up pitching," and that in the late 1920s Harry Warner of Warner Brothers Pictures asked, "Who the hell wants to hear actors talk?" How is that for knowledgeable experts seeing the future?

I have suggested that the Finance partner be accountable for being the agent of change because he or she is more likely than other partners to know about changes occurring in other parts of the organization and outside the company. But any partner can take the lead. It does not have to be Finance. The important point is that someone must be accountable for predicting change in the external environment and initiating change within the organization, that is, challenging the status quo all the time.

There are many other beliefs that I could set forth regarding the Finance function's role in "Partnering for Performance."[SM]

However, beliefs are personal and developed over a period of years, and are not necessarily right or wrong. My 11 beliefs discussed above on the Finance function's role in "Partnering for Performance"SM may challenge traditional views held by others in this matter. But I believe they can enhance an organization's efforts to achieve its objectives and goals.

As business units and Finance shift from their traditional adversarial or avoidance roles to more effective partnering efforts (and many companies today have made or are making such shifts), all partners should be aware of what Finance should bring to the table.

CONTRIBUTIONS OF FINANCE

Educate the team. But keep in mind that partners on the team will not see a need to be educated—particularly on financial matters where they believe their knowledge from handling their own personal finances is directly transportable to their organization's finances. The Finance partner must persist in clarifying the many misconceptions about financial principles. Let's just take one, the importance of cash.

Cash—not earnings—is the true measurement of any business's or unit's performance! Simply put, "Cash is cash." There is no judgment in cash as there is in accounting earnings (LIFO versus FIFO, accelerated versus straight-line depreciation; capitalized software development versus expensed, etc.). I repeat, there is no judgment in cash—it is what wealth you have available for the shareholders after collecting from your customers and paying your employees and bills. Privately owned or nonpublic companies seem to understand this much better than public companies forced to report earnings each quarter. Perhaps this says something about how our securities markets operate and the role of securities analysts. For example, the DuPont Company announced second quarter 1995 earnings that were a company record and up substantially over the prior year ($1.70 versus $1.16 per share), but the stock fell over two points (about 3½ percent) because earnings were a few cents less than analysts' expectations. This example is by no means unusual!

There is yet another way to view the importance of cash. Strong cash flow means a healthy company! Think about AT&T's

recent acquisition of McCaw Cellular. AT&T paid over $12 billion for McCaw, which never reported operating earnings. In fact, in some years before the AT&T acquisition, McCaw reported significant losses. AT&T, however, not only targeted McCaw for significant strategic reasons but also recognized McCaw's strong cash flow performance. I think the reader would have to agree that AT&T is not a naive company. It saw a financially healthy growth company where the lack of reported earnings was irrelevant—because of its strong cash flow.

Another concept the Finance partner should bring to the team is the importance of, and focus that should be given to, returns (on assets, equity, cash, etc.) and not just profit margins. Similarly, teams should know how to better manage receivables and inventories or lower fixed costs and breakeven points. In other words, they must recognize the levers people in the business units can pull to improve returns and cash flow.

Support the partners with world-class services. The Finance team is usually responsible for operating many of the company's transactional systems (e.g., accounts receivable, accounts payable, payroll, expense reimbursement, and fixed assets). Such systems interface with other units within the company and, most importantly, with outsiders—customers, suppliers, and government regulators (such as the IRS). These systems and their smooth, reliable operation should be taken for granted by the other business partners on the team, or, stated another way, (1) should not cause them any problems with their customers, suppliers, or employees and (2) should provide them with the timely, insightful information they need.

World-class to me simply means delivering these services at the lowest cost with total accuracy. If the Finance function can do this, then it can free up its staff from transactional activities and focus on more value-adding analysis activities (competitive analyses, cost structure analyses, etc.). In so doing, the Finance contribution can support the partners by enhancing relationships with important outsiders and insiders, delivering useful, accurate, low-cost information to help the business units achieve their objectives, and providing considerable analyses to support such efforts. How the old Finance function does this—sometimes referred to as re-engineering—is an important consideration, but not my focus here.

Set the example by ensuring that excellence is the standard for all the partnership's activities. Accept nothing less than the best. Finance must bring this mind-set to the team's activities for all partners to observe and learn from.

I believe the one thing a business, a unit, or any other type of enterprise cannot tolerate is the status quo if it is to grow and continue to succeed. This view firmly rejects the oft-repeated adage, "If it ain't broke, don't fix it." This is a recipe for mediocrity at best, because if you always do what you always did, you will always get what you always got. This is just not good enough for any organization, much less a business in a constantly changing, complex, globally competitive business environment.

Excellence or quality involves everyone in an organization doing his or her job a little better every day. No drastic change! No rocket science! Just continuous improvement by everybody every day in all they do. Imagine the power of this—the improvement—over a period of years.

Communicate openly with all partners. Effective communication is the glue that holds any organization or relationship together because it keeps everyone informed on a timely basis on matters that impact or may impact their responsibilities and accountabilities. Failure to communicate effectively, efficiently, and in a timely manner will, at a minimum, hamper achievement of goals and objectives and, at a maximum, deny achievement altogether. Miscommunication as well as failure to communicate can only lead to problems—litigation, wars, messy divorces—all of which might be avoided with good communication. A business team is no different than any other collection of people.

I envision a new Finance partner that willingly shares information with the other partners. For perspective on this, a short while ago I read a wonderful book called *The Great Game of Business*,[2] that strongly suggests the key to business success is sharing *all*—repeat, *all*—financial information with *all*—repeat, *all*—employees. This book was an eye-opener as to what they do in their businesses, and how they have succeeded.

Do your best to see that all the partners are having fun. Not to have fun at what you do everyday for a living, I believe, is a personal

---

2 Stack, Jack and Bo Burlingham (Doubleday 1994).

tragedy. After all, during our working careers, we spend many hours on the job—much of the time we are awake. Fun is an important component in achieving goals and objectives; its absence in a partnership will impair performance.

I have set forth (1) some of my major beliefs on how and why the Finance function should partner equally with other units of an organization, (2) some areas where I believe Finance can contribute to achieving effective results for the partnership team, and (3) some reasons why in today's globally competitive world Finance and its business partners must work together more effectively. Some further thoughts for the CFO, his or her team, and the business partners follow:

- *The "Partnering for Performance"*^{SM} *concept is much broader than just Finance and the business units.* It is applicable to all groups within an organization: marketing, manufacturing, technology, human resources, and so on.
- *No one individual or group has a monopoly on knowledge.* Learn from each other.
- *Finance is not a business unto itself.* It must support the total organization and each of its individual parts.
- *Finance is much more than a bookkeeper.* It has broad knowledge of what is happening inside an organization and on the outside, such as economic changes, impact of taxes, the global competitive situation, and foreign currencies. As such, business partners would be sacrificing a valuable resource—a true competitive weapon—by excluding the Finance team from their decision-making process.
- *Finance needs to change past ways and "solicit" partnerships.* It cannot have an attitude that it will "wait for the phone to ring." When invited to the table as a full partner, it must make a value-adding contribution to be invited back.
- *There is little risk and great reward in inviting Finance to become your partner.* All organizations (particularly for-profit enterprises) take risks, so why not take one on Finance where the upside potential is tremendous?
- *Every Finance team member must act as if his or her career depends on helping others in the organization achieve their goals and objectives.* The fact is, it does now and it will more so in the future.

As chief financial officer of Northern Telecom, I played a principal role in the early 1990s in writing the following statements for Finance:

- *Mission:* To provide our businesses and the corporation with significant competitive advantage and our shareholders with superior financial returns on their investment.
- *Objective:* To provide the highest-quality, proactive, innovative, cost-effective, timely, value-added services and support to the businesses and the corporation by being a full business partner.
- *Policy:* Services and support are provided with the highest degree of integrity and commitment by a highly motivated, dedicated, well-trained, highly skilled, and professional team of Finance employees, each of whom, in an environment of openness and trust, has fun and derives career fulfillment.

I believed in these statements then and I believe them more so now as cost cutting and reduced levels of employment, along with newer concepts of managing (such as self-empowered employees) and re-engineering of work make the Finance role more vital for an organization's future success. My beliefs and observations discussed in this chapter have only been reinforced with the passage of time, as I continue to observe Finance's role in organizations. I encourage the reader to embrace "Partnering for Performance"SM as a new and better way to achieve his or her goals and objectives.

17

⑥ RELATIONS WITH EQUITY INVESTORS

A. Nicholas Filippello
Vice President, Financial Communications, and Chief Economist,
Monsanto Company

One of the overriding concerns of every chief executive officer and chief financial officer of a major, publicly owned corporation today is the creation of shareowner value. While the period of frequent hostile takeovers may be fading, an era of shareholder activism is rising in its place. Individuals are still the ultimate beneficial owners of most of corporate America. But increasingly those shares of ownership are being managed by major investing institutions for the benefit of public and private pension plans, insurance plans, mutual funds, and trusts.

GROWING IMPORTANCE OF INSTITUTIONS

Institutional investors represent a growing percentage of corporate America's ownership, increasing from less than 10 percent of U.S. equities in the early 1950s to about half by the 1990s. Furthermore, institutions account for more than half the ownership of New York Stock Exchange firms and well in excess of half for many manufacturing firms or large firms serving industrial (as opposed to consumer) markets. These institutions are becoming more informed and more willing to exert their influence. Building effective relationships with these shareowners requires a sound financial communications program and a mutual understanding of what *relationship investing* means to shareowners and to the corporation.

Institutional management and ownership of equities have now reached such magnitude that many institutions have made a major shift in the way they view their ownership of corporations. In the past, institutions simply tended to vote with their feet. If they disagreed with the way a company was being managed, they were more disposed to sell the stock than to challenge management.

Today more shares are held by index fund and value-oriented managers, and ownership positions have become so large that to sell out could undercut investment values and increase the cost of managing funds. Therefore, institutions are becoming increasingly active with managements and boards of directors. Hence, the rise in what is being called relationship investing, where management and institutional investors have begun to view the creation of shareowner value as a shared responsibility and a partnership effort. Whereas institutional activism in the 1980s often centered on social issues, the focus in the 1990s is on financial performance.

This trend should not be viewed as a threat to management, but rather as a recognition that these institutions—charged with fiduciary responsibility for the invested funds of their constituents—represent the owners of the corporation. There need be no conflict between management and owners if it is recognized that the goal of both is the creation of value. For example, management's personal long-term financial incentives must be linked closely to those of the corporation's owners for both to receive value. And, it is helpful for shareowners to understand that link.

INFORMING THE INVESTOR

The most important element in attracting and retaining satisfied shareowners is financial performance. There is no substitute for an aggressive and credible strategy along with a successfully executed plan to attain corporate goals. However, it is also vital that investors and potential investors have a solid understanding of the corporation, its products, its markets, its strategy, its goals, and the economic forces that drive financial performance. Therefore, a positive relationship with shareowners must also include an effective communications program between the company and the financial community. Good communications can provide a working partnership with a more stable, long-term–oriented investor constituency and, in some cases, can enhance access to capital markets.

There are five basic premises on which a sound financial communications policy is based:

1. The equities market is reasonably efficient over time. That is, it incorporates publicly known information into its expectations of future financial performance and into its assessment of risk.

2. Fair and appropriate sustained market value will be attained only where the financial community has an accurate understanding of the markets and major conditions affecting the corporation's various businesses, of corporate and financial strategies, and of key risk and success factors.

3. The optimal level of financial and other disclosure increases with the complexity and breadth of the businesses in which the corporation is engaged.

4. The equity market's required rate of return for a given company will reflect confidence in and credibility of management as well as risk factors associated with the general market, the businesses, corporate strategy, or financial structure.

5. Shareholding institutions will become increasingly active in exercising their power to influence managements and/or boards of directors. Accordingly, they are more likely to exercise their influence in a responsible manner if they are well informed about the company, its operations, and its strategies. It is, therefore, in the company's interest to have well-informed shareowners.

WHAT DRIVES THE STOCK PRICE?

Most modern models of stock price determination are based on the expected net present value of the future stream of some measure of financial performance, such as net cash flow, dividends, or economic value added. Actual market value, over time, is determined by the aggregate expectations of market participants regarding future financial performance, discounted back to the present by the market's required return adjusted by some measure of risk.

In practice, expectations of future financial performance are determined by the combination of trends in past performance and of the effectiveness of the company's program to communicate its strategy, critical success factors, opportunities, risks, markets, and competitive environment.

The discount factor, or required rate of return, applied to future financial results is unique for any given company and is a function of market interest rates, the general risk associated with the equities markets at any point in time, risk factors peculiar to the industry or industries in which the company operates, and company-specific risks that may reflect such factors as the product portfolio, potential legal liabilities, perceived opportunities or vulnerabilities, and, importantly, the credibility of management.

The best that any company can expect from reasonably efficient financial markets is long-term fair valuation of the company's securities. This is where a sound financial communications program can add value. In order for securities analysts and investors to do an adequate job of developing accurate expectations of future financial performance, they must have a sound understanding of the company's direction, its product portfolio, the markets served, and the company's likely position in these markets. In fact, recent studies suggest that a solid investor relations program can positively influence stock prices.

The need for a credible financial communications program increases with the complexity of the firm and its businesses. A one-product, consumer-oriented, low-technology company can get by with minimal communications because its businesses can be easily understood by investors, and regular financial reports tend to speak for themselves. Many industrial or even service-based companies, however, are dealing with complex technologies, multiple markets, environmental costs or risks, and a host of other factors that must be considered by the investor.

Of equal importance is the effect that a credible financial communications program can have on the discount factor that the market implicitly assigns to a company's expected flow of future earnings, dividends, or cash flow. That discount rate can properly be viewed as the rate of return on investment required by the incremental buyer of the company's stock.

This expected return reflects the investors' perceived risk of owning the company's stock. In turn, that perception of risk will be influenced by the investors' confidence in management, the credibility that management has built over time, and the investors' understanding of and comfort with the company's strategy and the various aspects of its operations.

It is a well-known maxim that the market does not like uncertainty. Uncertainty increases perceived risk, which (everything else equal) will depress the company's stock price. A successful financial communications program, therefore, will seek to make investors as informed as possible within the bounds of legal requirements or the protection of competitively sensitive information. One-on-one communications, complemented with timely written and/or telecommunication-based updates on issues and events of interest, provide a sound communications foundation for the company and financial community.

This is relatively easy to do when business conditions are favorable, when earnings are moving up, and when news releases are announcing positive developments. It is far less easy, but even more important, when the news is not positive. It is tempting to clam up and delay the dissemination of bad news. However, it is during these times that candid, open communications can significantly enhance a company's credibility.

If a company develops a reputation for being straightforward and truthful during difficult times, the opportunity grows for the discount rate applied to valuation of the stock price to be reduced as confidence in management increases. Likewise, the stock price will eventually reflect reduced uncertainty once the prospects for financial performance have again brightened.

FINANCIAL AUDIENCE

The audience for a financial communications program falls into four broad categories, each carrying a different weight of priority depending on the size and makeup of the company. The first is sell–sell analysts. These are the analysts working for brokerage firms or investment banking firms. Their primary role is research with a heavy emphasis on specific industries and companies. The best of these analysts can be an important resource for the company.

Many will maintain regular, frequent contact not only with the company, but with its competitors, suppliers, and customers as well as government regulatory authorities who may have some influence over the company's products or markets. As such they can often provide a credible "third-party" voice in taking the company's message to the rest of the financial community. Additionally, because of their in-depth knowledge of the industry and their contacts, they can frequently be a source of information that may not otherwise be readily available. Therefore, a good investor relations officer will maintain a close relationship with this group through frequent discussions and meetings, and will be a conduit for two-way communications between analysts and management.

The second group is the buy side of the Wall Street community. For most big-cap publicly traded companies this is by far the most important group because they represent the investing institutions that own the stock and/or make the buy and sell decisions. While many buy-side portfolio managers and analysts will be influenced by the work of sell side analysts, increasingly they are doing their own research and require more direct contact with the companies that they own or are considering as an investment. Consequently, an ever greater amount of effort is being undertaken by companies to identify appropriate target institutions and to communicate their messages to them.

The third audience is individual investors. While individuals have, over time, invested increasingly through institutional intermediaries, they still account for about half of the ownership of U.S. equities. At one extreme a consumer products company that is literally a household name will view individual investors and customers frequently as one and the same. It may have a significantly higher than average percentage of its shares owned by individuals and have an opportunity to get extra mileage from its advertising dollar.

At the other extreme an industrial intermediate or business services company may be a household name only in Wall Street offices and be virtually unknown to the average person on the street. For this firm a program to communicate directly with millions of individual investors is unlikely to be cost-effective. In this case it makes sense to rely on third-party information, such as brokerage house reports and the press, as the primary means of information transmission to interested individual investors. Exceptions to this approach might be in the company headquarters' hometown or in locations where the company has a large employment base and high public visibility.

Finally, the financial press is a critical audience. Obviously financial news coverage can influence individual investors but, in these times of rapidly reported electronic journalism, institutional analysts and investors can be influenced as well. Many financial journalists have a broad spectrum of coverage and thus may be less well informed about the company than the most knowledgeable Wall Street analysts. Therefore, it is imperative that these relationships be cultivated by getting to know key reporters, responding to their questions, and providing them with background material. It is also useful to get them together with the CEO periodically when there is an important message to get out to investors.

It is important that the investor relations officer be viewed by the press as a reliable source of information and that the reporter feels that he or she is receiving treatment equivalent to that of a securities analyst. Nevertheless, in most cases, analyst briefings and press briefings should be conducted separately. The company has a far greater ability to guide and control the focus of a press story on a one-on-one basis than if there are analysts in the same room who may divert the reporter's attention to issues that are tangential or undesired from the company's perspective.

TYPES OF INVESTORS

Segmenting the investor portion of the financial audience a different way, a company's shareowners fall into three broad categories, each of which has its own requirements. The first is traders, speculators, and arbitrageurs. These people provide a service in that they create added liquidity to a company's stock, but they have no lasting interest in the company. On a day-to-day basis they can dominate the movement in the stock's price. Therefore it is important to make pertinent facts available on a timely basis to this group. But it is impractical and not cost-effective to devote much of the company's resources to communicating with people who have no lasting interest in the fundamentals.

The second group, passive investors, can range from individual investors to the company's employees and retirees to managers of large index funds. The characteristic that they have in common is that they tend to buy and hold, trading only infrequently. Consequently, they tend to have little day-to-day impact on stock price. Nevertheless, for a variety of reasons, these are desirable shareowners, notwithstanding the fact that public pension index funds are sometimes the institutions most likely to take activist corporate governance positions. Again, it is important that company information be made broadly available to this group through the wide dissemination of annual reports and other investor-oriented materials. However, there, too, it generally is not cost-effective to devote significant resources to proactive investor relations efforts that target passive investors.

It is the third group, which can be called active investors, that is the logical target for investor relations programs in most companies with a substantial institutional ownership. These investors tend to be institutions managing pension funds, mutual funds, trusts, or insurance companies with the intent of beating average market returns. They tend to engage in research on the fundamentals of the company or industry. Some invest on the basis of industry sector rotation through the economic cycle. Others invest on the basis of expected earnings momentum or on underlying or long-term potential value.

This last group, the value-oriented and growth-oriented investors, are the most cost-effective targets of a company whose management objectives are clearly aligned with the creation of shareowner value. These are the investors who ultimately will determine the equilibrium or efficient value of the company's stock. Finance theory would suggest that the price of a company's stock is set by the incremental (or marginal) investor. On any given day that incremental investor may be a trader or speculator who drives the price above or below its equilibrium value. Longer-term, however, it is more likely to be a sophisticated investor—comparing the estimated potential net present value of future financial performance to the current stock price—who sets the trend.

The most effective investor relations program will target what has sometimes been called the "lead steers" among the value- or growth-oriented investing institutions. Target institutions can be identified by examining the size of equity portfolios managed, investment criteria, and investment philosophies. The ideal target will be large enough to take a significant position in the company's stock, will be sophisticated in its analysis, and will have an investment philosophy that is consistent with or parallel to the management philosophy of the company.

These are the institutional investors who can be the single most important factor in driving the long-term valuation of a company's stock. These investors will require more than standard financial disclosures and accounting statements. They will require nonfinancial information as well, including management philosophies toward its businesses and toward its shareowners. It is with this group that relationship investing can have its greatest payoff.

WHAT INFORMATION MUST BE COMMUNICATED?

If the ultimate purpose of investor relations activities is to facilitate fair market valuation of the company's securities, the principal objective is to promote investor understanding of the company. Four general areas require frequent, ongoing communication between the company and investors:

1. Product portfolio and markets served.
2. Current business conditions and outlook.
3. Corporate strategy.
4. Sources of potential surprise.

PRODUCT PORTFOLIO AND MARKETS SERVED

It is essential that the existing and potential investor understands what the company is all about—that is, what are the key products and product groups of importance to the company and what are the primary end-use and intermediate markets served. Good institutional analysts will be unwilling to rely solely on the company's expectations for its prospects. Rather, they will need to build up sales and profit projections of their own in order to make judgments regarding the company's earning power and potential attractiveness as an investment.

Providing product/market information can be relatively straightforward for a company selling a few products directly into well-defined, readily identified consumer markets. In these cases simple identification of major products may be sufficient.

For many large, diversified industrial companies that sell intermediate products (i.e., sell to other companies rather than to consumers), the job requires a much greater degree of education. Here, it is necessary to trace for the investor the chain of demand, beginning with the end-use markets ultimately served, through the intermediate consumer industries service, identification concerning the company's position within those particular markets as well as critical success factors. While it would be unproductive to disseminate market information in such detail that it can be digested by only the most dedicated analyst, sufficient information should be made available to allow the investor to understand the chain of demand for the company's products. The objective is to give the analyst/investor sufficient information to allow an independent estimate of sales and earnings prospects without providing so much as to help competitors.

CURRENT BUSINESS CONDITIONS AND OUTLOOK

Value-oriented investors tend not to be as concerned with quarterly earnings as is generally thought. Nevertheless, competitive pressures within segments of the institutional investing community and among sell side analysts place current earnings prospects high on some analysts' list of priorities. Institutional estimates for the current quarter, the current year, and the following year are constantly being revised and massaged to be as up-to-date as possible. Consequently, a major portion of day-to-day investor relations activities centers on current business conditions and the outlook for principal markets or factors that could affect near-term financial results. In conducting these activities with the investment community, it is crucial to be ever mindful of the basic legal prohibition against divulging any material information unless and until it has been publicly disclosed by a press release or equivalent public statement.

Major financial institutions employ their own economists who generally work closely with industry analysts in developing projections on which to base independent sales and earning projections for individual companies. Nevertheless, the typical analyst wants to know how the company views its own business prospects and what kind of assumptions regarding the external business and economic environment are being utilized for internal planning. More importantly, however, the analyst will be critically interested in recent developments in orders, shipments, pricing, and inventories. Where this type of information can be shared without compromising competitive considerations or legal requirements, it is beneficial to do so. It is almost always in the company's best interest to help analysts do their jobs and to "be smart" relative to the company's performance capabilities from ongoing operations.

CORPORATE STRATEGY

Oliver Wendell Holmes once said, "[T]he great thing in this world is not so much where we stand as in what direction we are moving." This is an undeniable truth in the valuation of corporate equities. The product and market information previously discussed is essential for investor understanding of where and what a company is today. But, a candid communication of strategy tells the investment community where the company intends to go.

A credible discussion of strategy must include an up-front analysis of any problem areas. What areas of the company may be underperforming? What alternatives are available to management? What objectives has management set to deal effectively with these problems? There is a natural tendency to want to minimize discussion of problem areas. But astute investors and analysts will know that the problems exist. Management can gain substantial credibility and confidence with the financial community by openly acknowledging their existence, identifying possible solutions, and presenting the options for plans of action.

A discussion of strategy must also include plans associated with ongoing product lines. This might include plans for market share gains, expansions into specific industrial or geographic markets, product improvements or process changes, or even "cash cow" or wasting asset strategies. It might also include a discussion of how the company plans to respond to changes in the competitive, regulatory, or economic environment.

Additionally, a discussion of strategy must focus on new products, areas of planned growth for the future, dividend payout and share repurchase policies, acquisition/divestiture strategy, areas of planned capital investment, and fields where research and development will be concentrated. In short, the company should attempt to answer the investors' question, "Where and what does the company want to be 2 years, 5 years, or 10 years from now and how does it plan to get there?"

Finally, it is critical to integrate a discussion of a growth or product strategy with a consistent financial strategy. Equity analysts will want to know how a growth strategy will be financed. How much can reasonably be financed through internally generated funds? What kind of debt expansion will be required? Is it likely that the company will raise funds in equity markets?

A credible, positive, well-understood growth and financial strategy can be a key element in building a healthy, sustainable price/earnings multiple.

SOURCES OF POTENTIAL SURPRISE

As stated before, the market reacts negatively to uncertainty. While uncertainty often is unavoidable, the company can seek to reduce it by openly discussing sources of potential surprise. If a company creates a reputation for hitting the market with negative surprises or failing to discuss candidly potential liabilities, competitive threats, or adverse product developments, then uncertainty will develop regarding the fundamentals of the company's earning power, financial stability, and management capability. Once such a reputation has been developed, market demand for the stock likely will be somewhat less than it otherwise might be if management were viewed more credibly. A natural result is a stock price that is depressed relative to its industry and its own potential.

Second only to consistency in importance is credibility. It is necessary to be as open and honest with analysts and investors as legal and competitive considerations will allow, and to be willing to talk in bad times as well as good. "No comment" or "trust us" statements in the face of adverse news or developments may simply fuel rumor and uncertainty. The result may well be a more negative stock price reaction than an open discussion of the situation would cause.

In fact, talking openly about potential negative developments can actually have a positive long-run impact on the stock price by enhancing the sense of comfort in management's credibility.

Some of our more successful investor relations initiatives at Monsanto have occurred during times of stress and significant downward pressure on the stock price. Two of these situations occurred when a major income-contributing product was confronted with a perceived threat to its continued viability, and when the loss of a product liability lawsuit stirred fears on Wall Street of catastrophic financial liability. In each case we pulled together the highest-ranking experts within the company to meet with financial analysts and investors to discuss the facts and answer their questions in a candid, no-hype manner. In one case the meeting was held in New York. In the other, the meeting was arranged quickly by conference call, one of the first such uses of widespread conference calls for investor–company communications. In each case, armed with the facts, analysts and investors were able to deal with the crisis in a rational manner and the plunge in the stock price was halted.

Apart from damage control, the company should routinely communicate with the investment community on a proactive basis. For targeted audiences, frequent personal interaction with the investor relations officer is a necessity. At Monsanto, we also involve members of executive management periodically throughout the year. typically, the CEO, CFO, and key operating heads will make presentations to company-sponsored or broker-sponsored meetings once or twice a year. In addition, they will often be available for groups of visiting analysts and investment managers.

The annual report, of course, should be the defining document of the company's performance and strategy. It is also the primary vehicle for conveying some of the more intangible aspects of the company that produce value, such as intellectual capital, the focus of research and development programs, or product brands. As such, the annual report should be much more than a legally required document. If done in a credible fashion, it can be an important vehicle for helping to communicate the quality, the values, and the strategy of the company not only to shareowners, but to employees, customers, suppliers, and other audiences as well.

OPTIMAL DISCLOSURE AND CHANGING TECHNOLOGY

In recent years there have been dramatic changes in the requirements and methods of communications among companies, their current and prospective shareowners, and securities analysts. The revolution in computer and telecommunications technology has resulted in a rapid acceleration in the speed of communications. Often within minutes of a development, messages are being transmitted from companies to securities analysts and then to their clients over facsimile machines, First Call reports (an on-line service that transmits analysts' or company reports to subscribing institutional investors), telephone conference calls, recorded telephone messages, or news wires.

There are obvious positives and negatives associated with these trends. On the positive side, we now have a more timely, efficient flow of information than ever before. This, in theory anyway, should lead to a more efficient market. On the negative side, however, instant communications lead to increased attention to near-term developments, changes in the outlook for quarterly earnings, and increased stock price volatility.

This accelerated speed of communications has put securities analysts under pressure to instantly interpret new information and frequently results in "sound-bite" analyses on First Call reports or cable television financial programs. Similarly, traders, speculators, and short-term–oriented investors rush to take advantage of fast-breaking information and shifting sentiments.

Nevertheless, the move toward instant mass communications can be turned to the advantage of the company and its shareowners. Just a few years ago, financial communications programs focused their first priority on brokerage-house securities analysts. This was done because of their magnified role in influencing the market and shaping investor attitudes. That system was far from adequate because information could not be disseminated in a uniform, timely manner. Many investors had to wait in line to hear the company's story or wait for the brokerage analyst's report to be issued.

Today, rapid mass communications allow for all interested analysts and institutional investors to receive information simultaneously. The current system is certainly more fair and more efficient, and it allows the institutional investor to make an independent judgment without waiting hours or days to receive relevant information.

As communications technology continues to progress, the accompanying side effect of increased stock price volatility will not go away. The company seeking to keep its shareowners informed has no choice but to play the game of instant communications. The market will react whether or not you provide your side of the story. Inappropriate market reactions will at least be minimized if market participants have access to all of the relevant information.

Despite, and perhaps because of, this increased market volatility, it is important for companies to understand who the various players in the market are and whose interests are aligned with theirs. You will not be able to avoid having the company's stock attacked now and then by traders and speculators whose only interest is a quick profit with no regard for the economic fundamentals. These may be the people who drive trading activity and movement in your stock price on any given day. However, experience and more than ample academic research suggest that, over time, it is the more patient investor, making decisions based on the economic fundamentals of a company, who determines the long-term trend of stock prices.

DELIVERING VALUE TO THE INVESTOR

It is important for companies to understand that the interests of management and fundamental-value–oriented investors are largely parallel. The interests of shareowners, management, employees, and all others who have a stake in the company's success will be served only if the corporation is financially healthy and if shareowner value is being created.

The fundamental-value shareowner will be attracted if the company can credibly and successfully manage the business for the creation of shareowner value. That does not require maximizing earnings quarter by quarter, but rather optimizing the corporation's resources to increase the net present value of future financial performance.

Such a program requires balancing the near-term performance and long-term growth of the corporation's current product portfolio, building tomorrow's product portfolio, enhancing the productivity of assets by reducing costs and improving processes, and divesting underperforming assets when appropriate. Additionally, cash must be invested where it can increase shareowner value and be returned to shareowners through dividends and share repurchases once the funding needs of the business and growth programs have been met.

The fundamental-value investor will also be attracted by an open, candid, consistent financial communications program. Such a program will provide for periodic personal interaction between investors and top management to build a base of knowledge and trust between management and the investment community. Management should be willing to articulate corporate and financial goals in a way that will build confidence on the part of the investor without creating unrealistic expectations.

Finally, it is vital that the company send reinforcing signals to investors through its actions. Investors will listen closely to what you say. But they will act based on what you do.

18

⑥ RELATIONS WITH PROFESSIONAL RESOURCES

Robert J. Chrenc
Executive Vice President and CFO, AC Nielsen

Today, it is possible to find consultants who claim to be experts in nearly every area of corporate endeavor. This chapter is not to provide an exhaustive list of those areas where consultants might be most helpful to chief financial officers, but rather to focus on how the CFO can use them most effectively.

CFOs normally have continuing relationships with their auditing firms as well as with tax and pension consultants and investment and commercial bankers. These relationships generally are historic in nature and are established to deal with fairly specific tasks. Most CFOs are adept at managing the costs of the services provided by these professionals. This chapter deals with the more ambiguous and complicated relationships where problems can arise. There are few senior executives who, in an age of specialization, rapid technological change and compressed business cycles, have not hired outside consultants and, once having done so, felt out of control.

The success of corporate–consultant relationships in an increasingly complex business environment depends on good communication, strong management, and clear-cut objectives within a framework of trust and openness. A successful relationship can be rewarding both to the CFO and to the organization. Consultants that I have talked to emphasize that the most productive relationships were those sustained over long periods of time. In such relationships, the consultants have developed a continuity with their clients that greatly enhances their ability to function in an expeditious, cost-effective manner.

WHEN OUTSIDE CONSULTANTS ARE NEEDED

Having achieved the CFO position, many executives presume competence in areas where they have neither professional training nor personal experience. There is a frequent human tendency among senior executives to underestimate the complexity and value of professionalism and experience in areas of unfamiliarity. Examples include organizational behavior, personnel administration, operations research, and other areas of management and management science. Knowledge of these areas may not have been critical to attaining the CFO position, but they are critical to excelling as a CFO. When confronted with a problem or issue in which the CFO has little or no formal training or experience, it would be wise to consider the help of a professional with the needed expertise.

Similarly, the staff of the typical CFO consists of people who have specific responsibilities and expertise in narrow areas. Thus, when confronted with difficult problems, especially in areas where neither the CFO nor any of the staff possess expertise (such as the re-engineering of a business process or function), the organization must look elsewhere for the required specialized competence. Given current staff work, internal personnel may have neither the time nor the experience to define or implement an appropriate solution to an important but complex problem.

One way to avoid the mistake of assuming there are simple solutions to complex problems is to discuss the problem with the right level of experienced professional. An example of an area in which outside experts can often help is staffing at senior management levels. Senior-level hiring decisions involve risk. The risk is usually not one of functional or technical competence, but rather one of ability to work successfully with the other senior executives in the organization and within, rather than against, the culture of the organization. Many senior executives, including CFOs, have a hard time seeing beyond the requirements of functional and technical competence. An organizational consultant with knowledge and experience in working with the internal culture as well as an understanding of technical competency criteria can quickly reduce the risks surrounding whether the potential senior executive hire will be able to succeed in the organization and strengthen the CFO's ability to perform effectively.

Furthermore, CFOs may want to use an outside consultant to deal adroitly with special situations. By using a consultant, it is possible to avoid unnecessary personal confrontations or highly charged emotional situations. For example, a CFO I know wanted to examine the functions and operations of his company's purchasing department. He believed that the head of purchasing perceived him to be interfering and biased when he had conducted even routine examinations. To accomplish his objective, the CFO hired a outside consultant acceptable to the head of purchasing. The CFO got the examination he needed, and the head of purchasing felt that the outside consultant was unbiased and fair.

Another CFO whom I interviewed for this chapter mentioned the use of an independent consulting firm to force domestic functional executives to focus on the need for a strong international leader. This need was not only obvious to some of the company's internal executives, but it was also the solution employed by many of the more successful international competitors. The internal resistance came from the strong domestic functional organization, which was concerned about the loss of prerogatives, responsibility, and power in the international region. This control would have to be given up to accommodate a relatively independent and autonomous international president.

In this case, an experienced and independent management consultant was engaged. He thoroughly researched the external environment, including the competition, and become sensitive to the internal corporate culture in the course of his work. The force and logic of his presentation created an opportunity for the firm to make a correct executive decision to install a semiautonomous, independent international president.

A key benefit to using consultants is that they bring a fresh, impartial perspective to a company's problems, business processes, and procedures. This objectivity, coupled with the consultant's industry expertise from other engagements, can be critical when reviewing internally completed staff work that supports important decisions and when the cost of error is significant. Such reviews can establish the credibility of the internal work and provide reassurance that the internal staff did not underanalyze a situation or issue. As an outsider, the consultant brings a perspective that is impartial and unbiased. Auditors do this, of course, when they audit a company's financial statements. But they also do so, for example, when they review the procedures in an accounting department or evaluate back-office functions and audit transaction processing procedures.

Another frequently effective and efficient use of outside professional resources is to assign them to action task forces made up of line managers. In this instance, the broader technical experience, along with more developed skills in working in task forces effectively, can be used as a lever to substantially ratchet up the effectiveness of the task force itself. This ratcheting up occurs when the outside consultant

- Serves as a meeting facilitator, keeping the task force focused on the most important issues.
- Keeps the task force focused on finding solutions that are within the capability of the organization and its available resources to implement.
- Helps the task force identify solutions that can be accomplished in a reasonable and acceptable period of time.

The use of consultants is most productive when viewed from the perspective of *change agents.* Their work is most productively viewed as interventional, which can improve

- The quality of management's decisions in specific instances.
- The effectiveness of management processes within the firm.
- The productive efficiency of the organization to function with its resources in its environment.

The best situation is when the external consultant not only facilitates implementation, but also, in doing so, transfers critical knowledge and capabilities to the internal staff, thereby ensuring continuing success long after the consultant is gone. This transfer of knowledge is a critical component of good change management. The external consultant can use his technical expertise, industry experience, and impartiality to facilitate organizational change and improve the chances of the successful outcome of the CFO's re-engineering or restructuring initiative.

In the instances cited above, the CFO who has developed a network of professional relationships has an advantage: the ability to access quickly and economically the required expertise with the assurance that effective solutions to the problem will be proposed. The most effective resource pool is the one that offers the greatest potential for insight and support in relation to those tasks most critical to the success of the CFO in his job. The corollary to this is that being able to access this resource pool as needed requires that the CFO develop not only a strong network, but also a solid understanding of the strengths and proven areas of expertise each resource can provide.

THE PROFESSIONAL RESOURCE NETWORK

There are several ways to identify professional resources and to inventory them for future use. Professional resources include not only consultants, but also peers who have achieved superior performance in areas important to an individual CFO's success. The CFO who has not taken the time and effort to become acquainted with a range of professional resources is at a professional disadvantage. High-performing CFOs do not "go it alone"; they have a broad, extremely competent network of professional resources available.

It is well known that access to a resource network is one of the principal benefits of membership and meeting attendance in organizations such as the Financial Executives Institute. Meeting regularly with successful peers to discuss mutual problems provides one of the most beneficial support networks available to an executive.

Networking with CFOs in other industries has the potential benefit of expanding one's resources to include a broader array of consultants and the ability to tap into new ideas on performance improvement. The objective is to establish an ever-expanding resource pool over the course of a career. Frequently, benchmarking your organization against one in another industry provides valuable insights into best practices. For example, a large domestic airline was able to improve its gate turnaround time and gain a significant competitive advantage by studying the race car pit crews of the Indy 500 and applying the crew's routine during a race to its own maintenance checks.

Developing a network of available professional relationships is a process that can be managed. The process involves identifying those professionals with superior functional expertise in areas that matter the most, particularly those with which the CFO is least experienced and knowledgeable. Assignments that the consultant finds at least marginally profitable should be awarded with sufficient regularity to maintain a professional's level of interest and test the chemistry of the relationship.

One financial officer actually maintained an active inventory of professional relationships that were carefully cultivated. The list was actively maintained, and professionals were added to and deleted from the list when appropriate. When specific expertise was required and a relationship existed, he was able to initiate an engagement with little time or cost expended in the search.

The same executive stated that he conducted ongoing searches for professional expertise. He felt those searches to be as important as searches conducted for the purpose of staff additions. His process was to identify candidates from sources such as peers, recruiters, and even periodicals. He would then contact the potential candidates and invite them to his office or to lunch or dinner to conduct his interview. Normally there would be enough mutuality of interest that even the most accomplished professional would succumb to the invitation. Peers who had successfully managed to overcome difficult problems were perceived to be the most valuable resources.

The objective is to construct an available support network of world-class professional expertise in those areas where the executive may need help. Most executive careers are a function of the individual executive's ability to perform independently and under stress, as well as create a superior internal and external support organization. It is a sobering notion that a career is as limited by the quality of the support organization as it is by the ability of the executive. This reality was summed up by an executive who commented that if he were only dependent on his own ability, he would have failed long ago.

BUILDING YOUR OWN NETWORK

The best sources for outside consultants are those you previously have used with success. They know your business and understand your organization. You can save both time and money by not having to educate them about your industry and your company. They get straight to the problem without requiring extensive background information.

A second source for outside consultants is the recommendation of other financial executives. Find out what their experience with various consultants has been, and get the names of those they think have performed especially well.

You can also learn about various consultants at meetings of professional societies and trade associations where you have an opportunity to meet them and discuss their qualifications and experience. Speakers may themselves be consultants or be able to recommend ones appropriate to your needs. Bylined articles in professional publications and trade journals may also provide potential leads.

You may want to use consultants with whom you are unfamiliar on a small, limited engagement to observe their performance. Such an engagement allows you to see the consultants in action requiring only a limited expenditure of time and money. It gives you an opportunity also to observe the personal "chemistry" among you, your staff, and the consultants. Staff feedback is an excellent indication of how well the consultants and their professional staff fit your consulting needs. Because so much consulting work entails organizational or otherwise sensitive issues, it is important that the consultants behave responsibly in the engagement. If you or your staff are uncomfortable with them, you will probably not be happy with their performance.

One of the more common techniques for evaluating the capability of a variety of professional resources is to accept proposals or invite presentations from a group of suitable candidates. This is an opportunity to compare competitors on a level playing field. It not only provides a forum through which you can determine which consultant to use for an immediate need, but can help in network building. This is true to the extent that you can assess the strengths and weaknesses of each player and store that information away for future use.

Often, several investment bankers will do presentations for a single proposed transaction even though the firm already has an ongoing investment banking relationship. Their hope is that they can show sufficient financing capabilities to get all or some of the business.

WHAT TO LOOK FOR IN A CONSULTANT

Typically, there are two types of consultants: problem solvers and facilitators. The first, the problem solver, is engaged to provide an analysis of and the solution to a problem. The organization itself takes responsibility for implementation or execution of the solution. The second, the facilitator, not only develops the approach or solution, but assists in implementation—in the best cases, transferring knowledge, expertise, and ownership of the solution to internal staff during the process. The complexity of the problem and the breadth of the organization it affects helps to determine what type of consultant you need.

Some of the most often mentioned attributes of the consummate consultant are

- Established reputation.
- Technical competence.
- Good professional staff.
- The right "chemistry."
- Industry familiarity.
- Breadth of resources.
- Sensitivity to client organization needs.

All of the consultants and professional resources interviewed mentioned the above characteristics as being crucial. Certain attributes, however, are relatively more important to particular areas of resource need as identified below.

Audit Firms

Auditors are the most commonly used consultants by CFOs. The more important reason for this, of course, is the SEC requirement that all publicly held companies must file audited financial statements. Many privately held companies also have their financial statements audited for a variety of reasons. For example, submitting audited financial statements to a bank may help in securing a loan. Auditors can be helpful in a wide variety of areas, including

- Internal control reviews.
- EDP controls.
- (Re)structuring of the finance function.
- Domestic and foreign tax planning.
- Management information systems.
- Internal audits.

Auditors, particularly "Big Six" auditing and professional services firms, are frequently retained when (1) the specific engagement crosses several functional areas (e.g., finance, business process redesign, and information systems) so breadth and depth of resources are critical and (2) an independent and credible "stamp of approval" is one of the objectives the CFO is seeking to achieve. Professional standards demand that the auditor maintain the highest standards of independence and objectivity.

Investment Bankers

Investment bankers offer capabilities that include

- The ability to arrange for outside financing.
- Experience and expertise in mergers and acquisitions.
- Experience and proficiency in innovating creative financial products.
- The ability to recommend, structure, and execute a myriad of financial transactions.
- Sound understanding not only of complex financial instruments of today's global marketplace, but also of where both the industry and regulation are heading.

Because the CFO's array of tasks, already broad, continues to expand in breadth and increase in complexity, investment banks are a valuable resource with respect to new financing instruments. For thousands of world-class corporations and financial institutions, derivatives have become a proven tool for competing successfully in today's business environment. While the value of derivatives is clear, important concerns have been raised regarding the challenges and risks they pose. Investment bankers and other financial consultants in these areas require specialized skills only recently available to even the most financially sophisticated CFOs.

Commercial Bankers

While most large companies would not only use commercial bankers to satisfy their financing needs, CFOs of smaller businesses use their commercial bankers as an important link in their network of resources. They not only advise on the appropriate alternatives to meet their financing needs (e.g., lines of credit, accounts receivable financing, equipment loans), but, because of their knowledge and contacts in a business community, they may be most valuable in identifying other consultants to address specific problems. The commercial banker is a valuable resource that almost every company has, but one that is often overlooked.

Professors and Other Experts

Frequently, an outside consultant may be utilized as an intellectual interlocutor. In this capacity, the CFO would be able to discuss freely innovative ideas with a respected, impartial mind that won't be threatened. Trust and intellectual integrity are crucial characteristics of a successful relationship.

Once overlooked or called upon infrequently, professors are now a frequently tapped resource. The CFO should not underestimate the academician's understanding of or experience with a particular business problem. Frequently, these professionals either were once active participants in the business community (many still are) or have completed considerable research in the field. Typically, they also have access to their own network of consulting expertise and are willing to give you access to it.

MANAGING PROFESSIONAL RELATIONS

The best external professional resources would, ideally, also be those who manage themselves the best. Unfortunately, such is not always the case. All too often the cobbler's child is barefoot. External professionals capable of great functional insights and contributions are often the worst managers of their own practices. As a result, it can be foolhardy to assume that a competent technical expert is also a competent project manager, especially one acting on your behalf.

The larger the externally managed project, the more important it is that it be disaggregated into appropriate bite-sized chunks with stand-alone milestones for review. The best position for the CFO to be in is one where the project can be stopped at any appropriate point. Projects should always be reviewed in the context of their bona fide alternatives. However, the alternatives of doing nothing or of stopping the project should always be discussed at each milestone of achievement or lack of achievement. This latter point cannot be overstressed. External consultants, even at their best, are under pressure to produce revenue. No matter how professional they may be, their best interests are not always the CFO's best interests. CFOs should assume the responsibility to see that projects are managed in their companies' best interests.

While it is important to define the scope of the assignment, and while it is helpful to limit the scope of the assignment, it is dangerous to limit the background to any assignment. It is not realistic to expect a consultant to make a knowledgeable recommendation with imperfect or intentionally biased information.

It is also important to manage expectations in relation to what even the best professional consultants can reasonably produce. For example, in a culture that is hostile and resistant to change, it is unreasonable to expect an external consultant to be able to position the need for change any better or worse than the internal executive. Expectations in relation to the value of accomplishments must be reasonable and achievable. The best consulting projects are those of limited scope and limited duration and that achieve their objectives. All too often, inexperienced executives will hire consultants to perform tasks that they themselves have failed to achieve over long periods of time. Despite popular notion, consultants, even the best of them, are only human.

HOW TO BE A GOOD CLIENT

They key question here is, What does it really take to ensure a successful, productive relationship? One of the most effective ways to get the most out of your consultant is to be a good client. An important aspect of the client–consultant relationship is openness and honesty. One way to ensure honesty from your consultant is by making an example of yourself. Make sure you provide him with adequate background information to enable an understanding of "where the firm is coming from." Additional areas of emphasis are

- Frequent communication.
- Good documentation.
- Periodic performance evaluation.

All of these items necessitate that a CFO maintain strong involvement with his consultants. Once you have engaged a consultant, you cannot simply wait for a final report. To get the maximum benefit from his services, a CFO should be actively involved on an ongoing basis. Keep in mind that getting the input of line managers is critical to the success of any project, but especially those utilizing external professionals. Taking responsibility for employee buy-in and commitment is critical.

All good relationships require *mutual dependability*. Don't delegate too much and don't take a hands-off approach. You are the principle contact for the consultant, and your personal involvement is essential. You should strive for an open, unbiased relationship. This includes making sure that a workplan calendar is in place and timing and deliverables are understood—by everyone. It also means making sure that both parties meet their commitments. An outside consultant cannot do much about company employees who don't meet deadlines.

To achieve a relationship of mutual dependability, trust and confidence are important. CFOs should choose a consultant with whom they can have an open, frank exchange. Don't be afraid to challenge conclusions. Ask for clarification when a point is unclear. Sometimes a consultant will offer negative news or opinions. Don't reject them; challenging and discussing those observations can be instructive.

ENGAGEMENT LETTER

An engagement letter should be required for all work done by outside consultants. The engagement letter should specify the approach, staffing, timing, deliverables, and fees. Engagement letters that only broadly cover work to be done and make expansive promises for improvement are to be avoided at all costs.

Engagement letters can range from one-paragraph statements of objective, scope, staff, duration, and fees to lengthy legalistic documents. The more costly and complex the projects, the more the need for specificity and detail. Greater initial detail reduces the probability of later misunderstanding and conflict. In many instances—particularly in large, complex projects—the engagement letter should be reviewed by a general counsel and bear his imprimatur.

The best consultants are often the most expensive. The issue is whether their utility value exceeds their cost. Frequently, expensive consultants are that way because of their experience and expertise. In-depth qualifications are frequently insurance against mediocre performance. In other words, by and large, you get what you pay for.

Determining what fees are appropriate is not a simple matter. There are no specific guidelines or standard costs. Some consultants charge a per diem plus expenses; others charge on an hourly basis. The rate charged depends on a variety of factors, including

- Qualifications and experience of the consultant, as well as the nature of the expertise.
- Complexity of the assignment.
- Support provided to the consultant.
- Level of expertise needed at various phases of the project.
- Timing.
- Changes in the scope of the assignment after it has begun.

In most cases, you should determine both the rate and the manner of billing in writing before the engagement begins. By establishing the fee arrangements before the work begins, you can save yourself misunderstandings, friction, and a poor working relationship.

In addition, it is helpful to detail explicitly the support the firm will provide to the consultant. A CPA firm, for example, that assumes a role of auditor or management consultant without a specific commitment of cooperation from the CFO for his staff most likely is set for a confrontation regarding access to information.

Investment bankers, on the other hand, often engage in proposals or actual work before specific terms are discussed. As mentioned above, this is an opportunity for the CFO to assess competence, while at the same time providing a marketing tool for the investment banker. In fact, much of the work involved in an investment banking proposal is frequently completed before the transaction is proposed. Although there are times when this causes unrealistic expectations, it is a result of the nature of the industry. Keep in mind that part of maintaining the professional resource network involves developing an awareness of expectations and managing expectations to your long-term benefit.

As mentioned earlier, large projects, especially complex ones, should be broken down into manageable pieces with formal periodic milestone review. This will enable the project to be restructured and the fees renegotiated as the project progresses.

Often, executives forget that some projects just may not be achievable. Consultants, in their enthusiasm and confidence, are prone to overestimate their own qualifications and expertise. Many projects that consultants undertake have not been done by them before. The notion that the project may not be doable for organizational or technical reasons is an idea that only the best consultants confront clients with. It is therefore, a mutual responsibility to demand and respond to regular progress evaluations.

You should also insist on demonstrable, measurable results. Not only should you ask for client references through which you can gauge experience and work style, you should also expect the consultant to articulate what measurable results can be expected within the defined project time frame.

Experienced users of consultants all feel that the engagement letter and fee negotiation process are perhaps the most important factors in a successful engagement. They are the most important factors because, during the process of negotiation, performance expectations and fee levels are established and are mutually agreed upon. Further, a well-prepared engagement letter should be the basis for periodic project performance review. Clients should be aggressive in insisting upon the most professional and comprehensive engagement letter. They should also be aggressive in holding the consultants to the terms of the engagement letter.

The best consultants not only encourage clients to participate in and challenge their work, they demand it. When a client feels uneasy about any part of the work in progress, he should discuss his feelings and uneasiness with the senior engagement manager. Clients who actively and appropriately participate in the engagement management process no only ensure the likelihood of successful project completion, but also frequently gain insights that lead to better and more informed executive decisions.

CONCLUSION

One CFO made the interesting comment that the most important personal goal in his life was continuous personal and professional growth. Executives who spend almost all of their waking hours working or thinking about their business must satisfy their need for professional growth in work-related activities. The executive who strives and is driven to be successful does not stop the work-week on Friday afternoon. Most very successful executives think, sometimes obsessively, about business problems when they are shaving or showering and even when they are engaged in leisure and family activities. Pressing problems cannot be dropped and forgotten easily.

One solution is to build a support network of individuals with relevant consulting skills who are available to assist in both relieving some pressures of executive life and also providing opportunities for continuing personal and professional growth. Continuing personal growth is achieved when the work done complements and extends the executive's skills, particularly in those areas that may be necessary to his future success but with which he has neither formal education nor practical experience. The executive who understands the process of continually shaping and reshaping consultant support as his career evolves has a significant competitive advantage over his peers who lack such a finely honed and ever-evolving professional support and personal growth system.

V

INTERNATIONAL FINANCIAL MANAGEMENT CHALLENGES

19

⑥ INTERNATIONAL RISK ASSESSMENT

Judy C. Lewent
Senior Vice President and CFO, Merck & Co., Inc.

Caroline Dorsa
Treasurer, Merck & Co., Inc.

Globalization has continued to intensify since 1986 when this handbook was last published. This trend eventually reduces general business risk ("diversification effect") as multinational corporations respond by diversifying their product lines, production locations, sources of raw materials, locations of product research, and so on. However, for the foreseeable future, complex issues of international financial risk will continue to represent a central element of the decision-making process, thereby making the CFO an essential business partner of global business executives.

The experience of the pharmaceutical industry suggests that foreign investment in mature European markets encounters, in many respects, only slightly more market or operational risk (e.g., currency and price control risk) than a similar project would face in the United States. Increasingly, however, new business opportunities are located in the emerging markets where the risk profile differs significantly from that of the United States and Western Europe.

What is the core of international risk assessment? It is a process of shaping and managing a firm's exposure to specific risks of the international marketplace. It is not a process whose objective is to remove all risk; this is not a logical objective for investors who wish to capture returns available from rapidly growing economies.

Risk assessment involves

Defining risk
Monitoring risk
Analyzing risk
Measuring risk
Managing risk

It is important to keep in mind that, despite a clearly defined risk framework, the assessment of international risk for an investment decision should remain specific not only to the type and location of a prospective investment but to the investor as well. An investment decision in one country might pose very different risk management issues for different investors. Further, these risks may be subject to change over time. For example, the collapse of many centrally planned economies (e.g., in Central and Eastern Europe) has created dimensions of business risk very different from the risks which existed when those nations were part of the Soviet sphere of influence. Similarly, these changing risk dynamics are different for a pharmaceutical firm than for a consumer products company. Different investors can also be expected to evaluate and assess risk differently in the same country and differently over different time periods. Finally, international risk assessment should be a dynamic, ongoing process that also assesses when and if to *disengage* from a foreign market or project.

The assessment of international risk can also extend beyond traditional *sovereign risk* (i.e., the *political risk* of government expropriation or civil unrest and the *transfer risk* of outward-bound cash flows). For example, it might include

• *Loss of technological advantage.* Protection of patents, trademarks, and copyrights may be weak or ineffectively enforced overseas; their introduction into an unprotected foreign market might entail risks to other international markets due to the subsequent export of pirated technology to those markets. This is an issue of particular concern in the pharmaceutical industry.

• *Gradual erosion of real prices.* Erosion of real (i.e., net of devaluation) prices for products sold in a foreign market may occur as devaluation outpaces a firm's ability to increase prices.

• *Financing and capitalization risks.* Financing and capitalization constraints (and opportunities) are governed by local law and custom and, as such, are subject to change at any time.

- *Market risk.* This is the fundamental operational business risk associated with producing or selling in a new market.

How then should a CFO approach such an analysis? Can standard capital budgeting techniques be used effectively as a framework for investment decision analysis given the varied dimensions of risk noted above?

DEFINING RISK

When beginning a risk assessment, the most important task is to isolate the risk factors critical to achieving your business objectives. For example, when analyzing political and economic risks, it is important to identify to what extent the local government and economy impacts the economics of the particular project under consideration. The health of a local economy is probably less relevant to the success of a factory whose entire output will be exported than to a factory being built exclusively to supply its local market.

All international projects are subject to the risks of changes in the political and economic environment of the host country, regardless of the duration of the investment. International projects whose returns are highly sensitive to the ability to generate cash flows beyond a short/medium-term projection period (i.e., its "terminal value") carry a somewhat higher degree of exposure to future political and economic developments because of the expanded time horizon. Further, where a project has cash flows in different currencies, identification of the currency and location (onshore/offshore) of cash flows is important.

Risks that must be specifically identified and defined often include political risk, economic risk, financing risk and exchange controls, and market risk.

Political Risk

Assessment of the extent to which foreign political decisions or events will impact your business must include an assessment not only of political leadership but also of the institutional framework and fundamental social acceptance of the political structure.

For example, the introduction of coalition governments into the Japanese political system in 1993 had little impact on investment activity. The locus of economic policy power remained unaltered within the well-established, well-accepted, stable bureaucracy. On the other hand, a political landscape dominated by a contest between supporters of market-based economic systems and supporters of centrally planned economies implies a higher degree of risk for a foreign investor. Although less prevalent than in the past, in extreme situations, this risk can manifest itself with the government's expropriating a subsidiary's business and assets.

A thorough risk assessment should also analyze the impact of potential local political instability on a business investment and should consider the likely costs of responding to such changes.

Economic Risk

This risk involves the manner and extent to which economic developments in the host county will adversely affect your business. Here, it is vital to analyze to what degree business results are a function of the health of the local economy. As previously mentioned, a factory producing a product primarily for the local market will be subject to the economic risks of that economy. Traditional measures of economic health include GDP growth, employment, and savings and investment rates (economic strength) as well as inflation/devaluation, external account balances, foreign debt, and currency reserves (economic balance). In addition, government management of its fiscal affairs is usually a leading indicator of future economic strength. In some instances, such as our own, this has a direct and immediate impact. In most overseas markets the government ultimately pays for most pharmaceuticals so inevitably prices and levels of reimbursement are influenced by the health of the local economy and the fiscal health of the government.

Financing Risk and Exchange Controls

A wide variety of local factors will influence the ability to finance and, as subsequent conditions require, refinance a project in a foreign location. In the case of a foreign subsidiary, there may be proscriptions against interaffiliate or cross-border financing or onerous capitalization/decapitalization rules and costs. There may be prohibitions against U.S. dollar–denominated financing or requirements that the investor finance in (expensive) foreign-currency–denominated debt from foreign financial institutions. Similarly, exchange controls may restrict repayment of such financing or dividend remittances. These risks should be incorporated into the risk assessment of a project through explicit adjustments to the assumed level of free cash flow.

Market Risk

Fundamental to any risk assessment is the basic analysis of a project's expected risks to market events (e.g., market share, competitive response, pricing flexibility). These factors are specific to each particular investment project, industry, and competitive environment.

MONITORING RISK

Now that we have defined many of the key risks, where do we obtain information on risk? The role of gathering business intelligence should be performed by every functional area of a multinational company. While there is certainly no lack of data in today's information explosion, the critical objective is to filter out "noise" and focus on the key factors affecting the risk of doing business in a country. Obviously, this function does not end once a decision to do business in a country has been taken—monitoring the risk factors defined above is a continuing duty that complements all of the risk management activities described later in this chapter.

The information resources available to the CFO can be divided broadly between published materials and data provided by expert consultants, economists, or other external business contacts, with some overlap between the two.

A good general starting point is to obtain country business guides published by different accounting firms or banks. Similar guides and other business promotion literature can also often be obtained directly from consulate offices of the country of interest. Different international advisory services and public institutions also publish intensively detailed compendiums of financial, banking, and tax regulations, national economic statistics and associated commentary, and detailed risk-scoring country studies. In terms of monitoring risk on an up-to-the-minute basis, aside from general-purpose news periodicals and computer access to business news wires, there are a host of current specialized newsletters that focus on specific regions or countries around the world.

With respect to rules and regulations, it is always prudent to obtain confirmation from local accounting/tax, banking, and legal advisers. These external contacts should also be utilized for their general knowledge of the country's political and economic situation.

ANALYZING RISK

A CFO needs to be an active participant in the development of a global risk strategy since many international business risks can be translated into the language of financial risk. A global risk strategy should explicitly identify key risks which must be addressed in any new project proposal; done well, this can provide both financial and operational decision-making frameworks. The strategy should articulate not only the common dimensions of risk to be incorporated into the project analysis but also the methodology by which they should be integrated into the analytical and decision-making processes. A well-developed strategy can also articulate where, within the organization, responsibility lies. For example, at Merck, measurement and assessment of sovereign risk lies within the Treasury function, market risk is the purview of the operating division, and so on. In a highly decentralized organization, responsibility for all dimensions may lie with the relevant operating unit with advisory support from expert corporate staff groups. Within Merck, nonmarket risk assessment is primarily a Finance area responsibility, handled within the Treasury Department as well as a separate group whose activities are specifically dedicated to capital investment analysis.

MEASURING RISK

A key role of a CFO is to find a common language with which to incorporate all of these factors so that decision makers can better assess the return and risk characteristics of alternative international projects when making decisions. The methods we have used successfully at Merck all have the discounted cash flow model as the core approach, upon which we have expanded to add new tools that capture the multiple dimensions of cash flow risk. A number of these methods are cited below.

A simple discounted cash flow model for the life of a project is the starting point of its financial evaluation. Incorporating international risk adjustments in the financial evaluation of the project can be accomplished through a variety of methods:

1. Shortening the required payback period.
2. Increasing the discount rate at which all project cash flows are discounted in computing net present value.
3. Adjusting the value of cross-border cash flows to reflect the assessment of aggregate international risk in the project.
4. Adjusting the value of individual components of cash flows of a project based on specific risk assessments.

Shortening the payback period is a simple, convenient way to screen projects. However, it penalizes projects with significant terminal values or cash flows in later years. Moreover, it is not altogether clear that international risks increase with the length of time a project requires to achieve a target return. Many economic risks are cyclical in their pattern. Further, many estimates of international risk factors (for example, currency exchange rates) can be made with more confidence over the long term than the short term.

Altering the discount rate (cost of capital) for all project cash flows, though also convenient, ignores the fact that not all flows are subject to the same risk. Frequently, the repatriation of a foreign subsidiary's local earnings may be subject to greater risk of exchange controls than the cross-border cash flows arising from the subsidiary's importation of raw materials or intermediate or finished products. Through rigorous analysis, project evaluation can go beyond the allocation of onshore versus offshore flows—the risks of each component cash flow can be evaluated and risk-adjusted. In addition, a simple discount rate adjustment, to the extent that it is considered a rough proxy for additional risk, can overpenalize the long-term project due to the compounding nature of the discount rate in calculating a present value. This suggests that a broadly applied discount rate adjustment could incorrectly characterize the project-specific factors capable of making a significant difference in the calculated value of expected cash flow returns.

At Merck, we have found that the tools available in advanced financial evaluation can be well suited to analyzing the types of risks discussed above. The ability of the CFO to think beyond a single point estimate and to provide financial analyses that highlight key risks and opportunities that assist decision making is crucial.

In addition to conventional sensitivity analysis, Merck's experience suggests that two analytical tools, Monte Carlo analysis and decision tree analysis, can be very useful in articulating the risk trade-offs of projects in a manner that enhances the ready comparability of many types of alternative investment projects.

Monte Carlo analysis (which is based on the simultaneous variation of multiple variables, each of which has been estimated using a probability distribution that best describes its potential range) can provide management with a good assessment of the range of expected results given the range of uncertainties of the input factors. The key to successful analysis is (1) a significant amount of upfront time to determine which factors are most important as well as (2) identification of the endogenous and exogenous factors that can cause their variation. These factors may relate to internal project development issues in marketing, but they may also relate to factors of international risk cited above. For example, how could political risks change the potential returns to a project? In Merck's business, political risks affect our long-term returns because in many countries the pharmaceutical payments are made directly from the government. Therefore, we might adjust the shape of our sales probability distribution as well as its maximum sales estimate in any year to reflect the fact that changes in the political situation might affect the climate for support of new technologies in the health care system.

Similarly, Merck looks at economic risks when evaluating investments in emerging markets. Again, because of our industry's direct dependence on government (i.e., taxpayer-financed) health care reimbursement, we are very concerned about the overall economic health of the countries in which we make new investments. We might change the slope of the growth of our sales distributions over time to reflect our assessment of the speed at which an emerging economy may grow and prosper. When combined with probability-based assessments of our own marketing and product plans, the output statistics from a Monte Carlo analysis (in the form of expected return and cash flow distributions) provide a powerful tool to estimate the long-term success of our strategic initiatives within the framework of the larger exogenous risks that we face.

The second tool that we have found useful, and onto which international financial risks can be easily added as an overlay, is the decision tree framework. A logically structured decision tree provides valuable insight about not only the level of commitment that a firm has to make to a new initiative, but also the timing of such commitments. For example, in Merck's business, product development is a long, risky process. When we combine this company-specific risk with the macro uncertainties of global investment initiatives, the value of a decision tree becomes clear. It is important for us to consider the size and timing of the investments needed to accomplish these initiatives. But it is also critical to consider when these investments need to be made relative to our own product development cycle (e.g., how close we are to the next new product requiring significant new marketing support in this region) and the economic health of the region (e.g., the launching of a new currency or inflation control program). By using the decision tree, we can highlight our investment commitment patterns through time. On top of this, we can overlay our estimate of the timing for resolution of the international risks that we know exist at the outset. For example, given the same expected level of return, we are more likely to undertake an international project in one emerging market if we know that our most significant capital investment comes much later in the process than in another emerging market where a higher up-front resource commitment might be necessary. The obvious reason is that the first approach preserves our strategic flexibility or, to put it more simply, keeps our options open. This logical business assessment can be captured easily using a decision tree tool.

Exhibit 19.1 shows a stylized example of the decision tree approach. The probabilities across the top estimate the likelihood of attaining approval for a drug by the regulatory authorities given knowledge of the product's characteristics at that point in its development. The present-value figures show the after-tax cash flow

E X H I B I T 19.1

Merck & Co., Inc., Licensing Candidate Decision Tree

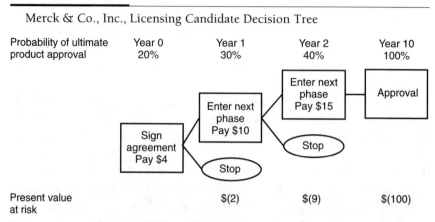

| Probability of ultimate product approval | Year 0
20% | Year 1
30% | Year 2
40% | Year 10
100% |

| Present value at risk | | $(2) | $(9) | $(100) |

at risk at each point in time should a decision be made to terminate the project. The decision nodes show the out-of-pocket costs to enter the next phase of development.

Finally, at Merck we have recently begun to use option theory as a tool in making investment decisions. Given the nature of our long lead time research investments, Merck has recognized that a portion of the value of a research project investment lies in the knowledge gained that may assist future projects. From a financial point of view, this can be thought of as the option value of a project because it is an investment that enables one to preserve or enhance strategic flexibility in the future. Merck has begun to use tools that incorporate option value in some of our project analyses.

As emphasized earlier, a prerequisite to managing international risk effectively is the identification and assessment of the specific risks to the business objectives of the project over the appropriate time horizon. An implication of this is that effective management of risks from a strategic point of view includes constant reassessment and remeasurement of risk to take account of the often quickly shifting landscape of international markets. This might be accomplished by updating the financial model or reassessing the probabilities of the occurrence of events originally thought to impact project returns. The Monte Carlo model and decision tree, for example, can be updated regularly.

Accounting Considerations

A CFO is also responsible for ensuring the integrity of a firm's financial statements. Accordingly, the extension of a company's activities into international markets requires an understanding of the relevant accounting dimensions to international risk assessment. It is recommended that a firm develop, in advance, a general policy that addresses the appropriate U.S. GAAP accounting treatment for international projects. This process can eliminate unnecessary surprises between the economics of a business strategy and the manner by which the investment and its expected future returns are reflected in the company's financial statements. Under certain circumstances, U.S. GAAP may prevent consolidation of foreign income on an accrual basis or, worse, may suggest the "expensing" of an entire investment in a foreign project at the time it is made, pending the future realization of project cash flows. It is important to know these policies up-front and to ensure that they are well understood and consistently applied in order to avoid unnecessary surprises.

Accounting for direct investment in countries with higher than normal risk sometimes results in cash basis rather than accrual accounting. Usually, the approach is followed if either of the following are observed:

1. Exchange controls or other restrictions raise serious doubts about an investor's ability to recover, in currency convertible to U.S. dollars, the original investment.
2. Political risks endanger an investor's ability to recover, in currency convertible to U.S. dollars, the original investment.

Future changes in circumstances may also have an immediate earnings impact; again, these accounting issues should be examined when assessing and structuring a foreign investment.

MANAGING RISK

Having identified and developed a framework for measuring and incorporating such risk assessment into project evaluations, how then can these risks be influenced or controlled? Broadly speaking, we believe it is helpful to categorize international risk management into (1) strategic actions that can be taken before conducting business with or in a country and (2) operational and financial tactics that are available once local business has been established.

Strategic Actions

In essence, strategic actions encompass the manner by which a multinational organization chooses to implement its overall business strategy in a foreign country. Such decisions are strategic in nature because they directly impact, over a lengthy period of time, the long-term commercial opportunities of the initiative and not just the short-term balance sheet or income statement implications. The spectrum of possibilities generally runs from only exporting finished product to that country to the establishment of an in-country subsidiary performing a vertically integrated range of importation, manufacturing, and marketing functions. Within the spectrum, a local presence can entail a representative selling office, a local licensee or franchise, export activities, and so on. The level of risk generally increases in direct proportion to the nature and scope of the activities one performs within the host country.

Operational Tactics

Although some of these operational tactics are often considered financial in nature, this area encompasses actions that maintain the future value of revenues and income, and minimize the erosion of asset values, usually as a result of exchange rate devaluation. The primary means of maintaining revenues under such circumstances is to increase prices in real terms (i.e., net of devaluation). In the pharmaceutical industry this is generally constrained by government price controls; hence, great emphasis is placed on cost control and productivity improvements. On the balance sheet side, the general goal is to reduce balance sheet exposure. Specific tactics here include reduced trade terms of sale, offering customers prepayment discounts, improving the collection process, minimizing idle cash, and other working capital management techniques.

Financial Tactics

The narrow definition of financial tactics focuses on the utilization of financing, investment, and hedging instruments. In its simplest form, financing with local currency or investing surplus cash in hard currencies neutralizes local-currency monetary asset exposures. Additional protection may be available through the use of forward exchange contracts and foreign currency call and put options. To a large extent, the more complex hedging instruments are generally not available or are highly illiquid in emerging markets at this point in time. Consequently, financial hedging activities generally focus on the simplest techniques in those economies with developing capital markets, despite the fact that the risk there can be the greatest.

Once the decision is made to enter an international market, the next question is how best to structure the investment so that the fewest non-operational risks need be retained. Obviously, operational or business risk cannot be diversified away if the project is to provide the opportunity for significant returns. A brief overview of some of the strategic, operational, and tactical approaches that the Merck Finance Area brings to managing international risks are discussed below.

Export Business

If the strategic decision is taken to expand business in a foreign market by means of direct exports to customers or distributors in a foreign market, the risks are straightforward:

- The commercial credit risk of the importer's ability and willingness to pay.
- The foreign exchange transfer risk of obtaining U.S. dollars or other hard currency in settlement.

Operationally, an exporter that invoices sales in U.S. dollars is not subject to devaluation (in U.S.-dollar terms) of the receivable/cash proceeds. But that exporter is at risk to the ability of the importer's central bank to convert its own currency to U.S. dollars. Conversely, an exporter that invoices in the currency of the importer is exposed to devaluation.

For export sales, negotiation of letters of credit, issued or confirmed by banks outside the jurisdiction of the country of importation, offers a well-established mechanism to control either commercial or transfer risk on an individual transaction basis. The cost of such guarantees varies directly with the market's perceived risk of nonsettlement by the central bank. Alternatively, government or quasi-government agencies such as Nederlandse Crediet

Maatschappij (NCM) in Holland, Compagnie Francais d'Assurance pour le Commerce Exterieur (COFACE) in France and the Export-Import Bank of the United States ("Ex-Im Bank") offers programs of export credit insurance for individual transactions or a portfolio of customers/countries, at negotiated premium rates reflective of the same perceived risks. A number of private insurers also offer export insurance through Lloyd's brokers in the UK.

Establishing Foreign Legal Entities

The strategic decision to establish a legal entity presence in a foreign nation and invest in fixed or working capital can be implemented in a variety of ways to reduce risk capital exposures. A firm's ability to utilize such alternatives will depend not only on the legal/financial environment in the host country but also on the nature of the underlying business and one's expectations regarding repatriation to the parent of future cash flows. If local cash flow is expected to be fully invested in the growth of the local business, transfer risk will represent a risk of secondary importance.

Alternative "wholly owned" legal structures include

Representative offices.
Branch of subsidiary or parent.
Full subsidiary corporations.

The selection of a legal entity form should optimize the project's cash flows by obtaining tax relief for start-up losses, permit tax-efficient repatriation of future profits, anticipate current and potential exchange controls, and allow for flexible business and financial responses to unexpected future events. Although the decision to establish an entity is a strategic one, operational and tactical solutions will need to be continuously applied to address these risks. For example, the likelihood of start-up losses at a new operating entity in the Philippines induced Merck to operate as a branch of a U.S. company, thereby reducing the risk of unutilized operating loss tax carryforwards.

Each host county will adopt a slightly different attitude toward such flows as royalties, interest, management fees, and transfer price transactions. This attitude is usually expressed in the form of exchange control constraints on fund flows or limits on deductions, for local income tax purposes, for certain expenses and fees paid to affiliated companies. Structuring the form of subsidiary/parent cash flows in this context can increase the likelihood of achieving a desirable consolidated return on the project.

The precise nature of one's business activities may *require* a specific form of operation. For example, some countries require the establishment of a subsidiary in order to manufacture in the host country; others may not allow you to have a subsidiary unless you manufacture. In certain Eastern European countries, for example, the legal form of operation determines the options on invoicing local customers. For example, in Hungary, Merck found that one may only import and invoice customers *in Hungarian currency* if a full subsidiary structure exists. We therefore concluded that such a legal entity was a necessity to more fully participate in the economy's growth.

Debt Financing, Guarantees, and Subsidiary Capitalization

Implementing the capital structure of a subsidiary provides many other opportunities to manage the risk profile of an international business initiative. Decisions regarding the financing of the subsidiary are central to the overall risk profile of a project and the traditional domain of a company's financial officers.

Consider, for purposes of illustration, a foreign subsidiary that imports some intermediate material, licenses a certain manufacturing technology, and manufactures, markets, and sells a product in the local currency. Such a full-fledged operation requires some degree of permanent capital and working capital financing. The financing of this project will be a key determinant of its risk profile. What lenders or institutions exist that are willing to assume some element of risk?

International Agencies
There currently exist a number of international institutions whose mandates encourage them to provide project financing as well as other consulting and project management services in, primarily, emerging economies. The most significant of these are OPIC (Overseas Private Investment Corporation), EBRD (European Bank for Restructuring and Development), and the IFC (International Finance Corporation, a subdivision of the World Bank).

These organizations can provide loans, loan guarantees, or direct (equity) investments in qualifying projects. However, even though these agencies exist to reduce the risk of investing in such foreign markets, like commercial lending institutions, they are sensitive to the "hard" (convertible) currency cash flows. This has resulted in the historical preponderance of large-scale, natural-resource–export–based projects supported by these organizations.

However, even if a contemplated project produces no immediate hard currency flows, the participation of one or more of these "preferred lender" institutions, even on a nominal basis, can provide considerable technical expertise in working with foreign central banks and, occasionally, better access to foreign exchange or commercial debt financing.

These organizations and the expertise they bring to a project are of particular value where the country is in transition from a centrally planned to a market-oriented economy and the legal infrastructure or tax regime is in a rapidly evolving state. The advisory role that such institutions play in counseling these governments makes them knowledgeable about the current business climate and operational roadblocks. For example, when considering investment during the early days of the former Soviet Union's transition toward a market-oriented economy, Merck found that a significant barrier to foreign investment was the difficulty in determining ownership and control of the country's enterprises and economic assets. International organizations committed to promoting direct foreign investment in emerging markets can play a very productive role in resolving such issues.

Commercial Banks

Debt financing from local institutions may be available to varying degrees based on the general development of capital markets in the host countries. Frequently, such lenders may look to parent-company or third-party guarantees for such debt or be unwilling or unable to commit debt financing for extended periods of time. Also, some countries restrict access to debt denominated in currencies other than their own. If this is the case, the CFO must consider the risk sharing attributes of a third-party lender with the possibility that "real" interest rates (interest rates net of inflation/devaluation) may be more expensive than a capital injection funded by the parent.

Inter-affiliate Lenders

Where possible, interaffiliate lenders may provide access to a stable source of financing. Of course, this is not a risk reduction technique per se, as the obligation for the funding remains within the corporate family. However, under certain circumstances, interest payments may be permitted in periods of currency shortage while dividends may not be allowed. Accordingly, interaffiliate debt, as an alternative to an equity investment, may be desirable.

Creating a Joint Venture

Another strategic risk reduction approach is the use of joint ventures (discussed at length in Chapter 20). Potential partners might include

Foreign (private) investors
International agencies
Foreign governments

To the extent that a partner shares in the business risks of a project, a firm's cash outlays (and risk) should be reduced. The identification, selection, and negotiation of a joint partner relationship can be difficult and time consuming but might ultimately be advantageous. In some countries, it is mandatory; in others, a partner with access to existing land or production facilities and knowledge of the local market or government institutions might represent a key element of success as well as a risk reduction opportunity. Merck chose to operate in this fashion in the People's Republic of China.

Further, there are interesting operational opportunities in a joint venture structure. It may be possible to structure such a relationship so that each partner receives a different return on the project. Local expenses and earnings can be shared among local partners while other joint venture cash flows (for example, fees and royalties) can be allocated in a different manner between the partners to recognize their differential contributions to the venture.

Hedging Currency Risk

As mentioned, certain economic risks, such as currency fluctuation, can often be hedged through the tactical application of financial market vehicles such as forward exchange contracts, options, or other similar transactions. The cost of such transactions, either to protect the value of current assets or to secure the U.S. dollar equivalent of future foreign currency cash flows, can be relatively easily incorporated into a project evaluation. Such mechanisms do not exist for all currencies in all markets, but the trend is definitely in the direction of increasingly efficient markets in a broader array of currencies.

When such mechanisms are not available, one can still usually resort to hedging via local currency financing to offset monetary asset exposure positions. The choice between financing in local currency (hedging) versus U.S. dollars (not hedging) involves the same risk/return trade-off analysis applicable to the analysis of hedging via forward exchange contracts. The local currency interest rate net of projected exchange rate changes should be compared to the dollar interest rate with appropriate sensitivity or probabilistic Monte Carlo analysis.

In practice, our experience in rapidly growing markets over the recent past has been that a consistent policy of *not* hedging currency risk in emerging countries is more economical than hedging all the time because high real risk premiums are already factored into local interest rates. As an example, Exhibit 19.2 compares the cumulative compounded local monthly interest rate to cumulative currency devaluation for Mexico from 1989 through 1994. Even with the maxidevaluation at the end of 1994, one would have paid far more to hedge all the time than to simply endure the exchange losses resulting from the devaluation of an exposed position. However, the optimal result would have been attained if one were especially astute with respect to timing the hedge to just prior to the maxidevaluation. Of course, this requires foresight and market timing ability which is often more a matter of luck than skill and is therefore not a reliable risk reduction strategy. Consequently, our own policy has been generally not to hedge in such markets but to selectively hedge on an exception basis when monitoring indicates the demonstrable possibility of singular adverse events occurring in a short time frame.

With respect to hedging short-term currency risk in the more developed economic and capital markets, there exists a wide range of competitively priced hedging vehicles with which to manage short-term fluctuations in the rates of currency exchange. In these international markets selective, regular hedging programs

EXHIBIT 19.2

Mexico's Cumulative Compounded Local Monthly Interest Rate versus
Cumulative Currency Devaluation

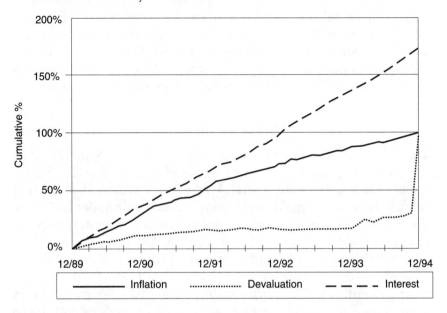

have proven effective in reducing the volatility of business results
with an acceptable cost trade-off.

Further, to the extent that a company depends on significant
flows of foreign currency to fund its U.S.-dollar commitments,
appropriate hedging strategies for anticipated revenues should
be considered. At Merck, one of our most significant cash flows
is the ongoing funding of research and development, which is
conducted primarily in the United States. However, we receive
significant cash flows from our operations in Western Europe
and Japan. In 1989, Merck began a long-term program to hedge
our foreign currency revenue exposures using long-dated options, which has allowed us to reduce the volatility of our expected cash flows over our planning horizon. This enables us to
ensure that our capital structure does not have to be altered as a
result of exchange rate movements in order to fund our long-
term commitments to R&D.

Sovereign Risk Insurance

Sovereign risk insurance policies typically afford protection against two classes of risk: expropriation risk and transfer (currency convertibility) risk. The lending provider of such insurance in the United States is Overseas Private Investment Corporation. The cost of such insurance, regardless of whether a foreign investment project qualifies for coverage under OPIC's terms, often provides a good indicator of the general risk profile of a country.

Other Techniques

There are many other operational solutions to managing business risk that may provide a superior return after adjusting for international risk. For example, a straightforward licensing strategy may reduce the need to make significant capital commitments. On the downside, a company cedes a certain amount of control over the manner in which their product is marketed by the licensee.

Subsidiary countertrade re-export programs should be considered to reduce transfer risk. Under a traditional countertrade arrangement, a U.S. exporter selling to a customer in a country with limited foreign currency reserves seeks to reduce its transfer risk by acquiring access to the hard currency proceeds of a successful exporter located in that foreign country. (See Exhibit 19.3.) This approach was successfully used by Merck in the mid-1980s in Brazil with various metal products when the local exchange control authority required a neutral balance between the nation's imports and exports. Typically a broker acts as an intermediary and arranges for the offshore exchange of hard currency from the U.S. parties for local currency and product from the foreign parties. This is done in a way that protects the U.S. exporter from the risk of nonpayment due to the potential imposition of exchange controls or the general unavailability of foreign exchange.

If the U.S. exporter can identify products that can be supplied by the foreign customer's country and that can be used in its own operations, then the U.S. exporter can control all of the currency flows and reduce the cost of accessing the hard currency. (See Exhibit 19.4) In the right situation, this structure can provide a predictable source of hard currency for use in purchasing high-margin product from the parent with reduced transfer risk.

EXHIBIT 19.3

Traditional Countertrade Structure

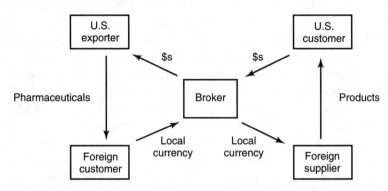

EXHIBIT 19.4

Counterpurchase Structure

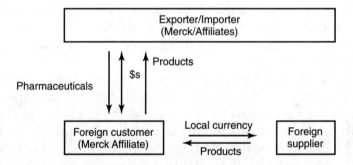

CASE STUDY

During the 1980s, many of the business risks described above were present in Argentina and were further amplified by both hyperinflationary conditions and a lack of support for intellectual property rights (a key issue for Merck given the nature of our product line). Consequently, the financial and operating divisions conducted a strategic review and, subsequently, embarked on a restructuring strategy during the late 1980s to improve profitability. It should be emphasized that the strategy entailed divergent approaches between the Human Health (pharmaceutical) division and the AgVet (agricultural/veterinary health) division, both of which conducted business in Argentina. Although not as well known, the latter division was (and still is) of significant importance to Merck in Argentina as a result of the size of the market for this product line. More importantly, the AgVet product line was much less encumbered by restrictive regulatory price controls than was the pharmaceutical business. Consequently, a key business objective was to alter strategically the risk profile of Merck's pharmaceutical division while retaining operating control over the AgVet business.

Similar to its approach to most markets, the traditional Merck operating structure was in place in Argentina at that time. This structure was a wholly owned affiliate that imported raw material ingredients to be formulated and packaged into finished-form products in a local plant and sold in the local market. Hence, Merck had both fixed and monetary asset exposure to country risks—especially those associated with currency devaluation in a hyperinflationary environment. The primary goals of the restructuring strategy were to reduce Merck's asset exposure and enter into a business arrangement with a local "partner" who could operate more effectively in Argentina's environment. At the same time, there was a desire to maintain upside potential should market conditions improve.

The result was the sale of the plant to a local pharmaceutical company along with a grant of a license/supply arrangement. This licensee would now import the raw materials for local manufacture in its newly acquired plant and, subsequently, sell finished products to local customers. However, to retain marketing control, the Merck affiliate would continue to maintain a sales force to promote the Merck product line to physicians and hospitals. The licensee would pay the Merck affiliate a fee for these marketing services in support of its product sales. In addition and most importantly, Merck retained an "option" on future improvement in the business through a "price sharing" arrangement. This structure provided for payments by the licensee to the Merck affiliate if in-market selling prices in real-dollar terms increased above contractually specified levels. This structure was subsequently modified to a profit-sharing arrangement. In either case, when Argentina's economic situation improved in the early 1990s, Merck exercised its options and owned a stake in the licensee's profitability. This feature best exemplifies how a financial structure was created to limit or reduce operational risk while allowing for positive future results.

At the same time, the wisdom of retaining the AgVet business became apparent owing to the more flexible pricing environment for this product line. As part of Argentina's economic liberalization program, it became feasible to price AgVet products on a dollar-indexed basis (i.e., to structure local-currency invoice terms in a way that ensured that the dollar value of the collection, at the time an invoice came due, was equivalent to its dollar value at the time the receivable was created). In this fashion, the local-currency monetary exposure to devaluation was effectively eliminated even though financial hedging instruments, such as forward exchange contracts, were not then available in Argentina.

As in other real world situations, after the restructuring, the arrangement encountered some bumps during Argentina's severely hyperinflationary period, which necessitated adaptation and modification underscoring the need for continuous monitoring and periodic format re-evaluation of the risk/return profile of international projects. Since 1988, there have been at least three major reviews of the Argentine business. The impetus for such reviews has come both from the finance area—particularly sensitive to financial market parameters such as exchange, financing costs, and the risk of capital barriers—and from operating management, who are more sensitive to product pricing and market conditions.

CONCLUSION

The CFO must be a full partner in the assessment of international risk trade-offs, especially given the extent to which the array of international risks has increased in recent years. The skills that the CFO traditionally brings to financial risk assessment can be transferred to international business risk assessment as well. It is critical that risk assessment be done consistently throughout the organization; the CFO can again assist in providing both the "language" and the structure to make this happen efficiently. At Merck, we have found that risk assessment, if done well, is not only an up-front analytical process, but also an ongoing project management function, in the same manner as a reassessment of marketing factors is part of the business process. It is also clear that international risk assessment often requires a more complex analysis than that required for a domestic project. The CFO not only manages the financial risks but can also be a partner in the risk management process with operating management through the extension of financial modeling tools to assess alternative operational solutions to risk reduction. The ongoing risk assessment and review process provides a good framework for ensuring that those processes are in place and working in a way that benefits the project and, ultimately, the firm's shareholders.

20

⑥ OVERSEAS ALLIANCES

Assessing the Potential Benefit from, Searching for, and Structuring Them

John L. Becker
Director of Business Development, Cummins Engine Company

Robert J. Sack
Professor of Business Administration, Darden Graduate School of Business Administration, University of Virginia

In this chapter we will review the reasons why a company might want to enter into an overseas alliance, the process that might be followed in identifying an overseas partner, and some of the factors that might be considered in structuring such a relationship. This discussion will focus on formal alliances, particularly joint ventures. Some ideas discussed in this chapter will apply to other less formal relationships such as a license with a local manufacturer or an agency agreement with a local distribution company, but the discussion here will assume that the circumstances justify a more participative, more active relationship.

In some larger companies development of overseas alliances will be the primary responsibility of a special unit, staffed with people who have experience in international business and in contract negotiation. In other companies development of overseas alliances will be managed case-by-case by individually established task forces. In any event, where the overseas alliance is potentially material, its development should be monitored by an oversight committee from senior management. The CFO should either be directly involved in the project development or be an active part of the oversight team. This discussion is designed to enhance the CFO's perspective on that development effort.

OPPORTUNITIES FOR AN OVERSEAS ALLIANCE

How does a management team identify an opportunity for an overseas alliance? The company's strategic planning process should include a regular analysis of the potential market for the company's products throughout the world, or the potential for application of the company's processes to the development of new products. Those discussions should target areas where there appear to be significant market opportunities, now or in the future, for an international partnership. CPC International provides an interesting illustration of that strategic thinking in its 1994 Annual Report. A copy of the company's two-page analysis "Business Extension 1992–94" is reproduced in Exhibit 20.1. Note the joint ventures established in South Africa (to re-establish the company in that country), Latin America (to combine forces with General Mills), and Mexico (to strengthen the company's position in the NAFTA market).

Except in unusual circumstances (e.g., where the elimination of apartheid made it possible for companies to move quickly into the South African market), the development of a new market area should proceed in a planned, logical progression. For example, once an opportunity has been identified, it may be wise to begin work in that area with an agency relationship and then evolve through a licensing agreement to a joint venture. Most importantly, the strategic plan for particular market opportunity should set out the type of relationship that would be most appropriate in that market, for the long term, and should outline a timetable for the evolution toward that goal. It pays to do that long-range thinking at the outset, because it is important to identify possible partners early on so as to have the time and the business opportunities to assess their potential. Similarly, it is recommended that the U.S. firm begin the implementation of that plan and begin working in the area, even on a limited basis, because that presence will provide an opportunity to cultivate the personal relationships required for any subsequent joint venture relationship.

In some markets, the near-term sales volume will be too small to otherwise justify a formal, joint venture relationship, but the long-term promise will be significant. In such a situation it may be important for strategic reasons to establish a joint venture with a domestic company early on to get a jump on the competition and

EXHIBIT 20.1   Business Extension 1992–94   Acquisitions, New Businesses, Joint Ventures (JVs)

Country	Brand/Business Name	Key Products	Strategic Contribution
North America			
United States	LeGoût brand	Soups, bouillons, gravies, entrées, desserts	Doubles CPC's foodservice business in U.S.; adds frozen food products.
United States	Henri's and Western brands	Pourable dressings	Adds to dressings capabilities; strong foothold in Midwestern markets.
United States	Iberia brand	Soups, bouillons, canned vegetables, oils	Builds Hispanic foods lines; provides vehicle for introducing other CPC Hispanic products.
Europe, Africa/Middle East			
Czech Republic	CPC Foods a.s.	Soups, bouillons, dressings	New business in newly opened market; dressings leader; exporting Hellman's mayonnaise to new businesses in Central and Eastern Europe.
Germany	Pfanni brand	Convenience potato products	Leading extendable brand, compatible with the Knorr brand; also contributes to the foodservice business.
Hungary	CPC Hungary Rt.	Soups, bouillons, desserts, dressings	New business in newly opened market; soups and bouillons leader.
Poland	CPC Polska SP.zo.o	Soups, sauces, bouillons, desserts	New business in newly opened market; also currently providing soups, bouillons, and desserts for new business in Russia.
Russia	CPC Foods Company Ltd.	Soups, sauces, bouillons, dressings	New business in newly opened market; first major international company to introduce soups, bouillons, and dressings.
Israel	TAMI	Soups, bouillons, dressings, deserts, cereals	Leading brands and market positions in new market for CPC.
South Africa	CPC Tongaat Foods	Soups, sauces, oils, desserts, starches	JV re-establishes CPC in South Africa; platform for extension into sub-Saharan Africa.
Turkey	Bozkurt brand	Bread spreads, desserts	No. 2 brand for jams and helva desserts; a sales organization to support CPC's soup, bouillons, and desserts.
Latin American			
Regional	International Dessert Partners	Baking and dessert mixes	JV combines CPC's organization and infrastructure with General Mills' expertise in dessert mixes.
Argentina	AdeS brand	Soya products	Unique, fast-growing nutritional beverages, with potential for geographic expansion.
Brazil	Vitamilho brand	Precooked corn flour to make dietary staple	Leader in huge Northeast Brazil market, extends CPC's participation in starch/basic nutritious foods business.
Chile	Juan Bas brand	Sauces, mustards, mayonnaise	Strong market leader in chili sauces.
Costa Rica	Don Luis & Maravilla brands	Soups, bouillons, sauces, dressings, desserts	Adds to CPC's no. 1 mayonnaise and sauce business; provides entry into bouillon and desserts categories.
Mexico	Arancia CPC	JV to produce corn-refining products	JV combines CPC's corn-refining business with Arancia business to strengthen CPC's position in Mexico and in the NAFTA market.
Venezuela	Ne-nerina, Polly brands	Processed cereals	Market-leading products; well-established distribution network utilized to strengthen CPC's existing Venezuelan business.
Asia			
China	CPC (Guangzhou) Foods Ltd.	Bouillons	New business in newly opened South China market; first major international company to manufacture bouillons.
China	CPC (Beijing) Foods Ltd.	Bouillons, dressings	New business in newly opened North China market; first major international company in dressings business.
Indonesia	P. T. Knorr Indonesia	Soups, bouillons, corn oil	New business in fast-growing market of 185 million people.
Sri Lanka	Kist brand	Sauces, jams	New business in fast-growing market; distribution for launch of CPC soups and bouillons
Vietnam	Representative Office	Bouillons, soups, dressings, bread spreads (imported)	Coordinating distribution by local companies to establish new business in newly opened market.

Source: 1994 annual report of CPC International.

lock up the best partner. The risk in such a preemptive strike is that
the partner may be discouraged with results in the early years,
which may sour the relationship for the longer term. That risk can
be managed, in part, by establishing a detailed business plan with
the partner, which makes clear the near-term costs and the long-
term potential.

Most strategic thinking looks for an attractive market potential
in a geographic area, but it may also be appropriate to look for opportunities to fill in a product line. It may also be appropriate to
consider a joint venture to exploit that product opportunity, particularly where two companies own complementary technology. For example, Cummins Engine Company and Wartsila, of Finland, have
formed a joint venture in Europe to produce two series of diesel engines above Cummins' current power range. These engines are
based primarily on Wartsila's technology, but benefit from Cummins' experience and designs for high-volume manufacturing. Sales
volume synergy comes from both companies' marketing systems.
In a similar way, two international companies might form a joint
venture to pursue a new technology together, pooling their basic research and sharing future development costs and risks.

The genesis of some overseas alliances will be a natural result of the company's strategic planning process. However, as
often as not, the idea for such an arrangement will come from
field salespeople who are frustrated with their inability to exploit
the market fully or who see an opportunity for a beneficial relationship with a local company. Because of their on-the-scene perspective, the field salespeople can be an important resource for
the firm, and the marketing organization should expect their
field people to act as intelligence gatherers; for example, they
should provide feedback on customer reaction to prices and new
products as well as on activities of the competition. But in addition to monitoring those ongoing business activities, the field
salespeople should be alert to possibilities for an overseas alliance. To help them see the possibilities for a joint venture, it
might be useful to keep those people apprised of kinds of relationships the company has been establishing in various parts of
the world. The development officer ought to be on the agenda of
regional sales meetings, and the company's successes with its
overseas alliances should be detailed in internal publications.

WHY CHOOSE A JOINT VENTURE AS THE FORM OF THE OVERSEAS ALLIANCE?

A company can approach an overseas opportunity with one of several structures, on a continuum as follows:

Sales Agency	License Agreement	Joint Venture	100%-Owned Subsidiary

From a number of standpoints, the best arrangements are the two extremes: a controlled sales agency and a 100-percent–owned operation. With both of those structures, the company earns the full benefit of all of the product sales and maintains control over the technology, the product, and its reputation. The middle two options are compromises and, although they bring distinct advantages, they carry some disadvantages as well.

A local sales agency will often be the lowest-risk approach to an overseas market because it requires little capital investment and because sales proceeds can be denominated in dollars or can be hedged or insured. However, agency agreements are not always practicable. In some developing countries (e.g., India, China, Brazil) constraints such as hard currency availability, import restrictions and duties, or even market price/currency values may make it impractical to ship completed products from the U.S. company's facilities to customers in that country. Further, the agency approach may require customer acceptance of some delivery inconveniences and shipping costs. Finally, the lack of control over the market area can make it difficult for a company to use an agency approach for any significant market penetration.

A wholly owned, local manufacturing facility could offer the best opportunity to earn the maximum payoff for a new market. But such an overseas investment carries significant risks such as those highlighted in the preceding chapters. It might be possible to manage most foreign exchange risk with hedging strategies or by borrowing locally a large share of the required capital. Nonetheless, the long-term nature of such an investment makes it very difficult to control effectively currency risk. More importantly, because the market is unfamiliar, it will be difficult for a U.S. company going into a new territory to establish an acceptable level of comfort with projections of revenues and costs. Unless the product has been firmly established in the marketplace or feasibility studies indicate that there is likely to be a cost-effective volume, many companies will be reluctant to commit the required investment and take on that kind of risk in a foreign environment on their own.

In addition to the financial investment, the development of a wholly owned manufacturing subsidiary overseas requires a similar investment of management talent. Because of the demands of working in a different environment, the people committed to such an enterprise must be the very best. Again, unless there is a cadre of people who have demonstrated that they can manage effectively in the local environment—the supplier, employee, customer, and regulatory communities—many companies will shy away from making such a commitment of money and management talent on their own. Absent the confidence as to product acceptance and management abilities, a license agreement or a joint venture that brings local capabilities is often the best alternative.

A license agreement that permits a local company to manufacture a product for sale in a particular market area does provide some return from the grant to use the company's technology, and that return can be earned without the cost or risk of any incremental capital expenditure. However, there are some significant disadvantages to a license form of expansion: Except for some industries, the return earned on a license is typically small, and few companies want to give up the promise of a more active involvement in a really significant market. Of more concern, a license agreement allows the local company to control the development of the market. In the best of circumstances, the local manufacturer develops the market according to its own needs for growth and is constrained by its own needs for capital. In a more skeptical scenario, the local manufacturer may be tempted to develop its own products to meet the needs of the market and allow the licensed product to atrophy. At the worst, even the most carefully written license agreement carries the risk that the local manufacturer will appropriate the licensed technology or the production process for purposes unintended by the licensor. Given that line of thought, in any market where the market potential is significant and where the technology is worth defending, a joint venture may be the better route to overseas expansion.

Perhaps the most common reason to enter into an overseas joint venture is to gain market access.[1] Notwithstanding a product's unique advantages, it may be very difficult to introduce that product into a particular market because of the dominance of local suppliers. Very often, a local supplier has local loyalties and a distribution network that is hard for an outsider to crack. Also, because of community ties or government regulations, a local supplier may be part of a vertically integrated chain of companies that control the end market. For example, U.S. automobile companies have reported significant difficulty penetrating the distribution system in Japan. A new Ford dealer in Tokyo says, "The market's open tariffwise, but behind the tariffs, it's very difficult."[2] Finally, because of wage rates, amortized equipment costs, tax breaks, and a number of other reasons, a local supplier can often compete with pricing—even if only on a short-term basis—in a way that effectively closes the market to outsiders. In those situations, a sales agency will not be practical. And, because of the risks inherent in a license agreement, a joint venture (cooperation with a strong local supplier) may become the best way to gain access to the local market expeditiously.

In a more positive vein, there are situations where a local company has such potential as to make a partnership attractive without regard to market opportunities in the area. The local partner may have a unique product, new technology, or an extraordinary group of people—any of which can supplement and leverage the U.S. company's position. Often there is a blending of reasons for a strategic alliance. For example, Cummins Engine and Komatsu have established a pair of co-operative joint ventures. One venture in Japan was set up to produce Cummins' midrange engines both for Cummins' customers and for use in Komatsu's earthmoving equipment produced in Japan; another venture in the United States was set up to manufacture a product based on

---

1. There may be situations where an overseas venture is suggested by wage rate differentials, supplier costs, tax rates, or natural resource opportunities. The discussion here, analyzing advantages and disadvantages of the several forms of overseas organization, applies equally to those alliances.
2. Quote attributed to Motoh Katsumata in Edith Updike, "Roadblocks, Roadblocks Everywhere," *Business Week*, June 19, 1995.

Komatsu's 30-liter engine for sale through the Cummins system. In addition to improved market access, both companies value various functional skills of the other and plan to master those skills for adaptation and implementation within their own respective companies.

All of the above discussion is linear, following the chart from a sales agency to a full ownership. But the structure of the relationship need not be so categorical. It may make sense to divide the concept of the business venture into its component elements and introduce quite a bit of creativity into the organization of the relationship. It is possible to pick and choose between a variety of organizational forms and then mix and match the most appropriate form to the organizational need. For example, an overseas relationship could be structured in any one of the above forms or any of these combinations:

1. Form a joint venture to manage the marketing of a product, and have that venture buy the product from a local company that manufactures the product under license from the U.S. partner, or vice versa.
2. Have the venture construct its facility with temporarily advanced funds, but then sell the facility to the local partner under a sales/leaseback arrangement.
3. Establish separate ventures for manufacturing, marketing, and financing a product in an area, and create different control and capital structures for each, according to the business it will undertake.

The objective of any such mix-and-match arrangement will be to gain the maximum advantage from the specialized structure with the lowest administrative cost.

ESTABLISHING THE JOINT VENTURE

Many companies are likely to find that their people will identify more opportunities for overseas alliances than the company can pursue. It will be useful to establish a procedure to filter out the most promising alternatives, and to keep track of the ventures in development so that their promise is realized. Once a concept for an alliance is outlined, Cummins follows an internal management process that has been refined to five steps:

1. "Charter" a feasibility study of the alliance.
2. Develop a "contract" for deliverables with management.
3. Have interim reviews during negotiations.
4. Obtain final approvals.
5. Begin operations, manage the results, and build the relationships.

Step 1: "Charter" a Feasibility Study

Defining the Concept

Field personnel or some other source within the company will be the first to identify an opportunity for an alliance and define a business concept for the project. The proponents of the project should be asked to describe why this project makes good business sense and spell out what the returns might be. Once this concept is defined and accepted, the project moves into the formal management review process.

Develop the Charter itself

To give form to the concept, a specific "charter" should be developed for the project. The written charter should identify the business logic for the project, compare this project against pre-established criteria,[3] and establish a defined team and budget. The charter should be understood to authorize the team to undertake a feasibility study with the potential alliance partner. In return for that authorization, the charter specifies the deliverables of the feasibility study. Finally, for the project team and for the company's overall management, the charter forms the basis for internal communications about the project.

---

3. Cummins has established an "Alliance Checklist" for this purpose. The Alliance Checklist is a set of questions inquiring into key considerations, which the company has determined are important to the success of any venture. It is used as an early screening device to help management focus on the most promising opportunities. Regardless of the form of the checklist used, it will be helpful for any management to have set out some success criteria in advance, perhaps based on previous experiences, to use as a benchmark for current proposals.

Perform the Feasibility Study

An initial feasibility study should be prepared, analyzing the market and the profitability for the venture. The marketing people working in the area are often the best resource for estimating sales price and volume levels; at a minimum they should be asked to corroborate the data gathered by the joint venture development staff. A cross-functional team, usually working in conjunction with the potential partner, will develop an initial operating plan for the venture including its operating costs and the capital that will be required. The feasibility study should also recognize the corporate resources required from the U.S. partner-firm, including the time of the task force staff and the additional people who may have to be involved in the development and implementation of the alliance. This will also be the time to clearly identify the qualitative factors that might help to justify this venture. If this initial definition demonstrates that the venture has sufficient promise, development of the idea can proceed to the next step.

Step 2: Develop a "Contract" for Deliverables with Corporate Management

Terms of the Contract

It will be important that the people representing the proposed partners in the venture are comfortable with the results of the feasibility study and the assumptions that underlie its results. Assuming that the feasibility study indicates that a joint venture could be profitable, the Cummins project team prepares for a "Step 2" review with senior management. This review explains the feasibility study, again compares the project against the Alliance Checklist, and documents a "contract" with management that governs subsequent activities. The contract identifies the deliverables both from the project team and from management as the project enters the formal negotiation phase of its development. The contract identifies, in detail, the resources and timing required for developing and implementing the project and establishing a clear set of "negotiating limits" within which the project team is authorized to commit the company. Depending on the specific alliance being negotiated, these "limits" might detail target ranges or positions on items such as

Ownership levels.

Management positions and alliance governance.

Transfer price formula and risk sharing.

Technology payments and control.

Capital investment and borrowings.

Input prices from partners.

Projected financial returns.

In turn, as its part of the contract, management agrees to provide the human and financial resources required for the detailed planning and negotiating phase of the project and commits in principle to undertake the project if the team stays within the negotiating limits.

Identify the People

As part of working out the contract with management, the implementation timetable should be developed, together with an assignment of responsibility. The early responsibilities are usually assigned to the development team, but the personnel of the U.S. company who will eventually be charged with managing the venture should be designated as early as possible in the development process and included as members of the negotiating team. This allows them to develop a strong relationship with the partner with whom they will be working and to build "ownership" in the negotiated agreements that will govern their future activities.

There are several trade-offs here. To make the opportunity inherent in the venture attractive to the best people, some of the key features of the venture must be outlined with a good deal of specificity. However, the venture will be more successful in the long run if the people who are to be responsible for the management of the business have been involved in the development of the operating plans. Bringing the people who will be responsible for the operations into the planning process early will pay subsequent dividends because they will own the operating plan. However, the planning process must begin well before there can be any assurance that the venture will become a reality. That uncertainty will create a risk for the company and for the people involved. The company must trade off the expected potential from a possible future joint venture operation against the cost of removing those skilled people from their current assignments. The individuals involved must also weigh the potential payoff from an interesting and challenging career opportunity against the risk that they will be in limbo if the project does not come to fruition. Top management should evaluate that risk in the same way as they evaluate any other business opportunity, considering the cost of being wrong against the rewards of being right. It is inappropriate, however, to ask employees to make that same hard-eyed analysis—the company must find a way to assure the employees that their career risks are minimal and their opportunities are enhanced by joining in this venture.

Negotiate an Agreement in Principle
There will have been a number of discussions between the teams representing the two partners during the process of developing the initial concept and completing the feasibility studies, but eventually those discussions (which entail much negotiating and establishing of positions) must become formal negotiations. There will be a point where the parties agree to push toward a definitive agreement. During the feasibility studies, the parties will have agreed on certain data, assumptions, and structures on which to base their projections. They will probably have agreed on the purpose of the alliance (What is its scope?), a general statement of the investment required (What is each party to bring to the table?), a set of financial projections (If we each do our job, what might the venture earn?) and, perhaps, the management plan (Who is to be responsible for what?). Having agreed on those fundamentals, the two negotiating teams ought then to agree on a timetable for the development of any interim documentation, such as a memorandum of understanding. In addition, at this time, the parties ought to have reached an agreement on the details of the contribution each part is to make, the process of due diligence that they will follow, and the development of the final documentation.

For the alliance to be successful, each party must be in a position to contribute something of value; if the contribution is too one-sided, the relationship will be strained and, if confronted with a period of business difficulty, that strain could collapse the venture. In the negotiations, it is important for each side to acknowledge explicitly the contribution the other is making, even if that contribution cannot be quantified. An explicit recognition of the contribution brought by each party sets a tone of mutual dependency and cooperation at the beginning; it also establishes the expectations each of the parties has for the venture and for each other.

It may be possible to delegate much of the negotiation to the development team or the management people who are to be assigned to the venture. However, in any significant venture the top people from each of the partner companies must be involved. Over the life of the venture, the partners will encounter changes in their needs and in the business environment of the venture. Adaptations will be required from everyone involved. The venture is more likely to be successful if the people at the top have come to respect each other, and if, based on that personal relationship, they develop a commitment to make the venture work. They will need several opportunities to meet and get a feel for each other as to ethical standards, business philosophies, and management styles. Written reports with background data help begin the association, but for most top management people it will take several personal assessments before the venture can become a real partnership. The venture will need an influential senior management sponsor on both sides who is committed to the partnership's success.

It is also important that the key people in the negotiations be able to demonstrate their international sensitivity. In many cases, the people from the overseas partner will have had some international experience, but that is not as often the case for the people from the United States. Unless the negotiating team representing the U.S. partner has international experience, they will be well advised to do some advance work before the discussions begin. The team ought to have an opportunity to travel in the overseas country and to do some reading on the country's history and culture. Even if it has been agreed that the venture will conduct its business in English, the negotiating team from the United States ought to have some familiarity with the local language so as to demonstrate their interest in the partner's society and to function more effectively in the local environment.

The above discussions suggest that the venture needs to be a collegial, friendly, personal partnership. Over the long term that will be true. However, it is also true that the venture is a business partnership. The formal negotiations establishing the venture will set the tone for the eventual working relationship, and it is important that both sides field teams who can communicate their business acumen and their knowledge of markets, operations, and finance in a clear, competent manner.

The negotiations toward an agreement in principle should cover the critical elements of the alliance, such as

- The fundamentals of the business plan, including a qualitative statement of the objectives of the venture and a quantitative projection of the expected results.
- A time plan for the continued development of the venture over its start-up or initial operating period.
- An outline of the contributions each party will make to the venture, including capital, people, equipment and facilities, product design, know-how, and technology. It should also include actions that either partner must complete outside the scope of the venture upon which the success of the venture depends.
- A plan for the delegation of authority, including the degree of authority that should be retained by the various supervisory and management bodies and their composition. The negotiations should also establish the basis for determining the compensation of the venture's management team.
- An outline of the venture's financial reporting structure, including an agreement as to the basis of the accounting to be used, the frequency of the reports that will be prepared, and the provisions to be made for internal and external audit.
- An understanding of the scope of due diligence work that each party will want to undertake before the agreement is finalized.

There are several trade-offs to be made in these face-to-face negotiations: On the one hand, it is important to have talked through as many of the critical issues as possible so as to avoid unpleasant debates later in the relationship. On the other hand, it is equally important for these discussions to focus on the really key issues, lest the negotiations get bogged down in minutiae and the parties become distracted by arguments over saving face. If there can be an agreement on what the key issues are, the details can be settled later.

Another trade-off entails an assessment of competition for affiliation with the overseas partner. If there are other parties courting this specific overseas partner in competition with the U.S. company, the company must make a judgment as to the appropriate level of detail and time expended in coming to an agreement in principle. The company may decide to accelerate the discussions and come to an agreement in principle at a broader level than might otherwise be advisable so as to preclude the overseas partner from negotiating with other parties. It will be important for the team to be satisfied that open issues can be resolved during the due diligence and final negotiation phases. On October 31, 1995, *The Wall Street Journal* carried a story announcing that Shanghai Automotive Industry Corp., China's leading car maker, had chosen General Motors as its partner for the production of vehicles, engines, and transmissions in a joint venture worth $1 billion. The article included these interesting quotes: "Observers say that GM beat Ford for the deal in large part by doing more to appease local demands for technology transfer, export rights and investment capital" and "A spokesman for Ford said the auto maker is 'disappointed. We, of course had worked hard on the project. We wish GM good fortune on it.'"[4]

Some issues will be more important than others—priorities will vary according to the circumstances. The negotiating team ought to have a short list of "must-haves" for each possible venture situation. In addition to the items detailed in the above listing, for example, it may be critical to agree on quality control provisions to protect a trade name or a product reputation. Where the manufacturing process entails environmental risks, it may be important to reach an agreement on appropriate controls. Where the

---

4. Gabriella Stern, "GM Is Selected over Ford by China for Joint Venture," *The Wall Street Journal*, October 31, 1995.

venture is to exploit a new technology, it may be important to get an agreement as to assignment of engineering personnel to the venture. Similarly, where the venture is to exploit a market, it will be important to specify the (experienced) people who will be assigned to the marketing team and to commit the parties to a marketing budget. In any area that is critical to the success of the venture, the negotiations must go beyond an agreement that each party will use its "best efforts."

Step 3: Have Interim Reviews during Negotiations

The negotiation effort will typically result, at some stage, in a Memorandum of Understanding between the parties. That interim agreement should serve as the basis for obtaining final buy-off from the decision makers in each organization. The degree to which interim milestones in the negotiations need to be approved by the decision makers will depend on the experience of the parties with joint venture negotiations and the authority vested in the negotiating teams. The more experience the company has had, and the more structured the venture development effort has become, the greater the delegation of authority to the negotiating team can be. But judgment will always be necessary. In every negotiation there will be areas of contention. People directly involved in the negotiations must be alert to those areas and ask for approval on an ongoing basis.

The Cummins process, at Step 2, develops a contract with management within which the negotiating team has approval to operate. Whenever the negotiations go beyond the negotiating limits agreed in the contract, the negotiating team is obligated to prepare an interim review for management and to seek either approval for revised limits or other instructions. Even where the negotiations are proceeding within the limits outlined in the contract, the simple passage of time may necessitate an interim review to confirm progress. Again, the circumstances will dictate the amount of time acceptable between reviews. The more complex the negotiations are, or the more important the venture is to the long-range plans of the company, the more frequent the management reviews should be. Cummins, for example, reviews each development project with senior management monthly.

Regardless of the degree of involvement of the top people in the ongoing negotiations, the final memorandum of understanding should be carefully reviewed with the senior decision makers so that the venture can be visualized in its entirety and the buy-off can be based on a realistic assessment of the plan. Obviously, it is better for the future of the relationship with the overseas partner if the negotiated arrangement can be approved without change; but it will, of course, be better to raise questions at this point and resolve them than to raise them at contract signing time—or later.

Step 4: Obtain Final Approvals

The Due Diligence Review

As part of the final buy-off, it is important to complete the due diligence review that should have begun when the contacts were first made. The due diligence process should include both objective and subjective elements. Cummins includes these types of questions in each of its four review steps:

- A review of the prospective partner's current audited financial statements. Does the partner have the capital to meet its commitments? Does it have sufficient liquidity? Are the trends of its business such that it can continue to meet its obligations, and not make demands on the liquidity of the venture?
- Interviews with prospective partner's business advisers, including an attorney, a banker, and an accountant. How do those people describe the business style of the partner's top managers? How do they rate the ethics of the company? Is there any question as to the partner's legal standing? Is there litigation or are there political problems on the horizon? Based on their knowledge of the partner's business, what do they think about the prospects for the venture?
- Interviews with key business associates of the prospective partner, including customers and suppliers. Is the relationship amicable or contentious? Has the relationship changed over time? How do those people describe the business style of the partner's top managers? How do they rate the ethics of the company?

- Physical inspection of the partner's facilities. Does it appear that the partner pays attention to maintenance? Does it appear that local managers pay attention to environmental risks? Is the facility safe for the employees? What is the attitude in the plant—do management and employees appear to cooperate willingly with each other?
- A review of local press coverage of the prospective partner and its top people. Do the company and its people have reputations as good citizens? Is there evidence that the reputations have changed over time?
- A review of the laws and regulations to which the venture will be subject. Will the laws or regulations preclude implementation of critical elements of the venture regardless of the fact that the overseas partner has agreed to them?
- A review of supporting elements in the economic environment of the host country. Are the assumptions made in the feasibility studies still valid? There are likely to be areas where the business practices in the host country differ from those in the United States. Do those differences carry any implications for the future of the venture?

The Final Documentation

The final documentation for the joint venture should include a written agreement that incorporates all the important points from the negotiated memorandum of understanding. The final documentation should include (1) an initial business plan reflecting the parties' understanding of the plans for the venture's first several years of operations and (2) the bylaws, incorporation papers, and other documents required for the operation of the venture itself.

The degree to which the negotiated agreement between the parties is documented will vary, depending on the perceived risk in the relationship and the business customs of the parties. In countries where professional business management is generally practiced, documentation tends to be more thorough because the parties accept the idea that potentially contentious issues ought to be anticipated and dealt with up-front. In countries where business traditions are based more on personal or family ties, an attempt to document promises, commitments, or procedures is often viewed as an affront to trust and honor. If the issues are contentious, that personal-affront/need-for-trust argument may be raised as a way of avoiding those issues. In such circumstances it will be difficult to push the need for documentation too far but, nonetheless, the final documentation should be as thorough as possible within the bounds of the relationship and should cover these points:

- Definitions of key terms (recognizing translation problems and cultural differences).
- Term of the venture: what its life is to be and how its assets and obligations will be handled upon dissolution.
- Warranties by the officers of the corporate partners as to their legal ability to enter into the venture, the accuracy of the data presented in the financial statements and elsewhere, and negative assurance that there is no other information that might be relevant.
- Scope of the venture: what territory is available to the operations of the venture and/or what product lines it may offer.
- Provisions for profit and loss sharing and for funding capital requirements; the form, amount, and timing of the initial capital contributions expected, and provisions for repatriation of earnings.
- Explicit provisions outlining who is able to bind whom in what circumstances.
- Procedures for making appointments to the oversight body and the management team, particularly where expatriates are to be assigned for any significant period.
- Procedures for establishing compensation (and expense allowances) for the management team, especially expatriates, if any.
- Procedures for the development and approval of the annual business plan as well as the plan's legal standing.
- Basis for establishing transfer prices; where the transfer price is to be based on market prices, a definition of *market* in these circumstances.
- Provisions for financial and qualitative reports to the venture partners, and for internal and external audits.

Step 5: Begin Operations, Manage the Results, and Build the Relationships

Establish the Operating Plan and Modify It

Once the venture begins operations, it is important for its managers to report on its activities, comparing results against the original plan. Management of the U.S. parent must commit extra attention to the venture in its early operations so as to be able to interpret its initial results and to take corrective action as might be required. The initial operations are sure to vary from the original plan and, after an initial period of operations, it will no doubt be necessary to develop a revised business plan for the ensuing years. The business plan is often the tool by which the parties agree to manage the venture, and this document can be an important form of communication between the oversight body and the management of the venture. Formal participation in approval of a regularly updated plan and scheduled measurement of performance against it are some of the most powerful management tools that the partners can employ. Regular participation in the planning and review process will alert the partners to business trends or problems requiring their intervention.

Development of a revised plan should form the basis of discussions between the partners as to the changes that might be required in the venture's operations, or the partners' activities on behalf of the venture. For example, the initial results of the venture may suggest that the parts supplied by one of the partners should be changed to meet local conditions. Or it may be that the people assigned to the venture are not working out; perhaps the expatriates have not accommodated themselves to the new, foreign environment, or perhaps the staff seconded by the local partner have not been able to meet the expectations of the venture's international customer base. It will be clear that, to make those discussions effective, the management of the venture must be able to report completely and objectively. It will be incumbent on the top people in the management of the partner firms to create an environment where the on-site people in the venture feel free to speak honestly to both partners. It will be tempting for each partner to rely on "their" people in the venture as the source of the real information, but that temptation must be resisted. If the venture is to be successful, there must be a spirit that ensures open communication between venture management and the managements of both partner firms.

Build the Relationship

It is important to think about the venture as part of a relationship. One of the goals should be the development of a working relationship with the partner that goes beyond the joint production of a particular product and beyond any other specific objective. Although the two venture partners may have been attracted to a joint venture because of the need of a particular set of customers for a particular product, the relationship is less likely to be successful if that product is its only raison d'être. Development of the venture should consider the possibilities for a broader relationship, and at any stage of analysis or implementation the possible larger nature of the relationship should be explored. A greater number of business linkages between the partners should enhance communications and provide a broader, more stable base upon which to resolve the inevitable problems that will arise in an international venture.

For example, Cummins Engine has been associated with Dong Feng Motors (DFM) in China as a licensee, and is investigating an expansion of that arrangement into a joint venture for the production of a broader range of engines. But, in addition to the engine business, DFM and Cummins' Fleetguard Division have already established a joint venture to produce filtration products for the Chinese market. In the same way, Cummins recently announced a joint venture with Tata Engineering and Locomotive Company (TELCO) for production of engines in India. Simultaneously, TELCO and Cummins' Holset division have agreed on a joint venture to produce turbochargers for the Indian market. Cummins' intent is to build broader, profitable bridges with both of these partners to help ensure the longevity of the relationships.

Manage the Results

The preceding chapter in this handbook outlines important ideas for successful monitoring of international operations. That discussion applies to overseas joint ventures as well as to wholly owned subsidiaries. A few additional comments may be appropriate to deal with the unique characteristics of the joint venture form of business.

Hedging and Currency Control

Chapter 28 suggested a number of procedures for the control of currency risks, with the understanding that the CFO has the ability to centralize treasury operations and manage currency exposures on a net basis. It is unlikely that the other partner in a joint venture will agree to the U.S. partner's control over the venture's funds, so other strategies may be required to manage the exposure facing the U.S. partner as a result of its investment in the venture. Typically, the U.S. partner will incorporate its anticipated or planned flows from the joint venture into its computations for net exposure—even though it must recognize that it does not have direct control over the internal management of the funds within the venture. There may be ways to manage that exposure even without direct control over the funds. For example, the local venture partner may be content to allow the U.S. partner to make its capital contribution in technology or patents. Or it may be that the venture partners can avoid making explicit capital contributions to the venture, and borrow the funding necessary with or without guarantees. Additionally, the partners could agree in advance to prompt repatriation of earnings, with the understanding that funding required for expansion is to be provided by additional bank loans. Finally, the partners could also agree to pricing the inputs to the venture in a currency that might help alleviate some of the currency exposures.

Monitoring and Flagging

To maintain the right up-front relationship between the venture partners, it might be a good idea to establish flagging devices in the venture agreement, with the understanding that they will be reported monthly to both partners and used as the basis for the discussions with the management of the venture. As discussed earlier, the business plan will typically be the basis for conversations about the results of the venture. In addition to the traditional report comparing results against plan, Cummins uses a simple communication device. At each quarterly board meeting of each of their joint ventures, the managing director will present to the board a single-page summary commenting on the critical issues in the plan with a red, yellow, or green flag signifying, respectively, off plan, near plan, or on plan. Subsequent details on "red" items include data, analysis, and action plans.

Audit procedures

The venture agreement must include provisions for audit of the venture's operations. Those provisions should include the timing of audit visits, and understanding that internal audits will be permitted and coordinated, a requirement that audit reports sent to venture management will also be sent to representatives of the partners, and a description of how the external audit team will be selected. It will often be appropriate for the venture to use local accounting standards because that will be the basis of accounting that local banks and suppliers expect. But in that case, there must be provision for conversion of those local generally accepted accounting principles (GAAP) statements into terms that will be usable for preparation of the U.S. partner's financial statements. Frequently, each partner will insist that the auditors it uses for its corporate accounts be engaged as the venture's auditor. Discussion between the partners and their auditors can resolve the issue, for example, by resorting to dual audit appointments or by providing for alternating roles for the two audit firms.

ACCOUNTING FOR THE JOINT VENTURE BY A U.S. PARTNER

The Consolidation Method

Where a partner owns a controlling interest in a joint venture, accounting standards in the United States require the use of the full consolidation method. Under today's interpretation of that rule, a "controlling interest" is understood to result from ownership of more than 50 percent of the venture's outstanding voting stock. Special circumstances might argue for the application of the substance of the rule, and against a strict application of the numeric guidelines. For example, a partner with a 45 percent interest might argue for the use of full consolidation where there are a number of other partners, none of whom own more than 10 percent. It would be expected, in that situation, that the 45 percent partner has control over the venture's board of directors and its operating management. In a reverse situation, a 60 percent partner might argue against the use of full consolidation because its ability to control the venture is blocked by specific provisions of the venture agreement, a bank covenant, or local law. Under today's interpretations it would be very difficult to apply "control" in such a substantive way. Current practice follows the 50 percent voting stock interpretation of control almost slavishly. That could change, however, if the Financial Accounting Standards Board (FASB) exposure draft on Consolidation Policies and Practices becomes GAAP. That exposure draft is discussed in the final paragraphs of this section.

Under the full consolidation method, the controlling partner includes all of the venture's assets and liabilities as well as all of its sales and expenses in its balance sheet and income statement. The interests of the other partners in the venture's net assets and net income are reported as minority interest in the controlling partner's financial statements. To accommodate the adding together that is required by the consolidation process, the statements of the venture will have to be restated in terms of U.S. GAAP if they are not already in accord with those standards, and then translated into U.S. currency in accordance with the requirements of SFAS 52.

The Equity Method

Where the partner owns enough of the voting stock of the venture to influence its direction, but not enough to control it, accounting standards in the U.S. require the use of the equity method. Convention has it that ownership of more than 20 percent of the venture's voting stock, up to 50 percent of the stock, is indicative of having influence but not control. Under the equity method, only the partner firm's share of the venture's net assets is included in the partner's balance sheet, and only the partner's share of the venture's net income is included in the partner's income statement. Before those net assets and that net income can be included in the U.S. partner's financial statements, the statements of the overseas venture must be restated to comply with U.S. GAAP and translated into U.S. currency, just as though the venture was to be consolidated. Where the venture is material to the reporting partner, the partner should include a footnote to its financial statements outlining the key details of the venture's assets, debt, and operations.

The footnote from Cummins' 1994 annual report to shareholders (Exhibit 20.2) clearly demonstrates the application of the equity method. Note that the carrying value of the investments in unconsolidated companies ($100.1) appears as an asset in the

EXHIBIT 20.2

Investments in Unconsolidated Companies ($ in Millions)

	December 31, 1994	1993
Consolidated Diesel Company	$ 33.1	$ 50.9
Kirloskar Cummins Limited	22.3	16.9
Behr America, Inc.	11.7	12.1
Other Investments	33.0	22.0
Carrying value	$100.1	$101.9

Included above in other investments at December 31, 1994 and 1993 were $17.7 million and $18.5 million, respectively, related to temporarily owned distributorships. Cummins' sales to these distributorships approximated $40 million in 1994 and $50 million in both 1993 and 1992.

Summary financial information for 50-percent-or-less–owned companies:

Earnings data	1994	1993	1992
Net sales	$913.6	$746.4	$695.9
Earnings before extraordinary item	14.8	3.4	14.4
Earnings	14.8	3.4	6.4
Cummins' share	5.6	.4	3.4

Balance sheet data	December 31, 1994	1993
Current assets	$199.4	$151.4
Noncurrent assets	186.0	207.0
Current liabilities	(146.3)	(127.0)
Noncurrent liabilities	(41.8)	(38.2)
Net assets	$197.3	$193.2
Cummins' share	$81.4	$82.7

Source: 1994 annual report of Cummins Engine Company.

"Investments and Other Assets" section of the company's 1994 balance sheet. That carrying value is more than Cummins' share of the investees' net assets. Based on the commentary in the exhibit we understand that that difference is due to the inclusion of temporary advances to those companies as well as Cummins' equity investments in them. If there were any significant amount of the goodwill included in the carrying value (because the interest in the venture was purchased at a premium from a third party), the amount of the goodwill would have been highlighted in the exhibit's text, and the amortization period disclosed. Cummins' income statement does not report the company's earnings from the ventures as a separate line item, no doubt because it is immaterial. That is typically the case. In fact, many companies include the earnings or loss from their ventures as part of consolidated cost of goods sold because they see the ventures as part of the overall production chain.

Implementation of the Consolidation and the Equity Methods

Where the full consolidation method is used, all intercompany transactions (e.g., sales by the partner and purchases of the venture) should be eliminated in the income statement, and unrealized profit (e.g., in inventory of the venture) should be eliminated from the income statement. Under equity accounting, no eliminations are required in the income statement, but unrealized profit in the venture's balance sheet should be eliminated. Under full consolidation, any difference between the partner's investment in the venture and its equity in the net assets of the venture will be allocated to other asset categories, most often goodwill, which in turn must be amortized to income. Under equity accounting, the difference between the partner's investment in the venture and its equity in the venture remains in the investment account. However, that difference must be amortized against earnings over a period in excess of 40 years, just like goodwill.

Proportional Consolidation

Equity accounting makes sense where the partner's share of the venture is, say, 35 percent, but it is conceptually awkward when the venture is equally owned, 50–50 by two partners. In those situations, the partners are often equally committed to the venture's obligations and may even share an obligation to share in its output, to cover its costs, and to contribute to its capital projects. As more and more business is done through alliances, some have argued for proportional consolidation. Under proportional consolidation, each partner takes its share of the line items from the venture's financial statements—the venture's individual assets, debts, revenues, and expenses—and includes that proportionate share in its own financial statements. That approach acknowledges the reality of the shared opportunity/obligation inherent in a joint venture. It also avoids the sometimes awkward "minority interest" presentation.

Unfortunately, proportional consolidation has not become accepted accounting in the United States except in a few unusual industry applications. The idea may be more completely developed in the future, but that development will depend on approval of the FASB.

The FASB's Consolidations Project

The Financial Accounting Standards Board has been working on a consolidations project since 1982. The work has resulted in one statement (SFAS 94, which requires consolidation of all majority-owned subsidiaries regardless of the nature of their businesses), several discussion memoranda, and one recent exposure draft. The most important issues the board is considering, which have the potential to impact joint ventures, are

- A suggestion that consolidation decisions be based on the degree of control exercised by the owner of the interest, rather than on the degree of voting stock owned.
- A suggestion that minority interest in a consolidated venture be treated as a separate component of equity on the partner's balance sheet, and not as a liability.
- A suggestion that, when a company presents segment information in accordance with SFAS 14, it defines *segments* as the business units management uses to manage the company's day-to-day operations.
- A challenge to the one-line presentation now used for consolidated equity investees, including a suggestion that proportional consolidation be allowed for real joint ventures.

The first two items have been addressed in an exposure draft released by the board in October 1995. That exposure draft does conclude that consolidation be based on a very broad definition of control, and it does conclude that minority interests should be shown as a part of the partner firm equity. In response to the exposure draft, the FASB received 158 written comments and heard from 26 people in a public hearing on February 26, 1996. It will take time for the board to work through the input it received, and to re-build a consensus among its members for any subsequent revisions to the exposure draft. Separately, the board had expected to issue an exposure draft of a new statement dealing with presentation of segment data in the first quarter of 1996, and may hold public hearings at a later date. There are no benchmark dates for the project on presentation of unconsolidated entities, at least as of Fall 1995; that portion of the overall consolidations project is still in the information gathering phase.

TAX ISSUES

The tax aspects of an overseas joint venture are very complex and could be the subject of a handbook all on their own. Because different overseas ventures will usually operate in different countries or will involve different products or services, it will be very difficult to generalize good tax practice from one venture to another. It will be important to have the counsel of a qualified tax practitioner, particularly during the time the overseas venture is under development and while its initial operations are being tested in practice. The venture should be designed to accomplish its strategic goal, not just to meet a tax objective. Nonetheless, tax costs must be considered in the feasibility studies conducted to assess the venture and tax counsel may be able to suggest ways to manage those costs. Similarly, where there are alternatives as to the location of the facility or the structure of the venture, it will be useful to include tax considerations in the cost/benefit analysis of those alternatives.

A number of tax factors can influence the design and operation of an overseas joint venture. If the overseas venture is structured as a partnership, the U.S. partner's share of the venture's earnings would be taxable both locally and in the United States as earned. In the partner's U.S. tax return, it would be allowed a foreign tax credit for its share of the local taxes paid by the venture. In the more usual case, where the venture is a local corporation owned in part by a local shareholder and a U.S. company, the tax status is both better and more complicated. Because the U.S. parent may not include an overseas venture in its consolidated tax return and because there is no "equity method" built into the tax code, the earnings of the overseas venture will be taxable in the United States only as distributed as dividends. The overseas venture will have paid local taxes on the earnings that produced those dividends, but the U.S. investor will only be entitled to a limited foreign tax credit. That "indirect foreign tax credit" is calculated initially as follows: Multiply the taxes paid or accrued by the venture during the year by the percentage that the dividends paid in that year are of the venture's undistributed earnings. The resulting foreign tax credit may not be used to reduce the taxes due on U.S. source income so the credit is limited to the lesser of (1) the foreign taxes paid or accrued or (2) the U.S. taxes attributable to that foreign source income. The resulting foreign tax credit is subject to other limitations and restrictions as well. Nonetheless, it will be important to consider (1) the tax rate in the local country and (2) the possibility that some portion of the earnings of the venture should be paid out to see whether there might be a benefit from a current foreign tax credit for the U.S. investor.

All tax planning for foreign tax credits assumes that the venture has its income and the U.S. parent has its income, but it will be immediately clear that those apparently objective incomes will be greatly influenced by transfer prices to and from the venture. Because of the influence the U.S. investor will have, it will be tempting to manage cash flow and currency exposures resulting from the investment in the venture by managing the transfer prices of goods and services provided to or bought from the venture. The parent firms may agree to almost any transfer price scheme that is acceptable to them, but the U.S. tax authorities will measure the relative income between the U.S. parent and the venture using prices that would prevail in an "uncontrolled" or arms-length transaction. Where the goods or services are commonly exchanged in the marketplace, the arms-lengthness of the transfer prices used will not be difficult to demonstrate. Current IRS regulations (regulations under Section 482, revised in 1994) acknowledge that there will be situations where there is no exactly comparable transaction in the arms-length market. So long as the differences can be compensated for, it may still be possible to rely on those "inexact comparables." Where the products or services are not commonly exchanged in the marketplace, the transfer price may have to be extrapolated by factoring out normal profit margins from the sales price of the end product, or factoring in normal profit margins from the cost of the goods or services transferred. The regulations detail six methods for establishing a transfer price—those alternatives are referred to as "specified methods." The taxpayer must be able to demonstrate that the transfer pricing method used is the "best method." The taxpayer's method will be evaluated against the reliability of the results considering the completeness of the data, the reality of the underlying assumptions, and the sensitivity of the results to deficiencies in the data and the assumptions. The U.S. parent must continually challenge its transfer pricing methodology to be sure that it (1) meets the IRS test of reasonableness and (2) demonstrates good faith:

> The new penalty regulations issued to implement OBRA 1993 [Omnibus Budget Reconciliation Act], however, reinforce the best-method rule by stating 'A taxpayer can reasonably conclude that a specified method [specified in the regulations] provided the most reliable measure of an arms-length result only if it has made a reasonable effort to evaluate the potential applicability of the other specified methods.[5]

The most serious problems in transfer pricing are likely to arise in connection with the sale or lease of trademarks or technology to the venture. "Regardless of which [transfer pricing method] is used, the transfer price [for an intangible should] attempt to approximate an amount that is 'commensurate with the income' that would be derived from the use of the intangibles."[6]

But the most important elements of the tax aspects of an overseas joint venture are not in the day-to-day operations of the venture, but more in the up-front planning for the venture. The planning for the venture must consider a wide variety of other, more complex factors, including the possibility of locating the facility in a U.S. possession to take advantage of a reduced tax rate, and the possibility that the venture could be considered a "controlled foreign corporation," which would make its earnings taxable to the U.S. parent, as earned. Clearly, in choosing the site for the venture, consider first and foremost the business objectives for the venture. And the ownership structure ought to be designed to deal with the most important overall business concerns. Nonetheless, in the same way that the investors will consider the currency exchange risk when they decide on a location for the venture and design its structure, there will be tax considerations as well. Again, the advice of good tax counsel, up-front, is sure to be worth the cost.

---

5. S. S. Lassar and T. R. Skantz, "New Transfer Pricing Documentation Requirements and Penalties," *The CPA Journal,* April 1995.

6. W. R. Sherman and J. L. McBride, "International Transfer Pricing Application and Analysis," *The Ohio CPA Journal* August 1995.

(Both articles cited in footnotes 5 and 6 demonstrate the transfer pricing methods with a case study/example. An additional case study is explored in Stephen Crow and Eugene Sauls "Setting the Right Transfer Price," *Management Accounting,* December 1994.)

⑥ CONTROLLING GLOBAL OPERATIONS

James M. Cornelius
Chairman, Guidant Corp.

Michael Grobstein
Vice Chairman, Ernst & Young International

"German Deficit May Hit Capital Markets"
Financial Times, May 17, 1996

"Gains in Asia and Europe Push Dollar Higher Against Yen"
The New York Times, May 21, 1996

"A New Latin America Faces a Devil of Old: Rampant Corruption"
The Wall Street Journal, July 1, 1996

"East European Trade May Soon Be Reviving"
The Wall Street Journal, July 22, 1996

As experience clearly indicates, the international business arena is dynamic, complex, and challenging. Larger multinational companies and firms establishing new foreign operations must cope with, among other matters, volatility in the movement of foreign exchange rates, changes in individual countries' restrictions on the flow of funds, hyperinflationary economies, devaluations, and political uncertainties. Increasingly, multinational companies face the tough question, What is the best control strategy to minimize the risks in our international operations in view of our financial and business objectives?

Achieving effective control over international operations requires a recognition that the international environment is different from the U.S. environment—that is, what works in the United States will not necessarily work in foreign operations. Determining the nature and extent of control necessary for an operation outside the United States requires an analysis of pertinent environmental factors. The identification and assessment of these factors for different types and sizes of operations provides a basis for measuring risk and for establishing appropriate, cost-effective controls designed to assist management in its pursuit of corporate goals.

The CFO of a multinational company works with a portfolio of business units operating in a variety of political, economic, and cultural environments. The risks of doing business and of earning targeted returns vary significantly in each of these environments. In addition, international political, economic, and cultural forces are dynamic, so CFOs must continually monitor these forces and measure their potential impact on operations. The CFO, in turn, must make or recommend appropriate adjustments that will cause the operating strategy to be responsive to the changing environment. These adjustments might include modifying the terms of doing business, hedging currencies, reorganizing international banking relationships, centralizing certain international financial activities, or changing the focus of the international internal audit function.

Ultimately, the CFO's role is to provide the expertise and judgment in the financial arena necessary to support line management in achieving corporate goals. The CFO does this by influencing operating as well as financial decisions with objective analysis of risks and potential rewards. The CFO's overall corporate perspective and basic understanding of critical economic variables provides the opportunity to combine this objective analysis with practical suggestions for dealing with investment and financing decisions in foreign operations.

CONTROL IMPLICATIONS FOR
THE GLOBAL ENTERPRISE

Large international companies have typically followed a common evolutionary pattern. This evolution begins with a purely domestic company that expands through the stages of exporter, multidomestic company, multinational company, and global enterprise. A multidomestic company is one that is in the earliest stages of international operations, having established limited foreign operations (e.g., sales offices, distribution centers, and manufacturing facilities) that serve the market needs of a particular foreign market. A multinational company is one where decentralized foreign subsidiaries are organized to perform a complete set of business operations for specified geographic markets, though it may have some functions centralized at parent company headquarters. A global enterprise is one that integrates and coordinates its activities on a worldwide basis.

The degree to which a company manages its operations from a global perspective has profound implications for international strategy and managerial and financial control and coordination. Every activity of a global company is affected, including the allocation of production tasks among different plans, the transfer of knowledge (e.g., process technology, production techniques, and best practices) across locations, the coordination of sales and service activities, sequence of product/service introductions in various markets, managing suppliers and distribution channels in various countries, and consolidation of financial and performance measures. Strategic alliances based in various countries add a further degree of complexity to the global enterprise. Complexity is also introduced by the multiple sets of economic, political, and cultural landscapes on which the global enterprise must operate. A multinational company may allow its subsidiaries a considerable measure of autonomy, but a global enterprise must ensure coordination among different activities that take place in different countries in order to integrate the business processes. The significant control implications that emerge in this environment place added responsibilities on financial management.

INTERNATIONAL FINANCIAL MANAGEMENT

International financial management may be effectively divided into three functions: treasury, controllership, and audit. Exhibit 21.1 lists the typical responsibilities under each function. In this chapter, we will discuss

- The use of environmental risk analysis to develop a control strategy.
- The case for centralized treasury management.
- The focus of the controllership function: designing financial reporting systems and analyzing operating results.

E X H I B I T   21.1

Financial Management Functions

Treasury

Cash management
Foreign exchange and interest rate exposure management
Monitoring environment risk (political/economic/cultural)
International banking
Resource allocation (investments/borrowing/capital structure)
Corporate risk management
Other (credit policies/pensions/investor relations)

Controllership

Financial reporting
General accounting
Cost accounting
Taxes (income, value added tax [VAT], customs duties)
Financial planning and analysis
Capital budgeting (facilities planning)
Profitability and performance reporting

Audit

Internal audit
External audit

- The role of internal audit and ideas for effective coordination with external audit.
- The critical need for good communication.

ENVIRONMENTAL RISK ANALYSIS

Defining Risk Factors

The country in which an operation is located is the primary consideration in determining the degree of control necessary for foreign operations. As discussed in Chapter 19, international risk assessment requires the CFO to examine the political, economic, and cultural factors that will impact operations. Inflation and interest rates, exchange and pricing controls, foreign investment incentives, and management practices are some of the specific factors that should be carefully reviewed. The assessment of the risks associated with these environmental factors, coupled with a definition of the size and scope of operations, provides the basis for structuring control strategy.

Exhibit 21.2 summarizes the key environmental factors that should be identified and analyzed to assess the degree of risk. In reality, the distinctions between political, economic, and cultural factors tend to be blurred; nonetheless, Exhibit 21.2 provides a useful checklist and analytical tool.

Clearly, different countries around the world present varying degrees of environmental risk to a multinational company trying to generate profits. But the political, economic, and cultural factors that cause these risks create a cross-current of problems and opportunities (the balance depending on the area of the world being analyzed). Less developed countries (including much of Latin America) and countries in the process of converting to free-market economies (including those in Eastern Europe and the former Soviet Union) present the highest risks. While Japan, Western Europe, and Canada present lower risks, these countries are certainly not without significant challenge. Exhibit 21.3 depicts the overall level of environmental risk associated with various countries and the effect of that risk on control requirements. The assessment of environmental risk is based on an overall analysis using the factors outlined in Exhibit 21.2.

Effect of Size and Scope of Operations

Once the degree of risk has been assessed, the next step is to define the level of investment and scope of activities to be controlled. For example, a small foreign operation may be selling on letters of credit—to a distributor. This operating commitment may evolve from a three-employee sales branch to a full-scale branch to an assembly operation with sales support, and to an integrated manufacturing and marketing operation that employs hundreds or thousands of people dealing in a number of different currencies. The key point is that as the operation evolves, so do the control requirements.

While few structural changes may be necessary in the initial stages of entering foreign markets, the need for controls increases significantly as a company expands to more than one country and

E X H I B I T   21.2

Environmental Risk Analysis

Locale Characteristics	Lower Risk and Stable Location	Higher-Risk Location	Vulnerable and Very-High-Risk Location
Economic			
Inflation rates	Consistently single-digit	Double-digit	Reaching triple-digit
Interest rates	Single-digit	Double-digit	Extremely high—triple-digit; difficult to obtain local financing for operations
Foreign exchange rates	Moderate changes	Not predictable	Volatile
Exchange controls	None	Some restrictions	Very difficult to remit funds to parent company
Economic growth rate	Median or above	Below median	Negative
Unemployment and termination costs	Low	Average	High
Political			
Exports	Many incentives	Some incentives	Few incentives
Import duties	None or low	Reasonable rates	Very high rates
Foreign investment incentives	Many	Few	None
Foreign ownership	Not restricted	Few restrictions	100 percent or even 51 percent owner-ship not allowed
Expropriation	Not likely	Some risk	High risk
Accounting and statutory reporting requirements	Similar to United States	Different from United States, but not onerous	Onerous
Taxes on income	Foreign investor treated the same—favorable tax treaties with United States	Some additional taxes and/or higher rates	High rates on foreign employees and investors
Product pricing	Not restricted	Few restrictions on certain commodities	Government-controlled product pricing
Cultural			
Productivity rate	Median or above	Slightly below median	Static or declining
Management practices	Similar to United States	Different, but not a problem	Difficult adjustment
Business ethics	Similar to United States	Different, but not an issue	High risk
Language	Similar	Different, but manageable	Difficult to master and assimilate

EXHIBIT 21.3

Relative Risk versus Financial Control

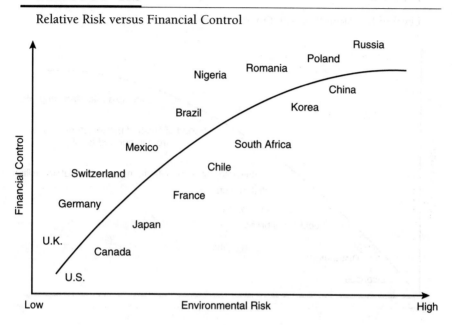

to full-service branches or subsidiaries. The CFO should have a plan to adapt the control strategy to changes in the scope of activity and environmental risks inherent in an evolving foreign operation, as shown in Exhibit 21.4.

CONTROL STRATEGIES

Evaluating the risks in managing foreign operations is a complex undertaking. However, the evaluation is critical to developing an appropriate control strategy. There are three dimensions to consider in developing a control strategy: environmental risk (as described above), growth, and business processes. In fact, the overall level of risk is multiplicative, as depicted in Exhibit 21.5's matrix, rather than additive. However, let's look at the individual items.

Growth

While growth in a business is usually considered a positive sign, there can be associated factors that challenge the ability to control

E X H I B I T   2 1 . 4

Level of Investment versus Financial Control

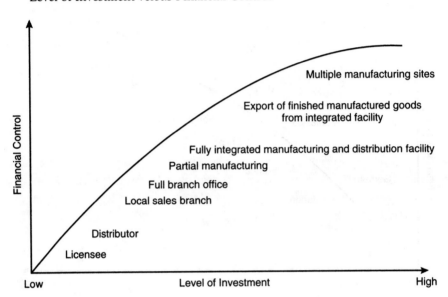

E X H I B I T   21.5

Pressures Influencing Control Strategy

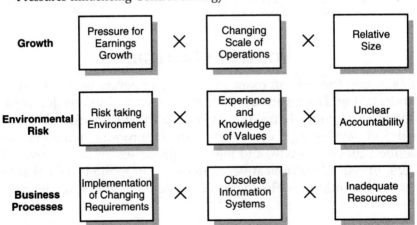

effectively. A rapidly expanding scale of operations over increasingly larger geographic areas is today a piece of the global strategic plan of many businesses. When new parts of the globe are added to an existing business structure, it is usually done with new people who do not have the knowledge of the global company's business ethics and values. The converse of the growth situation is in strategic downsizing in search of earnings growth. Both of these situations can lead to potential financial errors due to inexperienced people.

Environmental Risk

The overall environmental risk analysis outlined in Exhibit 21.2 and earlier chapters is clearly an essential element in developing a control strategy. However, in many cases, culture may be the critical factor that transforms an otherwise low-risk situation to one of high risk. Inadequate information resulting from a culture that avoids "bad news," is too sensitive to customer wants, or is unclear on accountability can have a disproportionate negative impact on the control objectives of the global corporation. Well-written, easily communicated guidelines of company policy are a must. In fact, they should be translated into local languages and reviewed by affiliate management and staff periodically.

Local management practices and business ethics that are not consistent with company operating philosophies create further challenges to effective control that challenge even closely monitored operations.

Business Processes

Finally, the adequacy of the business processes that are heavily reliant on today's computer technology represent another area of control focus. The changing requirements of managing a dynamic global business coupled with the fast-paced changes in computer and telecommunications technology can lead to processing inefficiencies or complete systems breakdowns if business processes are not adequately upgraded and maintained.

Exhibit 21.5—a matrix of these global internal control considerations—highlights the pressures that must be considered in developing an effective control strategy.

The remaining sections of this chapter describe several essential elements of an effective control strategy for multinational companies. The practical considerations and examples should help guide the reader in designing a tailored control strategy.

THE CASE FOR CENTRALIZED TREASURY MANAGEMENT

One of the principal concerns of the CFO of a U.S. multinational company is how to design and maintain a financial control strategy that minimizes the risks associated with doing business in foreign currencies and yet allows line management the freedom to pursue profitable business opportunities in international markets. Floating exchange rates have been an integral part of global economic activity for two decades and despite many attempts by governments to manage their relative values, the currency markets continue to be as volatile as ever. A recent example was seen in the current crisis brought on by the realignment of European currencies in the fall of 1992 and of the Mexico peso in the winter of 1995. In this environment an appropriate financial control strategy is difficult to define, but it is fair to conclude that the interrelationships of interest rates, currencies, and equity markets in the global marketplace will impact normal business activity and therefore deserve to be actively monitored and managed.

To meet the challenge of international financial control, many companies have formed a global treasury function with the day-to-day responsibility for managing individual foreign entity cash flow, capital structure, and working capital—through an existing network of local or regional treasurers—in a manner that reduces the negative impact of foreign currency fluctuations on overall corporate earnings. The global treasurer has the responsibility of evaluating the potential risk of adverse currency movement against the cost-effectiveness of strategies to protect against that risk. By developing a seamless, worldwide exposure management program, the company can benefit from participation in global financial markets. A centralized program does not necessarily have to be located at corporate headquarters. For example, one can consider alternatives such as a finance center in the Netherlands or a coordination center in Belgium, each of which can provide specialized services worldwide.

There are several proven advantages for centralizing the treasury function:

1. Centralized cash management will optimize cash flow and minimize borrowing costs and unfavorable tax effects.
2. Centralized foreign exchange management will help avoid losses. Uncoordinated efforts to minimize losses from fluctuations in exchange rates will, at a minimum, increase the costs of covering exposures and may well result in inadvertently creating exposures. For example, centralized foreign exchange management avoids having two different locations take offsetting hedging positions. Stated another way, effective foreign exchange management requires (1) centralized definition and consolidation of exposures and (2) a level of expertise that the local operation may not possess or be able to afford.
3. Improved communications between corporate financial management and operating unit financial management will facilitate (1) coordination of various related financial management functions and (2) more effective implementation of operating strategies.
4. The consolidation of operating unit treasury functions may provide opportunities for eliminating redundant tasks and positions. Integrating common activities, along with more efficient automation, can lead to significant cost savings.
5. Local management will be relieved of certain administrative responsibilities and can concentrate on manufacturing and marketing efforts.

Centralizing the treasury functions listed in Exhibit 21.1 provides necessary corporate oversight and helps minimize the cost of duplicating the specialized talent and experience necessary to carry out these functions in each country. However, some level of local or regional treasury management also is essential since cash must be collected and deposited efficiently and bills and taxes must be paid on a timely basis. Local or regional treasury personnel are also well situated to provide the global exposure management group with timely information on changes in exposures. In addition, maintaining local banking relationships will help reduce the cost of short-term, seasonal financing. However, centralized

E X H I B I T   21.6

Suggestions for Managing Exchange Risk

Strategic Control Objective	Treasury Program
1. Reduce banking costs of foreign currency conversions through intercompany netting of payables and receivables, denominated in the same currencies.	Coordinating cross-currency flows between affiliated companies with a multilateral netting or clearing system will reduce the amount of currency conversion and enable the company to receive same-day value of transaction. Leads and lags can also be used to manage financing and/or currency exposure and to set intercompany terms for the same purpose within the exchange control regulations and tax rules of each country.
2. Reduce transaction costs and prices paid to third parties by including third-party payments in the netting/clearing process.	Savings can potentially be realized in two ways when third parties are added to a multilateral clearing system. For example, suppose that a third-party vendor located in France supplies material to companies in France, Italy and the UK. Lower prices can often be negotiated by combining the volumes of all three purchasers, paying the supplier in francs, and making a single payment each month. In addition, the combined payment will reduce transaction costs.
3. Hedge specific local entity or corporate cash transactions with foreign exchange contracts.	The global treasury group determines when transactions may be hedged and by what entity. The gross amount will be based on the next hedge requirement after considering expenses and tax effects. Transactions that might be hedged include recorded and future foreign currency obligations, such as royalties, dividends, and intercompany and third-party obligations. In addition, risks from certain anticipated transactions may be hedged using foreign currency options.
4. Centralized exposure management for subsidiaries with nondollar functional currencies by denominating intercompany balances in foreign currencies.	Foreign exchange risk can be better managed and controlled in a central location.
5. View the use of proxy currency hedges very cautiously.	Proxy hedging was a very popular strategy for many years. However, the volatility in cross-rates, which began with ERM realignment in 1992, has significantly reduced the number of efficient proxy hedges. In addition, various developments in accounting rules limit both the instruments and opportunities for proxy hedges when using futures and forwards. However, a proxy hedge generally may be used with foreign options.

E X H I B I T   21.6   *Continued*

Suggestions for Managing Exchange Risk

Strategic Control Objective	Treasury Program
6. Have a very clear understanding of the financial objectives and the accounting treatment for each objective.	It is essential to have a clear, complete understanding of the firm's financial objectives and how each exposure and hedge will appear in the financial statements. Efficient risk management also requires that the market value of each position be monitored on a continuous basis.
7. Obtain insurance coverage to protect high-risk monetary or nonmonetary assets in politically sensitive countries.	The corporate risk manager may use insurance policies to protect company assets from political risk, including expropriation of assets and/or currency inconvertibility. One example is the federal government's Overseas Private Investment Corporation (OPIC) program for less developed countries. Commercial insurance policies that cover the same two risks globally or on a country-by-country basis are also available.
8. Lock in lower interest costs, reduce foreign exchange risks, and ensure credit availability in a specific country by executing an interest rate and/or a currency swap. (Usually a financial intermediary is necessary to match the parties.)	Arbitrage gains can be realized by swapping the strong financial reputation of a multinational in one country for the favorable reputation of a multinational in another country. For example, a U.S. parent company might deposit $5 million at 6 percent for five years in the U.S. branch of an Italian bank and receive a preferential 10 percent borrowing rate on an equivalent amount of lire for its Italian subsidiary. The Italian bank would then lend the U.S. dollars to an Italian customer in the United States who has excess lire in Italy, allowing each party to realize an overall interest rate savings.
9. Use multicurrency credit lines and investments to hedge foreign currency exposure or to reduce global borrowing costs.	Affiliate working capital requirements can be met by a multicurrency borrowing strategy. For example, Swiss francs might be borrowed by a Canadian affiliate because of a lower interest cost associated with the Swiss currency. However, the new exposure to the Swiss franc must be watched closely and hedged if the risk becomes too large.[1]
10. Establish long-term currency protection for a predictable foreign currency receipt or disbursement.	Besides using financial tools such as protection predictable foreign options or currency swaps, the purest currency receipt or disbursement solution is to intentionally create an opposing exposure. For example, a contractual flow of foreign currency receipts can be directly offset by intentionally borrowing in that currency. Similarly, an existing purchaser's arrangement can be changed to the currency where you need to create a liability. In short, the global marketplace may force one to accept an exposure, but because it is global, it is now much easier to offset than before.

1 Taking advantage of interest differentials in borrowing is viable only if the company has offsetting cash flows expected in the currencies in which the debt must be repaid. Otherwise current savings in interest costs could be more than offset by future exchange losses.

management of these relationships, including the establishment of appropriate transaction authorizations, is a critical control point.

IDEAS FOR MANAGING EXCHANGE RISK

Exhibit 21.6's list of strategic objectives and treasury programs is not meant to be all-inclusive, but it does illustrate the actions that a global company can take to deal with the risks inherent in doing business in international markets.

When foreign exchange management is centralized as part of the international treasury function and placed under the control of experienced executives, it can potentially save a multinational company millions of dollars. An important caution: Management must establish parameters that eliminate speculation, including monthly (or more frequent) reporting to senior management of positions, volume, and nature of transactions. There must be a real economic and accounting risk that merits the foreign exchange transaction. In addition, the authorization process for entering into foreign exchange should be clearly established.

Exchange rate risk and inflation tend to be linked over time. In addition, political factors have a bearing on exchange rate risk. For example, the referenda in Denmark and France on the Maastricht treaty during 1992 led to unprecedented volatility in all currency markets. No one can predict the impact of such confrontations on exchange rates. And no one can control exchange rates; they can only control their exposure level by managing their foreign exchange risk.

THE FOCUS OF GLOBAL CONTROLLERSHIP

The traditional controllership functions require extensive attention at the local business unit level. The local finance director does, however, need direction from corporate financial management so that worldwide consistency can be achieved. Guidelines for general and cost accounting practices and the basis for performance measurement, along with a structure for financial reporting, are key areas where such direction is required. This section provides suggestions on (1) key measures in monitoring and evaluating performance and (2) common problems to avoid.

Analyzing Global Results

Monitoring trends and flagging problems in a foreign operation require analysis that goes beyond net income. Because of the exposures to inflation and exchange fluctuations, the focus should be on cash flow and working capital with emphasis on intercompany accounts above prescribed limits. In measuring performance, the following are particularly useful for international operations:

Asset turnover. High turnover helps minimize risk of loss from inflation or currency devaluations.

Sales per employee. Monitoring headcount to control personnel additions will keep the operation efficient. If the operation experiences a downturn, it also will protect against the significant termination costs that are required in many foreign countries.

Net cash flow. Relating cash flows to intercompany account balances will highlight how effectively local managers manage their liquidity, as well as inventory and receivable balances.

Return on investment. Meaningful evaluation of ROI requires adjustments for environmental risks and cost of capital.

The analysis of operations should consider who has responsibility for setting intercompany prices and making various financial decisions. Of course, when responsibility is changed, so should accountability change. Local managers should not be rewarded or penalized for matters over which they have no control. For example, if the local manager is not responsible for the capitalization of the operation or managing foreign exchange risk, then interest charges and the effect of foreign exchange gains and losses should be eliminated from profit and loss calculations used to measure performance. Other methods must then be established to control working capital movement and capital expenditures.

Analyzing Financial Reporting Systems

There are three common pitfalls in financial reporting control systems designed for international operations:

• *The system is not decision-oriented.* Although significant effort is directed toward developing information for corporate and regional management, it is more important that major systems be designed to provide information for planning, controlling, and improving the individual operations. The system should highlight areas that are not within the range of budgets or other expectations, and these variance conditions should trigger action. An effective decision support system is in sharp contrast to a system designed merely to maintain the books and records and to report results up the line.

• *The system does not address the unique aspects of international operations.* The following usually warrant special consideration in the system design:

Joint ventures/minority interest.

Exports/imports.

Local requirements for accounting/reporting/tax.

Consolidation needs for multicurrency operations.

• *The system is too complex for the size of the operation.* The standard corporate package may not be appropriate for all overseas operations. If the operation is a simple one, it does not need a sophisticated system. In most cases, it will be beneficial to consider overall system needs for the various operations within a country or region. This analysis will help determine automation strategy, as well as where systems can be consolidated. Centralizing accounting and reporting systems for all operations within a country or region will eliminate the administrative burden from marketing and production operations, especially for those that are too small to justify the resources.

Audit Role in International Control

Cost/Benefit Considerations

Internal audit can perform an important role in the control of overseas operations. However, a company should make a cost/benefit analysis to determine whether it makes sense to have internal auditors travel overseas from their U.S. headquarters or to establish an internal audit function at a regional location (for example, London) to handle certain overseas operations.

If operations are decentralized, it becomes more important for internal auditors to have an ongoing program of review that covers these operations. On the other hand, if control is centralized, it becomes questionable as to whether internal audit involvement can be cost-justified. A company should assess the likelihood that internal audits (both financial and operational) will result in suggestions for efficiencies that could lead to significant cost savings. If the primary role of internal audit is viewed as one to identify potential cost savings, then a regional overseas base or ongoing overseas travel by a U.S.-based international audit group may well be justified.

Many corporate directors, as well as chief financial officers, believe that internal auditors should focus on control effectiveness rather than operating efficiencies. In this case, integration with the efforts of the external auditors becomes important. If the internal and external auditors are using the same audit methodology to conduct their audits, external auditors can realize the benefit of the internal audit efforts and minimize the work they would otherwise be required to perform.

The extent to which external auditors can rely on internal auditors in overseas operations is, in most cases, more limited than the extent to which they may be able to rely on them in domestic operations. This is because of the separate statutory audit reports required of subsidiaries in many countries outside the United States. The audit of a subsidiary in the United States ordinarily has no separate audit report requirements, so less than a full audit can be performed. Some of these limited audits can often be handled by internal auditors with only a review required by the external auditors to meet their professional standards. However, for operations outside the United States, the external auditor can delegate only a small portion of his work to the internal auditors because of the need to have separate audit opinions expressed on the subsidiaries' financial statements.

Nonetheless, significant benefits can be gained from integration of audit efforts at operations outside the United States. The following should be considered:

1. Internal auditors based in the United States who travel overseas will have a difficult time abroad because of language difficulties and a lack of understanding of local

business customs. Some public accounting firms will provide their foreign based personnel to function as internal auditors and to accomplish the objectives of the internal audit assignment without experiencing the language problems, along with the high travel costs, that are obviously associated with this type of assignment.

2. International accounting firms can offer an English-speaking staff person based abroad to work with the visiting U.S. internal auditors to help with language translation and to help explain local business customs, accounting, and tax requirements.

3. Internal auditors could have personnel from one of the company's other overseas operations temporarily assigned to internal audit. This person should have a financial background and appropriate language capability.

4. Internal audit personnel should meet with the local external audit executives serving the company's overseas operations to review problems noted in the previous audit and to discuss any other areas of concern. These meetings assist in directing internal audit emphasis and help provide early resolution of accounting issues.

5. To avoid duplication of effort and facilitate the internal auditors' work, internal audit should seek access to the external auditors' work papers. Similarly, the external auditor should receive any internal audit reports relating to the company's overseas operations as well as have an opportunity to review related work papers to identify important accounting issues that may require their follow-up.

6. If the company follows a program of internal control evaluation that is consistent with the methodology used by its external auditors, there are opportunities for further efficiencies.

Many companies believe that the benefits of maintaining an audit function to develop personnel and to provide additional opportunities to identify operating efficiencies and control weaknesses more than justify the cost. However, other companies are challenging the cost-effectiveness of maintaining an internal audit function,

EXHIBIT 21.7

Audit Program Decision Diagram

	B—moderate-priority locations	A—key locations
High	• Specific procedures in selected areas of higher exposure	• Extensive audit procedures annually
	C—low-priority locations	B—moderate-priority locations
Low	• Analytical review and ongoing monitoring procedures	• Specific procedures in selected areas of higher risk
	Low	High

and some have concluded that their external auditors may be able to do the job for less. The outsourcing of internal audit functions to external auditors can range from virtually the entire department to certain specialized functions (e.g., information systems auditing). Companies need to balance cost reduction objectives with the development benefits obtained from rotating financial and operating personnel through the internal audit function.

Setting Audit Priorities
Once a decision is made for internal audit to become involved in audits of operations outside the United States, the next step is to set priorities. Some type of risk analysis methodology should be used so that resources can be effectively allocated. A structured approach to setting priorities also will facilitate responding to questions from management and audit committees about the extent of audit coverage and the reasons why some locations are being visited and others are not.

Exhibit 21.7 (an audit program decision diagram) is an example of one way to summarize how a risk analysis can help set priorities. To determine whether a location should be classified as A, B, or C, some type of quantitative analysis should be made considering the various risk factors as well as the exposure (materiality) of the operation. The risk factors should include (1) environmental risks (see Exhibits 21.2–21.5) (2) overall quality of internal control, (3) management's ability to make accurate estimates, (4) complexity of operations, and (5) recent changes in key personnel and information systems. Multiple factors might be used to measure materiality (for example, sales, assets, operating expenses, and head count).

Attaching weights to these various risk factors as well as considering the materiality of each location will provide a basis for (1) a quantitative assessment of each operation and (2) listing the operations in order of their risk and exposure. For example, those operations that exceed a certain point total would be classified as A, the key locations. Extensive audit procedures would be performed at these locations on an annual basis. The extent of internal audit procedures would depend on the involvement of external audit and cost-effectiveness of providing the service. B locations would require less extensive procedures, and areas of audit emphasis would be rotated. For example, there may be a policy that would require internal audit to perform some procedures at least every two years. C locations—the low priority ones—would require only analytical review procedures annually and ongoing monitoring of results. Visits by internal audit would depend on (1) whether external auditors provide full statutory audit procedures and (2) the results of the ongoing financial analysis. Depending on the results of these factors, internal audit might plan to visit these C locations on a 24-to-28–month rotation program.

Regardless of the methodology used to set priorities, corporate operating management should provide input to the planning process. This involvement is essential for several reasons:

1. It provides an opportunity for internal audit to get up-to-date insight into management concerns. This information can then be used to modify the results of the quantitative analysis to respond to current risks.
2. It provides for a mutual understanding of audit objectives and improved cooperation with local managers.
3. It sets the stage for an increased interest in audit results and corrective actions.

Good Communications Are Critical

Effective communication between corporate headquarters and the company's overseas operations is particularly important. A good example of the need for effective communications took place recently when a large U.S. multinational acquired a company in the United Kingdom. The financial manager of the acquired company had never met face-to-face with financial management of the acquirer so he was not familiar with the parent company's stated policy against accumulating funds at the local level. When he accumulated funds and invested them at a favorable interest rate, he thought he was performing in the parent's best interest. Unfortunately, the value of the pound dropped against the dollar, and several hundred thousand dollars were lost. If the local financial manager had been aware of the policy against accumulating funds at local operating companies, he would have avoided the loss by forwarding the funds to corporate and reducing the intercompany balance. The problem was a direct result of poor communications.

Maintaining effective communications in a multinational environment is not an easy task. One way to help make sure all financial managers are "hearing the same message" is to conduct annual financial conferences on a worldwide or regional basis. These provide an excellent open forum to discuss operating developments and to review corporate policies. These conferences also provide an opportunity for the CFO to emphasize to local financial managers the importance of (1) maintaining effective internal controls and (2) keeping open lines of communication with corporate headquarters. The cost of these conferences is more than offset by the improved lines of communication.

CONCLUSION

Control of global operations to achieve desired profits while maintaining risks within acceptable levels is a challenge to every CFO who operates in the international arena. It requires establishing controls proportionate to the risk and investment involved. Risk can be measured by identifying and assessing pertinent political, economic, and cultural factors.

The degree of risk and level of investment have a direct bearing on how a company should be organized. The higher the risk and related investment, the greater the need for centralization. In particular, centralization of treasury functions provides a variety of benefits that help minimize both the risk and cost of doing business outside the United States. Most controllership functions require ongoing attention at the local level; however, corporate financial management needs to provide the direction and structure for fulfilling these functions.

The key point to remember when considering internal audit as an element of control over international operations is the cost-effectiveness of the function. A CFO should look at the opportunities for identifying areas for operating efficiency, as well as the need to oversee the effectiveness of the local operation's internal controls. Whether overall control is centralized or decentralized will influence this decision. And it is essential that the internal audit effort be integrated with that of the external auditors to avoid duplication of effort and to maximize cost-effectiveness.

Ultimately, however, thoughtful planning and good communication are the keys to an effective financial control strategy.

INDEX

Delivery guarantees, 32, 284
Demand forecasting, 200
Demographic information in
  business forecasts, 57, 58
Deployment skills, 185
Derivatives
  over-the-counter market,
    248
  in pension asset portfolios,
    247-248
Developing countries
  acquisition decisions
    within, 164
  agency agreements in, 371
  growth opportunities, 41-43
  hedging activities, 355
  market forecasts, 49-51
  risk assessment, 401
Diamond, Sidney, 69, 73, 81, 87,
  88, 92, 95, 98, 99, 102, 107, 109
DiBianca-Berkman Group, 302
Disclosure
  legal considerations, 318
  optimal, 322
  standards, 117
Disney, 209
Distribution resources planning
  systems in supply chain
  management, 290-291
Divestment opportunities, 160
  evaluation, 164
Dodge, William E., 225
Dong Feng Motors, 387
Dorsa, Caroline, 343
Downsizing, 71
Dozier, Glenn J., 143
Due diligence process, 383-384
DuPont Company, 182, 298, 304
DuPont two-step formula, 134
Dwyer, Tom, 112, 113

Early retirement plans, cost-
  shifting through, 238
Earnings per share, 151-152
  importance of cash flow,
    144
Eastern Europe
  currency constraints, 357
  market forecasts, 49-51, 53-
    54
  risk assessment, 344, 401,
    403
  unstable infrastructures, 358
EBRD (European Bank for
  Restructuring and
  Development), 357
Economic cycle volatility, 43-46
Economic risk, 346
  cost side, 60
  defined, 59
  revenue side, 59-60
  scenario analysis, 64-65

Economic value
  added methodology, 166
  as a performance
    measurement, 171, 172
Economic value added model,
  148
Effective tax rate
  book-tax difference, 215
  effect of reductions, 215
  as a performance measure,
    214
Electronic data interchange
  (EDI), 90, 200
  for efficient receivables, 205
  importance of, 79
  in supply chain
    management, 289
  trends, 105, 106
Electronic funds transfer, 90
Electronic journalism, 315
Electronic linkages, 79, 84, 90-91
  to customers, 105
  to suppliers, 71-72
E-mail global networks, 84
  trends, 79, 91
Emerging markets
  evaluation, 36
  forecasts, 48-54
  hedging instruments, 355
  risk assessment, 37, 350-351
  unstable infrastructures, 358
Employee empowerment, 21-22
  for improved inventory
    control, 201
  relationship to
    accountability, 13
  with shareholder mind-set,
    33
Employee exploitation, 27
Employee Retirement Security
  Act of 1974 (ERISA) effect on
  pension management, 227
Employee training as a
  performance measure, 174
End-user computing, 90
Entrepreneurial process, 185
Environmental competitiveness
  as a performance measure, 174
Equity investments on
  international projects, 357-358
Equity method of accounting,
  390-392
Ethical principles, 17
  in cost management, 32
  or decision making, 24-26,
    301
  for managers, 21, 301
  and tax concerns, 29-30
Ethics codes, 23-24
Europe
  currency crises, 406
  financial service
    availability, 406

Europe—*Cont.*
  market forecasts, 49-51, 52-53
  risk assessment, 343
European Union (EU) market
  forecasts, 49-51, 52-53
Event-oriented applications,
  106-107
Excess capacity, 101
Exchange control constraints,
  357, 410
Exchange rate risk, 37, 60, 354-
  355, 406-410 political factors,
  410
Executive incentive programs,
  158, 178, 214, 310
Executive information systems,
  90, 305 access to, 14
Export credit insurance, 356
Export income, 222
Expropriation risk, 362

Fabozzi, F., 240
Facility planning, 9
FCIA (United States), 355
FIFO inventory, 152
Filippello, A. Nicholas, 309
Finance team integration, 295-
  308
Financial Accounting Standards
  Board (FASB) exposure draft
  on Consolidation Policies,
  393-394
Financial communications
  programs, 310-313
Financial Executives Institute,
  329
Financial Executives Research
  Foundation, 14
Financial goals, 14
  cash-flow-related versus
    earnings-related, 144
  communication of, 152-153,
    310-313
  driving business decisions,
    165
  in global corporations,
    159-160, 162-163
  investor perspective, 150
  lender perspective, 150-151
  linked to incentive pay, 158,
    310
  management perspective,
    151
  selection criteria, 143
  and shareholder value, 157
  using peer group
    evaluation, 144-145
  workers perspective, 151
Financial institutions
  as business partners, 19
  views on privately held
    companies, 124